BEYOND NAMES FOR THINGS
Young Children's Acquisition of Verbs

BEYOND NAMES FOR THINGS
Young Children's Acquisition of Verbs

edited by

Michael Tomasello
Emory University
William E. Merriman
Kent State University

LEA LAWRENCE ERLBAUM ASSOCIATES, PUBLISHERS
1995 Hillsdale, New Jersey   Hove, UK

Lawrence Erlbaum Associates, Inc., Publishers
365 Broadway
Hillsdale, New Jersey 07642

Cover design by Jan Melchior

Library of Congress Cataloging-in-Publication Data

Beyond names for things : young children's acquisition of verbs /
   edited by Michael Tomasello, William E. Merriman.
      p.   cm.
   Includes bibliographical references and index.
   ISBN 0-8058-1250-4 (alk. paper)
   1. Language acquisition. 2. Grammar, Comparative and general—
Verb. 3. Grammar, Comparative and general—Syntax. I. Tomasello,
Michael. II. Merriman, William Edward.
P118.B49 1995
401'.93—dc20   94-21937
                                                              CIP

Books published by Lawrence Erlbaum Associates are printed on acid-free
paper, and their bindings are chosen for strength and durability.

Printed in the United States of America
10 9 8 7 6 5 4 3 2 1

Contents

Part III The Role of Argument Structure

CHAPTER ONE

Introduction:
Verbs Are Words Too

William E. Merriman
Kent State University

Michael Tomasello
Emory University

In the closing 200 pages or so of their encyclopedic work, *Language and Perception*, Miller and Johnson-Laird (1976) offered a thorough account of adult verb semantics and identified numerous gaps in our knowledge of how the meanings of verbs change during childhood. Few lexical developmentalists heeded the call for research, however. Most chose to study other kinds of terms instead, most notably object labels. It is actually only within the last 5 years that the empirical literature on verb meaning acquisition has grown to the point where an edited volume on the topic has become a realistic possibility.

We do three things in this introduction: identify some causes of the field's near obsession with object labels, consider why investigators have recently begun to turn their attention to verbs, and finally, present a synopsis of each chapter in the book.

DOMINANCE OF THE OBJECT LABEL

Although some studies of the semantics of children's verbs were published in the 1970s and early 1980s, and the research programs of a few persons such as Eve Clark, Janellen Huttenlocher, and Dedre Gentner included this lexical domain, much more attention was paid to children's acquisition of object labels. Several factors promoted this overriding interest in names for things. These words were judged to be particularly well suited for (a) pitting

1

Clark's and Nelson's early theories against each other, (b) examining the development of natural categories, (c) investigating early developing capacities for class logic, (d) exploring the relation between word meanings and nonlinguistic concepts, and (e) studying word learning without needing to know much about linguistic theory, much less having to choose between rival accounts. Finally, the belief that object name learning is the simplest kind of lexical acquisition undoubtedly played a role.

Clark's and Nelson's Theories

Semantic feature theory (Clark, 1973) and functional core theory (Nelson, 1974) dominated the field of early lexical development in the 1970s. The central predictions of the former were that youngsters' terms would be overgeneralized and interpreted as synonymous with related terms until differentiating features were acquired. Although the theory covered all types of words, the empirical projects that addressed it primarily concerned object labels and relational terms other than verbs (e.g., quantitative, spatial, and temporal words).

One impetus for the research on object labels was the conflict between Clark's (1973) proposals and Nelson's (1974) theory, which was exclusively concerned with names for things. From an analysis of overextensions, Clark concluded that early noun intensions consisted of one or two static perceptual attributes, most frequently shape. In contrast, Nelson contended that children did not give as much weight to such features as they did to object function. The question of the relative importance of shape, function, and other attributes in young children's generalization of novel object words has guided many investigations ever since (see Merriman, Scott, & Marazita, 1993, for a recent example). A current recasting of the question is whether youngsters assume by default that a novel word will be extendable to all similarly shaped objects. This operating principle has been given a variety of names—*Shape* (Landau, Smith, & Jones, 1988); *Object Kind* (Hall, Waxman, & Hurwitz, 1993); *Categorical Scope* (Golinkoff, Hirsh-Pasek, Mervis, Frawley, & Parillo, this volume).

The two theories also clashed regarding the prevalence of object name overextensions. Nelson (1974) noted instances of both conventional mapping and underextension, and Anglin (1977) followed with further evidence of the latter as well as methodological arguments for why analyses of children's production might overestimate the frequency of overextension. Numerous studies of the nature of naming errors have since filled the pages of books and journals. Nearly all have focused on object labels, even though most of young children's adjectives and verbs have extensions and so could be assessed with respect to this issue.

Natural Categories

The emphasis on object names was also maintained by the ecological turn taken in the scientific study of categorization in the 1970s. Labov (1973) showed how the boundaries of common object name extensions were not fixed but could be altered by perceived functional context (e.g., something that looked more like a cup than a bowl would be called "bowl" if it was being used to hold cereal). This result challenged the classical analysis of word intensions as immutable sets of individually necessary and jointly sufficient features. The death blow to this analysis was delivered by Rosch and Mervis (Mervis & Rosch, 1981; Rosch, Mervis, Gray, Johnson, & Boyes-Braem, 1976), who demonstrated in a host of processing tasks the nonequivalence of the various members of a natural object category and of the various object categories in a natural class inclusion hierarchy. Some members/categories were judged to be better than others; these prototypical members/basic level categories were verified fastest and served as the reference points to which other members/categories were compared. Rosch (1975) also provided evidence for the special status of focal colors, ideal geometric forms, round numbers, and landmark spatial directions, but she did not address actions and their descriptions.

Research on natural categories supported a new theoretical framework for early object word meaning acquisition; it was given its fullest explication by Mervis (1984, 1987). The important tenets were that basic level object names are learned first, that these names affect how more general or more specific labels are acquired, that underextensions involve primarily atypical category members, and that overextensions involve objects that are shaped like prototypical members of basic level categories.

The interest in nonclassical classes prompted a rash of lab studies that explored how youngsters interpreted novel count nouns for artificial object categories that possessed the kind of family resemblance structures found in the real world (Horton & Markman, 1980; Kossan, 1981; Markman, Horton, & McLanahan, 1980; Mervis & Pani, 1980; Ward et al., 1989; White, 1982). The results supported numerous claims about how the effect of various kinds of input depended on the typicality and homogeneity of the objects named. Some conclusions stimulated further theoretical and empirical work, including studies of whether the kind of object name input that adults present to children depends on object typicality or the hierarchical level of the label being introduced (e.g., Callanan, 1985).

Others (e.g., Carey, 1985; Gelman, 1988) probed children's sensitivity to the predictability of the hidden attributes of an object (e.g., whether it has a spleen) from the natural category to which it belongs and/or from evidence of such attributes in other members of its category. Although in some studies youngsters were asked to gauge the likelihood of action capabilities (e.g., "eats worms"), the focus was the perceived informativeness of object category membership. Markman (1989) proposed that count noun forms are understood to be inductively deeper than other types of words (i.e., lead to inferences of a greater number of attributes).

Even though they are as natural as any other lexeme, verbs have been largely ignored by the ecological revolution. Although they can be construed as having a typicality structure, Bowerman (1978) is the only scientist to have noted such a gradient in the early use of such terms (e.g., Eva's *kick*; Christy's and Eva's *open*). Because there is no clear action analog to the basic level object category, there has been no corresponding line of inquiry in the action domain.

Class Logic

A central concern of Piagetian theory is the development of the logic of classes and more specifically, the development of multiple classification and class inclusion reasoning. An important component of performance on Piaget's class inclusion problem is children's assessment of the reference of the terms involved. When asked, "Are there more dogs or more animals?" with respect to an array of five dogs and three cats, for example, interpretation of the reference of *dogs* and *animals* is critical to how the question is answered (Markman & Seibert, 1976; Smith & Rizzo, 1982). In this research, the referring expressions have nearly always been noun phrases that designate sets of objects. Thus, the study of how children learn to interpret and find referents for object words has held the promise of contributing to our understanding of children's difficulties with certain problems in class logic.

Verb versions of the Piagetian inclusion problem have not been investigated. One could show children several actors acting and ask, for example, "Are there more people walking or more people moving?" (Wilkinson's, 1976, request that children compare standing and sleeping cows comes closest.) The problem is clearly easier to engineer with object labels, and perhaps places less of a burden on attentional resources when in this form; these are probably the main reasons that verbs have not been used. However, given that the semantic organization of most verbs approximates a matrix more than it does an inclusion hierarchy (Huttenlocher & Lui, 1979), verb versions might yield different results—ones not necessarily attributable to differences in processing load.

Piagetian theory also has a lot to say about children's understanding of relations. But here again, verbs have lost out. Even though all sorts of relations are encoded by verbs, cognitive developmental research has focused on others (e.g., "taller than," "more/less/the same"). At the heart of the Piagetian analysis is the claim that children have difficulty conceiving of an entity as belonging to more than one class or as participating in more than one relation. The first possibility has prompted many investigators to explore the manner in which children integrate the extensions of basic-level object names with those of superordinate and subordinate ones (Anglin, 1977; Callanan & Markman, 1982; Macnamara, 1982; Taylor & Gelman, 1988; Waxman, Shipley, & Shepperson, 1991).

Markman (1992) drew together research on both the class inclusion problem and the development of object label hierarchies around an alternative to the Piagetian idea. She suggested that even though children can interpret two names as referring to the same thing, they simply do not expect them to overlap this way (i.e., they assume mutually exclusive word extension by default). This idea unites several disparate observations—the fewer mistakes children make with collection than with class inclusion problems, the tendency for the superordinate object names in most languages to be mass nouns, youngsters' disposition to map novel count nouns onto objects they cannot already name rather than onto ones they can.

Other researchers have come to the mutual exclusivity (ME) hypothesis via a different route, namely, by considering how the acquisition of new names might function to correct overextensions of old ones (Barrett, 1978; Merriman, 1986; Merriman & Bowman, 1989). Given these empirical roots, it should be no surprise that nearly all of the work that has expressly addressed the ME principle, or the related Novel–Names–for–Nameless–Categories principle (Mervis & Bertrand, in press), has concerned object labels— until now (see Merriman, Marazita, & Jarvis and Golinkoff et al., this volume).

Relations Between Word Meanings and Nonlinguistic Concepts

The manipulability of small objects makes possible a number of ways of assessing children's nonlinguistic organization of them. Sorting and sequential touching can be taken to indicate what are, to use Brown's (1958) phrase, behavioral equivalence classes. The availability of such measures makes it a relatively simple matter to compare developments in object word learning with those in the nonlinguistic classification of things (see Markman & Hutchinson, 1984) as well as to evaluate the correlation between these developments (see Gopnik & Meltzoff, 1987, 1992). Also, sets of objects that possess various static attributes or relations can be constructed, and children can be asked to handle them in various ways (e.g., to complete a pattern or to imitate what the experimenter does to them). Responses can then be related to measures of mastery of the relevant attribute or relational terms (see Levine & Carey, 1982; Rice, 1980; Smith, 1984).

Manipulation measures are not readily devised for actions because actions cannot be touched or moved from one pile to another. One could have children sort cards depicting various actions, but this necessarily removes their dynamic quality, which is a defining component. Although there are ways other than manipulation to assess nonlinguistic concepts (e.g., attentional and memory procedures), only a handful of studies have applied these to actions. Tomasello (this volume) identifies ways in which the field's view of the conceptual basis of lexical development would be different were verb learning to supplant object label acquisition as the paradigmatic case.

Linguistics

Researchers have needed only a smattering of knowledge about syntax, morphology, or phonology to address the leading issues in object word meaning acquisition. This is not to say that a deeper understanding of these topics would not have promoted the discovery of important phenomena in this domain; Macnamara's (1982, 1986) contributions are the best counter-evidence. Also, a clear current trend is the study of the interplay between novel noun interpretation and knowledge of linguistic structures in early development (see Soja, 1992; Walley, 1993). In contrast, children's verb meaning acquisition has always been characterized as intimately intertwined with the mastery of more formal aspects of language. For example, the late-developing errors in verb use that Bowerman (1978, 1982) scrutinized are instructive regarding developmental change in both the semantic representations of verbs and beliefs about their syntactic privileges. From children's inappropriate use of causative constructions (e.g., "I'll jump that down"), Bowerman concluded that they must have discovered a common semantic element in the verbs used in such constructions, namely, action that causes a change in an entity's state or location, and that they must have adopted the erroneous rule that any verb that specifies this type of action is acceptable within the frame N–V–N–locative/state term.

Because of its relative independence from linguistic theory, object word meaning acquisition may have become a favorite for graduates of developmental psychology programs where the primary training tends to be not in linguistics but in Piagetian and information processing approaches to basic cognitive phenomena. It is no accident that the few persons who have recently explored the structural bootstrapping of verb meaning tend to be well grounded in the current linguistic-theory-laden research on syntactic development.

Perceived Simplicity

Investigators may have just perceived object name learning to be simpler than learning action or stative verbs and thus may have chosen to study object names on the assumption that science should start with the simplest cases. Gentner (1982) proposed that this greater simplicity, or naturalness, is responsible for the more rapid early acquisition of nouns than verbs. Even if the perception of greater simplicity is inaccurate, as Gopnik and Choi (this volume) contend, it may still have influenced the direction of research.

The canonical use of a novel English count noun in speech to youngsters involves drawing their attention to an object and labeling it (e.g., "That's a spoon"). This event can be recreated in lab training studies with fair confidence that the findings will be relevant to natural object name acquisition. As long as the object is unfamiliar and static, it can be safely assumed that the child will take the name to refer to the entire object, rather than to something else (e.g., one of its parts; Markman & Wachtel, 1988). Furthermore, whether in the lab or the real world, one can establish whether speaker and listener achieve joint attention to an object word's referent by monitoring eye gaze (Tomasello & Farrar, 1986).

In contrast, as Tomasello (this volume) has documented, there is no canonical novel verb input. The most frequent way in which action words are introduced is either as part of a command (e.g., "Pick up that toy") or in reference to an impending, possibly planned, action (e.g., "Let's put a bandaid on that" or "Do you want to get up?"). Even if one succeeds in constructing a lab analog for one of these kinds of input, the results may only generalize to a minority of real-world verb cases. Also, it is often not clear what the child will take the spoken word's reference to be. For example, what will he or she consider to be the point at which the action referred to by "putting a bandaid on" begins—searching for the bandaid, pulling off its backing, moving it toward the skin? Without a clear notion of the boundaries of the event, joint attention to the verb's referent cannot be assessed; reference cannot be directly inferred from eye gaze. According to Gentner (1982), this uncertainty is the source of the difficulty that young children allegedly have with verb meaning acquisition.

Two other factors make the acquisition of the simplest verbs a more complicated matter than that of the simplest nouns (from the researcher's point of view, not necessarily the child's): limited temporal availability and the self–other distinction. Many actions can be inspected only for a brief period; once the action ends, further analysis of it must rely on processes other than direct perception, such as remembering and reasoning. For example, once a person has kicked a ball, the act of kicking can no longer be observed; it can only be remembered or inferred from the flight of the ball. Investigators may have viewed this restriction as an impediment to action word learning. In contrast, an object can be directly encoded as long as it remains in view; it may even be possible to handle it or view it from a variety of perspectives.

Except for labels for oneself or one's body, object names refer to external things. In contrast, actions can be performed by either oneself or another person. This duality creates unique complexities for both the acquisition of action words and the scientific study of this process (Huttenlocher, Smiley, & Charney, 1983). Different information may be available when one performs an action versus when one observes it; intentions and kinesthetic cues would seem more salient in the former, whereas the latter delivers more visual information about changes in the entire body of the actor during the movement. For this reason, a verb that a child learns for his or her own action may not be extended to the same action carried out by someone else, and vice versa. Also, comprehension of an action word can be tested by asking children either to produce a referent themselves (e.g., "Kick the ball") or to point to/look at someone else doing so (e.g., "Which man is kicking the ball?"), and results of the two tests may differ in interesting ways.

These complexities may have caused those interested in lexical semantic development to steer clear of verb meaning acquisition until the presumably simpler case of object word learning had received an adequate treatment. Although it can be debated whether this last goal has been achieved, many child psychologists have turned their attention toward verb learning in recent years. In many of the contributions to this book, previous developmental research on object words remains a dominant reference point for the interpretation of findings regarding verb acquisition.

RECENT INTEREST IN VERB SEMANTIC DEVELOPMENT

Just as there are many reasons why object labels dominated the field of lexical development during the 1970s and 1980s, several causes can be identified for the recent surge of interest in verb meaning acquisition.

The Appeal of a New Frontier

As already argued, some who have concerned themselves exclusively with how youngsters learn names for things may have decided that few interesting questions remain to be asked about this topic. Thus, they have shifted their attention to verbs and other lexical domains that are as important as object labels but less well charted.

Search for General Acquisition Principles

Others have clearly chosen to study verbs for the sake of testing the limits of word learning principles that were developed for object names (Golinkoff et al., Merriman et al., this volume).

Verbs' Rise to Prominence in Linguistic Theory

Much of the information that linguists used to assign to syntactic rules is now embedded in the lexical entries for individual verbs, including such things as the argument roles that fill out their meaning. This is true of approaches as diverse as Lexical Functional Grammar (Bresnan, 1982) and Cognitive Grammar (Langacker, 1987). Thus, child language researchers who are especially linguistics-friendly have fixed on questions in verb meaning acquisition because of the implications of the answers for syntactic development. The allure of a new frontier has likely motivated them as well.

Although many developmentalists have neither the time nor inclination to master the latest linguistic theories, they do keep abreast of the general trends in this field, as these are communicated through secondary sources. The greater role now given by linguists to verb meaning has been featured in several such summaries (Bates, Bretherton, & Snyder, 1988; Bloom, 1991; Pinker, 1989; Tomasello, 1992).

Theories of Syntax-Semantics Relations

We suggested that researchers of the past may have been daunted by the fact that the acquisition of verb semantics is clearly intertwined with syntactic development. A great deal of order has been given to this complex nexus by two recent theories: Gleitman and her colleagues' account of how syntactic knowledge facilitates, or bootstraps, verb semantic development (Gleitman, 1990; Landau & Gleitman, 1985), and Pinker's (1989) proposals concerning the manner in which knowledge of verb semantics plays the reciprocal role in syntactic development. According to the former, children learn which aspects of verb meaning are predictable from the set of syntactic frames in which a verb appears and use this knowledge to constrain their hypotheses about the meaning of a new verb. According to the latter, children's assignment of verbs to both broad and narrow semantic classes determines the particular syntactic structures that children allow them to enter. Several predicted patterns of acquisition can be derived from each theory, prompting researchers to make counterproposals as well as to conduct decisive tests (see Braine & Brooks, this volume).

Individual and Cultural Differences

Many English-speaking children accumulate a large stock of nouns early in development, but others get by with a much smaller set and rely more heavily on pronouns and all-purpose phrases (Bates et al., 1988; Nelson, 1973, 1981). Some evidence suggests that these two groups of children are exposed to language differently, depending on the functions their parents are trying to achieve in speaking to them. Cross-cultural and cross-class comparisons suggest that Western middle-class parents of first-born children are unique in their preoccupation with object naming; in other groups, much more emphasis is placed on the use of language to regulate the attention or behavior of others for the sake of achieving certain social or instrumental goals. This research has promoted the turn toward verbs by showing that learning names for things is far from the universal first step in language acquisition.

Event Cognition

Finally, although interest in the development of class logic and natural categories has compelled investigators toward the study of object label acquisition, there has been a fair amount of research over the past 10 years or so on young children's representations of temporally extended events (see Bauer & Mandler, 1992; Nelson, 1986). As developmentalists become secure in their understanding of these cognitive structures, they will be more likely to attempt to establish how words for actions, processes, and mental states map onto these representations (see Tomasello, 1992, for suggestions).

THE CURRENT VOLUME

The contributions to the book are organized around three themes: earliest words for actions and events, basic principles of verb learning, and the role of argument structure. Because Maratsos and Deák (chapter 14) provide critical commentary on the chapters, we will merely summarize the main points here.

Earliest Words for Actions and Events

The acquisition of English words for events, objects, and persons in the single word period is the focus of Patricia Smiley and Janellen Huttenlocher's opening analysis. Although a term's prominence in input is found to be generally predictive of how soon a child starts to use it, there are exceptions to this relation in each lexical domain. The authors attribute these to two processes: toddlers' active search for ways of expressing certain perceptual notions, and their inability to learn words that convey concepts that are beyond them. Regarding early event words, it is proposed that these encode something about how the movement or outcome component of a physical event looks (e.g., *up* or *allgone*) but do not express anything about its perceived cause. Once concepts of intention and other subjective states become available for expression, youngsters not only begin to use several change-of-state verbs to express their goals (e.g., *get, find, make*), but also start to produce and comprehend their own names and the personal pronoun *I*.

Alison Gopnik and Soonja Choi do not merely find fault with the field's fixation on object labels; they convict it (Gentner, 1982, in particular) of having overestimated the ease with which these words are acquired compared to event words. Three causes of this inaccuracy are identified: over-representation in research samples of English-speaking, middle-class, first-born children, whose mothers tend to give frequent lessons in object naming; the "odd" way English-speaking toddlers first refer to events; and the salience of nouns relative to verbs in English sentence structure. According to the authors, English- and adult-centric researchers have been put off by the syntactic heterogeneity and semantic unconventionality of the English words first used by children to encode events and have been misled by English's far-from-universal tendency to drop verbs or bury them in the least salient positions in utterances. Korean and Japanese, by contrast, are verb-final and frequently allow noun elision, and children learning these languages tend to hear more verbs and fewer nouns per utterance than those who grow up listening to English. Moreover, most of the aspects of events that young children want to talk about are well expressed by Korean verbs. The Whorfian consequences are well documented: Not only do Korean toddlers acquire verbs more quickly and object names less quickly than their English counterparts, but performance on conceptually related problem-solving tasks is also affected.

Susan Braunwald addresses the relation between the acquisition of verbs and grammatical development in the second year of life. Her diaries of the early speech of two English-speaking sisters (J and L) indicate that a proto-SVO structure emerged for both between the 19th and 20th month despite L's knowledge of many more verbs than J and production of them from a younger age. The abrupt increase in the syntactic complexity of J's utterances coincided with a dramatic spurt in verb acquisition. In contrast, L's grammatical development and verb accumulation proceeded in a continuous fashion, with the exception of the 22nd month, when the former accelerated and the latter slowed up a bit. Interesting possibilities regarding the way verb learning may either promote or compete with syntactic development are discussed.

Basic Principles of Verb Learning

Michael Tomasello continues the campaign against the object-word bias, especially as he finds it embodied in Markman's (1992) structural principles account of lexical development. He advocates an alternative social-pragmatic approach (see also Bruner, 1983; Nelson, 1985), which emphasizes the communicative skills that both children and adults bring to the task of conveying and deciphering intended meanings. Toddlers' problem of characterizing lexical reference turns out to have an entirely different structure for action than for object words; the latter tend to be used in ostensive contexts (i.e., where the referent can be viewed as its name is spoken), but the former do not. Moreover, in some situations 24-month-olds are actually less likely to learn novel verbs when these are used ostensively than when used to designate impending or completed action. Thus, an old adage must be amended: Talk about the here and now is sometimes not as easily understood as talk about the real soon or the just then. Finally, 2-year-olds show remarkable sophistication in determining the referent that adults intend a novel verb to have. Impending actions that are identified by speakers as having occurred accidentally are readily dismissed, and knowledge of the structure of a repeated event is used to infer the action that a speaker intended to perform but could not carry out.

The next two chapters present efforts by those who have advanced operating principle accounts of children's object word learning to extend their frameworks to verb learning. Merriman, Marazita, and Jarvis make alterations in a laboratory paradigm used to assess expectations about novel count noun reference. The basic procedure is to pair an object or action that youngsters can already name with one they cannot and to ask them to identify the likely referent of a novel word. Although scores of studies with the noun version have been published and some findings are well replicated, viable theoretical accounts have tended to proliferate rather than die out. The firmest claim is that children who are 2½ years or older assume by default that novel count nouns will designate object categories that are mutually exclusive with those of familiar object labels.

The verb results are striking for their lack of correspondence with the noun findings. Whereas 2-year-olds' tendency to map a novel noun onto an unfamiliar entity is weaker than 4-year-olds', the mapping effects of the two age groups are comparable for noncausative action words. Whereas stimulus pre-exposure reduces 2-year-olds' mapping preference for objects but not for actions, it has the opposite effect on 4-year-olds' performance. Of the many ways suggested for integrating these findings, perhaps the hypothesis most worthy of further research is that children learn from experience that novel verbs are more likely than novel nouns to violate the Mutual Exclusivity principle in a default situation.

After summarizing Frawley's (1992) characterization of the structure of adult motion verbs, Golinkoff, Hirsh-Pasek, Mervis, Frawley, and Parillo argue for a close correspondence between the basic semantic components of this kind of term and the image-schemas that Mandler (1992) has claimed infants construct from viewing events. The bulk of the chapter, however, concerns six principles that purportedly guide youngsters' interpretation of novel object and action words. The first three, *Reference* (that a new term refers to a physical entity), *Extendability* (that it can be generalized to entities that resemble attested referents), and *Object/Action Scope* (that it refers to a whole object unless a name is already known for the thing, in which case it refers to the object's action), are claimed to emerge around the child's first birthday for object words and possibly later for action words. The most controversial of these dicta is Object/Action Scope; it ascribes to children the kind of bias that Tomasello and Gopnik and Choi contend is only found in researchers. After these three heuristics have been in use approximately 6 months, the remaining three are said to become functional: *Categorical Scope* (that a novel noun designates a basic-level object category and a novel verb designates a category of all "actions which appear to require the same semantic components"), *Novel Names–Nameless Categories* [N3C] (that a novel word will map to a previously unnamed entity), and *Conventionality* (that unconventional word uses will eventually be replaced by conventional ones). Although the authors do not address the alternatives to N3C posed by Merriman et al. in the preceding chapter, they have done so elsewhere (Golinkoff, Mervis, & Hirsh-Pasek, in press).

Katherine Nelson examines evidence and arguments regarding the relative dominance of nouns over verbs in English child language and presents a preliminary study of the early development of event words that can be used as both nouns and verbs (e.g., *help, walk*). Although some current theories imply that the acquisition of such dual category terms should be problematic, results do not support this hypothesis. Although most 20-month-olds tested restricted their production of these terms to a single category, they comprehended both uses. Also, contrary to some theorists' suggestions, not all of these event terms were initially treated as verbs.

Douglas Behrend classifies the processes that can influence verb meaning acquisition according to whether these emanate from the child, the environment, or knowledge of language structure. Following Merriman and Bowman (1989) and Markman (1992), he views child-driven processes as default expectations about the meanings of novel words. His studies indicate that toddlers and preschoolers assume that an action's result, rather than its manner or instrument, is the most important semantic component for extending a just-learned verb to a novel event. However, this operating principle is not nearly as robust as the corresponding Shape, or Categorical Scope, principle for object words. Environmental forces can readily modify it: Children who hear the same verb applied to three result-variable, manner-invariant actions realize that manner is central to the verb's meaning and result is not.

There have been several demonstrations of how information about the syntactic privileges of a verb influences children's interpretation of it (see next section). Behrend extends this structural approach to include information about the grammatical morphemes a verb can take. Specifically, children tend to give greater weight to result than manner when a novel verb is only introduced in the past tense (i.e., marked with an *-ed* inflection) than when it only occurs in the present progressive (i.e., marked with an *-ing* inflection). This bootstrapping effect is somewhat fragile, however.

Argument Structure

Anne Lederer, Henry Gleitman, and Lila Gleitman argue not only that children use the sentence frames in which a verb appears to identify its argument structure but also that verb meanings would not be learnable otherwise. If the novel verb *glorp* occurs in an NP–V–NP–PrepP sentence, for example, it can be safely inferred that the term encodes an action that causes an affected entity to move or change in a certain way. Although such structural information does not uniquely specify the verb's meaning, it does increase the likelihood of the learner entertaining a correct or nearly correct interpretation of the verb. In the empirical part of their chapter, the authors succeed in achieving a crucial subgoal for their theory, namely, demonstrating that verbs that occur in similar syntactic frames in mothers' speech to children tend to have similar meanings.

Letitia Naigles, Anne Fowler, and Atessa Helm make several important contributions to this structural approach. Young children's interpretation of familiar verbs is found to be frame compliant; that is, children tend to assign a novel meaning to a familiar verb when it is presented in a frame in which it has never before occurred. Adults, on the other hand, are verb compliant; they refuse to alter the semantics of a familiar verb just to reconcile it with an unattested frame.

The study of children and adolescents with Down syndrome sheds considerable light on the cause of this developmental shift. These groups are found to be less verb compliant than normal-IQ children of the same chronological or mental age but equivalent in this regard to those of the same "syntactic age." Because the extent to which children make a term comply with its frame varies greatly from verb to verb, Naigles et al. conclude that both syntactic and lexical knowledge acquisition play major causal roles in the transition to verb compliance. Several findings challenge specific claims of the leading theory of the acquisition of argument structure (Gropen, Pinker, Hollander, & Goldberg, 1991; Pinker, 1989).

The limits of the argument structure approach are brought out by Matthew Rispoli's studies of the acquisition of Japanese. Because this language allows the core arguments of a predicate to be omitted, and because even youngsters as old as 5 have little comprehension of the Japanese system of case markings, syntactic bootstrapping cannot play much of a role in early verb learning. Yet Japanese children are remarkably successful in figuring out the meanings of many verbs and in identifying the types of predicates in which the verbs can occur. The author argues that children's success is largely due to their acquisition of knowledge of the relation between various kinds of predicates and speech acts.

Children also need pragmatic rather than syntactic knowledge to learn the argument structure of certain English verbs, namely, intransitives that take indefinite null complements (e.g., *eat*). Only transitive forms of these verbs are permitted when that which undergoes the action is discourse accessible. For example, if someone said, "We got a whole lot of bacon," it would be inappropriate to ask for some by saying, "Can I eat?" Not all intransitive verbs share this restriction (e.g., if told, "Your beard is scratchy," you could reply, "I just shaved" or "I just shaved it"). A transcript analysis shows that the discourse contexts in which transitive forms of *eat* are obligatory are learned before the age of 3.

Like Naigles et al., Martin Braine and Patricia Brooks challenge aspects of Pinker and Gropen's account of how children come to realize that certain verbs are not to be used in certain argument structures. The authors question the claims that verbs are assigned to narrow subclasses based on rather idiosyncratic aspects of meaning and that rules characterizing the permissible argument structures for each subclass are acquired. Braine and Brooks propose instead that argument structure privileges are learned on a verb-by-verb basis. If a child has had experience with a verb, he or she may use it in an unattested frame if its meaning is compatible with the general semantics of the frame. However, once the argument structures for a verb have been "solidly learned" (i.e., observed frequently and recently enough), unattested argument structures will be judged to be inappropriate. In a pilot experiment in which both preschoolers and adults were taught novel verbs that could be assigned to one of Pinker and Gropen's proposed semantic subclasses, subjects' willingness to use a verb in an unattested frame was unrelated to its subclass membership.

CONCLUSIONS

Until five years ago, the field of early lexical development had been rather neglectful of verb learning and rather obsessed with children's acquisition of names for things. We have traced this bias to an attempt to decide between Clark's and Nelson's theories of the 1970s, interest in the development of natural categories and class logic, the availability of direct means for assessing the language–cognition relation, and the apparently simple, linguistics-free nature of the topic. The recent shift toward verb meaning is attributable to a variety of factors: the appeal of a new frontier, the search for general acquisition principles, the central role given to verb meaning in current linguistic formulations, the guidance provided by two recent theories of how syntax and verb semantics might bootstrap the development of one another, individual and cultural differences found in the composition of early lexicons, and progress in research on the nature of young children's event representations.

The contributions to the book are divided according to three issues: earliest words for actions and events, basic principles of verb learning, and the role of argument structure. These clusters are not exhaustive. Limitations of time and space have prevented us from incorporating research on other important aspects of verb meaning development, such as deixis, implicit notions of causality, or reference to mental states. Our hope is that the research we have included will promote further investigation of all aspects of the semantic development of this fundamental class of words.

ACKNOWLEDGMENT

Preparation of this chapter was supported by NICHD Grant HD-25958 to William E. Merriman.

REFERENCES

Anglin, J. M. (1977). *Word, object, and conceptual development.* New York: Norton.
Barrett, M. (1978). Lexical development and overextension in child language. *Journal of Child Language, 5,* 205–219.
Bates, E., Bretherton, I., & Snyder, L. (1988). *From first words to grammar: Individual differences and dissociable mechanisms.* New York: Cambridge University Press.
Bauer, P. J., & Mandler, J. M. (1992). Putting the horse before the cart: The use of temporal structure in recall of events by one-year-old children. *Developmental Psychology, 28,* 441–452.
Bloom, L. (1991). *Language development from two to three.* New York: Cambridge University Press.
Bowerman, M. (1978). The acquisition of word meaning: An investigation of current conflicts. In N. Waterson & C. E. Snow (Eds.), *The development of communication* (pp. 263–287). New York: Wiley.
Bowerman, M. (1982). Reorganizational processes in lexical and syntactic development. In L. Gleitman & E. Wanner (Eds.), *Language acquisition: The state of the art* (pp. 319–346). New York: Cambridge University Press.
Bresnan, J. (1982). *The mental representation of grammatical relations.* Cambridge, MA: MIT Press.
Brown, R. W. (1958). How shall a thing be called? *Psychological Review, 65,* 14–21.
Bruner, J. (1983). *Child's talk.* New York: Norton.
Callanan, M. A. (1985). How parents label objects for young children: The role of input in the acquisition of category hierarchies. *Child Development, 56,* 508–523.
Callanan, M. A., & Markman, E. M. (1982). Principles of organization in young children's natural language hierarchies. *Child Development, 56,* 1093–1101.
Carey, S. (1985). *Conceptual change in childhood.* Cambridge, MA: MIT Press.
Clark, E. V. (1973). What's in a word? On the child's acquisition of semantics in his first language. In T. E. Moore (Ed.), *Cognitive development and the acquisition of language* (pp. 65–110). New York: Academic Press.
Frawley, W. B. (1992). *Linguistic semantics.* Hillsdale, NJ: Lawrence Erlbaum Associates.
Gelman, S. A. (1988). The development of induction within natural kind and artifact categories. *Cognitive Psychology, 20,* 65–95.
Gentner, D. (1982). Why nouns are learned before verbs: Linguistic relativity versus natural partitioning. In S. Kuczaj, II (Ed.), *Language development* (Vol. 2, pp. 301–334). Hillsdale, NJ: Lawrence Erlbaum Associates.
Golinkoff, R. M., Mervis, C., & Hirsh-Pasek, K. (in press). Early object labels: The case for lexical principles. *Journal of Child Language.*
Gleitman, L. R. (1990). The structural sources of verb meaning. *Language Acquisition, 1,* 3–55.
Gopnik, A., & Meltzoff, A. N. (1987). The development of categorization in the second year and its relation to other cognitive and linguistic developments. *Child Development, 58,* 1523–1531.
Gopnik, A., & Meltzoff, A. N. (1992). Categorization and naming: Basic level sorting in eighteen-month-olds and its relation to language. *Child Development, 63,* 1091–1103.

Gropen, J., Pinker, S., Hollander, M., & Goldberg, R. (1991). Syntax and semantics in the acquisition of locative verbs. *Journal of Child Language, 18,* 115–151.

Hall, D. G., Waxman, S. R., & Hurwitz, W. M. (1993). How 2- and 4-year-old children interpret adjectives and count nouns. *Child Development, 64,* 1651–1664.

Horton, M. S., & Markman, E. M. (1980). Developmental differences in the acquisition of basic and superordinate categories. *Child Development, 51,* 708–719.

Huttenlocher, J., & Lui, F. (1979). The semantic organization of some simple nouns and verbs. *Journal of Verbal Learning and Verbal Behavior, 18,* 141–162.

Huttenlocher, J., Smiley, P., & Charney, R. (1983). Emergence of action categories in the child: Evidence from verb meanings. *Psychological Review, 90,* 72–93.

Labov, W. (1973). The boundaries of words and their meanings. In C-J. Bailey & R. Shuy (Eds.), *New ways of analyzing variation in English.* Washington, DC: Georgetown University Press.

Landau, B., & Gleitman, L. R. (1985). *Language and experience: Evidence from the blind child.* Cambridge, MA: Harvard University Press.

Landau, B., Smith, L. B., & Jones, S. S. (1988). The importance of shape in early lexical learning. *Cognitive Development, 3,* 299–321.

Langacker, R. (1987). *Foundations of cognitive grammar.* Stanford, CA: Stanford University Press.

Levine, S., & Carey, S. (1982). Up front: The acquisition of a concept and a word. *Journal of Child Language, 9,* 645–658.

Kossan, N. E. (1981). Developmental differences in concept acquisition strategies. *Child Development, 52,* 290–298.

Macnamara, J. (1982). *Names for things: A study of human learning.* Cambridge, MA: MIT Press.

Macnamara, J. (1986). *A border dispute.* Cambridge, MA: MIT Press.

Mandler, J. (1992). How to build a baby: II. Conceptual primitives. *Psychological Review, 99,* 587–604.

Markman, E. M. (1989). *Categorization and naming in children: Problems of induction.* Cambridge, MA: MIT Press.

Markman, E. M. (1992). Constraints on word learning: Speculations about their nature, origins, and domain specificity. In M. R. Gunnar & M. P. Maratsos (Eds.), *Modularity and constraints in language and cognition: Minnesota symposium on child psychology* (Vol. 20, pp. 59–101). Hillsdale, NJ: Lawrence Erlbaum Associates.

Markman, E. M., Horton, M. S., & McLanahan, A. G. (1980). Classes and collections: Principles of organization in the learning of hierarchical relations. *Cognition, 8,* 227–242.

Markman, E. M., & Hutchinson, J. (1984). Children's sensitivity to constraints on word meaning: Taxonomic vs. thematic relations. *Cognitive Psychology, 16,* 1–27.

Markman, E. M., & Seibert, J. (1976). Classes and collections: Internal organization and resulting holistic properties. *Cognitive Psychology, 8,* 561–577.

Markman, E. M., & Wachtel, G. F. (1988). Children's use of mutual exclusivity to constrain the meanings of words. *Cognitive Psychology, 20,* 121–157.

Merriman, W. E. (1986). Some reasons for the occurrence and eventual correction of children's naming errors. *Child Development, 57,* 942–952.

Merriman, W. E., & Bowman, L. L. (1989). The mutual exclusivity bias in children's word learning. *Monographs of the Society for Research in Child Development, 54* (3–4, Serial No. 220).

Merriman, W. E., Scott, P., & Marazita, J. (1993). An appearance–function shift in children's object naming. *Journal of Child Language, 20,* 101–118.

Mervis, C. B. (1984). Early lexical development: The contributions of mother and child. In C. Sophian (Ed.), *Origins of cognitive skills* (pp. 339–370). Hillsdale, NJ: Lawrence Erlbaum Associates.

Mervis, C. B. (1987). Child-basic object categories and early lexical development. In U. Neisser (Ed.), *Concepts and conceptual development: Ecological and intellectual factors in categorization* (pp. 201–233). Cambridge, MA: Cambridge University Press.

Mervis, C. B., & Bertrand, J. (in press). Acquisition of the novel name–nameless category (N3C) principle. *Child Development.*

Mervis, C. B., & Pani, J. R. (1980). Acquisition of basic object categories. *Cognitive Psychology, 12,* 496–522.

Mervis, C. B., & Rosch, E. H. (1981). Categorization of natural objects. In M. R. Rosenzweig & L. W. Porter (Eds.), *Annual Review of Psychology* (Vol. 32, pp. 89–115). Palo Alto, CA: Annual Reviews Inc.

Miller, G. A., & Johnson-Laird, P. N. (1976). *Language and perception.* Cambridge, MA: Harvard University Press.

Nelson, K. (1973). Structure and strategy in learning to talk. *Monographs of the Society for Research in Child Development, 38* (1–2, Serial No. 149).

Nelson, K. (1974). Concept, word, and sentence: Interrelationships in acquisition and development. *Psychological Review, 81,* 267–285.

Nelson, K. (1981). Individual differences in language development: Implications for development and language. *Developmental Psychology, 17,* 170–187.

Nelson, K. (1985). *Making sense: The acquisition of shared meaning.* New York: Academic Press.

Nelson, K. (1986). *Event knowledge: Structure and function in development.* Hillsdale, NJ: Lawrence Erlbaum Associates.

Pinker, S. (1989). *Learnability and cognition: The acquisition of argument structure.* Cambridge, MA: MIT Press.

Rice, M. L. (1980). *Cognition to language: Categories, word meanings, and training.* Baltimore, MD: University Park Press.

Rosch, E. (1975). Cognitive representations of semantic categories. *Journal of Experimental Psychology: General, 104,* 192–233.

Rosch, E., Mervis, C. B., Gray, W. D., Johnson, D. M., & Boyes-Braem, P. (1976). Basic objects in natural categories. *Cognitive Psychology, 8,* 382–439.

Smith, L. B. (1984). Young children's understanding of attributes and dimensions: A comparison of conceptual and linguistic measures. *Child Development, 55,* 363–380.

Smith, L. B., & Rizzo, T. A. (1982). Children's understanding of the referential properties of collective and class nouns. *Child Development, 53,* 245–257.

Soja, N. (1992). Inferences about the meanings of nouns: The relationship between perception and syntax. *Cognitive Development, 7,* 29–45.

Taylor, M., & Gelman, S. A. (1988). Adjectives and nouns: Children's strategies for learning new words. *Child Development, 59,* 411–419.

Tomasello, M. (1992). *First verbs: A case study of early grammatical development.* New York: Cambridge University Press.

Tomasello, M., & Farrar, M. J. (1986). Joint attention and early language. *Child Development, 57,* 1454–1463.

Walley, A. C. (1993). The role of vocabulary development in children's spoken word recognition and segmentation ability. *Developmental Review, 13,* 286–350.

Ward, T. B., Vela, E., Peery, M. L., Lewis, S., Bauer, N. K., & Klint, K. (1989). What makes a vibble a vibble: A developmental study of category generalization. *Child Development, 60,* 214–224.

Waxman, S. R., Shipley, E. F., & Shepperson, B. (1991). Establishing new subcategories: The role of category labels and existing knowledge. *Child Development, 62,* 127–138.

White, T. G. (1982). Naming practices, typicality, and underextension in child language. *Journal of Experimental Child Psychology, 33,* 324–346.

Wilkinson, A. C. (1976). Counting strategies and semantic analyses as applied to class inclusion. *Cognitive Psychology, 8,* 64–85.

PART ONE

EARLY WORDS FOR ACTION

Conceptual Development and the Child's Early Words for Events, Objects, and Persons

Patricia Smiley
Pomona College

Janellen Huttenlocher
University of Chicago

Our purpose in this chapter is to explore the nature of early concepts by examining the nature and order of emergence of children's word meanings. Word meanings are often used as an index of concepts, but as we argued elsewhere (Huttenlocher, Smiley, & Ratner, 1983), the meanings children assign to words may reflect children's conceptual development, the ways parents use words, or both of these factors. In order to evaluate the relative influence of conceptual development on lexical acquisition, we examine both child word meanings and parent use of words. In particular, we examine the extent of correspondence between children's and parents' use of words for events, objects, and people in the single-word and early multiword periods. These comparisons allow us to make inferences about the nature of children's earliest event, object, and person concepts and about change in the nature of these conceptual categories over time.

We are especially interested in the acquisition of words for events. In the adult language, events are encoded by verbs that express the various relations that hold among entities. Many of these verbs encode the intentional causation of movement or change by people. In child language, however, verbs are not among the first words acquired (Gentner, 1982; Goldin-Meadow, Seligman, & Gelman, 1976; Huttenlocher, Smiley, & Charney, 1983). Several studies, including ours, indicate that children encode events early but they employ a variety of words, including many nonverbs, to do so. Our method—examining the development of child word meanings over time in the context of parent input—allows us to address some important issues in word learning and in the early conceptualization of events. We explore the reasons for the relatively late acquisition of verbs (e.g., they may be hard to extract acoustically from adult sentences, and/or concepts of intentional action may be inaccessible to young children) and for the early acquisition of the first event words (e.g., they may be salient in parent speech, and concepts of intentional action may be accessible to young children, or they may encode a more primitive understanding of events).

To anticipate the thrust of our discussion, the data we present on child word meanings and parent word use in various domains indicate that both parent word use and conceptual development play major roles in lexical acquisition. We argue that although input helps children acquire particular words, the order of acquisition and the nature of word meanings chiefly reflect the accessibility of certain conceptual categories at different points in time. We discuss the changing sensitivities of the child's cognitive system that seem to guide the emergence and growth of the early conceptual scheme.

THE NATURE OF THE EARLY CONCEPTUAL SYSTEM

As we outline in the next section, our method relies on assessing the extent to which input affects the particular words children acquire at different points in time and the meanings children assign to those words. This approach has implications for addressing a larger question as well, namely the extent to which the child's conceptual system responds to or resists the language environment. Other researchers (e.g., Gelman, 1990b; Spelke, Breinlinger, Macomber, & Jacobson, 1992; Turkewitz & Kenny, 1982) recently proposed that the perceptual and conceptual systems are designed to process certain aspects of experience in a particular order and that this facilitates growth and integration in those systems. The approach we take may provide another way to determine whether the conceptual system is constrained to develop (i.e., to make use of input) in a particular sequence and to specify the nature of that development. It may also allow us to identify those concepts that are primitives and that provide the basis for other concepts that emerge later.

More specifically, different relations between child and adult word use lead to different conclusions about the responsiveness of the conceptual system over time. For example, if the meanings children assign to the words they acquire mirror adult word use, especially if these matching patterns of use are restricted in some way (e.g., child and parent use *shoe* only for the child's sandals or *drink* only for the dog drinking from a water dish), this would suggest that the child's conceptual system is relatively responsive to input. That is, input may focus the child's attention on certain nonlinguistic contexts, enabling the child to form certain concepts and attach words to them.

On the other hand, if the child acquires words whose meanings do not correspond to adult word use (e.g., child uses *ball* for different balls despite parent use only during a catch game with a particular ball or *get* just for the child's acts despite parent use for a range of people getting things), this would suggest that the child's conceptual system is relatively resistant to the range of contexts in input. That is, although input may help the child to learn words, exposure to words in context may not account for the formation of the child's concepts. Using such data, we can determine the ways in which input affects word learning and can infer the nature of concepts that are accessible to the child at different points in development. Using conclusions drawn about various conceptual domains over time, we can assess the overall responsiveness of the conceptual system to the language environment.

ASSESSING CHILD WORD MEANINGS, PARENT INPUT, AND THE COURSE OF CONCEPTUAL DEVELOPMENT

In this section we discuss in more detail the methods we use to assess child word meanings and parent input and to analyze patterns of correspondence in these sets of data. Our evidence for the nature of child word meanings in various domains comes from production and comprehension studies in the period of single-word speech (before about 20 months) and in the subsequent period of early multiword speech. Spontaneous production data allow us to examine those sets of instances for which the child uses a word, and this is a potentially powerful method for assessing the nature of word meanings. Many researchers (e.g., Bloom, 1973; Bowerman, 1980; Piaget, 1962) noted that child word usage is sometimes narrower or broader than appropriate adult use. Such patterns have been used to infer that children have immature word meanings. However, children use words not to inform us about their word meanings but rather to serve their particular communicative needs. Thus, children may have adultlike word meanings but a limited range of communicative purposes, or they may be unable to specify fully their communicative intent because they produce only one word at a time. Of course, it is also possible that these kinds of productive uses reflect truly non-adultlike word meanings.

To determine whether non-adultlike word use reflects immature word meaning or the child's communicative needs, techniques of elicited production and comprehension are particularly useful. If the contexts for spontaneous production of some words are restricted or if particular words are not produced at all, one can either elicit production to an exemplar of a category or set up comprehension tasks to assess responses to critical category instances. If the contexts of spontaneous production are too broad, comprehension tasks can be used to define the boundaries of what the child considers appropriate instances. For example, one can present arrays of instances similar to or associated with category instances to test hypotheses of overgeneral or complexive word meanings.

Because we are interested in the development of the child's categories, we do not examine production or comprehension of words in relation to single instances of a (potential) category, as others did (e.g., Barrett, 1986; Bloom, 1973; Reich, 1976). Single instance uses of words do not provide information about the nature of a category. They may be examples of the child's earliest attempts to catch on to the word-to-world matching game (Gleitman, 1990), initially matching words to whole event representations (Barrett, Harris, & Chasin, 1991). Further, most reports of words for single instances indicate that they are early and often short-lived, either falling out of use or soon extending to other category instances. We examine words applied to a range of distinguishable instances in the single-word and multiword periods to determine whether early categories are adultlike or non-adultlike in nature and whether they change over time.

To determine the extent to which lexical acquisition reflects changing conceptual abilities or learning from parent word use, we examine the relation of various aspects of parent input to the nature and order of emergence of child word meanings. Three major aspects of input may affect lexical acquisition, namely the frequency with which words are used, the salience of words in input sentences, and the range of instances to which words are applied. These characteristics of input may have different specific effects on two aspects of word learning: Frequency and salience of use of particular words may affect which words are acquired as well as the order of emergence; the contexts in which parents use words (i.e., the range of instances covered) may affect the nature of meanings the child assigns to words.

With regard to the particular words the child acquires and the order in which they are acquired, the words learned first may be those that occur more frequently and saliently than other words in parent speech. That is, if particular words are presented frequently, are said with stress, and occupy salient positions in parent utterances, forming new concepts or mapping words to established concepts may be promoted. On the other hand, the effects of frequency and salience of particular words in input may not be powerful. Even a very few uses may enable the child to learn words if a particular concept is accessible. Conversely, even highly frequent and salient words may not be learned if the child is not yet capable of forming the concepts they encode. These two cases, in which effects of input frequency and salience are weak, suggest that conceptual development exerts strong enabling or limiting effects, respectively, on which words are acquired. Finally, parents may never produce certain words; in such cases, the child's failure to acquire words would be uninformative about the state of conceptual development.

Note also that the perceptual salience of words in sentences may change with age. For beginning language learners, words that are stressed and presented alone or not deeply embedded in the stream of speech are more salient (Fernald, McRoberts, & Herrera, in press; Messer, 1981; Ninio, 1985).

For more advanced language learners, in contrast, even words that occur in the middle of sentences are salient, especially if they are stressed, presumably because the child uses lexical knowledge already acquired to analyze more complex sentences (Fernald et al., in press). Thus, even if certain concepts are equally available and nonlinguistic contexts equally transparent across age, older learners may have an advantage in forming those concept–word mappings.

Further, the natural linguistic contexts or embeddedness of words in utterances varies for different word classes. For example, in English, object names and the child's own name are more likely to occur in simple sentence frames or alone (e.g., "Shoe; that's your shoe" or "Jeremy!") than are verbs (e.g., "Mommy's getting your shoe, Jeremy" but not "Getting"). If the words acquired first occur in more straightforward linguistic contexts and those acquired later occur in more complex linguistic contexts, it would be impossible to disentangle the effects of input salience and conceptual development. That is, if input sentences are difficult to process acoustically, children may not acquire certain words, even if they already possess those concepts or are capable of forming them. This may be the case for verbs; examining the meanings of early nonverbs, therefore, may help determine whether young children's failure to acquire verbs is due to a conceptual limitation.

With regard to the nature of the word meanings the child acquires, the nonlinguistic contexts in which parents use words may enable children to map words on to concepts they already possess, or input may help children to form concepts that are potentially available (see also Nelson & Lucariello, 1985). In general, adult usage may or may not include the full range of appropriate uses (e.g., Harris, Barrett, Jones, & Brookes, 1988), and as we suggested previously, the range of contexts to which children apply words may match or diverge from adult usage. Matches between child word meanings and adult usage suggest either that children make use of parent speech in forming concepts or children already possess those concepts and map words on to them. Mismatches strongly suggest that conceptual development exerts a major influence on the nature of the word meanings acquired. Further, in cases of divergence, partially overlapping child meanings indicate that children conceptualize a phenomenon in a non-adultlike way, and absent child meanings indicate that children are incapable of forming a particular concept.

PLAN FOR THE CHAPTER

Our plan for the rest of the chapter is to examine the words children learn, the nature of child word meanings, and the nature of parent word use for different classes of words in order to make inferences about the roles of input and conceptual development in lexical acquisition. First, we review data from studies of child language and parent input in the single-word period, focusing on words for events, objects, and people. For each word class, we compare our data on child word meanings and parent input with those of other researchers, review relevant nonlanguage studies, and draw conclusions about the role of input in word learning and about the nature of the child's early concepts. We also examine the order of emergence of concepts within the single-word period to determine whether some concepts are more accessible than others.

Second, we review data from child language studies in the early multiword period of speech, focusing on new words for events and people and on changed meanings for words acquired in the single-word period. We again interpret the child data in the context of parent input and compare our data with those of other researchers before drawing conclusions about the nature of concepts in this period of development. We then describe the course of early conceptual development based on the nature and order of emergence of the child's concepts in the single- and multiword periods, placing the evolution of event concepts in the context of developing notions of objects and persons. Finally, we discuss the ways in which changing sensitivities of the conceptual system may account for the nature and order of emergence of these important aspects of the young child's conceptual scheme.

EARLY MEANINGS OF EVENT, OBJECT, AND PERSON WORDS

Event Words

Consider, as we did in an earlier paper (Huttenlocher, Smiley, & Charney, 1983), the kinds of event representations that may be accessible to children as they learn their first event words. Events consist of the movements of animate or inanimate entities, either singly or in relation to one another, that in some cases result in changes in existing states of affairs. Because events are observable, they may be represented on the basis of some aspect of their appearance. However, they may also be categorized on the basis of unobservable causal relations between entities or, when behaviors of persons are involved, on the basis of intentions that guide behavior.

Events that consist of human actions are produced by the self as well as by other people, and the observable and unobservable aspects of movement or change are different when the self is a participant rather than observer of action. That is, when a person initiates movement or change in the self or in an object, movement in the object and some bodily movements are observable. In addition, feelings of moving and of possessing a goal are potentially accessible to the self. In contrast, when another person initiates movement or change, movement of the other's body and any object is fully observable, whereas the person's subjective states are not and must be inferred.

We proposed (Huttenlocher & Smiley, 1991; Huttenlocher, Smiley, & Charney, 1983) that if the child represents observable aspects of events and groups instances of events together on the basis of similarity of appearance, then events that involve perceptually simple movements may be among the first to be categorized. These include events in which single entities move in ways that vary little from instance to instance. Thus, categories of simple movements of animates (e.g., actions like walking or kicking) may be early. Events that involve more than one entity, even if one of the entities is a person, may also be perceptually simple if the movements of both entities are similar or if the child's focus is on the movement of only one entity. For example, events in which two objects move in similar ways (e.g., "object launchings" in which one object approaches along a path and a second object is launched along that path) are recognizable in infancy (e.g., Leslie, 1982) and may be represented on the basis of their appearance. Even events that involve perceptually complex movements (e.g., the movements involved in fixing or opening things) can be represented on the basis of similarity of appearance if the outcome state (e.g., intactness or openness) is perceptually simple and salient. Further, the child may well see simple movements or states of the self, other persons, and objects as similar to each other. As Piaget (1954) argued, 1-year-olds' imitations of novel observed actions (e.g., opening the mouth after watching a matchbox being opened) suggest that even infants appreciate parallels in movements of different entities.

On the other hand, if the child represents events in terms of their unobservable aspects, category instances can be grouped together on the basis of a similarity in the causal relation between entities, whether the movement or change involved is perceptually simple or complex. Thus, for events in which one object produces movement in another, events in which animates move alone, or events in which a person performs various movements to achieve a result (e.g., the movements involved in fixing a toy, a seam, or a teapot), the child may represent one entity as the cause of movement or change. For events with people, the child may also represent the person as the possessor of particular inner states (i.e., intentions or goals) that motivate actions.

We proposed (Huttenlocher & Smiley, 1991; Smiley & Huttenlocher, 1994) that certain patterns of use of single words provide evidence for the child's event representations. If children represent similarities in the appearance of events, they may use words to encode events with perceptually simple movement patterns and apply these words to events regardless of the entity in which the movement occurs—the self, other people, or objects. They may also use words for events with perceptually complex movement patterns if these movements result in salient outcome states, again regardless of whether change is produced by self or other. These words may be produced after the event occurs, when the outcome is salient.

In contrast, if children represent similarity in causal relations for events involving two objects, they may encode the relational event by producing words at the start of such events or as they progress (e.g., "push" as an object starts to roll toward or as it hits a second object). If children represent similarity in causal power or intentions of persons who produce movement or change in themselves or in objects, they may also tend to use these words in particular ways—prior to self-action, when their own goals are salient, and after others' actions, when the achieved goals are salient (see Hutten-locher, Smiley, & Charney, 1983, on multiword uses). However, children may apply words only to self instances at first because the self has privileged access to inner states. Although it has been suggested that uses of words to request that others perform certain actions provide evidence that children represent others' goals (Edwards & Goodwin, 1986), they may not. When making requests, children may be thinking of their own goals or imagining the outcome of a desired action (Huttenlocher, Smiley, & Charney, 1983; Smiley & Huttenlocher, 1994; see also Budwig, 1989). Requests may suggest that children conceptualize the animate or instrumental capacities of other people but not their intentional states.

The data on which our assessment of children's first meanings for event words is based come from the spontaneous speech of 10 middle-class children (5 boys and 5 girls; 8 first-borns and 2 second-borns). Their utterances and contexts of use were audiorecorded for 5 hours a month during the single word period, starting at a median age of 13 months and ending at a median age of 19.5 months. For each child, the final month of the single word period was the last month in which no more than 5% of utterances contained more than one morpheme. We analyzed words that were produced by four or more children and used in contexts of entity movement or change to determine whether children used their words to encode appearance-based categories of simple movement or salient changes of state in entities, or goal-based categories of actions produced by the self or other people (Huttenlocher & Smiley, 1991; Smiley & Huttenlocher, 1994).

We identified 17 words; here we review our major findings for 14 of them (excluding the performatives *hi, byebye,* and *nightnight*). They included several types of words in the adult language—four spatial prepositions (*down, up, off, out*), four verbs (*open, ride, rock, sit*), two adjectives (*more, my/mine*), one adverb (*there*), and one noun (*door*)—and two words that appear mainly in child-directed speech (*allgone, uhoh*). We began our examination of the contexts of use of event words by determining whether children used these words in contexts where events were present or absent.

We found that a majority of uses for almost all the early event words (except for *more, open,* and *ride*) occurred when event instances were present; we based our conclusions about word meanings chiefly on these uses. However, "absent instance" uses were also easily interpretable—they were primarily requests for action in appropriate circumstances.

When we considered the present instance uses, we found commonalities across instances, so we could ask what kinds of events were encoded with early event words. Ten words were used in contexts that involved simple movements of entities that varied little from instance to instance. In particular, the paths of those entity movements were very similar. For example, directed vertical motion was most common for *down,* motion away from some entity for *off,* motion toward another entity for *my/mine,* putting two objects in contact for *there,* and change in posture for *sit.* Occasionally, movements in the opposite direction occurred (e.g., taking out for *there;* going up for *down*).

For these 10 words, we looked at present instances to determine whether the perceptually simple movements occurred in a range of entities. That is, we tried to determine whether the child encoded movement types independent of the kind of entity that moved. Three words (*door, my/mine,* and *there*) were used for movement of a certain kind in inanimate objects, one word (*ride*) for movements of an object or a person on an object, and the other six words for movements of both people (e.g., getting *up* or going *out*) and objects (e.g., a toy horse made to go *up* a hill or a doll taken *out* of a truck). Thus, as a group these words were used for movement occurring in both animate and inanimate entities, and when words were used for events involving people, instances involved both the self and other people. These uses suggest that for these 10 words, children group instances on the basis of similarity of appearance of particular kinds of movement in a variety of physical entities.

The other four words (*open, allgone, uhoh,* and *more*) were applied to events with movements that varied from instance to instance, but three of these had perceptually salient outcome states that could be categorized on the basis of appearance. *Open, allgone,* and *uhoh* were used for events in which entities moved in perceptually complex ways but the resulting outcome states of openness, absence, or disarray were perceptually simple. These words, like those for simple movement, were applied to events produced by both the child and other people. In fact, about 40% of uses of *allgone* and *uhoh* were for observed events, and a majority of uses of *open* were requests for other people to enact events. Further, *allgone* and *uhoh* were often used for pre-existing states of absence or disarray when only the object states and not the movements that brought them about were salient. These uses suggest that for these three words, children group instances on the basis of similarity of appearance of salient outcome states of certain kinds, regardless of how they come about.

The last word we examined, *more*, was also used for events in which movements of entities varied widely across instances (e.g., movements involved in somersaults, procuring objects, or turning the handle of a jack-in-the-box). These movements were sometimes produced by the child and often requested of an adult, and the word use almost always involved a second instance of a particular event. These uses suggest that children group instances on the basis of a notion of replication (perhaps a non-appearance-based category) of interesting effects, regardless of the entities involved.

Thus, for most of the early event words we examined, there is evidence to suggest that the child represents the similarity in aspects of the external appearances of events. However, movement in persons and in objects is always produced by a person, so it is possible that the child represents not just movement or change of state but a conceptually more complex relation—intentional human action or causation of change in objects by persons. Suggestive evidence that the child does not yet represent intentional human action came from two sources: the child's use of words for events produced by self and by others and the timing of utterances in relation to events produced by self.

Our earlier work on children's verb meanings (Huttenlocher, Smiley, & Charney, 1983) showed that verbs first acquired in the early multiword period were initially applied only to self-action, both in production and comprehension, and when applied to self-action were produced prior to acting. These data suggested that at first the child encoded only self-goals. In contrast, for the early event words, we found uses for events initiated both by the child and by other people but, as for verbs, uses during child-initiated events were far more numerous. A strong bias toward self-action uses may indicate that the child is not easily able to encode events initiated by other people or that the child has no reason to talk about others' actions. To determine the source of bias, we attempted to elicit production of several different words for observed events from several children by drawing the child's attention to an adult engaged in an activity (e.g., sitting down for *down* or struggling to remove a shoe for *off*) and saying, "Look! What's Mommy doing?" For all the words we tested, children produced words for the observed events; their elicited productions occurred in the same month or one month after the child's first use for self-movement. Further, the spontaneous uses of words for instances involving other people were just as compelling as self-uses (e.g., saying "off" as a sibling took off her shoe, "rock" as a boy rocked on a playground horse, "there" after the observer put a dress on a doll) and often occurred in the same month but always within a month or two of the first uses for self.

Uses of words for events produced by self and by others may mean that children encode intentional action in the single-word period or that children encode movement or change in different entities but not intentionality. We reasoned that if children produce words prior to initiating movement or change (as they do with verbs), the words may encode intention or the causal relation between self and object movement. We found that for 9 of the 10 simple movement words, the majority of uses occurred when events were ongoing. The percentages were similar for movements of the self versus self-produced movement of objects, suggesting that the child focuses on the motion of an entity rather than on the causal relation between self and object movement. For *there* as well as for *open, allgone,* and *uhoh,* the majority of self-uses were after the completion of the event, when the achieved result was salient. Further, *uhoh* was sometimes used for clearly accidental events.

Thus, this aspect of the data fails to provide evidence that intentional causation of movement or change is the child's focus. Note, however, that single-word speech data are not conclusive with regard to this issue; because the child produces only one word, it is impossible to know with certainty whether the child represents events in terms of movement or change in single entities or instead, in terms of a relation between an initiator and an object. Indeed, the preponderance of self-action uses during apparently goal-directed activities is consistent with the notion that the child is at least in the process of acquiring a sense of self as a cause of self- and object-movement. As Gopnik (1988) argued, use of words during self-initiated activities may indicate that the child is grappling with this cognitive problem.

Accounts from other laboratories support our interpretation of word use. That is, other researchers also emphasize the child's grasp of perceptual commonalities among instances of movement and change in entities. Others report that in the single-word period some event words cover movements in the child, other persons, and objects, with object movements produced by both self and other (Choi & Bowerman, 1991; Edwards, 1978; Edwards & Goodwin, 1986; McCune-Nicolich, 1981); that some words are used to name self-action as well as to request actions of others involving a variety of entities (Tomasello, 1987; Tomasello & Farrar, 1984); and that some early event words are used for events with salient outcome states (Edwards & Goodwin, 1986; McCune-Nicolich, 1981; Tomasello, 1987; Tomasello & Farrar, 1984). Further, Tomasello and Farrar (1986b) reported that novel words for two kinds of appearance-based event categories—simple movements (spinning) and salient changes of state (hiding)—can be trained in the single-word period.

In contrast, some researchers (Gopnik, 1981, 1982; Gopnik & Meltzoff, 1985, 1986) claimed that children do not represent perceptual similarities among events but rather similarities in aspects of self-action. Gopnik and Meltzoff argued that the referential uses of many early event words encode similarities in the child's plans—their outcome, success, or failure—across a variety of kinds of movement or change. In particular, they propose that *down, up, off,* and *gone* encode outcomes of child plans, *there* encodes the success of plans, and *uhoh* encodes the failure of plans. One part of their argument rests on the proposal that the movements of entities involved in events (e.g., downward motion for events of throwing, falling, or sitting; detaching motion for events of taking off or pulling apart) are essentially dissimilar in appearance and that the child's plan to achieve outcome states is the common element among these instances. Although the extent of perceptual similarity among instances is a matter of coders' judgments, Gopnik and Meltzoff (1986) proposed that at least some early event words encode notions that seem to depend on the child's noticing similarities in appearance across various instances of entity movement, namely notions of "gravity" and "attachment." Bowerman (1989), also, argued that children perceive various attachment or separation events involving two small objects as similar.

The second part of their argument involves an interpretation of data from productive word use and performance on cognitive tasks. For example, Gopnik and Meltzoff (1984, 1985, 1987) showed that the use of *there* after a variety of completed child actions and the solution of several means–ends tasks without trial and error (e.g., placing a necklace in a bottle, using a string to get an object, stacking rings in order on a post and avoiding a solid one) emerge simultaneously. They argue that these converging data show that *there* encodes the success of the child's goal-directed actions. The data may indicate that the child is in the process of constructing a self with intentions. However, they are also consistent with the idea that the child is learning to manipulate more than one object in space.

In summary, there is support for the notion that in the single-word period, the child focuses on the perceptually available aspects of events. In addition, some aspects of the data are consistent with the emergence of a concept of self as an initiator or possessor of goals. However, as we argue in later sections, there is strong evidence from nonlanguage studies of conceptual development as well as from studies of later word use that the self as a cause of movement or change is not fully represented until around the second birthday.

Parent Use of Movement/Change Words. To explore the possible effects of parent word use on the child's acquisition of particular words and on the meanings of those words, we discuss evidence for frequency, salience in utterances, and nonlinguistic contexts of some event words from our own and others' research. In our work, we examined uses of content words, including event words, in a sample of 21 middle-class mothers (Huttenlocher, Haight, Bryk, Seltzer, & Lyons, 1991) as well as uses of four spatial terms (*down, up, off,* and *out*) in a sample of 11 middle-class mothers speaking to their 16-month-olds (Goodman & Huttenlocher, in preparation). These data were taken from four hours of videotaped interactions between each mother and her child at home.

We found a strong positive association ($r = .65$) between the frequency of parent use of content words and the age of children's acquisition of those words (Huttenlocher et al., 1991). For the spatial terms in particular, the most frequent words in mother speech were *down* and *up* (Goodman & Huttenlocher, in preparation); these were also the words used by the greatest number of children (10 and 9 children, respectively) in a comparable sample (Smiley & Huttenlocher, 1994). In addition, some early event words occur in very salient linguistic contexts. *More* and verbs for salient changes of state (e.g., *blow up*) are often used as single words (Ninio, 1985), and spatial terms often occur as particles, either alone or at the ends of adult utterances and with primary stress, as in "Do you want up?" (Tomasello, 1987). In the Goodman and Huttenlocher (in preparation) data, the four spatial terms were used both as prepositions (nonsalient, embedded uses) and as verb particles. However, three of the four words appeared frequently in perceptually salient positions—between 49% and 61% of uses of *down, up,* and *off* were either in final position or alone—and these were the three words with high frequencies of use in the child data. Thus, children's early acquisition of particular event words may be due in part to their frequency and accessibility in input sentences.

In contrast, only certain aspects of mothers' use of words in nonlinguistic contexts are mirrored in children's word meanings, namely the observable aspects of events. Parents use event words for simple movement or change (Barrett et al., 1991; Harris et al., 1988; Ninio, 1985) and for movement in a variety of entities (Choi & Bowerman, 1991; Goodman & Huttenlocher, in preparation), and these uses are mirrored in child word meanings. In addition, English- and Korean-speaking parents produce different kinds of appearance-based meanings (path of movement vs. tightness of fit), and these meanings are acquired early by their English- and Korean-speaking children, respectively (Bowerman, 1989). Thus, exposure to words in such contexts may affect the acquisition of particular word meanings.

Goodman and Huttenlocher's (in preparation) work shows that certain other meanings for event words are conveyed by parent use, yet these meanings are not acquired by children. Mothers in that sample produced a majority of spatial terms for present instances prior to events (perhaps because mothers encoded their own goals, expressed goals for their child, or anticipated the child's goals), but children in our comparable sample produced event words while movement was ongoing. In this respect, child usage diverges from mother usage and may reflect children's insensitivity to the conceptualization of goals.

Further, although mother uses of spatial terms for existing locations of objects were not frequent at 16 months (between 4% and 14% of uses for the four terms; Goodman & Huttenlocher, in preparation) child uses in the single word period were almost nonexistent—only 1% of uses (see also

Gopnik & Meltzoff, 1985; Greenfield & Smith, 1976). The absence of state uses of event words by children in the single word period may be due to children's inability to conceptualize the perceptually complex spatial relation between an object and its location. However, such uses are also less frequent than movement uses in mother speech, and they are presumably not as salient in mother utterances, occurring embedded among other words in prepositional phrases.

In sum, the parent input data suggest that word frequency and relative salience in input sentences may have salutary effects on learning particular event words. The input data also suggest that parent use of these words in contexts of simple movement and salient change of state influences the child's acquisition of meanings, whereas parent use in contexts of intentional action does not. The restriction in child use to ongoing movement suggests that a concept of intentional action, even for the self, is inaccessible in this early period. Finally, whereas some mother uses are for locations, almost no child uses encode locations, but this may be due to characteristics of input or conceptualization.

Related Studies of Event Concepts. The results of related nonlanguage studies strongly suggest that children in this period of language-learning appreciate parallels in observable aspects of movement or change in people and objects but not intentional causation of movement or change by people. That is, the nonlanguage data support a model of conceptual development that is consistent with our analyses of the patterns of child word meanings and adult speech. Two kinds of studies are relevant: studies of perception of object movement and studies of imitation of others' movements and production of change.

With respect to perception of object movement, before one year of age infants distinguish events involving different types of movement of single objects (Ruff, 1985) and of two objects (Leslie, 1982; Leslie & Keeble, 1987). The latter include events in which one object is "launched" by another versus events in which a target object is launched without contact or after a delay. The "smooth launch" events are more likely to be perceived as new events if they are reversed (i.e., with the launched object becoming the launcher) than are the "anomalous launch" events (Leslie & Keeble, 1987).

Although this finding suggests to some (e.g., Mandler, 1992) that infants grasp the causal nature of certain physical events, Cohen (Cohen & Oakes, 1993; Oakes & Cohen, 1990) found that infants do not group instances of causal or noncausal events together but rather perceive associations between particular objects and the events in which they occur. These data support Piaget's (1954) argument that categorization of events in which movement in one object is caused by another may be based on expected associations between successive object movements rather than on an understanding of cause–effect relations. A notion of causality involves recognizing not only that one object movement normally succeeds another but also that the first provides the force that brings about the second (Huttenlocher & Smyth-Burke, 1987; Leslie, 1982).

Contrasting children's perception of events consisting of just object movements with events consisting of human action on objects may provide evidence about their understanding of the causation of object movement. Leslie's (1982, 1984) studies show that before 8 months, infants discriminate the caused movement of an object in contact with a hand from the "magical" movement of an object that is not in contact with a hand (but they do not distinguish between similar events with two objects). However, these findings may show simply that the child's expectations for hand–object and object–object movement relations are different. Golinkoff (Golinkoff, Harding, Carlson, & Sexton, 1984) reported that even at 16 months children perceive as similar events in which chairs move spontaneously or are caused to move by a person, perhaps because they focus only on entity movement. At 2 years they perceive the events as dissimilar, perhaps because they recognize people as the sources of movement in objects. Similarly, data from Gleitman's laboratory (reported in Gleitman, 1990; Naigles, 1990) show that linguistic expressions of movement *caused by* an animate versus movement *in* an animate are distinguished at around 2 years.

Young children's imitations of others' movements also provide evidence that movement in entities is conceptualized before movement of objects caused by people. Thus, by about one year, infants imitate familiar and novel bodily movements that are visible or invisible to the self (Guillaume, 1926/1971; Masur, 1991; Piaget, 1951; Uzgiris & Hunt, 1975) as well as simple movements on objects (Hanna & Meltzoff, 1989, 1991; Meltzoff, 1988) and novel effects caused by movements on objects (Guillaume, 1926/1971; Piaget, 1951). That is, they treat instances of bodily movement in self and other as well as self- and other-produced movement in objects as similar. For the instances involving the production of novel effects in objects, Guillaume (1926/1971) argued that if children understand that an initiator's movements caused the interesting effects, they should replicate the model's movements exactly. Only at around 2 years of age do children imitate precisely the nature of a model's movements in producing effects on objects (McCall, Parke, & Kavanaugh, 1977; Nadel-Brulfert & Baudonniere, 1982). It is possible that 1-year-olds understand the causal power of persons to create change even though they imitate only effects and not the precise movements involved in creating those effects. However, the convergence of McCall et al.'s data with those from Golinkoff's laboratory suggests that they do not.

Taken together, the word use data from children and parents and the data from studies of event perception and imitation suggest that events are at first conceptualized on the basis of similarities in appearance of movements or achieved change of state in entities (including people) and not on the basis of intentional causation of movement or change by people. That is, event words are not early substitutes for verbs; they encode more primitive notions of movement or change in any entity. We turn to another class of word meanings acquired in the early months of speech, namely words for small objects.

Object Words

As for events, many object types share aspects of appearance, whereas other object types share critical internal properties despite dissimilarities in surface appearances. Thus, one way in which children may represent a class of objects is on the basis of similarity in appearance across instances. However, because objects often occur in contexts of movement and change, children may group instances of objects together on the basis of a different perceptual similarity—the simple events in which objects occur. Alternatively, children may conceptualize objects not on the basis of such perceptual similarities but rather on the basis of similarities in their "insides."

With respect to these possibilities, research shows that by 2½ years, children can infer that even dissimilar-looking objects share nonobservable properties or processes (e.g., "eats dirt," "moves by itself"), especially when a category label is provided (Gelman & Coley, 1990). Younger children (up to 16 months) make inferences about common function only when objects look alike (Baldwin, Markman, & Melartin, 1993). It may be that infants have strong expectations that object appearance and nonobvious properties are corre-lated; however, it is not yet known whether they could also make inferences that dissimilar-looking objects share such properties if a category label were provided.

With respect to the view that event contexts figure in children's early conceptualization of objects, Nelson and her colleagues (Gruendel, 1977; Nelson, 1974, 1983; Nelson & Lucariello, 1985) suggested that in the single-word period, children form some object-related categories in which an event is the basis for grouping instances. Gruendel (1977) reported that at least some words for objects reflect such groupings (e.g., one child's use of "hat" encoded the event of *putting on* hats, buckets, paper, or keys).

In our study of object word meanings (Huttenlocher & Smiley, 1987), we analyzed spontaneous production of object words in the single-word period by the 10 children whose event words we discussed previously. Several specific analyses of word use were designed to determine whether object word meanings include commonalities in appearance and/or events in which objects tend to occur. First, in contrast to earlier studies (e.g., Bowerman, 1980; Piaget, 1962) that drew conclusions about word meaning by examining the range of unique uses of words, we examined the relative frequencies of each kind of use and identified commonalities within the types of uses.

We found that the majority (23 of 25) of the most frequent words (i.e., those used by 4 or more of the 10 children) were used over 80% of the time for present, appropriate instances of objects (see Table 1, Huttenlocher & Smiley, 1987). Our analysis indicated that the present instances to which names were applied formed a set based on perceptual similarity, with occasional broader application than the adult category. For example, "ball" was used primarily for kinds of balls but also for Christmas ornaments, eggs, and oranges. These overgeneral uses were probably attempts to stretch a limited vocabulary to fit children's communicative purposes (see Huttenlocher, 1974). Thus, our data on present instances suggest that object-word meanings cover perceptually similar instances of objects of particular kinds.

Second, whereas some earlier research (e.g., Bloom, 1973; Bowerman, 1980; Piaget, 1962) treated uses when category instances were not present as evidence that children named related aspects of context (e.g., a habitual location or event) with object words, we analyzed these uses in terms of other possible communicative functions that words might serve. This analysis supported our assessment of the nature of word meanings based on the present-instance uses. By and large, absent-instance uses were interpretable as appropriate contexts for comments on the recent or habitual presence of the named objects (e.g., saying "cookie" for a schoolbag where a child recently noticed a cookie or "ball" for Mommy's racquetball racquet) or requests for the named objects (e.g., saying "cheese" while reaching and looking at the refrigerator). (See Tables 3 and 4, Huttenlocher & Smiley, 1987.) These data provide evidence against an interpretation of word use that suggests that events or locations in which objects are encountered are components of children's representations of objects.

Third, whereas earlier studies of events occurring during object word use highlighted only a few words (e.g., Gruendel, 1977), we analyzed all frequent object words. Event contexts were very frequent—only 17% of uses occurred when an object was stationary. Of special interest were those contexts in which similar objects were always involved in the same event ("object-specific action") or a range of dissimilar objects occurred in a single event, as in Gruendel's examples of *baba* and *bat*. Analysis of all 25 object words showed that whereas general object-handling actions (e.g., getting or pointing at an object) were very common, object-specific acts (e.g., throwing a ball, eating an apple) were relatively infrequent. (See Table 3, Huttenlocher & Smiley, 1987.) Only a few object words had a substantial proportion of object-specific uses (between 20% and 43% for *light, bat, shoe, apple*, and *sock*). Thus, these few words could encode either "object of a kind" or "object of a kind + event-with-object." In a further analysis of the objects involved in object-specific events, we found that these were almost always appropriate objects of one kind and that when other objects were present, most were perceptually similar. It was never the case that a diverse set of objects was involved in a particular event. In addition, the perceptually similar objects were no more likely than appropriate objects to be involved in an object-specific event than in an object-general event, suggesting that the child's focus is on the class of objects, not on the event.

In summary, our analyses indicated that object word uses encode objects of particular kinds, grouped by their common shape, and do not encode notions of event-with-object. Although objects were often involved in events, the range of action contexts was broad in most cases and even for those objects for which certain action contexts were quite salient, the proportion of uses in those contexts was relatively small. Thus, our data indicated that object word meanings are adultlike—they encode object types, abstracted from the events in which they occur.

Other researchers also noted that most object words cover an appropriate range of instances—that is, a perceptually similar set of instances—from the start (Bowerman, 1980; Gruendel, 1977; Harris et al., 1988; Macnamara, 1982; Rescorla, 1980) and that older children reliably extend newly learned names to similarly shaped exemplars (Golinkoff, Hirsh-Pasek, Bailey, & Wenger, 1992). Further, many novel object words are extended on the basis of form, especially when the salience of object function (i.e., the number of possible object-specific actions) is low (Nelson & Bonvillian, 1973; Ross, Nelson, Wetstone, & Tanouye, 1986). Although words are usually extended to instances on the basis of perceptual (shape) similarity, functional overextensions and the minority of uses during object-specific acts suggest that object function is also a component of meaning. Interestingly, awareness of the possibility of common function for a range of different-looking objects may be more developed among advanced language-learners, rather than characterizing the youngest language-learners. Lucariello (1987) found that both beginning (mean MLU = 1.07) and advanced (mean MLU = 1.53) language learners extended words for novel objects on the basis of similarity in form but only advanced learners overgeneralized to perceptually dissimilar objects that varied widely in form but not function from the original exemplar (e.g., a ladle instead of a baster used to serve a liquid).

Thus, beginning speakers' word use reflects sensitivity to similarities of shape. Even though object function is not lost on young children—saying "hat" while putting keys on the head may constitute a playful, metaphorical use of the word that relies on knowledge of object function—and even though older children are able to create new object groupings on the basis of functional similarity despite wide variation in form, children of all ages conceptualize objects apart from the events in which they can occur.

Parent Use of Object Words. Analyses of several aspects of the uses of object words by middle-class mothers shed some light on the role of input for the acquisition of object words. The frequency of mothers' use of particular object words at 16 months was strongly related ($r = .77$) to children's age of acquisition of those words over the period from 18 to 24 months (Huttenlocher et al., 1991). Preliminary data from a subset of this same corpus of mother speech showed that placement of object words in utterances was very salient—70% of object words occurred alone or in last position in utterances. Mothers' use of many common nouns as single-word utterances is also reported by Ninio (1985), and other research shows that object names are often stressed in utterances, especially when attention is jointly focused (Messer, 1981; Tomasello & Farrar, 1986a).

A study of cultural differences in these input characteristics shows that they affect acquisition of object names as a class (Fernald & Morikawa, 1993). Whereas Japanese mothers present more object labels in single-word utterances, American mothers provide more object labels, use more adult forms, are more consistent in the forms they use, and present object labels more often in stressed, salient positions (e.g., at the ends of questions). According to mother report, American children's noun vocabularies are almost twice as large as Japanese children's. Further, other research shows that the nonlinguistic contexts of object naming may promote mapping of words to context. Naming very frequently accompanies joint attention to objects (Harris et al., 1988; Ninio, 1985), and naming in these contexts is strongly correlated with the size of later noun vocabularies (Akhtar, Dunham, & Dunham, 1991; Della Corte, Benedict, & Klein, 1983; Tomasello & Farrar, 1986a).

We do not have data on the range of uses of object names by adults from our sample of mother speech, but Harris et al. (1988) found that mothers used object words across a range of appropriate contexts and that for the earliest uses of object words, children's most frequent contexts of use mirrored those of their mothers. In sum, frequency of use and linguistic and nonlinguistic salience appear to affect the acquisition of object words as a class; frequency is also highly related to the acquisition of particular words. Although we do not have much data on the kinds of instances mothers talk about, the fact that children's object words have adultlike meanings from the start suggests either that children possess adultlike object concepts prior to word learning or that they construct them through hearing adults use object words in a range of appropriate contexts.

Related Studies of Object Concepts. Studies of differential attention to perceptually similar objects and of appropriate use of new object exemplars show that very young children form object groupings based on similar shape and also that they are sensitive to the functions of objects within these groupings prior to or in the early months of language-learning. Thus, by 9 months, children sequentially touch similar instances of one of two contrasting types of geometric forms. Shortly after one year, children touch first one type and then the other (Ricciuti, 1965; Starkey, 1981); they differentially manipulate or attend to realistic category and noncategory members (Mandler & McDonough, 1993; Mervis, 1985; Ross, 1980), and their selection of category instances is stable (Mervis, 1985). Between 12 and 18 months, they use new object exemplars in specific and appropriate ways (e.g., Lowe, 1975; Lucariello, 1987), even if words for the objects are not produced (Lucariello, 1987; Mervis, 1985). Even some categories that emerge by 24 months, namely substances, are formed prior to learning relevant language and apparently without the benefit of input (Soja, Carey, & Spelke, 1991). If some categories of material kinds—objects and substances—are formed without language input, this suggests that conceptual development may operate independently of parents' word use in the acquisition of at least some word meanings.

Thus, our data and those of other language and nonlanguage researchers suggest that object word meanings cover instances of objects that share form, that appropriate function is part of object knowledge, and that some concepts may be acquired without language input. The role of parent speech for some object and substance terms may be to permit pairing words with established concepts rather than to assist in the formation of concepts themselves. There is a substantial effect of frequency of parents' use on the particular words acquired; however, the nature of object word meanings may reflect primarily the influence of children's conceptual development— that is, the early accessibility of appearance-based concepts of small objects.

Person Words

Like event words, words for persons can capture the visible and/or internal similarities among instances. Although people have different visual perspectives on the self and others as well as differential access to experiences of inner states by self and other, adults group instances of persons on the basis of similarities in appearance or subjective states, when appropriate (Huttenlocher & Smiley, 1990). Class names (e.g., *baby, woman*) and proper names are used to encode the physical identity of people, whereas possessive pronouns (*my, your, her*) and first person pronouns (*I, you, she*) are used to encode subjective states of possession and participation as agent or experiencer, respectively. Further, adults use class names and proper names to refer to both self and certain others at the same moment, but they use possessive and first-person pronouns to refer to either self or other on different occasions. That is, pronouns are linguistic shifters (e.g., Charney, 1980); the same words refer to either self or other, depending on the conversational role (speaker or hearer) a person fills.

Given that person words can capture similarities in either physical or subjective aspects of people and that rules of language use are complex for some person words, on what basis do young children group together instances of self and other? With regard to the physical identity of individuals or classes of people, children may represent the perceptual similarity among instances, as they do for other kinds of objects. If people are grouped together or recognized as individuals on the basis of appearance, instances of both self and other may be included. On the other hand, because children have less access to physical appearance of the whole self (except in the mirror), they may fail to include the self and apply these words only to other people at first.

With regard to possession, children may apply words (proper names or possessive pronouns) correctly on the basis of the similarity in appearance of a person in habitual physical contact with certain objects. Alternatively, children may represent these relations on the basis of subjective feelings of ownership. In either case, uses for objects to which the self or other has enduring ownership relations, not just temporary use relations, would be most convincing that a child has a notion of possession. However, it is difficult to determine whether such uses reflect appearance- or internal-state-based categories. If meanings included only òwned objects and were restricted to the self, children might conceptualize ownership in terms of subjective states, because there is direct access to inner states only for the self.

With regard to conceptualizing the intentional agency of persons, certain kinds of uses of person words (proper names and pronouns) suggest that children understand intentionality. In particular, as for event words, uses of self words prior to acting suggest that children conceptualize the self as an intentional agent. Uses of words for other people during not-yet-successful attempts to achieve certain kinds of goals may indicate that children conceptualize others' intentions. In contrast, uses of person words during simple movements produced by other people are not as convincing. In fact, words used for other persons during movement may encode only physical identity; that is, movement may draw attention to the presence of a particular person (Huttenlocher & Smiley, 1990; see also Frye, Rawling, Moore, & Myers, 1983). As for event words, requests using person words indicate only that the child understands the animate or instrumental capacities of people, not necessarily the intentional nature of their actions (Huttenlocher & Smiley, 1990).

Our data come from analyses of the contexts of use of person words in the single-word period by the 10 middle-class children whose event and object word meanings we discussed previously. We review here preliminary data on words for people (presented in Huttenlocher & Smiley, 1990) and include a closer look at the use of *my/mine* (Smiley & Huttenlocher, 1994), which we classified as an event word.

We found that words for other people (e.g., *mommy*, siblings' names) are acquired in the first few months of speech. A majority of names for all kinds of people are said when an appropriate person is present. *Mommy* and *daddy* seem to be used both as class and as proper names at first, but other words (e.g., *Becky*) are used only as proper names. These uses for present, appropriate instances suggest that children represent other people as physical entities with a certain appearance.

Person words are also used in requests when people are present or absent, and the proportion of request uses is greater than for either event or object words. In addition, the nature of requests is unique for person words. When object and event words are used, the object or event is requested; when a person's name is used, the request is for an object or action, to summon the named person, or to make a nonspecific request (i.e., to complain). All three kinds of uses suggest that children represent other people as entities that can move on their own and function as instruments of goal fulfillment. In related work on categorization of animate and inanimate exemplars, Mandler (1992; Mandler & McDonough, 1993) suggests that 9- to 11-month-olds group animals as "self-starters"—sources of their own movement—and distinguish them from perceptually similar inanimates.

Do the child word-use data suggest that people are conceptualized not just as animate instruments but also as intentional agents or causes of object movement? Uses when people are engaged in some goal-directed activity independent of the child were relatively rare—less than 10% of all uses. Instead, word use often occurred when children noticed adults entering or leaving the room, when children greeted adults, and when children gave objects to adults; similar uses were noted by other researchers (e.g., Greenfield & Smith, 1976). As we pointed out previously, these uses do not provide compelling evidence that others' intentions are encoded. People's appearances and disappearances and their role as object recipients may draw attention to them as entities. Such uses may also reflect the child's understanding of their animate nature.

There is another reason to suppose that children do not conceptualize other people as agents. One might expect that the self would be conceptualized first in this regard. As we argued previously, the abundance of uses of event words for movement or change of the self may indicate that a child is starting to conceptualize the self as an intentional agent. However, in the single-word period, our data showed that children do not acquire a word to name the self, and to our knowledge there is no systematic study of children's comprehension of their own names. Names for people are restricted to proper or class names for others in the early months of language-learning. Further, the personal pronoun *I*, which may occur in intentional self-action contexts, is not acquired.

Only the pronouns *my* and *mine* were produced in the single-word period, and like other event words, these words seem to encode a kind of simple movement in objects. In our data, *my* and *mine* were used similarly and primarily for moving an object toward a person (Smiley & Huttenlocher,

1994). There were uses of *my/mine* when the child or another person moved objects toward themselves, but uses when other people obtain objects may encode the conditions that normally precede the child's moving that object toward the self. In addition, compared to most other event words, a greater percentage of *my/mine* uses named pre-existing states (e.g., the child holding an object). Thus, *my/mine* could encode either a movement with a consistent appearance that ends in a salient outcome state or a notion of possession for the self or for both self and other.

Because *my/mine* was used primarily for movements initiated by the child, it could encode possession. However, two other aspects of usage suggest that an adultlike notion of possession is not encoded. First, the objects moved toward or held by the self were not predominantly child-owned; a third were clearly others' possessions (e.g., mommy's necklace). Other researchers' observations of the contexts of use of *my* are very similar—*my* occurs during actions of grabbing for objects that often do not belong to the child (Charney, 1980; Deutsch & Budwig, 1983; Edwards, 1978). Second, even if children's notions of possession are broader (including all sorts of objects) than adults', it is unlikely that the relation between objects and self is explicitly encoded. As we noted, children have no other words for self, not even their proper names. Thus, this early pronoun seems to be linked with movement or change and a "self-assertive feeling," as Cooley (1908) suggested.

In sum, the only words for people acquired in the single-word period are names for other people, and these seem to encode both appearance and movement potential (animacy) but not intention (agency). The only self word acquired early, the possessive pronoun, like other event words, seems to encode movement or change of a particular kind and not a notion of possession. Thus, neither words for other people nor words for self seem to encode the unobservable, subjective states of persons.

Parent Use of Person Words. We have preliminary data on parent use of several person words from 2½-hour observations of each of our 11 mothers speaking to her 16-month-old. The person word *mommy* was used fairly frequently—167 uses by eight mothers—and a majority of these uses were in salient positions, either the first or last word in the utterance. About half of the uses were in contexts of varied mother actions, and half were when no action was occurring. Thus, frequency and salience of use of *mommy* may be sufficient for the child to acquire this word; however, the range of adult use of *mommy* is not mirrored in child use—children used *mommy* only during a few actions (e.g., coming and going). As we suggested previously, these activities may draw attention to mother as an entity capable of movement in fulfillment of the child's goals but not as an agent in her own right.

Mothers used the word *my* but much less frequently and saliently than *mommy*—only 35 uses by 8 mothers—and almost every use was in medial utterance position. In comparison, *your* was very frequent—a total of 415 uses by all 11 mothers—and primarily in medial positions. Despite the discrepancy in frequency of use of *my* and *your* and the relative inaccessibility of the possessive pronouns in the stream of speech, children acquire the words *my* and *mine*, suggesting that the movement of objects toward a child is a conceptually accessible (and powerful) idea. As Charney (1980) argued from experimental comprehension data, young children acquire this word with restricted meaning because at first they conceptualize just the speaker role (for whom *my* is appropriate) only for themselves.

Finally, the child's name was among the most frequent words in mother speech at 16 months—533 uses by our 11 mothers—and it occurred in salient positions, alone or in last position. Further, names were used in salient nonlinguistic contexts: when offering things to the child, when calling the child, and so on (Huttenlocher & Smiley, 1990; Ninio, 1985). Despite these input characteristics that may promote conceptual development and word learning, children did not acquire the proper name for self until the early multiword period, several months after the acquisition of names for objects and other people. This pattern suggests that a concept of the overall appearance (and perhaps other characteristics) of the self may be inaccessible to the child throughout the single-word period, preventing word learning.

Related Studies of Self-Recognition. Studies of children's facial self-recognition corroborate the finding that the self is not explicitly conceptualized early on, even as an entity with a particular physical appearance. In the single-word period (prior to about 20 months) children engage in mirror exploration, looking at and playing with their image (Stipek, Gralinski, & Kopp, 1990), but at most only a small minority (Lewis & Brooks-Gunn, 1979; Priel & deSchonen, 1986; Stipek et al., 1990) label a picture of themselves with their own name. In contrast, by 24 months, a majority of children produce their own name to label a picture of themselves (Lewis & Brooks-Gunn, 1979; Stipek et al., 1990) or react to rouge on their faces (Priel & deSchonen, 1986), and these behaviors are characteristic of almost all children by 30 months (Bullock & Lutkenhaus, 1990). Further, a comparison of Bedouin and urban Israeli children shows that the emergence of self-recognition behavior at 20 to 26 months is independent of experience looking at the self in a mirror (Priel & deSchonen, 1986).

Order of Emergence of Early Meanings
for Object, Event, and Person Words

Each of the types of word meanings acquired in the single-word period seems to reflect conceptual development and in particular a sensitivity to the similarity in appearance among instances to which words are applied—similarity among objects or persons of a kind, similarity among movements in entities, or similarity among changes of state in entities. A consistent ordering in the emergence of these meanings for most children would suggest that even among these appearance-based categories, one of them is conceptually prior to the others, or that they are equally accessible but the relative frequency or salience of mother use across word types contributes to the observed ordering. If there is no particular ordering in the emergence of these meanings, each may be a conceptual primitive, and sensitivity to appearance of instances, whether of types of entities or of movement or change, underlies early word meanings.

Our data on the order of acquisition of object, movement and change, and person words come from two sources, the longitudinal study of 10 children cited throughout this section and the longitudinal study of 11 children and their mothers from which the parent data reported in this section were taken. For the sample of 10 children we have 5-hour observations at monthly intervals, starting with each child's first month of speech. For the sample of 11 children, we have 4-hour observations at bimonthly intervals, starting at 16 months. We counted a word class as acquired for a particular child in the month during which the child had at least two meaningful uses of at least one word in the class (e.g., one naming use of *mama* in the first month of speech and two request uses in the second month would count as person words acquired by the second month of speech). Because the classes of object and event words are larger than the class of person words, we also included comprehension data for person words when it was available.

The sample of 10 children yields the best evidence on order of emergence because we have measures of production and comprehension. We first examined the order of emergence of object versus person words for each child in their first four months of speech (see Table 2.1). As shown in Table 2.1 (footnote c), two children (B2 and B5) produced only one spontaneous use of a person word (*mommy*) during the first four months of sampling. However, we had tested their (and G5's) comprehension of *mommy* in months prior to their first productive use, and they responded reliably in the month shown. Using the combined production and comprehension data, we see that object words were acquired before person words by five children and that person words were acquired before or simultaneously with object words by five children. Thus, there was no privileged order of acquisition of these two word classes.

We then compared the order of emergence of object/person words (using the average of the months in which object and person words appeared) and movement/change words. This analysis showed that object/person words were acquired before movement/change words by 6 children and that movement/change words were acquired before or simultaneously with object/person words by 4 children. Again, there appears to be no preferred order for acquisition of these two word classes.

TABLE 2.1
Age of Acquisition of Event, Object, and Person Words

Subject[a]	First Month of Speech	Word Class		
		Event	Object	Person
G1	11	13	11	13
G2	13	15	14	14
G3	13	16	15	14
G4	13	13	13	16
G5	14	15	15	16 (15)
B1	13	16	13	15
B2	13	—[b]	13	16 (14)[c]
B3	13	13	13	14
B4	13	15	15	13
B5	21	21	23	23 (20)[c]

[a]G1–5 indicate female subjects; B1–5 indicate male subjects.
[b]B2 did not acquire any event words during his first 4 months of speech; his first event word appeared in his 5th month of speech.
[c]Month in parentheses indicates when children reliably comprehended *mommy*. B2 and B5 each produced *mommy* only once in the first 4 months of speech.

Finally, of the full sample of 21 children, a total of 19 (9 of 10 and 10 of 11) had begun to speak before 16 months. We treated this age as a benchmark and found that 15 of the 19 children had produced both object/person and movement/change words, 3 had produced only object/person words, and one had acquired only movement/change words by 16 months. Clearly, within and across children, none of these word classes has priority over the others in very early language-learning.

Similarly, Gopnik (1988) reported that for referential uses of object/person words and movement/change words ("cognitive-relational" words in her breakdown) there is no preferred order of production. For 27 subjects across two studies, 13 produced object/person names before movement/change words, and 14 produced object/person words after or at the same time as movement/change words (see Tables 2 and 4, Gopnik, 1988). Several other researchers also found that novel words for simple movements and for small objects can be trained in the same early period from 15 to 17 months (Oviatt, 1980; Schwartz & Terrell, 1983; Tomasello & Farrar, 1986b).

LATER WORD MEANINGS

We have described the nature and simultaneous acquisition of some classes of word meanings in the single-word period. Some of the words have adultlike meanings from the start—object words encode objects of a kind, abstracted from their contexts; words for other people, after some initial overgeneralization, pick out particular individuals; and *allgone* and *uhoh*, which are not marked for cause or intention even in the adult language, encode salient effects on objects. In contrast, other early words do not have adultlike meanings—*door* and *there* encode kinds of movement or change and *more* encodes repetition of events. The early person word *my* appears not to encode possession, and other words for self are missing. *Down, up, off,* and *out* encode direction of movement but not location. The early verbs *open, ride, rock,* and *sit,* are used for movement or change produced by different people, as they are by adults, but they appear not to encode intentional acts, even for the self.

Because we do not have all the relevant parent input data, we cannot be certain for many of the words children acquire whether childlike meanings reflect childlike concepts or instead mirror restrictions in the range of use by adults. That is, *door* may only have been used by parents as doors were opened for the child, *there* may only have been used by parents in the context of placing objects in or on other objects, and *open* may have been used primarily for outcome states.

For some word meanings, however, available input and acquisition data suggest that the failure to acquire word meanings reflects the relative accessibility of concepts. For example, although parents used the child's name frequently and saliently, it was not acquired. Although parents used spatial terms saliently and prior to movement events produced by self and other, children did not use these event words to announce their intentions. On the other hand, the absence of locational meanings for the spatial terms and the absence of other verbs for intentional actions in the single-word period may be attributable to their occurrence in medial, nonsalient positions in parent utterances. For these cases, data from the multiword period are helpful in determining whether the concepts these words encode are inaccessible to the younger child or whether the words are difficult to extract and map onto concepts.

Old Words with New Meanings and New Words

We have argued that in the single-word period, children acquire a set of word meanings that reflect their ability to group category instances by appearance. In particular, we suggested that events appear to be conceptualized in terms of observable movement or change in entities. We next present evidence that in the early multiword period, events are no longer conceptualized in terms of movement or endstates but rather in terms of intentional action, initially just for the self. This development is reflected in changes in the meanings of event words as well as in the acquisition of many new verbs for goal-directed action. This shift toward conceptualizing internal states is also reflected in the acquisition of self words that appear to encode agency.

The data on the change in meanings of event words (spatial prepositions and *my*) come from our longitudinal study of 10 children in the early multiword period (through MLU 2.5) (Smiley & Huttenlocher, 1994). We found that some uses of spatial terms were unchanged from the single-word period; there were uses for movement in people or inanimates, produced by both the child and other people. These uses occurred in a variety of linguistic contexts, with a majority functioning as verb particles (e.g., "Take shoe off") and the next highest proportion as the main event word (e.g., "Doggie out"). Constructions with the spatial term as the main event word or "predicate" raised the question of whether these words encode intention in the early multiword period. Compared to utterances with verbs acquired in this period, utterances with spatial terms as predicates almost never had person words in first position (e.g., "Nicky out"), constructions that might encode intentionality. Instead, spatial terms appeared most frequently with inanimates in first position (e.g., "Horsey up") or with no other word in first position (e.g., "Off truck"), suggesting that the words still encoded movement in some entity rather than movement caused by a person.

In addition, the four spatial terms were no longer used exclusively in contexts of movement in entities. In this later period, uses of *down, up, off,* and *out* for pre-existing states increased, and linguistic contexts of use reflected this new meaning component. The words appeared in location phrases such as "Want down table" and "I take my spoon out a there." Other researchers (e.g., Gopnik & Meltzoff, 1985; Stockman & Vaughn-Cooke, 1992; Tomasello, 1987) also reported that the meanings of spatial terms evolve to cover both directed movement and location, as they do for adults. With respect to this change in meaning, Bowerman (1989) suggested that younger children may at first conceptualize only symmetric two-entity movements in which object roles are not marked, whereas older children may represent the specific asymmetric relations between smaller and larger (supporting or containing) objects (see also Gopnik & Meltzoff, 1986).

The early event word *my* also acquired a relational meaning in the early multiword period (Smiley & Huttenlocher, 1994). Whereas early uses of *my/mine* encoded movement of a wide range of objects toward the child, later uses of *my* were primarily stative (the child holds an object) and the proportion of uses for child-owned objects was twice as large as for the single-word uses. The linguistic structure of the child's multiword utterances also reflected the shift toward a relational meaning. Almost all utterances contained NPs with *my* as a noun modifier, juxtaposing the person word and the object word (e.g., "My hands hurt," "Me putting my socks on"). These uses suggest that *my* encodes an enduring relation between objects and the self and perhaps a subjective state of possession. However, uses for objects belonging to other people persisted, suggesting that children's notion of a possessive relation is somewhat broader than adults'.

Along with the new relational meanings for the spatial terms and a more fully developed notion of the subjective state of possession, children acquired words for the self. Data from our group of 10 children showed that between 20 and 24 months, children acquired both their own names and the first person pronoun *I*, in either order, within a span of 1 or 2 months (Huttenlocher & Smiley, 1990). The simultaneous acquisition of these words, despite differences in linguistic complexity, suggests that a concept of self that includes both the particular appearance and the actor/experiencer role of the self emerges all at once. (See Budwig, 1989, for a closer analysis of uses of particular self words for particular functions.)

Finally, a large number of verbs were acquired in the early multiword period. The most frequent verbs in child speech were "change" verbs; these are not defined by the nature of the movements involved in carrying out the action but rather by the achievement of a change of state created through a range of appropriate movements (e.g., *find, get, make*) (see Table 5, Huttenlocher, Smiley, & Charney, 1983). The vast majority of verbs, like event words, occurred when the child was acting or requesting an action. In contrast to the uses of earlier event words, when verbs were used in relation to present instances of events they were produced as the child began to act and in utterances with the child's name or the personal pronoun *I* in first position. In addition, words that encode experiences of desire, namely *want* and *need*, were acquired and used exclusively for child states; the only uses for other people were routinized (e.g., "Want this?" while handing over objects). Together, these data suggest that unlike event words of the single-word period, later-emerging change verbs encoded children's goals of causing change.

In contrast, there was substantial evidence that children in this period do not yet encode others' intentions to cause change. First, because children rarely used change verbs for others' actions, we attempted to elicit such uses by drawing the child's attention to others' actions. Although we were able to elicit early event words as descriptions of others' movement or change, our attempts to elicit change verbs as descriptions of other people's actions were unsuccessful. Second, our comprehension study of verbs applied to other people's actions showed that children at first applied only some verbs to others' actions. Movement verbs (e.g., *bounce, kick, wave*) were learned much earlier than change verbs (see Table 3, Huttenlocher, Smiley, & Charney, 1983). Even the transitive versions of the appearance-based movement verbs (e.g., a person kicking a hat vs. kicking one's foot) that involve two entities and are perceptually more complex than the intransitive versions were much easier for children than the goal-based change verbs that involved two entities.

Thus, in the early multiword period, the word meanings data suggest that children conceptualize self-action in terms of goals but at the same time categorize others' actions only on the basis of the consistent appearance of bodily movements. The application of verbs to observed events in which other people cause change through variable means occurs later and may depend on the child's ability to infer that others' variable movements, like their own, are organized around goals of achieving some result. Some support for the view that goals are important in organizing perceptual information about human action comes from Behrend (1990), who found that when 3-year-olds (and adults) were asked to extend newly acquired novel verbs to new instances of observed events, the kind of change produced (i.e., the goal of the action) was the most informative component, more informative than either the movements of entities or the instruments used.

Parent Use of Words for Location and Intentional Action. Although the word meaning data strongly suggest that children re-conceptualize events in terms of intentional human action in the early multiword period, these data alone do not indicate whether this shift is due to changes in the nature of parent speech to children or to a fundamental conceptual change that originates in the child. We next examine data on parent usage to determine the extent of influence of input on these new meanings. There are limited data on parents' use of spatial terms for location, suggesting that such uses may increase markedly over the multiword period. Goodman and Huttenlocher (in preparation) found that at 16 months, between 4% and 14% of uses of the four spatial terms encoded existing object locations; Messer (1981) reported that locative descriptions in a laboratory play setting increased sevenfold between 14 and 24 months. Thus, the change in frequency of occurrence of location uses (as well as their position in the middle of parent utterances) may help explain children's later acquisition of location meanings for these words.

Because data on the frequency, salience, and contexts of parent use of verbs are also fairly scarce, we next review accumulating data from several laboratories. Parent frequency of use of particular verbs may be expected to affect children's acquisition of those verbs. Huttenlocher et al.'s (1991) finding of a strong positive correlation between parent frequency of use and child age of acquisition of particular content words suggests that there may be such a relation for verbs. In addition, salience of verbs in parent utterances may change with age as linguistic knowledge increases. Indeed, Tomasello and Kruger (1992) reported that certain characteristics of parent input affect verb learning at 21 but not at 15 months, perhaps because increasing linguistic knowledge helps children extract verbs from mother utterances.

The frequency and salience of verbs relative to words in other classes can also reveal the effects of input on lexical acquisition. In both English and Korean, verbs have a frequency advantage over nouns in parent input; in mother speech to their 12- to 17-month-olds, verb tokens are about twice as frequent as noun tokens (Au, Dapretto, & Song, in press). However, in English, verbs are three times less likely than nouns to receive primary stress (Messer, 1981), and verb tokens are no more likely than noun tokens to appear in salient, utterance-initial or -final positions (Au et al., in press). In contrast, in Korean, verbs are twice as likely as nouns to occur in these salient positions (Au et al., in press; see also Gopnik & Choi, 1990).

One study suggests that these characteristics of input affect verb learning; Choi and Gopnik (1993) reported that verb spurts (10 or more new verbs in one monthly session) preceded noun spurts for six of their nine Korean subjects. On the other hand, the number of nouns and verbs learned before the verb spurt (at about 19 months) was approximately equal for these children, and for the other three children, noun spurts occurred first. Further, Au et al. (in press) found that Korean children (at 17 and at 23 months) knew many more nouns than verbs, just like their English-speaking peers; this finding corroborates more extensive cross-linguistic data presented by Gentner (1982). Note also that several of the earliest Korean verbs encode salient changes of state or simple movements (Choi & Gopnik, 1993; Gopnik & Choi, 1990), as do early movement or change words in English. Thus, the greater availability of verbs in Korean input may primarily affect the acquisition of words that encode the movement or change aspect of events. If this is so, as Keil (1990) pointed out, the data patterns observed across cultures (i.e., similar representations despite dissimilar environments) probably reflect the operation of a powerful cognitive constraint.

Moreover, the order of acquisition of verb meanings for self and other that we observed in our study (Huttenlocher, Smiley, & Charney, 1983) was not related to the nature of parent use. Huttenlocher, Smiley, and Ratner (1983) examined parents' uses of two types of verbs for child and adult action, namely simple movement verbs and change-of-state verbs. There were three major findings: Adults used both kinds of verbs to describe the child's as well as their own actions, but uses for children's action were about twice as frequent as for adults' action. Parents' uses of movement verbs were somewhat more biased toward children's action than were change verbs. However, parents used one of the change verbs that children produced most frequently (*get*) more often for their own than for children's actions.

The overall bias in parents' use toward child-action contexts is consistent with children's initial verb meanings, but the extent of the bias does not account for children's complete failure to apply change verbs (especially *get*) to others' actions at first. Moreover, the stronger bias toward children's actions for movement verbs does not explain children's earlier application of movement verbs to others' actions. Huttenlocher, Smiley, and Ratner (1983) also found that the distribution of parents' uses at 24 months was similar to that at 16 months, so input cannot easily account for the shift in meanings from self to others' actions or the shift from movement verbs to change verbs for others' actions. Thus, the early restrictions in children's verb meanings probably reflect an initial inability to conceptualize goal-directed actions of other people.

Recent evidence suggests that another aspect of input may indeed promote the formation of a notion of intentional action for both self and other. Tomasello and Kruger (1992) reported that the size of children's verb vocabularies is related to the timing of mothers' use of verbs—prior to the child's actions, when the child's goals presumably are salient, and after her own actions are completed, when the aims of her movements are most apparent. Tomasello (1992) speculated that impending and completed contexts of use may be best for learning change-of-state verbs for which organizing goals and/or salient outcome states are important, whereas ongoing contexts of use may be best for movement verbs that are repetitive and simple in appearance.

SUMMARY AND CONCLUSIONS

Input, Conceptual Development, and the Acquisition of Word Meanings

In this chapter we examined, within and across two early periods of language learning, the nature of children's word meanings and the nature of parents' word use in order to draw conclusions about the roles of adult input and conceptual development in lexical acquisition. We focused particularly on parent and child use of event words in order to understand how young children conceptualize events. We examined two other classes of words— object and person words—in order to place event concepts in the broader context of the child's developing conceptual scheme.

Our method involved examining different patterns of correspondence between parents' use and children's word learning. In brief, matches between parent use and child use suggest a relatively strong role for parent input; mismatches, a relatively strong role for conceptual development. To review the findings, studies of early word meanings showed that children learn words for events, objects, and persons in the single-word period. Studies of input suggested that the particular words children acquire are sufficiently frequent and salient in parent speech to permit young children to learn them. For example, there was a relation between input salience and acquisition of particular event words in comparable parent and child samples as well as a strong effect of frequency of exposure on the acquisition of particular object words. Some words are learned despite lower frequency and salience, however. For example, the event word *my* is used relatively infrequently by mothers and primarily in medial utterance position (and, presumably, in contexts of mothers' possessions). Nevertheless, children acquire this word early, suggesting that the movement category it initially encodes is salient and that children may "seek" to learn this word (Gopnik & Choi, 1990; Shatz, 1987).

Studies also showed that children's event words have only partially adultlike meanings, whereas names for objects and other persons are adultlike from the start. Especially notable is the absence of intentional action meanings for the earliest event words; in addition, the spatial terms and *there* do not have locational meanings, and *my/mine* does not encode possession at first. Data on the nonlinguistic contexts of use of these early words by parents are scarce, so it is not entirely clear what role parent use plays in the nature of meanings acquired. The few studies of input showed that parents use the spatial terms and object words across a range of appropriate contexts. However, nonlanguage studies of object and substance categories suggest that some concepts are formed independently of parent word use. Thus, for some early movement or change categories and for object categories, exposure to words in parent speech may enable children to map words onto concepts if they are already in place or may promote the acquisition of both categories and words.

We also observed certain mismatches between parent word use and the words or meanings children acquire, suggesting that the conceptual scheme does not always develop in response to contemporaneous input. In the single-word period, although parents produce words prior to events that involve human action and sometimes use spatial terms to encode location, children do not use these words for intentional action (even for the self) or location. In addition, although children acquire the word *my* and their parents presumably use it appropriately in contexts of personal possession, children's use reflects a simpler notion of object movement. And, despite informative parent use, children do not acquire their own names. Further, in the early multiword period, even when children have more language and adult uses of verbs cover instances of self- and other-action, children do not initially acquire full verb meanings.

As we discussed, failure to acquire some of these words or meanings in the single-word period may be explained in terms of characteristics of parent input and children's limited language knowledge. However, for several words in both the single and early multiword periods, the inaccessibility of relevant concepts appears to be the more important factor. Thus, the self words (i.e., child name, first person pronouns, self-action meanings of change verbs) are acquired simultaneously in the early multiword period regardless of differences in salience in parent utterances or in linguistic complexity, and verbs are extended to include others' actions after several months without a shift in the distribution of parent uses. These developments suggest that concepts of intention and other subjective states are initially inaccessible but that once the relevant concepts are available, mapping words to concepts may be straightforward.

Nevertheless, it is possible that input supports the acquisition of some of these later emerging categories (i.e., identity of the self, intentional action for other people) in subtler ways. Timing of parent utterances in relation to events seems to affect acquisition of verbs. In addition, that parents use their children's names and verbs for their own (parents') actions for many months before children acquire these words or meanings suggests that the categories may develop through cumulative effects of exposure to words in context rather than through immediate and powerful effects of conceptual change. We need systematic and detailed data on timing and contexts of parent use over the course of the single-word and early multiword periods to begin to address this question.

In addition to the roles of adult input and conceptual development in accounting for lexical acquisition, children's developing language knowledge no doubt allows them to learn new words or meanings by taking advantage of input in new ways. For example, knowing words for objects and other people may enable the child to attend to verbs in sentences that encode the goal-directed movements of a person on an object. Further, knowledge of certain word meanings may enable children to form more conceptually complex groupings of experience. For example, possessing categories of movement or change in entities may enable children to make sense of movements and outcome states they observe during parent use of words for goal-directed action, permitting them ultimately to learn that those movements are organized by intentions to achieve certain outcomes or goals.

In sum, language input, conceptual development, and language knowledge play important roles in early lexical acquisition. Over the first two years of language learning, children are exposed to many classes of words, often spoken in appropriate, informative contexts. Nevertheless, only some classes of words are acquired early in language learning; the effects of input appear to be limited when categories are unavailable to the child. Words that are acquired later in language learning appear to depend on important changes in the child's conceptual scheme and language knowledge, changes that enable the child to use parent input in different ways over this time span.

Event Words and the Development of the Conceptual System

Our analyses suggest that children's event word meanings reflect a dramatic change in the conceptualization of events from the single word to early multiword periods. At first, events are represented in terms of the movements and outcome states of animate and inanimate entities. As we saw, the child categorizes movement and change across these entities but also makes primitive distinctions with regard to person movement—other people are treated as if they can move on their own, and many kinds of self-movement are particularly salient. Later, events that consist of child action, especially those involving the production of movement or change in objects, are conceptualized in terms of intended outcomes. Still later, events that consist of others' actions are represented in terms of intentions that organize the observable aspects of those events.

These longitudinal data lead us to propose that orderly changes in sensitivities of children's conceptual system underlie the changes in representations of events, objects, and persons that we have described. Others argued (Gelman, 1990a, 1990b; Keil, 1990) that changing attentional sensitivities bias children to attend to aspects of input that are pertinent to the formation of concepts. The data we have presented suggest the nature of some of these attentional biases. In forming their first categories, children appear to group instances on the basis of perceptual similarity; the regularities children extract from a varied nonlinguistic environment and from the stream of adult speech reflect this sensitivity. Further, the appearance-based categories children form—of directed movement, salient changes of state, objects, and other people—may have a special status as primitive elements in the child's conceptual scheme. They emerge very early and seem not to depend on the prior emergence of other concepts. In addition, they may support the later acquisition of perceptually more complex notions involving relations among two or more objects that may be appearance-based in whole or in part.

By the early multiword stage, certain other aspects of meaning become accessible as a sensitivity to certain nonobvious properties of events and persons arises. Children's categories of self-action and possession evolve and appear to be based on commonalities in internal states. These internal state categories may also be regarded as primitive elements in the child's conceptual scheme; they are ontologically distinct from the appearance-based categories that emerge earlier (see also Keil, 1990). In addition, they may support the later acquisition of adultlike internal state categories that cover both self and other. Children may recognize the analogous relation between observable and unobservable aspects of events in which the self and other people participate.

It is not yet clear how children's sensitivity to psychological states, including intentions, develops. Rather than emerging full-blown at 20 to 24 months, a notion of intention may gradually coalesce through learning about object movement or change and self-action in infancy. That is, infants are sensitive to certain cues to physical causality including "point of contact" between objects (Brown, 1990), successive object movements (Leslie, 1982), and object transformations (McCune-Nicolich, 1981). In addition, we noted that some aspects of early word use—the strong bias toward self uses and the uses of words for other people to summon or complain—show that infants are sensitive to persons as distinct from other entities in their ability to generate movement and to make other objects move. Others (e.g., Mandler, 1992) argued that these cognitive achievements indicate that infants under 12 months represent human causation of events. In our view, the infant's knowledge of object movement, together with knowledge of the special movement properties of animates and in particular, the child's own experiences of exerting force on objects, may enable the child to bootstrap his or her way toward a partial notion of human causality by the end of the single-word stage (20 to 24 months).

As Gleitman (1990) reminded us, language has a role in the acquisition of a notion of psychological causation. She argued that categories of internal states cannot be acquired unaided or just by word-to-world mapping because there are no observable referents for these words in the world. Instead, sentence-to-world mapping helps delimit the portions of experience to which these words refer. Thus, mental state verbs occur in a restricted range of subcategorization frames, namely with sentence complements, that may powerfully predict the semantics of the verbs. Change-of-state verbs, similarly, have their own set of informative subcategorization frames that contrast with those for verbs of emotion or perception. Further, the NPs that serve as subject terms of such sentences include words for the child and other persons, highlighting the range of members in the categories of agent or experiencer.

Thus, children's sensitivities first to perceptually simple aspects of experience and later to psychological causation, along with informative language input and a developing ability to utilize it, may allow the child to form at first childlike and later adultlike representations of events in the second and third years of life. As Fischer and Bullock (1981) put it, the patterns of data we observed challenge us to explain why certain representations are actualized by the conceptual system at various points in time. These changes in sensitivity of the cognitive system, operating in a rich language environment, may help explain more precisely the evolution of the child's conceptual scheme.

ACKNOWLEDGMENT

The research reported in this chapter was supported by a grant from The Spencer Foundation to Janellen Huttenlocher.

REFERENCES

Akhtar, N., Dunham, F., & Dunham, P. (1991). Directive interactions and early vocabulary development: The role of joint attentional focus. *Journal of Child Language, 18*, 41–49.
Au, T. K., Dapretto, M., & Song, Y. K. (in press). Input versus constraints: Early word acquisition in Korean and English. *Journal of Memory and Language.*
Baldwin, D., Markman, E., & Melartin, R. (1993). Infants' ability to draw inferences about nonobvious object properties: Evidence from exploratory play. *Child Development, 64*, 711–728.

Barrett, M. (1986). Early semantic representations and early word-usage. In S. Kuczaj & M. Barrett (Eds.), *The development of word meaning* (pp. 39–67). New York: Springer-Verlag.

Barrett, M., Harris, M., & Chasin, J. (1991). Early lexical development and maternal speech: A comparison of children's initial and subsequent uses of words. *Journal of Child Language, 18,* 21–40.

Behrend, D. (1990). The development of verb concepts: Children's use of verbs to label familiar and novel events. *Child Development, 61,* 681–696.

Bloom, L. (1973). *One word at a time.* The Hague, Netherlands: Mouton.

Bowerman, M. (1980). The structure and origin of semantic categories in the language-learning child. In M. Foster & S. Brandes (Eds.), *Symbol as sense: New approaches to the analysis of meaning* (pp. 277–299). New York: Academic Press.

Bowerman, M. (1989). Learning a semantic system: What role do cognitive predispositions play? In M. Rice & R. Schiefelbusch (Eds.), *The teachability of language* (pp. 133–169). Baltimore: Paul H. Brookes.

Brown, A. (1990). Domain-specific principles affect learning and transfer in children. *Cognitive Science, 14,* 107–133.

Budwig, N. (1989). The linguistic marking of agentivity and control in child language. *Journal of Child Language, 16,* 263–284.

Bullock, M., & Lutkenhaus, P. (1990). Who am I? Self understanding in toddlers. *Merrill-Palmer Quarterly, 36,* 217–238.

Charney, R. (1980). Speech roles and the development of personal pronouns. *Journal of Child Language, 7,* 509–528.

Choi, S., & Bowerman, M. (1991). Learning to express motion events in English and Korean: The influence of language-specific lexicalization patterns. *Cognition, 41,* 83–121.

Choi, S., & Gopnik, A. (1993, April). *Nouns are not always learned before verbs: An early verb explosion in Korean.* Paper presented at the Stanford Child Language Research Forum, Palo Alto, CA.

Cohen, L., & Oakes, L. (1993). How infants perceive a simple causal event. *Developmental Psychology, 29,* 421–433.

Cooley, C. (1908). A study of the early use of self-words by a child. *Psychological Review, 15,* 339–357.

Della Corte, M., Benedict, H., & Klein, D. (1983). The relationship of pragmatic dimensions of mothers' speech to the referential-expressive distinction. *Journal of Child Language, 10,* 35–44.

Deutsch, W., & Budwig, N. (1983). Form and function in the development of possessives. *Papers and Reports on Child Language Development, 22,* 36–42.

Edwards, D. (1978). The sources of children's early meanings. In I. Markova (Ed.), *The social context of language* (pp. 67–85). New York: Wiley.

Edwards, D., & Goodwin, R. (1986). Action words and pragmatic function in early language. In S. Kuczaj & M. Barrett (Eds.), *The development of word meaning* (pp. 257–273). New York: Springer-Verlag.

Fernald, A., McRoberts, G., & Herrera, C. (in press). Effects of prosody and word position on lexical comprehension in infants. *Journal of Experimental Psychology: Learning, Memory and Cognition.*

Fernald, A., & Morikawa, H. (1993). Common themes and cultural variations in Japanese and American mothers' speech to infants. *Child Development, 64,* 637–656.

Fischer, K., & Bullock, D. (1981). Patterns of data: Sequence, synchrony and constraint in cognitive development. In K. Fischer (Ed.), *Cognitive development* (pp. 1–20). San Francisco: Jossey-Bass.

Frye, D., Rawling, P., Moore, C., & Myers, I. (1983). Object-person discrimination and communication at 3 and 10 months. *Developmental Psychology, 19,* 303–309.

Gelman, R. (1990a). First principles organize attention to and learning about relevant data: Number and the animate–inanimate distinction as examples. *Cognitive Science, 14,* 79–106.

Gelman, R. (1990b). Structural constraints on cognitive development: Introduction to a special issue of *Cognitive Science. Cognitive Science, 14,* 3–9.

Gelman, S., & Coley, J. (1990). The importance of knowing a Dodo is a bird: Categories and inferences in 2-year-old children. *Developmental Psychology, 26,* 796–804.

Gentner, D. (1982). Why nouns are learned before verbs. In S. Kuczaj (Ed.), *Language development* (Vol. 2, pp. 301–334). Hillsdale, NJ: Lawrence Erlbaum Associates.

Gleitman, L. (1990). The structural sources of verb meanings. *Language Acquisition, 1,* 3–55.

Goldin-Meadow, S., Seligman, M., & Gelman, R. (1976). Language in the two-year-old. *Cognition, 4,* 189–202.

Golinkoff, R., Harding, C., Carlson, V., & Sexton, M. (1984). The infant's perception of causal events: The distinction between animate and inanimate objects. In L. Lipsitt & C. Rovee-Collier (Eds.), *Advances in infancy research* (Vol. 3, pp. 125–165). Norwood, NJ: Ablex.

Golinkoff, R., Hirsh-Pasek, K., Bailey, L., & Wenger, N. (1992). Young children and adults use lexical principles to learn new nouns. *Developmental Psychology, 28,* 99–108.

Goodman, J., & Huttenlocher, J. (in preparation). *The development of locative categories and prepositions in language production and comprehension.* University of California, San Diego.

Gopnik, A. (1981). Development of non-nominal expressions in 1- to 2-year-olds. In P. Dale & D. Ingram (Eds.), *Child language—An international perspective* (pp. 93–104). Baltimore: University Park Press.

Gopnik, A. (1982). Words and plans: Early language and the development of intelligent action. *Journal of Child Language, 9,* 303–318.

Gopnik, A. (1988). Three types of early word: The emergence of social words, names and cognitive-relational words in the one-word stage and their relation to cognitive development. *First Language, 8,* 49–70.

Gopnik, A., & Choi, S. (1990). Do linguistic differences lead to cognitive differences? A cross-linguistic study of semantic and cognitive development. *First Language, 10,* 199–215.

Gopnik, A., & Meltzoff, A. (1984). Semantic and cognitive development in 15- to 21-month-old children. *Journal of Child Language, 11,* 495–513.

Gopnik, A., & Meltzoff, A. (1985). From people, to plans, to objects. *Journal of Pragmatics, 9,* 495–512.

Gopnik, A., & Meltzoff, A. (1986). Words, plans, things, and locations: Interactions between semantic and cognitive development in the one-word stage. In S. Kuczaj & M. Barrett (Eds.), *The development of word meaning* (pp. 199–223). New York: Springer-Verlag.

Gopnik, A., & Meltzoff, A. (1987). Early semantic developments and their relationship to object permanence, means-ends understanding, and categorization. In K. E. Nelson & A. vanKleeck (Eds.), *Children's language* (Vol. 6, pp. 191–212). Hillsdale, NJ: Lawrence Erlbaum Associates.

Greenfield, P., & Smith, J. (1976). *The structure of communication in early language development.* New York: Academic Press.

Gruendel, J. (1977). Referential extension in early language development. *Child Development, 48,* 1567–1576.

Guillaume, P. (1926/1971). *Imitation in children.* Chicago: University of Chicago Press.

Hanna, E., & Meltzoff, A. (1989, April). *Peer imitation in the second year of life.* Paper presented at the Biennial Meeting of the Society for Research in Child Development, Kansas City, MO.

Hanna, E., & Meltzoff, A. (1991, April). *Learning from others in infant daycare: Remembering and imitating the actions of another.* Paper presented at the Biennial Meetings of the Society for Research in Child Development, Seattle, WA.

Harris, M., Barrett, M., Jones, D., & Brookes, S. (1988). Linguistic input and early word meaning. *Journal of Child Language, 15,* 77–94.

Huttenlocher, J. (1974). The origins of language comprehension. In R. Solso (Ed.), *Theories in cognitive psychology: The Loyola Symposium* (pp. 331–368). Hillsdale, NJ: Lawrence Erlbaum Associates.

Huttenlocher, J., Haight, W., Bryk, A., Seltzer, M., & Lyons, T. (1991). Early vocabulary growth: Relation to language input and gender. *Developmental Psychology, 27,* 236–248.

Huttenlocher, J., & Smiley, P. (1987). Early word meanings: The case of object names. *Cognitive Psychology, 19,* 63–89.

Huttenlocher, J., & Smiley, P. (1990). Emerging notions of persons. In N. Stein, B. Leventhal, & T. Trabasso (Eds.), *Biological and psychological approaches to emotion* (pp. 283–295). Hillsdale, NJ: Lawrence Erlbaum Associates.

Huttenlocher, J., & Smiley, P. (1991, April). *Early words for movement.* Paper presented at the Biennial Meetings of the Society for Research in Child Development, Seattle, WA.

Huttenlocher, J., Smiley, P., & Charney, R. (1983). Emergence of action categories in the child: Evidence from verb meanings. *Psychological Review, 90,* 72–93.

Huttenlocher, J., Smiley, P., & Ratner, H. (1983). What do word meanings reveal about conceptual development? In T. Seiler & W. Wannenmacher (Eds.), *Concept development and the development of word meaning* (pp. 210–233). Berlin: Springer-Verlag.

Huttenlocher, J., & Smyth-Burke, T. (1987). Event encoding in infancy. In P. Salapatek & L. Cohen (Eds.), *Handbook of infant perception* (Vol. 2, pp. 209–231). New York: Academic Press.

Keil, F. (1990). Constraints on constraints: Surveying the epigenetic landscape. *Cognitive Science, 14,* 135–168.

Leslie, A. (1982). The perception of causality in infants. *Perception, 11,* 173–186.

Leslie, A. (1984). Infant perception of a manual pick-up event. *British Journal of Developmental Psychology, 2,* 19–32.

Leslie, A., & Keeble, S. (1987). Do six-month-old infants perceive causality? *Cognition, 25,* 265–288.

Lewis, M., & Brooks-Gunn, J. (1979). *Social cognition and the acquisition of self.* New York: Plenum.

Lowe, M. (1975). Trends in the development of representational play in infants from one to three years: An observational study. *Journal of Child Psychology and Psychiatry, 16,* 33–47.

Lucariello, J. (1987). Concept formation and its relation to word learning and use in the second year. *Journal of Child Language, 14,* 309–332.

Macnamara, J. (1982). *Names for things.* Cambridge, MA: MIT Press.

Mandler, J. (1992). How to build a baby: Conceptual primitives. *Psychological Review, 99,* 587–604.

Mandler, J., & McDonough, L. (1993). Concept formation in infancy. *Cognitive Development, 8,* 291–318.

Masur, E. (1991, April). *Transitions in representational ability: Infants' language-related and -unrelated imitation across the second year.* Paper presented at the Biennial Meetings of the Society for Research in Child Development, Seattle, WA.

McCall, R., Parke, R., & Kavanaugh, P. (1977). Imitation of live and televised models by children one to three years of age. *Monographs of the Society for Research in Child Development, 42* (5, Serial No. 173).

McCune-Nicolich, L. (1981). The cognitive bases of relational words in the single word period. *Journal of Child Language, 8,* 15–34.

Meltzoff, A. (1988). Infant imitation after a 1-week delay: Long-term memory for novel acts and multiple stimuli. *Developmental Psychology, 24,* 470–476.

Mervis, C. (1985). On the existence of prelinguistic categories: A case study. *Infant Behavior and Development, 8,* 293–300.

Messer, D. (1981). Non-linguistic information which could assist the young child's interpretation of adults' speech. In W. P. Robinson (Ed.), *Communication in development* (pp. 39–62). London: Academic Press.

Nadel-Brulfert, J., & Baudonniere, P. (1982). The social function of reciprocal imitation in 2-year-old peers. *International Journal of Behavioral Development, 5,* 95–109.

Naigles, L. (1990). Children use syntax to learn verb meanings. *Journal of Child Language, 17,* 357–374.

Nelson, K. (1974). Concepts, word and sentence: Interrelations in acquisition and development. *Psychological Review, 81,* 267–285.

Nelson, K. (1983). The derivation of concepts and categories from event representations. In E. Scholnick (Ed.), *New trends in conceptual representation* (pp. 129–149). Hillsdale, NJ: Lawrence Erlbaum Associates.

Nelson, K., & Lucariello, J. (1985). The development of meaning in first words. In M. Barrett (Ed.), *Children's single-word speech* (pp. 59–86). New York: Wiley.

Nelson, K. E., & Bonvillian, J. (1973). Concepts and words in the 18-month-old: Acquiring concept names under controlled conditions. *Cognition, 2,* 435–450.

Ninio, A. (1985). The meaning of children's first words. *Journal of Pragmatics, 9,* 527–546.

Oakes, L., & Cohen, L. (1990). Infant perception of a causal event. *Cognitive Development, 5,* 193–207.

Oviatt, S. (1980). The emerging ability to comprehend language: An experimental approach. *Child Development, 51,* 97–106.

Piaget, J. (1951). *The origins of intelligence in children.* New York: Norton.

Piaget, J. (1954). *The construction of reality in the child.* New York: Basic Books.

Piaget, J. (1962). *Play, dreams, and imitation in childhood.* New York: Norton.

Priel, B., & deSchonen, S. (1986). Self-recognition: A study of a population without mirrors. *Journal of Experimental Child Psychology, 41,* 237–250.

Reich, P. (1976). The early acquisition of word meaning. *Journal of Child Language, 3,* 117–123.

Rescorla, L. (1980). Overextension in early language development. *Journal of Child Language, 7,* 321–335.

Ricciuti, H. (1965). Object grouping and selective ordering behavior in infants 12 to 24 months old. *Merrill-Palmer Quarterly, 11,* 129–148.

Ross, G. (1980). Categorization in 1- to 2-year-olds. *Developmental Psychology, 16,* 391–396.

Ross, G., Nelson, K., Wetstone, H., & Tanouye, E. (1986). Acquisition and generalization of novel object concepts by young language learners. *Journal of Child Language, 13,* 67–83.

Ruff, H. (1985). Detection of information specifying the motion of objects by 3- and 5-month-old infants. *Developmental Psychology, 21,* 295–305.

Schwartz, R., & Terrell, B. (1983). The role of input frequency in lexical acquisition. *Journal of Child Language, 10,* 57–64.

Shatz, M. (1987). Bootstrapping operations in child language. In K. E. Nelson & A. vanKleeck (Eds.), *Children's language* (Vol. 6, pp. 1–22). Hillsdale, NJ: Lawrence Erlbaum Associates.

Smiley, P., & Huttenlocher, J. (1994). *An emerging lexicon: Acquiring words for events.* Unpublished manuscript, Pomona College.

Soja, N., Carey, S., & Spelke, E. (1991). Ontological categories guide young children's inductions of word meaning: Object terms and substance terms. *Cognition, 38,* 179–211.

Spelke, E., Breinlinger, K., Macomber, J., & Jacobson, K. (1992). Origins of knowledge. *Psychological Review, 99,* 605–632.

Starkey, D. (1981). The origins of concept formation: Object sorting and object preference in early infancy. *Child Development, 52,* 489–497.

Stipek, D., Gralinski, J., & Kopp, C. (1990). Self-concept development in the toddler years. *Developmental Psychology, 26,* 972–977.

Stockman, I., & Vaughn-Cooke, F. (1992). Lexical elaboration in children's locative action expressions. *Child Development, 63,* 1104–1125.

Tomasello, M. (1987). Learning to use prepositions: A case study. *Journal of Child Language, 14*, 79–98.

Tomasello, M. (1992). *First verbs: A case study of early grammatical development.* Cambridge, England: Cambridge University Press.

Tomasello, M., & Farrar, M. (1984). Cognitive bases of lexical development: Object permanence and relational words. *Journal of Child Language, 11*, 477–493.

Tomasello, M., & Farrar, M. (1986a). Joint attention and early language. *Child Development, 57*, 1454–1463.

Tomasello, M., & Farrar, M. (1986b). Object permanence and relational words: A lexical training study. *Journal of Child Language, 13*, 495–505.

Tomasello, M., & Kruger, A. (1992). Joint attention on actions: Acquiring verbs in ostensive and non-ostensive contexts. *Journal of Child Language, 19*, 311–333.

Turkewitz, G., & Kenny, P. (1982). Limitations on input as a basis for neural organization and perceptual development: A preliminary theoretical statement. *Developmental Psychology, 15*, 357–368.

Uzgiris, I., & Hunt, J. (1975). *Assessment in infancy: Ordinal scales of psychological development.* Urbana: University of Illinois Press.

CHAPTER THREE

Names, Relational Words, and Cognitive Development in English and Korean Speakers: Nouns Are Not Always Learned Before Verbs

Alison Gopnik
University of California, Berkeley

Soonja Choi
San Diego State University

The idea that object names are acquired well before words encoding actions and relations, first proposed by Gentner (1982), is still widely accepted. The related idea that object names form the most significant early semantic category is also widely held. The reasons that have been advanced to explain this purported dominance vary. Gentner's original discussion suggested that the early predominance of object names reflects a universal set of underlying cognitive principles. Still other accounts suggested that naming is less a cognitive universal than a linguistic one. Discussions of the early naming spurt, for example, often treat this development as an indicator of some new level of general linguistic skill (e.g., Halliday, 1975; McShane, 1980). The "constraints" literature suggested a rather different kind of universalist explanation, in this case a universal constraint on the types of concepts early words can encode. Markman (1989) even proposed a generally applicable principle, the whole object constraint, that makes children assume that early words refer to object classes. In fact, the constraints literature has exclusively focused on object names and categories, although the hypotheses are intended to be quite generally applicable.

All these different explanations propose universal cognitive or linguistic principles. They also assume that the data to be explained are universal: Children always use object names in their early speech well before they talk about actions, relations, or events; and naming is the most important semantic function of early speech. In this chapter we outline a number of reasons to doubt that these empirical claims are correct. In our studies English-speaking children frequently used not only object names but also words that encoded events and relations, although these words were rarely verbs. By many measures these words were as significant as names. Moreover, we have compared English speakers to Korean speakers. Korean-speaking mothers used more verbs and fewer nouns than English-speaking mothers in their speech to children. Furthermore, Korean-speaking mothers encouraged actions markedly more than English speakers during play sessions. For Korean-speaking children, the dominance of relational words was even more marked than for English speakers. In addition, Korean-speaking children, unlike English speakers, used words that were verbs in the adult language to encode early concepts of actions and relations. Many Korean-speaking children had a "verb spurt" similar to the object naming spurt in English.

For both English and Korean speakers, the uses of object names and relational words were closely and specifically related to particular cognitive developments. Relational words encoding aspects of actions and plans (verbs in Korean, words from other syntactic categories in English) were consistently tied to the understanding of relations between means and ends, whereas object names were consistently tied to classification. Korean speakers were advanced in means–ends understanding and delayed in understanding of classification relative to English speakers. The differences between the two groups reflect specific links between semantic and conceptual developments, supporting what we have called the *specificity hypothesis* (Gopnik & Meltzoff, 1986, 1987, 1993).

RELATIONAL WORD USE IN ENGLISH SPEAKERS

Even in the literature on English speakers, the predominance of object names may be an artifact of measurement techniques and subject selection. The most significant measurement problem stems from the fact that, in all languages and for adults as well as children, there are more different nouns than verbs. Because listing word types is the most common way of assessing very early language, nouns automatically dominate our immediate impression of early language. In a diary study, for example, nouns seem disproportionately significant because more actual examples of different nouns are recorded. Gentner's (1982) claims were based on these measures. However, it is important to note that the greater number of nouns than verbs is true of all adult languages. If our only knowledge of English were a dictionary, we might also get the misleading impression that nouns are more significant than verbs in adult English, because there are far more entries for nouns than verbs. The questions are whether children's early language, relative to the adult language, is somehow disproportionately focused on nouns and if so, whether this reflects the sort of universal principles described previously.

In addition, there is considerable variation in naming practices among English-speaking mothers, as we and others have noted, and this variation is reflected in differences among children. We and others have found that some mothers consistently use more nouns in their speech to children than other mothers do. These differences are reflected in the children's language (Goldfield, 1986; Gopnik & Meltzoff, 1993; Hampson & Nelson, in press). Object names are particularly likely to be the focus of explicit pedagogy by English-speaking middle-class mothers. These individual differences are particularly important because the mothers and children who seem to place most emphasis on names, labeling objects in picture books or playing the "naming game," tend to be middle-class mothers of first-born children, who are disproportionately well-represented in child language samples.

In fact, words that do not encode objects or object classes, often described as relational words (Bloom, 1973), are very commonly reported among the earliest words in many languages, including English (Bloom, 1973; Dromi, 1987; Gopnik, 1982; Nelson, 1973; Tomasello, 1992). The class of such words is smaller than the class of object names. Nevertheless, in our own studies such relational words were dominant in a number of other ways. In a longitudinal study of the first words of nine 15- to 21-month-old children, for example, there were several indications that relational words played as important a role as nouns (Gopnik, 1980) in early language. In this study, the spontaneous speech of 9 children, all second- or third-borns from a variety of social classes, was video recorded and transcribed. Three children were recorded every two weeks from age 12 months to 24 months, 3 were recorded every month from 15 to 21 months, and 3 were recorded every month from 18 to 24 months. As in previous studies there were more types of object names than of non-nominal words overall and for individual children (333 names to 138 non-nominal words). However, overall there were more tokens of non-nominal expressions than of object names (4,252 utterances of names and 6,504 non-nominal utterances), and this pattern was found for 8 of the 9 individual children. The overwhelming majority of these non-nominal utterances (3,838) could be accounted for by just a few non-nominal words, namely the canonical relational words, *that, there, no, more, oh dear* (the British version of *uh oh*), *up, down, in, out, on,* and *off.* Children used these 11 relational words almost as often as they used all 333 recorded object names.

Relational words were also more likely to be used consistently throughout the months in which language was recorded. Seventy-two percent of the object names occurred in only one of the longitudinal recording sessions, whereas 58% of the non-nominal expressions and 25% of the canonical relational words appeared only once. Relational words were also more likely to be used by several different children. All of the 11 canonical relational words were used by 5 or more children, whereas only 23 of the names (6%)

and 21 of the non-nominal expressions (15%) were used by 5 or more children. Moreover, all of the children used at least some non-nominal words as soon as they used their first object name.

Measuring dominance or importance is tricky, of course. However, it appears that the number of tokens of a lexical type, its consistency of use across time and across children, and its first appearance, are all as important measures as the recorded number of word types. On all these measures relational words are just as dominant, if not more dominant, than object names in early vocabularies.

Thus, even among English-speaking children the evidence for an early predominance of object names is not as overwhelming as it may seem. By looking at a restricted measure of dominance, the number of types of a particular word that occur in early vocabulary, and a rather restricted class of mothers and children, the literature may have established an impression that is fundamentally misleading.

The relative neglect of relational words may also have to do with "adultocentric" views of semantics and cognition. It is commonly if tacitly assumed in the literature that the child's language is largely interesting insofar as it converges on the adult language. This notion is elevated to a principle in the constraints literature. This emphasis has led investigators to neglect important parts of the child's semantic system that are quite different from the adult system. In adult language, nouns encode object classes, as do the nouns in early child speech. However, for adults, verbs are the quintessential alternative class of words, the words that typically encode actions and re-lations. However, for English-speaking children, early conceptions of actions and relations are not encoded by verbs but by words from a rather odd assortment of syntactic categories (from the adult point of view). These include prepositions, participles, and even exclamations (Bloom, 1973; Gop-nik, 1982; Tomasello, 1992).

Similarly, the concepts encoded by early nouns, largely concepts of ba-sic-level object categories, are at least superficially similar to those encoded by adult nouns (but see Mervis, 1987, on child-basic categories). However, the concepts encoded by early relational words may be quite different from those encoded by standard adult English verbs. These early words typically encode abstract and in some ways unusual events and relations, particularly events and relations involving the child's plans and the appearance and disappearance of objects (Gopnik, 1982, 1984; Gopnik & Meltzoff, 1985).

KOREAN SPEAKERS AND RELATIONAL WORDS

In addition to focusing on a relatively narrow aspect of early language development (vocabulary size) and a relatively narrow range of children, studies of early semantics have focused on a few European languages, particularly English. In the continuum of linguistic types, English is at the far end of the analytic–synthetic spectrum. English is, in fact, atypical in its reliance on word order and its scant use of morphological variation. Moreover, nouns are generally obligatory in English sentences.

In contrast, Korean and Japanese, languages with closely related structures, have a very rich verb morphology, depend on different verb endings to make important semantic and pragmatic distinctions, and are verb-final. Pragmatic rules in Korean and Japanese allow massive noun ellipsis, particularly in informal conversation where the context is clear and present (Clancy, 1985). Parental speech in these languages, which occurs in precisely such a setting, often consists of highly inflected verbs with few nouns, very much in contrast to North American English parental speech. We present data in this chapter showing that Korean-speaking mothers consistently used fewer nouns and more verbs than English-speaking mothers (see also Gopnik & Meltzoff, 1993); Fernald and Morikawa (in press) reported a similar pattern for Japanese-speaking mothers.

Studies of early cognitive and linguistic development in these children provide an informative contrast to studies of English-speakers. If the alleged predominance of early object names reported in the literature is the result of universal cognitive or linguistic principles, then we will also see this pattern in children speaking other languages. On the other hand, if this impression is at least partly the result of features of specific languages and of specific input to children, we may see a different pattern of semantic development in these children. Because verbs in Korean and Japanese express concepts encoded by relational words in English, we expect that children will use verbs in these contexts. In addition, because verbs are both more commonly used and more salient than nouns in these languages, we may find that children learning these languages will show even earlier and more elaborated encoding of actions and relations than English speakers.

This possibility is in line with recent work on other areas of early semantic development. Bowerman (1989) and Choi and Bowerman (1991) suggested that semantic development is not simply the result of universal cognitive or linguistic processes. Instead, semantic development reflects linguistic differences from the very beginning of language. For example, Korean verbs may make different distinctions than English ones. Korean locative verbs distinguish between movements that result in a tight fit and a loose fit but do not distinguish between relations of support and containment. One preposition may be used for the actions of slipping a hand in a glove and putting a picture on the wall (tight fit), whereas another may be used for putting an apple in a bowl or a coat on a chair (loose fit). English prepositions, in contrast, distinguish between support and containment but not tight and loose fit. The recent studies suggest that these distinctive semantic patterns are also reflected in children's speech from the time they begin to talk.

Korean-speaking children use spatial verbs to talk about movement and the tight fit/loose fit distinction but do not distinguish support and containment. This finding suggests that semantic development is shaped by particular language-specific structures from a very early period.

Even more intriguing is the question of cognitive development in these children. According to all the universalist accounts, the cognitive development of the Korean speakers should be similar to that of English speakers. In Gentner's (1982) account, for example, it is precisely the underlying universal cognitive structures that are responsible for the universal pattern of language development. According to the various linguistic accounts of the naming spurt, this development is due to linguistic factors that are quite independent of other cognitive abilities. Similarly, in Markman's (1989) account, cognitive development proceeds on its own independent course; constraints simply determine which concepts are chosen to be linguistically encoded.

On the other hand, some particularist accounts recently suggested that stronger relations between language and cognition may exist and that linguistic differences may lead to cognitive differences. If a distinction is clearly marked in the adult language, children may more easily acquire the conceptual distinction itself as well as the word for that distinction. On this view there is an active interaction between linguistic and cognitive development. We might advance the Vygotskian (Vygotsky, 1962) or perhaps even Whorfian (Whorf, 1956) idea that the acquisition of particular linguistic forms motivates the development of the related cognitive abilities: Language may actually facilitate cognition. In particular, the fact that a concept is encoded clearly and saliently in the adult language may make it easier for the child to learn. The Choi and Bowerman (1991) findings suggest that this may be true of Korean locatives. A number of other recent cross-linguistic studies make similar suggestions about various aspects of language (Sera, Rettinger, & Castillo-Pintado, 1991; Shatz, 1991; Slobin, 1985; Weist, Wysocka, & Lyytinen, 1991). Although they suggest such an outcome, none of these cross-linguistic studies included any nonlinguistic cognitive measures.

We have been conducting a series of studies of the early semantic and cognitive development of Korean- and English-speaking children, with particular emphasis on the acquisition of nouns and verbs (Gopnik & Choi, 1990; Gopnik & Meltzoff, 1993). The general picture that emerges from our semantic studies is not one of children universally concentrating on nouns and object naming in their early language. Rather, object naming appears to be one semantic and cognitive stream developing in parallel with others. Features of adult input and of the child's cognitive interests and concerns may make this stream more or less dominant. Children whose mothers use many object names or are deeply concerned with categorization problems may show a particular dominance of names, whereas children who hear a different pattern of linguistic input or are concerned with other cognitive domains may be less likely to emphasize this area of development. These children may talk about actions and relations earlier, more frequently, and with more elaboration.

CROSS-LINGUISTIC DIFFERENCES IN INPUT

The grammatical characteristics of Korean versus English should themselves make for input differences; such differences were found empirically in Japanese speakers (Japanese and Korean are closely related languages) (Fernald & Morikawa, in press). However, these differences had not been empirically tested for Korean speakers. Do the Korean speakers hear more verbs and fewer nouns than English speakers?

Twenty English-speaking mothers and 11 Korean-speaking mothers were tested with their 18-month-old children. A large complex dollhouse with typical furniture and family figurines was presented for 5 minutes, and mothers were asked to play with the house with the children. Their spontaneous speech was recorded and transcribed. We then compared the numbers of utterances, nouns, and verbs from the English-speaking mothers with those from Korean-speaking mothers. Korean-speaking mothers produced significantly fewer nouns and more verbs per utterance than English-speaking mothers (Korean mean NPU = .292, English = .455, $t = -2.035$, $p < .01$, one-tailed; Korean mean VPU = .608, English = .512, $t = 1.865$, $p < .05$, one-tailed). Also, Korean-speaking mothers produced twice as many verbs per utterance as nouns, whereas English-speaking mothers did not show a difference.

Pragmatic analyses of maternal input in the two language groups also show a stronger tendency of Korean-speaking mothers to direct their children to engage in activities rather than to label objects. These mothers frequently used verbal encouragements for activities. For example, they said, "nehe pwa" ("put [it] in") or "nwule pwa" ("push [it]") as directives or "mokyok haney" ("[The doll] is taking a bath") to describe what the children were doing (note that the nouns and pronouns in the English glosses are not included in the Korean utterances). This type of activity-oriented utterance occupied 45% of the mothers' speech. In contrast, labeling or asking names of objects (e.g., "chimtayya" ["(It's a) bed"], "ike mweya?" ["What is it?"]) accounted for only 9% of their speech. English-speaking mothers showed a different pattern. These mothers produced activity-oriented utterances 25% of the time and labeling utterances 24% of the time. In other words, English-speaking mothers spent an equal amount of time between encouraging or describing actions and labeling when they interacted with their children. They did not particularly emphasize actions during play.

SEMANTIC AND COGNITIVE DEVELOPMENT
IN KOREAN SPEAKERS

Are these differences in input reflected in the children's language? There is already some evidence in the literature on the very early language of Korean- and Japanese-speaking versus English-speaking children. A number of investigators noted that Korean- and Japanese-speaking children use verb morphology productively earlier than English-speaking children but use fewer and less varied names (Choi, 1986, 1991; Clancy, 1985; Fernald & Morikawa, in press; Rispoli, 1987; Tanouye, 1979). In a longitudinal study of 5 Korean speakers, we found that these children consistently acquired a naming spurt later than English speakers (Gopnik & Choi, 1990). More significantly and surprisingly, however, we also found that the Korean speakers were significantly delayed in the development of nonlinguistic classification abilities relative to the English speakers, although they were not delayed in other areas of cognitive development. Among English speakers there is a close and specific relation between the development of classification and the development of object naming (Gopnik & Meltzoff, 1987, 1992, 1993; Mervis & Bertrand, 1993).

We wanted to explore this finding further, but we also wanted to investigate another possible relation between linguistic and cognitive development. The Korean emphasis on verbs might make concepts encoded by verbs—concepts involving actions, plans, and goals—particularly salient to young children. During the one-word stage there are significant changes in children's understanding of these concepts. The clearest evidence for this comes from children's performance on means–ends tasks that involve designing actions to accomplish particular goals (Piaget, 1953; Uzgiris & Hunt, 1975, 1987). If an absence of nouns leads to a delay in classification, a stress on verbs may lead to an acceleration of these areas of development.

Such a pattern of development, a kind of double dissociation between the two languages and the two types of cognition, is also important from a methodological perspective. The delay in classification in the Korean speakers may be due to many general factors, motivational or stylistic differences, general cultural differences, and so on. These explanations become less likely if Korean speakers are actually advanced in other areas of cognition, particularly if these areas are also related to specific features of linguistic structure that are salient in Korean.

The first study reported here investigated how Korean children develop means–ends and classification abilities in comparison to English speakers and how the development of those abilities related to semantic development. The subjects were 9 Korean-speaking children living in Southern California and in Berkeley, 5 girls and 4 boys. None of these children were subjects in the Gopnik and Choi (1990) study. Eight of the children were cared for by monolingual Korean parents or grandparents and spoke only Korean. One of the children also used some English. Children were approximately 15 months old at the first visit (M = 450.77 days) and were tested for 6 months at 3- or 4-week intervals. These children were compared to the 12 children reported in Gopnik and Meltzoff (1987) and Gopnik and Choi (1990). These children were all monolingual English speakers and were similar ages as the Korean sample (M = 470 days at the first visit).

All 9 children received six cognitive tasks adapted from the Uzgiris and Hunt scales (Uzgiris & Hunt, 1975). These included two object permanence tasks and four means–ends tasks. The two object permanence tasks were finding a simply invisibly displaced object (Task 13) and finding a serially invisibly displaced object (Task 14). The four means–ends tasks were using a string to obtain an object, using a stick to obtain an object, placing a necklace in a bottle, and avoiding placing a solid ring on a post (Tasks 9–12). Six children also received three categorization tasks using objects and procedures that were similar to those used by Gopnik and Meltzoff (1987, 1992), Ricciuti (1965), Starkey (1981), and Sugarman (1983). In these tasks the children were presented with mixed-up arrays of objects from two categories; we observed whether they spontaneously sorted the objects into appropriate groups (for more details on administration of these tasks, see Gopnik & Meltzoff, 1986, 1987; Uzgiris & Hunt, 1975, 1987).

As in previous studies we counted children as having attained the highest level of ability if they solved the most difficult serial invisible displacement task (Task 14) or if they solved any one of the three most difficult means–ends tasks using insight (Tasks 9–12). That is, they determined the correct method of solving the task immediately, without a period of trial-and-error groping. In particular, this meant that the child immediately pulled the giraffe to him or herself with the rake, dangled the necklace bead by bead into the bottle, or discarded the solid ring without even trying to place it on the post. In earlier studies, children's abilities in these areas, determined by these same criteria, were related to the use of relational words in English speakers (Gopnik & Meltzoff, 1984, 1985, 1986; Tomasello & Farrar, 1984, 1986).

The scoring procedures for the categorization tasks were the same as those used by Gopnik and Meltzoff (1987), Ricciuti (1965), and Sugarman (1983). Children achieved exhaustive grouping, the highest level of classification, if they systematically placed objects of different kinds into physically distinct locations. Typically this involved making two separate piles on the table or placing all the objects of one kind into one of the experimenter's hands and all of another kind into the other hand. Children were scored as having achieved a level if they displayed the appropriate behavior on any one of the three sorting tasks.

Parents received the Early Language Questionnaire used by Gopnik and Meltzoff (1987); it was translated into Korean and administered and scored by a native Korean speaker. This questionnaire lists 12 different types of early social and relational words, such as words for success and failure, location, and disappearance. It also has a section for parents to list any other words their children use. Children's spontaneous speech during the sessions was also analyzed. We focused on two types of relational language: the use of words encoding either success or failure and the use of words encoding disappearance. In previous studies of English- and Korean-speaking children we found that success/failure words were related to means–ends tasks, whereas disappearance words were related to object-permanence tasks (Gopnik & Choi, 1990; Gopnik & Meltzoff, 1986). As in Gopnik and Meltzoff (1987), children were scored as having acquired a naming spurt if they developed 10 new names in a 3-week session. This is comparable to the criterion used in other studies of the spurt (Bloom, 1973; Corrigan, 1978; Goldfield & Reznick, 1990).

The data for the Korean speakers is displayed in Table 3.1. Like English speakers, Korean-speaking children used words to encode concepts of success, failure, and disappearance. Unlike the English speakers, however, these children used verbs to encode these concepts. The most common forms were *eps-ta* for disappearance (used by six children) and *twaytta* for success (used by six children). *Eps-* and *twae-* are Korean verb stems meaning *cease to exist* and *become*, respectively. Children used these words with the modal suffix *-ta*, which denotes perceptually salient events (Choi, 1991). In addition, two children used the Korean verb *issta*, meaning roughly *exist*, and one

TABLE 3.1
Age in Days at Which Korean-Speaking Children
Achieved Cognitive and Linguistic Milestones

| Subject | Cognitive Measures | | | Language Measures | | |
	Object Permanence	Means– Ends	Exhaustive Sorting	Disappearance	Success/ Failure	Naming Spurt
1	531	489		574	511	673
2	475	454		500	475	628
3	555	470		555	470	569
4	445	509	586	424	509	586
5	474	548	597*	424	445	521
6	478	478	631	478	478	672
7	605	474	567	537	496	670
8	442	496	554*	428	442	554*
9	646	487	576	688*	576	688*
Means	516.8	489.4	585.2	512	489.1	615.6
Medians	478	487	581	500	478	628

*These children did not accomplish this skill by the end of the testing session. For calculation purposes they were assigned a date 3 weeks after the end of testing session, the earliest age at which the skill could be acquired.

child did not use a disappearance word at all. Children also used the verb *an nawa* (roughly *not come out*) generally to encode failure. This parallels similar uses of words like *stuck* or *heavy* in English—children extend a word that applies to a particular instance of failure to the more general category (Bowerman, 1978; Gopnik, 1982). Finally, children used the exclamation *uh* for failure and used the exclamation *ya!* for success. Both these exclamations are standardly used in similar contexts by adult Korean speakers. The one bilingual child used the English *uh-oh* to indicate failure.

The pattern of emergence of the three types of linguistic developments (success/failure words, disappearance words, and the naming spurt) for the Korean speakers differed somewhat from that of the English speakers. For the English speakers, there were no significant differences between the three types of linguistic developments. For the Korean speakers, however, there was a significant delay of the naming spurt compared to the other two types of words, which were encoded by verbs. All nine of the children developed a success/failure word before a naming spurt, and eight of the children developed disappearance words before the naming spurt, and one child developed a success/failure word but neither a disappearance word nor a naming spurt ($p < .01$, by Wilcoxon test in both cases).

For the English speakers the three types of cognitive ability emerged, on average, at almost exactly the same age (see Table 3.2). Moreover, there was no consistent ordering among these developments. In particular, 6 of the 12 English-speaking children acquired the highest level of means–ends ability only after they acquired the highest level of categorization. In contrast, the three measures did not emerge together for the Korean-speaking children (see Table 3.1). In particular, all 6 of the children acquired means–ends abilities before they acquired categorization abilities ($p < .05$, Wilcoxon), as did 4 of the 5 Korean-speaking children reported in Gopnik and Choi (1990).

Thus, the Korean speakers showed a rather different pattern of semantic and cognitive development than the English speakers. More strikingly, there were absolute differences in performance on these measures for the Korean speakers versus the English speakers. There was a significant difference

TABLE 3.2
Median Age in Days at Which Children Acquired
Cognitive and Linguistic Abilities

	Cognitive Measures			Language Measures		
Language	Object Permanence	Means–Ends	Exhaustive Sorting	Disappearance	Success/ Failure	Naming Spurt
Korean	478	487	581	500	478	628
English	516.5	525.5*	510*	519	519*	550*

*$p < .05$ by Mann-Whitney U test

between the Korean and English speakers' performance on the categorization tasks. The Korean speakers were significantly delayed on this measure compared to the English speakers (M_{Korean} = 19.2 months, $M_{English}$ = 17.2 months, $p < .01$, Mann-Whitney). Similarly, there was a significant difference between Korean and English speakers' development of a naming explosion (M_{Korean} = 20.3 months, $M_{English}$ = 18.3 months, $p < .05$).

Intriguingly, however, the opposite pattern held for the development of means–ends abilities and success/failure words. Korean-speaking children were significantly advanced in both these areas of development compared to the English speakers (means–ends: M_{Korean} = 16.1 months, $M_{English}$ = 17.2 months, $p < .05$; for success/failure: M_{Korean} = 16.1 months, $M_{English}$ = 17.1 months, $p < .05$; all by Mann-Whitney test). Finally, there were no significant differences between the two language groups on object permanence or disappearance measures (see Tables 3.1 and 3.2).

In a second study, we compared the cognitive development of 10 additional Korean speakers with 30 additional English speakers in a cross-sectional study (the data from the English speakers are reported in Gopnik & Meltzoff, 1992). The mean age for the Korean speakers was 17.6 months, with a range of 17.0 to 20.0 months; for the English speakers it was 17.8 months, with a range of 16.8 to 18.8 months. Both groups of children received the same cognitive measures as the children in the longitudinal study. As in the previously reported study, the English-speaking children were about evenly split on the cognitive measures: 50% of the children passed the means–ends task, and 46% passed the classification task. In contrast, the Korean-speaking children showed substantially better performance on the means–ends measures (80% passing) and substantially worse performance on the categorization measures (10% passing). In other words, these children showed the same pattern of development as the children in the longitudinal study.

THE VERB SPURT

These studies suggest that the linguistic differences between mothers' speech in Korean and English are indeed paralleled by the children's semantic and cognitive development. The Korean speakers clearly acquired some verbs earlier than English speakers and showed a naming spurt later, if at all. However, in these studies we focused on a subset of verbs, namely those that encoded success and failure—verbs similar to the relational words used by English speakers. Was there a more general preponderance of verbs over nouns in the Korean speakers' early language? We have followed longitudinally (once every 3 or 4 weeks) the lexical development of 8 Korean-speaking children by recording their spontaneous speech during an hour-long free play at each session and through the Early Language Questionnaire completed by their parents. These children included 6 of the children in the longitudinal study reported above and an additional 2 children. When parents reported new words they also provided the contexts in which the child used them. It was often the case that the new words reported by the parents were spontaneously used by the child during the free play session. The mean age of the children at the first recording session was 14 months and at the last recording session was 22 months (details of this study are reported in Choi & Gopnik, in press).

These longitudinal data show several interesting phenomena. First, Korean children as young as 15 months old productively and appropriately use words that are clearly verbs in the adult language even in their earliest language (e.g., *cwuta* [to give], *ppayta* [to take out/off of fitted ground]; see Table 3.3). In most cases, these verbs were appropriately inflected for requests, questions, and declaratives. (In some cases, the children used only the first syllable of the verb.) Second, 6 of the 8 children had a verb spurt, a session in which 10 or more new verbs were learned. The children were all under 22 months old when this happened ($M = 18.6$ months). Moreover, for 5 of these children the sharp increase in verbs occurred before a naming spurt. Three of the children had sessions in which they had cumulatively acquired more different types of verbs than nouns, the opposite of the adult pattern, even in Korean.

It is interesting to note that at the verb spurt period, 3 children also showed marked development in verb morphology. That is, the children used the same verb with different verb suffixes that relate to mood and modality (Choi, 1991). This is characteristic of the adult grammar in Korean. This suggests that these children differentiated between nouns and verbs and were acquiring new verbs as full-fledged verbs.

Table 3.3 lists the verbs that were produced by at least three children during the study period. The semantic content of these early verbs was quite similar to the semantic content of early relational words in English. Many of the new verbs specified particular types of locative actions (e.g., peeling off a piece from an object or being carried on a specific part of the body). Others specified aspects of success and failure, disappearance, or request and rejection of request. As in English, however, the early words did not generally refer to simple actions (e.g., run or walk)—the uses we think of as prototypically verb-like in English (see also Tomasello, 1992).

In general, then, the Korean-speaking children talked about the same kinds of actions and relations that are discussed by young English speakers. However, the salience of verbs in the adult language seemed to lead the children to make more fine-grained and elaborated distinctions within this semantic field. Moreover, each individual child expressed more of the semantic distinctions from the set of relevant concepts than were expressed by individual English speakers.

TABLE 3.3
Verbs Used by Korean-Speaking Children[a]

Locative Verbs[b]	Activity Verbs	Disappearance Verbs	Success/Failure Verbs	Request/Rejection Verbs
yelta (open)	bata (do)	epsta (not exist)	twaytta (done)	cwuta (give)
ppayta (take out/off from tight space)	cata (sleep)	issta (exist)	an tway (not done)	pota (try)
tatta (close)	takkta (wash)			silhta (don't want)
kkita (put in/on to tight space)	mekta (eat)			
kata (go)				
ota (come)				
ancta (sit down)				
ilenata (get/stand up)				
nakata (go out)				
nebta (put in)				
pikhita (move over)				
ttelecita (fall)				
pesta (take clothes off)				
kkat (peel off)				
anta (carry in arms)				
epta (carry on back)				
thata (ride)				
milta (push)				
kkuta (turn off)				

[a]These verbs were produced by at least three children during the study period. In this table, the verbs are suffixed with the citation form -ta.
[b]Verbs denoting spontaneous or caused motion.

76

CONCLUSION

These findings cast doubt on the propositions that children always learn object names before they learn words that encode actions and relations, that they learn nouns before verbs, and that object names necessarily predominate in early vocabularies. These propositions largely arise from the peculiarities of verbs in English rather than from the peculiarities of young children's semantics. English verbs simply do not encode the kinds of actions and relations that young children want to discuss. In English and related languages, children use other types of words to encode concepts of actions and relations. In Korean, these concepts are encoded by verbs, and very young children learn verbs.

In this sense the children themselves are determining which aspects of the adult language they will acquire. All young children seem to be interested in both object categories and certain types of events and relations, interests that reflect their nonlinguistic cognitive development. Children acquire words in the adult language that are relevant to these particular interests. If these words are also significant in the adult syntax (as in the case of nouns in English or verbs in Korean), so much the better. If there is no simple match between syntactically significant categories and cognitively relevant ones, as in the case of English relational words, the children will adopt, and sometimes adapt, words from a variety of sources.

However, early semantic development is shaped by the specific types of input that the child hears as much as it is shaped by the child's interests and cognitive motivations. In fact, our studies suggest that the child's cognitive interests and motivations may be shaped by this input. First, the timing of different semantic developments may be quite different: The Korean-speaking children in our study learned verbs before English speakers and had a naming spurt later than English speakers. Second, the resulting pattern of development was different—developments that were roughly contemporaneous in English speakers were ordered in Korean speakers. Third, the actual semantic content of the children's language was different. The Korean speakers had a considerably larger and more differentiated verb vocabulary than the English speakers, even if we count early relational words as comparable to early verbs. The English speakers had a more elaborated and differentiated vocabulary for objects.

Moreover, and perhaps most surprisingly, the children's linguistic differences were reflected in their cognitive performance in a (dare we say it) positively Whorfian way. Just as the Korean-speaking children used verbs earlier, so they acquired means–ends skills relevant to actions and relations earlier. Just as the English speakers showed a more elaborated naming vocabulary earlier, so they also showed a more advanced understanding of object categorization.

Thus, there appears to be a very thorough bidirectional interaction between cognition and language in this period. The picture is not, as the more universalist accounts suggest, one of a universal process of conceptual development and an independent process of semantic development that latches on, as it were, to linguistically relevant concepts. Rather, children's early words encode the specific types of cognitive concerns that grab them at the moment, but those cognitive concerns themselves are shaped by the specific language the child hears. Children seem to be shaping their conceptual structures in line with the specific types of inputs they hear as well as shaping their interpretation of that input in line with their specific conceptual structures. To reiterate a metaphor we have used before, semantic and conceptual development are much like theory change in the history of science, with an interplay between interpreting new evidence in light of existing structures and revising existing structures in light of new evidence (Gopnik, 1984, 1988). To use a rather different metaphor, children simultaneously seem to be constructing a coherent account of the world they live in and a coherent account of the language they hear, and both these processes may interact in development.

ACKNOWLEDGMENTS

Research reported in this chapter was supported by NSF grant DBS9213959. We are grateful to Andy Meltzoff for helpful comments on an earlier draft.

REFERENCES

Bloom, L. (1973). *One word at a time: The use of single word utterances before syntax.* The Hague, Netherlands: Mouton.

Bowerman, M. (1978). The acquisition of word meaning: An investigation into some current conflicts. In N. Waterson & C. Snow (Eds.), *The development of communication* (pp. 263–287). London: Wiley.

Bowerman, M. (1989). Learning a semantic system: What role do cognitive predispositions play? In M. L. Rice & R. H. Schiefelbusch (Eds.), *The teachability of language* (pp. 133–169). Baltimore: Paul Brookes.

Choi, S. (1986, December). *A pragmatic analysis of sentence ending morphemes in Korean children.* Paper presented at the Linguistic Society of America, New York, NY.

Choi, S. (1991). Early acquisition of epistemic meaning in Korean: A study of sentence-ending suffixes in the spontaneous speech of three children. *First Language, 11,* 93–119.

Choi, S., & Bowerman, M. (1991). Learning to express motion events in English and Korean: The influence of language-specific lexicalization patterns. *Cognition, 41,* 83–121.

Choi, S., & Gopnik, A. (in press). Early acquisition of verbs in Korean: A cross-linguistic study. *Journal of Child Language.*

Clancy, P. (1986). The acquisition of communicative style in Japanese. In B. Scheifflin & E. Ochs (Eds.), *Language acquisition across cultures* (pp. 213–250). New York: Cambridge University Press.

Corrigan, R. (1978). Language development as related to stage 6 object permanence development. *Journal of Child Language, 5*, 173–189.

Dromi, E. (1987). *Early lexical development.* New York: Cambridge University Press.

Fernald, A., & Morikawa, H. (in press). How mothers talk about objects in Japanese and English. *Child Development.*

Gentner, D. (1982). Why nouns are learned before verbs: Linguistic relativity versus natural partitioning. In S. A. Kuczaj (Ed.), *Language development: Volume 2. Language, thought and culture* (pp. 301–334). Hillsdale, NJ: Lawrence Erlbaum Associates.

Goldfield, B. A. (1986). Referential and expressive language: A study of two mother–child dyads. *First Language, 6*, 119–131.

Goldfield, B. A., & Reznick, J. S. (1990). Early lexical acquisition: Rate, content, and the vocabulary spurt. *Journal of Child Language, 17*, 171–183.

Gopnik, A. (1980). *The development of non-nominal expressions in 12-24-month-old children.* Unpublished doctoral dissertation, University of Oxford.

Gopnik, A. (1982). Words and plans: Early language and the development of intelligent action. *Journal of Child Language, 9*, 303–318.

Gopnik, A. (1984). The acquisition of "gone" and the development of the object concept. *Journal of Child Language, 11*, 273–292.

Gopnik, A. (1988). Three types of early words: The emergence of social words, names, and cognitive-relational words. *First Language, 8*, 49–70.

Gopnik, A., & Choi, S. (1990). Do linguistic differences lead to cognitive differences? A cross-linguistic study of semantic and cognitive development. *First Language, 10*, 199–215.

Gopnik, A., & Meltzoff, A. N. (1984). Semantic and cognitive development in 15- to 21-month-old children. *Journal of Child Language, 11*, 495–513.

Gopnik, A., & Meltzoff, A. N. (1985). Words, plan, things and locations: Interactions between semantic and cognitive development in the one-word stage. In S. Kuczaj & M. Barrett (Eds.), *The development of word meaning* (pp. 199–223). New York: Springer-Verlag.

Gopnik, A., & Meltzoff, A. N. (1986). Relations between semantic and cognitive development in the one-word stage: The specificity hypothesis. *Child Development, 57*, 1040–1053.

Gopnik, A., & Meltzoff, A. N. (1987). The development of categorization in the second year and its relation to other cognitive and linguistic developments. *Child Development, 58*, 1523–1531.

Gopnik, A., & Meltzoff, A. N. (1992). Categorization and naming: Basic-level sorting in eighteen-month-olds and its relation to language. *Child Development, 63*, 1091–1103.

Gopnik, A., & Meltzoff, A. N. (1993). Words and thoughts in infancy: The specificity hypothesis and the development of categorization and naming. In C. Rovee-Collier & L. Lipsitt (Eds.), *Advances in infancy research* (pp. 223–255). Norwood, NJ: Ablex.

Halliday, M. (1975). *Learning how to mean: Explorations in the development of language.* London: Edward Arnold.

Hampson, J., & Nelson, K. (1993). Early relations between mother talk and language development. *Papers and Reports on Child Language Development.*

McShane, J. (1980). *Learning to talk.* Cambridge, England: Cambridge University Press.

Markman, E. (1989). *Categorization and naming in children: Problems of induction.* Cambridge, MA: MIT Press.

Mervis, C. (1987). Child-basic object categories and early lexical development. In U. Neisser (Ed.), *Concepts and conceptual development: Ecological and intellectual factors in categorization* (pp. 201–233). New York: Cambridge University Press.

Mervis, C., & Bertrand, J. (1993). Acquisition of early object labels: The roles of operating principles and input. In A. Kaiser & D. B. Gray (Eds.), *Enhancing children's communication: Research foundations for intervention* (pp. 201–233). Baltimore: Brookes.

Nelson, K. (1973). Structure and strategy in learning to talk. *Monographs of the Society for Research in Child Development, 38*(1–2), 1–136.

Piaget, J. (1953). *The origins of intelligence in childhood.* New York: Basic Books.

Ricciuti, H. N. (1965). Object grouping and selective ordering behaviors in infants 12 to 24 months old. *Merrill-Palmer Quarterly, 11,* 129–148.

Rispoli, M. (1987). The acquisition of the transitive and intransitive action verb categories in Japanese. *First Language, 7,* 183–200.

Sera, M., Rettinger, E., & Castillo-Pintado, J. (1991). Developing definitions of objects and events in English and Spanish speakers. *Cognitive Development, 6,* 119–143.

Shatz, M. (1991). Using cross-cultural research to inform us about the role of language in development. In M. H. Bornstein (Ed.), *Cultural approaches to parenting* (pp. 139–153). Hillsdale, NJ: Lawrence Erlbaum Associates.

Slobin, D. (1985). The cross-linguistic study of the language-making capacity. In D. Slobin (Ed.), *The cross-linguistic study of language acquisition* (pp. 157–256). Hillsdale, NJ: Lawrence Erlbaum Associates.

Starkey, D. (1981). The origins of concept formation: Object sorting and object preference in early infancy. *Child Development, 52,* 489–497.

Sugarman, S. (1983). *Children's early thought: Developments in classification.* Cambridge, England: Cambridge University Press.

Tanouye, E. K. (1979). The acquisition of verbs in Japanese children. *Papers and Reports on Child Language Development, 17,* 49–56.

Tomasello, M. (1992). *First verbs.* New York: Cambridge University Press.

Tomasello, M., & Farrar, J. (1984). Cognitive bases of early language: Object permanence and relational words. *Journal of Child Language, 11,* 477–493.

Tomasello, M., & Farrar, J. (1986). Object-permanence and relational words: A lexical training study. *Journal of Child Language, 11,* 477–493.

Uzgiris, I. C., & Hunt, J. (1975). *Assessment in infancy: Ordinal scales of psychological development.* Urbana, IL: University of Illinois Press.

Uzgiris, I., & Hunt, J. (1987). *Infant performance and experience: New findings with the ordinal scales.* Urbana, IL: University of Illinois Press.

Vygotsky, L. (1962). *Thought and language.* Cambridge, MA: MIT Press.

Weist, R., Wysocka, H., & Lytinnen, P. (1991). A cross-linguistic perspective on the development of temporal systems. *Journal of Child Language, 18,* 67–92.

Whorf, B. L. (1956). *Language, thought, and reality: Selected writings.* Cambridge, MA: MIT Press.

CHAPTER FOUR

Differences in the Acquisition of Early Verbs: Evidence from Diary Data from Sisters

Susan R. Braunwald
University of California, Los Angeles

In this chapter, I describe the emergence of verbs in the cumulative lexicons of two sisters, Joanna and Laura, henceforth J and L. Diary data from 12 to 24 months for J and L were compared in order to investigate how a toddler begins to acquire the actual words that will function as verbs in the endstate language. Individual differences in the *process* of J's and L's acquisition of verbs were found in these data. These differences are described in terms of a continuum of developmental synchrony-to-asynchrony in the integration of the form, meaning, and relational function of the girls' first verbs.

From a theoretical perspective, the topic of the acquisition of verbs and the description of their mental representations is complex and controversial (Barrett, 1983; Bates, Bretherton, & Snyder, 1988; Berman, 1988; Gentner, 1978, 1982; Jackendoff, 1983; Maratsos, 1988, 1991; Pinker, 1989; Tomasello, 1992). I do not define the mental representations of J's and L's first verbs. However, I do address the *issue of developmental dissociations and asynchronies in the overt process of the girls' early verb acquisition* (cf. Bates et al., 1988). I use the detailed, longitudinal diary data to confirm the premise that "there seem to be some qualitatively different ways to make the transition from first words to grammar" (Bates et al., 1988, p. 3).

A fundamental problem in research on the emergence of verbs is to define what counts as a verb in a toddler's early language production. There are two basic options for selecting a unit for the analysis of first verbs. One option is to rely upon the meaning and function of a word and to disregard the form (Tomasello, 1992). Thus, words such as *out, down,* and *off,* which function as action words (Huttenlocher & Smiley, 1991) or as predicates

(Tomasello, 1992), are counted as examples of emergent verbs. The other option is to focus on the form of the word regardless of its nascent meaning and actual function. Any word that functions as a verb in the endstate language, English, is the unit of analysis (Smith & Sachs, 1990).

In this chapter, the term *verb* refers to the form of the word. Words such as *get*, *go*, and *want* are counted as examples of emergent verbs, and their forms are used as a basis for tracing their development over time. When the word is the unit of analysis, the process of the girls' initial acquisition of verbs can be described from the developmental perspective of their known cumulative lexicons.

There is a precedent for comparing diary data from siblings to investigate the development of word meanings, including verb meanings (Bowerman, 1976). Two more recent diary case studies, one on lexical acquisition during the one-word stage (Dromi, 1987) and the other on first verbs in word combinations (Tomasello, 1992), relate directly to the choice of the developmental comparisons in this chapter. J's and L's known cumulative lexicons provide a developmental basis for identifying similarities and differences between the girls in the process of conjoining the phonological form, referential meaning, and grammatical function of their first verbs.

This chapter begins with a description of the diary data and the methods of analysis that were used. The data on J and L are first presented individually. Then, their developmental strategies for acquiring verbs are compared.

THE DIARY DATA

The diaries on J and L are not new. Their mother kept them during the late 1960s and early 1970s. At that time, she was the girls' primary caregiver, and keeping the diaries was her full-time professional commitment. A detailed theoretical and methodological discussion of these diaries is available elsewhere (Braunwald & Brislin, 1979a).

J and L are the daughters of college-educated parents. They lived with their parents and a cat (who was an important topic of their early language). J is 2 years, 9 months older than L and is left-handed. L's daily life and her sources of interpersonal experience were related to her place in the family as a second child (cf. Dunn, 1988; Peters, 1983).

Method of Data Collection

Criterion for Entering Data into the Diaries. Emergent structure was the only criterion for entering data into both diaries (Braunwald & Brislin, 1979a). Emergent structure was defined as any type of novel language use regardless of the correctness of the form or the clarity of the meaning. (In the examples, the first entry is from J's diary and the second from L's diary.) The following examples illustrate the incorrect but emergent use of: (a) the phonological form (e.g., "Eoiyo" [Fiona], "Cockle me" [Tickle me]), (b) the syntactic form (e.g., "Vac fraid Jo-Jo" [Jo-Jo is afraid of the vacuum], "Cooking Sue" [Sue is cooking]), (c) the semantic relation between a form and its referential meaning (e.g., "Baby leaf" [Small or little leaf], "Tata on" [Glasses on]), and (d) the pragmatic function of the utterance (e.g., "Hi baby!" [how L requests more food]).

The criterion of emergent structure was easy to use, and discrete and minor changes in language production were noticeable. Indeed, at the age of 4, even J, in her role as the older sibling (Dunn, 1988), recognized examples of L's newly emerging language (e.g., "Laura said blocks" and "Sue, write mine").

Compiling the Cumulative and Verb Lexicons. The method for recording the words in the cumulative lexicon was the same for J's and L's diaries. Any consistent pairing of a phonetic form with a discernible meaning was counted as a word. The form of these words, including verbs, could be conventional (e.g., *car, go,* etc.), homophonous (e.g., *bite* [noun] and *bite* [verb], etc.), or idiosyncratic (e.g., *lola* [pacifier], *kaking* [rocking], etc.). If a word was used consistently and frequently it was recorded in the lexicon even if its meaning was too opaque to be known with any degree of certainty (e.g., L's early use of *cry*). All uses of ambiguous words were recorded in the daily diary notes.

New words were entered in the daily diary notes along with contextual information. They were also recorded and dated on the monthly vocabulary lists that were compiled as each new word occurred. The lexicons were reviewed on the child's month birthdate. A computer-verified cumulative lexicon for each girl was derived from the daily entries and the monthly word lists (Braunwald, 1989).

The verb lexicons for both girls were compiled by reading through the daily diary notes and entering each new verb-like form onto a computerized cumulative list. Each girl's list of verbs was cross-checked by a computer search for those words in her cumulative lexicon. The girls' verb lists were compared to determine the words that they knew in common.

The Scope of the Diaries

J's Diary. It is important to explain how and why the scopes of the two diaries differ. The data from J are modest in scope in comparison to the diary study of L. At the time that J's diary record was kept, the idea of "rich interpretation" (Bloom, 1973; Brown, 1973) had not yet been proposed. Although there are some context notes in J's diary, they are not sufficiently systematic.

There is a second (circumstantial) limitation to the data from J. From 12 to 19 months of age, J's language production was limited. At 19 months, J literally leaped into expressive language as she simultaneously began to increase her lexicon and to use verbs. Prior to 19 months, there were very few observable clues to explain how J integrated the form, meaning, and function of her first verbs.

Despite the important limitations in J's diary, it is theoretically valuable. J's diary contains a complete record of her lexical acquisition, daily entries of her emergent language, and monthly summaries of her language development. Moreover, much of the information in her diary relates specifically to the emergence of verbs.

L's Diary.   The diary study of L helped to define a standard for the modernization of the diary method (Braunwald & Brislin, 1979a). There are many details in the systematic context notes and monthly summaries. There are also audio-recorded control data. The data analysis in this chapter is based on the handwritten diary record. However, my intuitions about this period of L's language development were enhanced by listening to the 18 hours of tapes.

The larger corpora on L is both an artifact and a diary record of her propensity to use language production as her primary strategy to acquire and to practice language. In contrast to J, L's early language production provided many examples of incremental developmental changes and informative errors. L's errors were a source of insight (cf. Bowerman, 1985) into the developmental complexity of the hurdles that toddlers must confront as they begin to acquire verbs.

Method of Data Analysis

The diaries from J and L are modern examples of the classical tradition of an atheoretical approach to data collection. There are no a priori and explicit theoretical assumptions that delimit the scope of the diary at the stage of data entry. Specific and well-defined theoretical issues are addressed at the level of data analysis.

It is impossible within the space of a chapter to describe in detail the wealth of information on the emergence of verbs that was found in the diary data. I have, therefore, tried to include data analyses and examples that address the development of verbs from two different theoretical perspectives. The first perspective is general and comparative. I present a broad overview of the developmental relation between lexical acquisition and the emergence of verbs first for J and L individually and then in comparison to one another. The figures in this chapter provide a graphic representation of this developmental scenario.

The second theoretical perspective is also comparative, but it is specific and detailed. I focus on the data from 20 to 22 months. The data from this transitional period in the girls' acquisition of verbs were analyzed and re-analyzed as the answer to one question led to another (cf. Bloom, 1991, for a rationale for this method of analysis).

Interpretation of the Diary Data

The diary entries describe a process that is in a constant state of flux. They describe new instances of language production that represent the cutting edge of each girl's performance at any given point in her development. Thus, many developmental milestones, which occur in samples of children's average language use at a later age, are found as rare events at an earlier age for J and L.

These data are descriptive, but they are not generalizable. "Small sample studies are extremely useful in showing us what is *possible*. They cannot tell us whether the same patterns are general or reliable" (Bates et al., 1988, p. 35, italics in original). The diary data from J and L show two distinctly different but developmentally possible strategies for acquiring verbs. However, they also indicate that chronological age was a common factor that influenced each girl's ability to consolidate the role of verbs in her language production.

THEORETICAL DEFINITIONS

Developmental Definition of a Verb

When form is the unit of analysis, the word may or may not function un-ambiguously as a verb in the child's early language production. Homonyms are a good example of this problem (cf. Nelson, this volume).

(1) J, 1;7.8, is looking at her own scraped knee.
    J: Papa *cut* knee? (Papa is J's grandfather.)
(2) L, 1;10.25, is expecting a friend, Lisa, to come over to her house.
    L: Lisa come my house, *visit.*

In Examples 1 and 2, the words *cut* and *visit* could be either a noun or a verb given the ambiguity of the situational and linguistic contexts. Developmental criteria are needed to decide if and when the phonological form, referential meaning, and grammatical function of a verb are conjoined.

Referential Meaning. I use two criteria, either separately or together, for ascribing the referential meaning of a verb to a word. One criterion is that the semantic content is verb-like in its meaning in a given situation. This judgment is based on how clearly the use of the word relates to the sequence of events in a given situation (Tomasello & Kruger, 1992).

(3) L, 1;6.15, dropped her pen on the floor and wanted it back.
   L: *Drop, drop, drop.*
(4) L, 1;6.25, is jumping from a ledge in a park.
   L: *Jump, jump.*

Thus, even a single word utterance may convey the referential meaning of a verb if there is a discernible link between the child's use of the word and a verb-like event in the situational context. There is no evidence that these one-word, verb-lexemes are serving a grammatical function.

The relational function of a word in the linguistic context is the second criterion for clarifying the referential meaning of a verb. In contrast to Examples 1 and 2, the linguistic context disambiguates the referential meaning of the words *cut* and *visit* in Examples 5 and 6.

(5) J, 1;9.8, is trying to cut hamburger.
   J: Jo-Jo *cut* meat.
(6) L, 1;11.10, is running into the kitchen to see M.
   L: I *visit* my mommy.

Thus, the explicit presence of the relational function of a verb in an utterance may contribute to the recognition of its referential meaning.

When the use of a verb is decontextualized, the clarity of its referential meaning depends upon the linguistic context and/or the listener's prior knowledge of the topic (cf. Braunwald & Brislin, 1979b). In Examples 7 and 8, L's new verbs emerged in decontextualized sentences. In Example 7, shared prior knowledge contributes to the listener's comprehension of two new verbs, *turn over* and *get scared.*

(7) L, 1;10.2, was turned over by a wave the day before. The family is at breakfast, and J is talking about the trip to the beach.
   L: Laura *turn over.*
   L: Laura *get scared.*
(8) One month and 9 days after Example 7, L, 1;11.11, is having her diaper changed when she spontaneously describes her experience at the beach.
   L: Water *tip* my *over.*
   L: Wave *tip* my *over.*
   L: I didn't like it.

In Examples 7 and 8, the referential meanings of four new words, the verbs *turn over, get scared,* and *tip over* and the noun *wave,* occurred in decontextualized sentences. In Example 8 the linguistic context is explicit. Any listener could figure out that L did not like being tipped over by a wave.

Grammatical Function. My criterion for attributing a grammatical function to a verb is conservative. I distinguish between the relational function of a verb in word combinations and its grammatical function in a sentence (cf. Tomasello, 1992). In Example 9 the verb *go* is part of a word combination.

(9) L, 1;6.1, comments on the fact that our visitors for the afternoon, including Daniel, just left.
   L: *Go* car.
   L: Daniel.

In Example 9, "Go car" is part of an incorrectly ordered vertical construction (Scollon, 1973) and is not yet integrated into the single grammatical sentence "Daniel go car."

The girls are credited with knowledge of the grammatical function of a verb when they can produce a three-part, correctly ordered sentence "in which both argument slots are filled appropriately" (Tomasello, 1992, p. 40).

(10) L, 1;10.26, The neighbor's dog, Eugene, suddenly begins to bark.
   L: *My bear Eugene.*
   L: *I bear Eugene.*
(11) L, 1;10.27, is getting ready for bed. L comments on a sound that she heard several days before in the same context. There is no sound to elicit this memory.
   L: *I bear Nestor riding bike.* (Nestor is a neighbor.)
(12) J, 1;10.26, sees an airplane. Her grandparents, Nanny and Poppy, come to visit by airplane.
   J: *Nanny, Poppy fly away airplane.*

In Examples 10, 11, and 12 word order is clearly serving as a semantic/syntactic device for conveying differentiated meaning in language production (Bloom, 1991). It is in sentences such as these, even if only verb-by-verb, that J and L demonstrated an unequivocal understanding of the grammatical function of verbs.

Use of the Term SVO. I use the term SVO in the text and the figures to refer to the production of sentences with a verb, such as Examples 5, 6, and 8 and 10–12. Because I am not describing the deep structure of the girls' grammars, the term SVO does not literally mean subject-verb-object.

Rather, SVO is used as an abbreviation to describe a developmental advance in the girls' abilities to produce the surface structure of a sentence. The intersecting line labeled SVO in the figures specifies the child's age at the time of her sixth spontaneous production of a structurally complete sentence (e.g., J's "Jo tie shoe" at 1;7.17 and L's "Laura do it" at 1;7.3).

J—SYNCHRONOUS EMERGENCE OF VERBS

J's pattern of lexical acquisition illustrates the simultaneous emergence of a verb qua form in her lexicon and its semantic meaning and relational function in word combinations. At 19 months and 4 days, the quality of J's expressive language changed dramatically. There was a steady increase in the growth of her vocabulary and a rapid onset in her ability to use verbs in sentences.

Word Combinations Without Verbs

By 18 months and 3 weeks, J frequently used two positional productive patterns and/or limited scope semantic formulae (Braine, 1976, 1988) to produce three-word combinations. In both formulae the word in first position was variable, and the two-word predicate was fixed. In response to the question, "Where's Dada?" J answered, "Dada bye-bye car-car." She varied this basic combination by substituting the name of the person who was "bye-bye car-car." J also used this positional pattern with the names of family members who went "wee-wee pot."

J was trying hard to talk and was just beginning to produce a limited number of spontaneous and linearly ordered word combinations without verbs. These included her first attempts to use word order to convey a consistent conventional meaning. She began to express alienable possession (e.g., "Mama purse," "Dada shoe," and "Cat wawa" [cat's water]). She also began to comment about and/or to describe things (e.g., "Milk cold" and "Nana kekat, cuckoo cat" [Grandma's kitty cat is a crazy cat]). Following this brief two-week period of systematic but limited use of word order, J suddenly integrated verbs into her linguistic repertoire and vastly expanded the scope of her language production.

The Emergence of Verbs

Beginning at 19 months and 4 days, J's language production reflected a developmental strategy that was insightful and analytic (Bates et al., 1988). Within a 4-day period, from 19 months and 4 days to 19 months and 8 days, J began to use verbs with correct word order. She began to produce SV sentences (e.g., "Sasha bow-wow bark" [Sasha, the dog, barks]), VO word combinations (e.g., "Pour milk" immediately after J poured milk from one glass into another), and her first SVO sentence (e.g., "Baby pick flower" in response to a picture in a book).

During the next 9 days, J met the criterion for productivity of five additional SVO sentences: "Mama dada go bye-bye car," "Timmy eat banana," "Peaowa (cat) broke balloon," "Peaowa (cat) fight black cat," and "Jo tie shoe." Moreover, there were no errors in the word order of her first 50 spontaneously produced utterances with a verb during the 18-day period between 19 months and 4 days and 19 months and 22 days.

This excerpt from my subjective summary note for J at 20 months of age captures the essence of the dramatic increase in her language production once she began to use verbs.

> Total vocabulary is 161 words. J uses these words in an infinite number of combinations so that the total effect is of adequate speech. She asks for what she wants and describes her own activities as she is doing them. For example, "Jo ride bike," "Jo-Jo eat food," etc. We can use language to explain things to J, and she will repeat our explanation. . . . She also talks to herself at great length. We hear her in her crib singing elaborate songs about Peaowa, mama, dada, and Jo-Jo's activities. Most obvious thing of all is her enormous love of language. She simply delights in any new word and in the sound of her own talking.

In summary, as J began to acquire verbs consistently in her vocabulary, she expanded the scope and power of her language production by varying her word combinations with them.

The Role of Verbs in J's Lexical Acquisition

The active emergence of verbs in J's vocabulary coincided closely in time with the onset of a general spurt in her rate of vocabulary growth as well as her productive use of SVO sentences. Figure 4.1 illustrates that from 19 months, J's overall vocabulary, and specifically her verb lexicon, developed steadily once she began to use SVO sentences in her language production.

As the total vocabulary curve indicates, J had an initial vocabulary spurt between 19 and 20 months. There was a 94% (78/83) proportional increase in the size of her vocabulary during this one-month period, and 33% (26/78) of these new words were verbs. During this same month J quintupled (26/5) the number of verbs in her vocabulary. Moreover, J began to use four of the five verbs from her prior vocabulary in sentences during this month (e.g., "Daddy *rock* Jo," "Peaowa [the cat] *walk* too," "Meat *cook*," and "Timmy *eat* banana").

The intersection of the vertical line labeled SVO with the vocabulary curves in Fig. 4.1 illustrates the developmental synchrony between the emer-

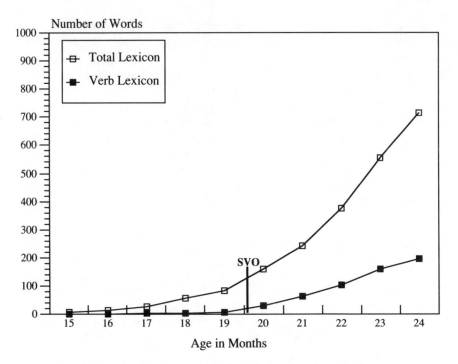

FIG. 4.1. Total verb lexicon and cumulative lexicon for J from 15–24 months.

gence of verbs in J's lexicon and the meaningful and grammatical use of these verbs in sentences. Thus, J's initial vocabulary spurt between 19 and '20 months coincided with the onset of her productive use of SVO sentences.

There was a second period of rapid vocabulary growth that involved the acquisition of many new words. From 22 to 24 months of age, J acquired 48% (341/715) of her total vocabulary at age 2. She also acquired 47% (92/196) of her total verb lexicon at this time. Thus, in J's case, the ability to use verbs in early sentences preceded the most active period of her vocabulary development.

Summary

Throughout the period from 19 to 24 months, J was concise and accurate with verbs, although her knowledge of morphology was minimal.

(13) J, 1;11.13, is at dinner and tells about a prior experience (cf. Bruner, 1990).
J: Kids in Jo playhouse.
J: Jo-Jo *go* in playhouse.
J: Kids *say* Jo *get out* playhouse.

(14) J, 1;11.23, sees squirrels in the park. The following utterances about squirrels were recorded during a 15 minute walk. "Squirrel *come down* here. Jo *hear* him. He *eat* nuts. Jo *give* squirrel nut. Jo *give* this squirrel nut. Squirrel *come up* this (bench). Bye-bye squirrel. *See* you later squirrel."

In reading through J's diary for the period between 19 and 24 months of age, there is an overall sense that she was in command of language. J did not begin to use verbs in language production prior to the integration of their form, meaning, and function in her mind. When the form, meaning, and function of verbs emerge this synchronously, they appear to be tightly interwoven developmentally.

L—ASYNCHRONOUS EMERGENCE OF VERBS

In contrast to J, L relied heavily on a production strategy that included rote output (Bates et al., 1988) as a mechanism for language acquisition. Thus, her diary data are a rich source of information about the incremental changes that led to the gradual integration of the form, referential meaning, and grammatical function of her first verbs. In fact, there was a clear developmental decalage between the emergence of verbs qua form in L's lexicon and evidence from her first sentences of an understanding of their grammatical function.

Linear Sequences Without Verbs

Early Word Combinations Between 15 and 16 Months. This very early period of word combinations without verbs is important because it clarifies the nature of L's first hypotheses about the form and function of language. The simplest developmental explanation of L's linguistic competence at this time is that she discovered two basic principles about the nature of language: that language is linearly sequenced in time (Veneziano, Sinclair, & Berthoud, 1990) and that a linear sequence can be used to negotiate a meaning with other people (Braunwald, 1978).

Between 15 and 16 months, L began to produce word combinations without any verbs. She began to try to combine one or more words into a sequential linear pattern. The first and least complex pattern consisted of multiple repetitions of the same word within a single intonation contour (e.g., "Baby, baby, baby" and "Out, out, out," both of which were requests to be put into the bathtub).

The second, more complex linear pattern involved the conjoining of a constant term such as *hi* or *bye* with a limited but variable group of high frequency words (e.g., about 10 words, including *baby* for self-reference and a term for each family member, including the cat). By 16 months, L's most advanced and frequent word combinations involved the word *hi* in either an initial or medial position. Some of these combinations with *hi* seemed to function as an expression of notice (e.g., "Hi bow-wow" to the sound of barking and "Car, hi car, hi car-car" as M drives into a parking lot). Thus, one of L's early sequential patterns with *hi* may have been a developmental precursor to her later use of verbs of perception, such as *see* (1;4.24) and *hear* (1;5.30), to express notice.

Social Use of Linear Sequences. A second general feature of L's language production between 15 and 16 months was her ability to use limited linguistic knowledge to serve multiple social purposes. She could use words to negotiate a meaning with another person.

> (15) L, 1;3.15, is playing with F's radio when J reprimands her.
> J: No, that's not for you!
> L: Dada, dada, dada.
> J: Don't turn it, okay.
> L: Kay.

During this early phase of language acquisition, differences in the meaning of the same linear sequence were expressed overtly at the juncture where language and context interfaced in social interaction. For instance, depending upon the situational context, "Hi baby" was a greeting to other babies, an expression of notice, and L's idiosyncratic way to request recurrence (e.g., "Hi baby! Hi baby!" as L holds up her plate for more meat; cf. Braunwald, 1978). The meaning of L's word combinations was not yet intrinsic to a surface or a deep structure. The differential meaning of her linear word combinations was embedded in the social interaction of the moment.

In sum, this early period of L's language production seemed to antedate both a pragmatic deep structure (Ninio & Snow, 1988) and a limited scope semantic formula (Braine, 1976, 1988). At 16 months and on the brink of uttering the first verb in her vocabulary, L appeared to understand two fundamental principles about language. She knew that she had to produce a linear sequence and that the meaning of such a sequence could be jointly negotiated. Armed with these two basic insights about the form and function of language, the toddler-linguist, L, began to tackle the dual problem of verb meaning and word order.

Developmental Steps in the Transition to Verbs

Combining Language and Action Without Verbs. There was no overt indication that L's first associations between language and action involved verbs. From 15 to 16 months, L's verbalizations that coincided with action were idiosyncratic and inconsistent (e.g., "Cookie, cookie, cookie" and "Hi kee, hi kitty, hi kitty" were both said as L chased the cat).

Between 16 and 17 months, the link between L's language and her actions became systematic. She began to say object words as she engaged in an action with that object (e.g., *bike* as L climbed onto her tike-bike; *towel* as L grabbed a towel). She also used conventional words to ask others to help her change locations (e.g., *down, up,* and *out*). She began to use the word *stuck* to indicate that she needed assistance to move herself (e.g., her arm was caught in the car seat strap) or to budge an object (e.g., a pull toy was caught on the doorjamb).

This coordination between L's language and her actions contributed to the impression that her words were meaningful and functional (Edwards & Goodwin, 1985). L's identification of an object was unambiguous when it was associated with an action (e.g., "Toe, toe" as L pulled her toes). This early conjoining of words with actions prior to verb meaning was a first step toward the ultimate coupling of actions with verb lexemes. L understood that the production of language could co-occur in time with an action.

Acquiring the Form of Verbs. Between the ages of 16 months and 8 days and 16 months and 29 days, L acquired the first six verb-like words in her vocabulary (*cry* at 1;4.8, *bark* at 1;4.18, *go* at 1;4.19, *cockle* [tickle] at 1;4.22, *see* at 1;4.24, and *blow* at 1;4.29). When the verb-like words *cry* and *bark* first emerged in L's language production, she did not seem to know their referential meaning or their grammatical function.

Cry was the first verb-like word in L's vocabulary. L acquired "Baby cry" in the context of a swimming lesson away from home. L cried in this situation and saw other babies who were crying (see Braunwald, 1978; Dromi, 1987; Nelson, 1991; Tomasello, 1992, for discussions of the relation between events and early word meaning). Although L already used the word *baby* (acquired at 1;2.22), the phrase "Baby cry" was a single unit (Lieven, Pine, & Dresner Barnes, 1992; Peters, 1983).

Initially, "Baby cry" was an unanalyzed form that L learned to understand through language production. Between 16 to 17 months of age, both the referential meaning and relational function of *cry* as a verb were indeterminate in 59% (27/46) of L's utterances with *cry*.

(16) L, 1;4.13, is taking her pacifier. (*Lola* is L's word for pacifier).
  L: Mommy.
  M: What?
  L: Lola.
  M: Lola what?
  L: Lola *cry*.
  M: No, lola doesn't cry.
  L: Hi *cry*.

The meaning and function of *cry* was opaque even in this example of a scaffolded vertical construction (Scollon, 1973). L used the word *cry* in 24% (11/46) of her utterances as if it were an appropriate association with the word *baby*.

> (17) L, 1;4.9, is looking at a picture of a baby on the back of a magazine. The context note contains the comment, "*Cry* in this instance does *not* mean 'cry' as far as I can tell."
> L: Baby *cry*.
> M: He's not crying.
> L: *Cry*, hi *cry*.
> L: Hi *cry*.

Thus, the referential meaning of *cry* as a verb was uncertain even when it was associated with the word *baby*.

Seventeen percent (8/46) of L's first utterances with the lexeme *cry* occurred with a possible referential meaning. In each case, L said "cry" in a situation in which the listener could discern a potentially meaningful relation between her word and the context.

> (18) L, 1;4.8, has soap in her eyes and is crying.
> L: Baby.
> M: Baby what?
> L: *Cry*.
> (19) L, 1;4.22, can hear J screaming.
> L: *Cry* Jo. (incorrect word order)

Although there are only eight examples of the potentially meaningful use of *cry*, these utterances are developmentally informative. They involved the decoupling of *cry* from the amalgam *Baby cry* so that *cry* functioned as an independent verb-like word in L's vocabulary.

Cry *and* Bark *in Linear Sequences With* Hi. Between 16 and 17 months of age, 20% (9/46) of L's utterances with *cry* and 33% (3/9) of her utterances with *bark* involved a word combination with *hi*, as in Examples 16 and 17. These infrequent but unusual linear sequences provide an important clue to the nature of the developmental transition that L was working out. Despite their verb-like form, *cry* and *bark* did not function as verbs in L's first word combinations with them.

L's first hypothesis about the grammatical function of *cry* and *bark* was that they could be integrated into her existing linear system of language production. To quote from the diary for L at 16 months and 8 days: "*HI* and *BYE* + a word continue to be her most frequent word combinations." Given

L's limited linguistic competence, it was permissible to replace *baby* and *bow-wow* with *hi* and to combine *hi* in an initial position with *cry* and *bark*. Moreover, there was no evidence that *hi* served some other function, such as an amorphous pronoun or the precursor to one.

Explaining the errors "Hi cry" and "Hi bark" has been problematic in previous analyses of these data (Braunwald, 1989; Braunwald & Brislin, 1979b). However, from the longitudinal perspective of their role in the acquisition of verbs, these utterances make developmental sense. There was no rule in L's language to prevent her from creating these novel and grammatically incorrect linear sequences.

L's utterances with *cry* and *bark* served an important transitional function in her language acquisition. They were the bridge between L's early fixed linear sequences and her subsequent more flexible approach to learning language. By 17 months of age, six verb-like words were present in L's vocabulary. L continued to use these words (*cry, bark, go, cockle* [tickle], *see*, and *blow*) throughout her second year. With each of these verbs, the developmental progression began with a meaning to communicate and gradually added the structure to do so conventionally (Clark, 1978; Levy, 1988).

The Emergence of Verbs

During a 2-day period (19 months, 2–3 days), L produced her first six grammatical sentences with a verb. Her production of these sentences occurred as part of an incremental process of change in her language production. These SVO sentences do not represent a dramatic entry into expressive language: "Laura sit chair," "Gluck (L's babysitter) change me," "Sue clean me" (used twice), "Gluck MeMe bite you" (MeMe at Mrs. Gluck's might bite me), and "Laura do it." Three of these sentences involve verbs from L's prior cumulative lexicon (*do* learned at 1;5.0, *sit* at 1;5.6, and *bite* at 1;5.6). The two new verbs, *clean* and *change*, express a subtle and idiosyncratic difference in word meaning. M and F "clean" L during a diaper change; any other person "changes" her.

The Role of Verbs in L's Lexical Acquisition

Figure 4.2 depicts the monthly growth of L's verb and cumulative lexicons from 15 to 24 months. The developmental relation between the number of words in L's verb and cumulative lexicons and her age at the time of her first SVO sentences is noteworthy.

The greatest proportional increase in L's total vocabulary occurred between 17 and 18 months. There was an 86% (85/99) increase in the size of her vocabulary during this one-month period. The most rapid proportional increase in L's verb vocabulary also occurred during the same month-long period. Between 17 and 18 months, L tripled (18/6) the number of verbs in her vocabulary.

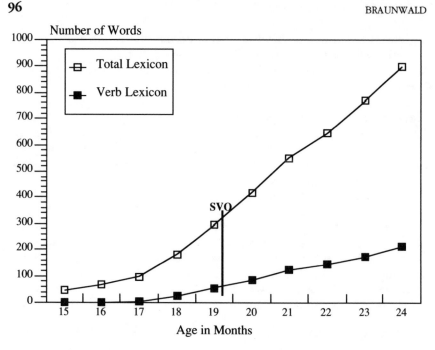

FIG. 4.2. Total verb lexicon and cumulative lexicon for L from 15–24 months.

L acquired 33% (301/899) of her total cumulative lexicon at age 2 prior to the production of her sixth spontaneous SVO sentence at age 19 months, 3 days. She also acquired 27% (58/215) of her total verb lexicon at age 2 before she produced early sentences. Thus, L knew the referential meaning of many different verbs before she began to combine them in hierarchically organized SVO sentences. This developmental pattern illustrates an asynchrony between L's acquisition of verb lexemes and her knowledge of their grammatical function in the organization of sentences.

Summary

Throughout the period from 16 to 24 months of age, L concentrated on communicating with her family. In reading through L's diary for this period, it is apparent that L relied heavily on a pragmatic-semantic strategy as her avenue into language.

(20) L, 1;4.13, takes all her turns in a routinized dialogue with M.
       M: Where's daddy?
       L: Bye-bye.
       M: Where's Jo-Jo?
       L: Bye-bye.
       M: Where's Laura?
       L: (L babbles in response.)

(21) L, 1;9.7, is carrying a crayon from the patio into the house.
    L: *Take* crayon me.
    M: You want to take the crayon with you?
    L: Yep, pocket.

Discourse in the negotiation of everyday life events seemed to play an important role in L's language development. In Example 22, L used the auxiliary verb *will* for the first time.

(22) L, 1;11.16, is climbing up after a banana.
    J: You can't get a banana.
    L: My *will* get banana.
    L: I *will* get banana.
    M: It's okay, she can get one.
    (M and J give L a banana.)

Thus, L capitalized on discourse with others as a way to understand and practice language.

There is never a sense that L was fully in command of language in the way that J was. She did not wait until she understood the meaning and grammatical function of verbs before she tried to use them. L made many mistakes in her production of verbs, but she also learned from these errors. Thus, L relied on language production as her primary way to grasp the principles of language (cf. Bates et al., 1988; Tomasello, 1992).

DEVELOPMENTAL COMPARISONS

This is not the first time that variation in the acquisition of verbs has been described in the language production of siblings (Bowerman, 1976). By the age of 2, both J and L had acquired substantial cumulative and verb lexicons. J knew 715 words, including 196 verbs. Her sister, L, knew 899 words, including 215 verbs. Throughout their second years, L always had a larger vocabulary than J did. Nevertheless, both girls acquired words that were typical of the verbs in a toddler's vocabulary.

Content

J's and L's verb lexicons at age 2 were compared to the 103 action words on the MacArthur Communicative Development Inventory: Words and Sentences (1993). The action words on the Communicative Development Inventory (CDI) are verbs that occur frequently in the vocabularies of toddlers between 16 and 30 months. Many of the action words on the CDI were found in both girls' verb vocabularies. Seventy-four percent (76/103) of the action words on the CDI were present in J's vocabulary at age 2, and 84% (87/103) were present in L's. Sixty-nine percent (71/103) of these action words were known by both J and L.

The vocabulary totals on the CDI represent vocabulary knowledge but are not an exhaustive list of a child's complete lexicon (Fenson et al., 1993). At age 2, both J and L knew many verbs that are not included among the action words on the CDI. Sixty-one percent (120/196) of the verbs in J's vocabulary and 60% (128/215) of L's were not found on the CDI.

When the girls' verb lexicons are compared to each other, 70% (137/196) of the verbs in J's vocabulary were found in L's total verb vocabulary. When L's larger verb vocabulary is compared to J's, 67% (144/215) of her verbs were found in J's total verb lexicon.

Rate of Development

Cumulative Lexicon. When the girls' rates of vocabulary development per month are compared, it is clear that the progression of J's and L's lexical acquisition differed. Figure 4.3 illustrates the number of new words that each girl learned per month from 15 to 24 months. J's rate of lexical acquisition began to increase at the time of the onset of the vocabulary spurt at 19 months. From 19 months onward, J learned many new words each month (range 78 to 180).

L's rate of lexical acquisition was consistently high (range 111 to 131) after the vocabulary spurt (17–18 months). The only exception to this rapid rate of lexical acquisition occurred between 21 and 22 months of age, when L's rate of lexical acquisition declined to 95 new words.

Verb Lexicon. Figure 4.4 shows a comparison of J's and L's monthly rates of verb acquisition from 17 to 24 months of age. Note the contrast in the rate of the girls' verb acquisition in relation to the production of SVO sentences.

There is an appreciable difference in the girls' rates of verb acquisition between 21 and 22 months of age. J rapidly acquired 41 new verbs, but L's rate of verb acquisition declined to a low of 22 new verbs. This difference in the rate of their verb acquisition at 22 months represents a change in each girl's developmental focus on language. Between 21 and 22 months, J actively increased the size of her vocabulary, whereas L began to improve the syntax of her utterances.

Percentage of Verbs in the Lexicon. Figure 4.5 shows a comparison of the percentage of verbs in each girl's cumulative lexicon from 17 to 24 months. Note that the production of SVO sentences coincided closely in

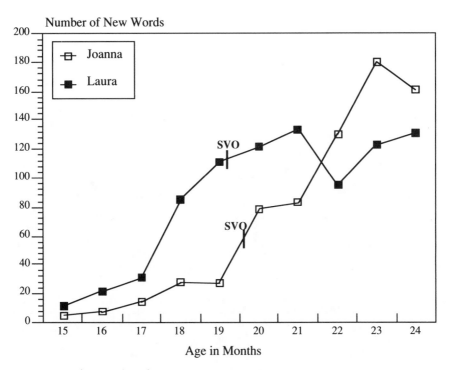

FIG. 4.3. Number of new words per month for J and L from 15–24 months.

time with the same proportion of verbs in the girls' total lexicons. Moreover, 20 months is the only age at which this proportional distribution of verbs was the same for both girls. Although the percentage of verbs in L's lexicon (from 17 to 19 months) was greater than J's, there was a proportional shift in the percentage of verbs in the girls' total vocabularies from 21 to 24 months. From 21 months onward, verbs constituted between 26% to 29% of J's total vocabulary at each month's birthdate and 23% to 24% of L's. In terms of absolute numbers, L always knew more words, including verbs, than J did. However, from 21 to 24 months verbs played a proportionally more important role in J's lexical acquisition.

The percentage of verbs in J's vocabulary reflected the same developmental trajectory as her rate of acquisition. Prior to 19 months, the percentage of verbs in J's total vocabulary was limited. Beginning at 19 months, J began to acquire many new verbs, and the proportion of verbs in her total vocabulary increased accordingly, from 6% at 19 months to a peak of 29% at 23 months.

The percentage of verbs in L's total vocabulary increased steadily between 17 and 24 months, from 6% at 17 months to 24% at 24 months. In contrast to the decrease in the absolute rate of her acquisition of verbs at 22 months, the proportion of verbs in L's vocabulary did not decline.

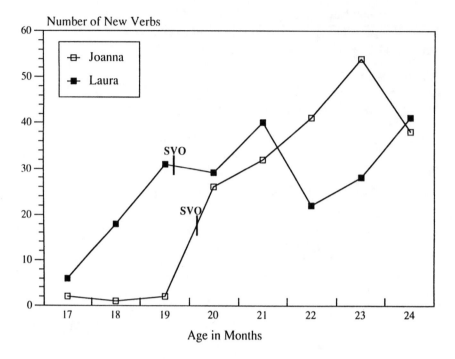

FIG. 4.4. Number of new verbs per month for J and L from 17–24 months.

The Emergence of Sentences

Between 19 and 20 months, J and L each made a basic and comparable developmental advance in the ability to use verbs. They both began to produce three-part, single organizational units built around verbs (e.g., SVO sentences). They began to produce transitive verbs with a subject and a direct object (e.g., "Jo-Jo get bike" as J intends to do so) and intransitive verbs with a qualification or additional information following the verb (e.g., "Laura sit chair" as L tries to climb into her car seat). Although this advance was far from a pervasive reorganization of the girls' use of verbs, it did signal the onset of the ability to produce a hierarchically organized structure with a subset of specific verbs (Ninio, 1988: Tomasello, 1992).

Patterns of Verb Use from 20 to 22 Months

The period between 20 and 22 months was analyzed in detail. All of the daily entries from both girls' diaries for this two-month period were coded. A total of 1,785 utterances, 322 for J and 1,463 for L, were coded in order to identify systematic patterns of acquisition for each girl.

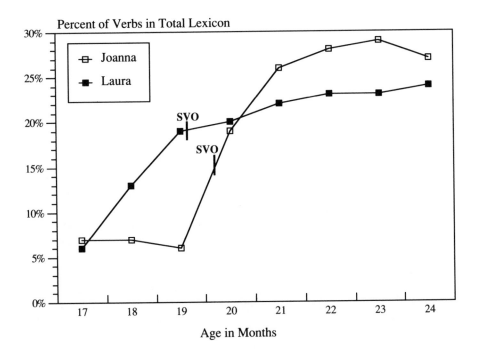

FIG. 4.5. Percentage of verbs in J's and L's cumulative lexicons from 17–24 months.

The period from 20 to 22 months was selected for developmental reasons. At 20 months, the proportion of verbs in J's and L's vocabularies was the same. Between 21 and 22 months, each girl appeared to shift her developmental focus. Whereas J began a period of active lexical acquisition, L began to produce more sentences.

The data were analyzed in many different ways. The important findings for this chapter concern the use of prior and new vocabulary in emergent language, the presence or absence of a verb in emergent language, and the presence or absence of a word in the pre-verb argument slot.

Between 20 and 21 months, 71% (103/145) of J's utterances with emergent language included a verb. J used new vocabulary, including new verbs, in 32% (46/145) of these novel utterances. Verbs made up 39% (32/83) of J's total new vocabulary for the month and 26% (63/244) of her cumulative lexicon at 21 months.

In the same period, 60% (435/724) of L's total utterances with emergent language included a verb. L used new vocabulary, including new verbs, in only 10% (71/724) of these novel utterances. Verbs made up 30% (40/133) of L's new vocabulary for the month and 23% (124/550) of her cumulative lexicon at 21 months.

Although both girls were acquiring open-class verbs, they were using different strategies to work out the grammatical function of a verb in a sentence. J, who was using a nominal style, could at 20 months produce many SVO sentences with either self or other as the referent (e.g., "Jo-Jo wear Mama shoe" and "Mama wear this shoe"). L included the pre-verb argument in 95% (111/117) of her utterances when she spoke of others (e.g., "Dee-Dee [J] eat Laura candy bar") but omitted it in 57% (98/173) of the utterances in which she was the referent (e.g., "Drop Laura bottle" as L drops her bottle).

Between 21 and 22 months, 71% (126/177) of J's utterances with emergent language and 70% (515/739) of L's contained a verb. Thus, J and L were using the same proportion of verb utterances in their emergent language. However, J was using a much greater proportion of new vocabulary, including verbs, than L was in these emergent utterances with a verb. Forty-two percent (75/177) of J's utterances with a verb involved new vocabulary, whereas only 6% (44/739) of L's did.

Verbs made up 32% (41/130) of J's new vocabulary and 28% (104/374) of her cumulative lexicon between 21 and 22 months. Verbs made up 23% (22/95) of L's new vocabulary and 23% (146/645) of her cumulative lexicon at 22 months.

As Figs. 4.3 and 4.4 illustrate, the rate of L's vocabulary and verb acquisition declined between 21 and 22 months. However, there is a developmental explanation for this decrease. To quote from the monthly summary in the diary for L at 22 months of age, "there appears to be a decrease in the acquisition of lexicon compared to the last few months, but this is overshadowed by the enormous leap in L's ability to manipulate syntax." L's pattern of verb use between 21 and 22 months illustrates this developmental change in her language production.

Between 21 and 22 months, L began to use the verbs in her existing vocabulary to produce many novel utterances. She included verbs in 70% (515/739) of her most advanced language and used 93 different verbs in 515 utterances. Of these 93 verbs, 71 were from her prior vocabulary, and 22 were acquired during the course of the month. At 22 months, there were 146 verbs in L's vocabulary. L used 64% (93/146) of them with emergent language during the preceding month.

The data from 21 to 22 months are replete with examples of L's progress in using the structure of language in new ways. For example, between 21 and 22 months, L's emergent language included 172 SVO sentences (e.g., "I see daddy blue car" and "Mommy read story me"). In contrast to the previous month, L produced pre-verb arguments in 73% (214/292) of those utterances in which she was the referent. L also used fixed and idiosyncratic social formulae with verbs as a way to fulfill her own social needs. For instance, the phrase *could I* emerged at 21 months and 17 days as L's formulaic routine for asking a yes/no question that functioned as a personal request (e.g., "More milk, could I?"). These are but a few of the many ways in which L began to expand her ability to use verbs in her language production.

Twenty-two months stands out as a landmark in both J's and L's development but for different reasons. At 22 months, J began the most active period in her lexical acquisition, adding 180 new words, including 54 verbs, in one month. At the same age, L was in the midst of using known words from her vocabulary, especially verbs, to create new meanings with the structure of language. Thus, each girl was actively expanding the scope of her earlier language skills.

Birth Order

J's style of language acquisition corresponded to the pattern that would be predicted for an upper SES and first-born girl (Bates et al., 1988). Her style of language production was analytic (Bates et al., 1988), referential (Nelson, 1973), and nominal (Bloom, 1991). She also used content words in the argument structure of her verbs.

> (23) J, 1;8.9 (no context note)
> J: Mama *give* Jo-Jo cookie nigh-nigh.
> (Mama gives Jo-Jo a cookie at bedtime.)

Note that J used nouns to fill the argument slots of the verb *give* and that she left out all of the obligatory morphemes.

L's style of language development in general and of verbs in particular was eclectic. The *dialogue cluster* (Bates et al., 1988), which involves labeling, imitation, and a tendency to answer questions and to engage in conversation, is an apt description of L's expressive language. Her style was also primarily pronominal (Bloom, 1991) once she began between 21 to 22 months to refer to herself in a pre-verb position in a sentence. Example 24 was selected to show the distinction between L's pronominal style with the verb *give* and her sister's nominal style with the same verb (see Example 23).

> (24) L, 1;9.3, is at Thanksgiving dinner and is showing her bottle to company.
> L: My mommy, daddy *give* it me.

L also had a tendency to subassemble the parts of a whole before she could put them together in a single correctly ordered sentence.

> (25) L, 1;8.25, is sitting in F's lap.
> L: *Sit* Daddy lap.
> L: Laura *is.*

Once again, but at a more advanced point in her development, L relied on an incorrectly ordered vertical construction (Scollon, 1973) to convey the complete meaning.

The Verb Island Hypothesis

The *verb island hypothesis* (Tomasello, 1992) predicts that children acquire the combinatorial rules of grammar verb-by-verb. Although the verb island hypothesis was not systematically examined in this study, it is relevant descriptively to differences in the emergence of verbs in J's and L's language production. The verb island hypothesis can be conceptualized as a variable that defines a qualitative difference between J and L in the grammatical organization of their first verbs.

At least superficially, L's asynchronous production strategy of verb acquisition is compatible with the verb island hypothesis. L seemed to be learning the grammatical function of verbs on a verb-by-verb basis when she first began to produce three-word sentences. In Example 26, L's word order with the verb *hear* is correct in the two-word combination but incorrect in the more complex attempt at a three-word sentence. Note the contrast between the correct use of the verb *hear* in Examples 10 and 11 and the incorrect use in Example 26.

(26) L, 1;7.16, The sound of children playing outside can be heard distinctly inside the house.
L: *Hear children.* (correct word order)
L: *Hear children.*
L: *Laura children hear.* (incorrect word order)
M: Yes I hear children. (acknowledgment, repair)
L: *Laura children hear.* (repetition of error)
A few minutes later, M is changing L's diaper and asks L about hearing the children.
M: Did you hear children?
L: *Hear children.* (correct word order)
L: *Laura children.* (verb deleted)

As the verb island hypothesis predicts, L figured out the relational function of the verb *hear* in a two-word combination. L could also produce "Laura hear." Yet she had not mastered the grammatical function of *hear* in a three-word sentence with a pre- and post-verb argument. At 19½ months, L was just beginning to use such three-word sentences infrequently, using only 11% (8/72) of the verbs in her vocabulary (*bite, break, change, clean, do, pour, rock,* and *sit*).

At 19½ months, J also was beginning to use verbs in three-word sentences. However, in sharp contrast to L, J could generalize her knowledge of the grammatical function of a verb to the many new verbs which were emerging in her vocabulary. Her new verbs were produced in the linguistic context of word combinations (e.g., "Get flower") and sentences (e.g., "Jo-Jo read book"). By 20 months of age, J's verb lexicon contained 31 words, and she used 84% (26/31) of these verbs in three-word sentences.

The emergence of verbs in J's language production seems to contradict the verb island hypothesis. However, given that J relied primarily on comprehension as her route into language acquisition, the pattern of her early verb acquisition is actually unknown. It is not possible to know from these naturalistic data whether J acquired information in comprehension in a verb-by-verb manner as the verb island hypothesis predicts.

CONCLUSION

J's Pattern of Acquisition

The form, referential meaning, and grammatical function of J's first verbs in language production were tightly yoked together as if they were indicative of a single, synchronous developmental advance. She actively began to add verbs to her vocabulary at 19 months, and she produced her sixth SVO sentence 17 days later. Thus, there appeared to be a system-wide and qualitative change in J's language production that began between 19 and 20 months.

Given the data on J, one could justifiably hypothesize that the swift and error-free onset of her language production is evidence for a maturational process—possibly one that is innately given (Chomsky, 1988) or constrained (Golinkoff, Jacquet, & Hirsh-Pasek, 1991). One could argue that the parameters of a specific language, English, were being set as a function of J's lexical acquisition (Pinker, 1989).

An alternative interpretation of these data is that a developmental progression, observed in L's expressive language, can occur covertly or internally through a process of comprehension. There are, in fact, anecdotal notes in J's diary from 16 months onward that describe her comprehension.

(27) J, 1;4.15, follows complicated directions: 1) She will fetch an item from another room. 2) If told that she is "going to go bye-bye," "take a bath," etc. she will begin to get ready for the event. 3) She will respond to verbal discipline such as "Not for Joanna," "Put _____ back," "Bring ____ to dada," and "Please don't touch."

Moreover, her dramatic advance in language production did not overshadow her progress in comprehension. In the summary note for J at 1;11.0, her mother noted "astounding comprehension as indicated by her answers, comments, and actions."

J developed the ability to produce SVO sentences without much actual practice in language production. However, it is possible that she was relying primarily on a comprehension strategy (Bates et al., 1988) during early language acquisition as her means to learn verbs (e.g., Tomasello, 1992) and to discover the organization of SVO sentences (Naigles, 1990). "Effective engagement can occur without verbal production clues from the child that this is happening . . . some children combine effective engagement and learning with remarkably low language production during learning" (K. E. Nelson, 1989, p. 292). If the form, meaning, and grammatical function of verbs are integrated covertly and internally, as they may have been for J, a sudden and qualitative change in language production is possible.

J abruptly and consistently began to acquire verbs in her vocabulary and to use them in meaningful, grammatical sentences. This pattern of verb acquisition is comparable to some of the children in Bates et al.'s (1988) longitudinal sample. These children got off to an average start during the earliest phase of language development but advanced rapidly once they began to use verbs.

> The discovery of verbs will of course be important for every child. However, for some children it seems to open new vistas and to present a more rapid way of breaking into language than that which they had previously used. These children suddenly move from the middle ranks toward the head of the class. (Bates et al., 1988, p. 111)

The emergence of verbs in J's expressive language marked the onset of sustained and rapid progress in the overall process of her language acquisition from 20 to 24 months.

In the brief span of 4 months, J learned 554 new words, including 165 verbs. By 24 months, she could use these words to create long sentences that described her own activities (e.g., at 1;11.12, "Nanny, Poppy take Jo out eat pancakes") and her observations of her world (e.g., at 1;11.25, "Cookie have raisin in it. Hole in it where raisin go in"). As her mother wrote in the summary note for J at 24 months: "In this year we (J and her family) have progressed from the physical reassurance and communication at one year to verbal communication . . . FANTASTIC TO WATCH HER LEARN TO TALK" (emphasis in original diary).

L's Pattern of Acquisition

In contrast to J, L's language production provided no evidence of a sudden burst of insight that led to understanding the grammatical function of verbs. L acquired her knowledge of verbs in a qualitatively different manner than her sister. Like Tomasello's daughter (Tomasello, 1992), L acquired her first verbs in a concrete, context-dependent, and often idiosyncratic way.

L began to acquire verb-like words between 16 and 17 months of age. From 17 months onward, L added meaningful verbs to her vocabulary. However, 2 months and 25 days elapsed between the emergence of the amorphous word, *cry*, in her expressive language at 16 months and 8 days and the production of her sixth spontaneous SVO sentence at 19 months and 3 days.

Given only the data on L, one would have to conclude that verbs are acquired as part of an incremental series of changes in language production. One would have to opt for a pragmatic-semantic foundation to the process of verb acquisition. In fact, there are many examples in this chapter in which L was clearly relying on a pragmatic-semantic approach to the structure of language (Ninio & Snow, 1988; Schlesinger, 1988; Tomasello, 1992). Social interaction in discourse played an important role in scaffolding L's understanding of the meaning and function of words, including verbs (cf. Vygotsky, 1962).

Explanation of Individual Differences

How can these two different empirical descriptions of the emergence of verbs be reconciled theoretically? The data from L help to answer this question. These data show that the form, meaning, and grammatical function of a verb were dissociable in L's early language production. These observed dissociations indicate that the toddler's developmental task is to conjoin the form of a verb in the endstate language with its conventional meaning and grammatical function in a sentence.

Although their strategies differed, J and L faced the same developmental problem in their initial acquisition of verbs. Both girls had to work out the complex relationship among a conventional form in the endstate language, an arbitrarily defined word meaning in their culture, a relational meaning in their linguistic system, and a communicative function in their language use. By 24 months of age, both J and L had solved this problem and developed the communicative competence to produce verbs in comprehensible sentences, although the process was far from complete.

The fact that J and L used different developmental strategies to acquire their first verbs in the endstate language was a real individual difference between them. The difference between J and L in the process of verb development was found in detailed longitudinal data from the same two children and was not a methodological artifact (Pine & Lieven, 1990). The data from J and L show that the process of the acquisition of verbs was variable, as a function of the child's chronological age and general strategy of language acquisition. The form, meaning, and grammatical function of a verb may, but need not, emerge simultaneously in language production.

Developmental Timing. The greatest proportional increase in the girls' total vocabularies coincided with the consistent use of the form of a verb in their language production. However, the developmental integration of the form, meaning, and grammatical function of verbs differed for each girl at the time of this vocabulary spurt. These differences in timing can be described in terms of a continuum of developmental synchrony-to-asynchrony.

In J's case, the onset of the vocabulary spurt and the acquisition of verbs in her vocabulary were synchronous with the emergence of verbs in SVO sentences in her language production. In L's case, the emergence of verbs qua form in her vocabulary preceded the ability to use the form in meaningful and grammatical sentences. There was an asynchrony between the onset of the vocabulary spurt and the production of verbs in SVO sentences.

In spite of individual differences between J and L in (a) the developmental process of the emergence of their first verbs, (b) the size of their respective verb and cumulative lexicons, (c) the rate of their vocabulary development, and (d) their age at the time of the onset of the vocabulary spurt, there was a comparable developmental watershed between 19 and 20 months. There was a striking developmental similarity in the timing of the onset of J's and L's first sentences with verbs (e.g., SVO sentences) and the only occurrence of the same proportional distribution of verbs in their total vocabularies at 20 months.

The period between 19 and 20 months marked a transition that involved verbs and led to "verbiness" (Bates et al., 1988) at 20 months. There was an observable and comparable organizational advance in the girls' ability to incorporate verbs into their language production. The data from J and L describe this onset of "verbiness," but they do not explain *why* this developmental advance occurred. Nonetheless, these data indicate that chronological age was an important variable that J and L shared at the time of this developmental transition in their acquisition of verbs.

It is clear that the individual differences between J and L related to variation in their initial focus on the linguistic and social input that became intake (Kuczaj, 1982) to the process of the acquisition of verbs. Bates et al. (1988) proposed a developmental reason why the intake to the process of the acquisition of verbs would be variable. They identified three partially dissociable and horizontally developing learning mechanisms—rote output or production, analytic production, and comprehension. They found that children differed in the proportion of their reliance on these three general cognitive learning mechanisms at a given point in development. Hence, there should be individual differences in one child throughout development (e.g., Bates' daughter Julia) as well as among different children at a given point in time (e.g., J and L from 16 to 19 months) based on the kind of environmental input that becomes intake.

In the absence of systematic information on the girls' language comprehension, it is not possible to reach a conclusive theoretical answer to the question of the etiology of their first verbs. However, the detailed description of the emergence of verbs in J's and L's language production is compatible with a cognitive theory (Bates et al., 1988; Bloom, 1991; Nelson, 1991; Tomasello, 1992). These data also implicate a comparable readiness between 19 and 20 months to tackle the problem of acquiring verbs.

The data in this chapter show individual differences between J and L in the overt process of their acquisition of verbs. At least in these diary data, in which minute developmental changes accrue over time, the observable process of the acquisition of verbs in language production was variable. Thus, one important aspect of a theory of the acquisition of verbs is the potential to identify and to explain normal individual differences in the process of children's initial development and use of verbs. The acquisition of first verbs creates a mind-boggling challenge to toddlers and to child language researchers who would like to explain this process.

ACKNOWLEDGMENTS

I wish to extend a loving thank-you to Jack, Joanna, and Laura Braunwald for their help in making my work possible. I would also like to thank Stephanie Geller, Arthur Parmelee, and Judyth Roberts for their encouragement over many years. Finally, I would like to thank William E. Merriman and Michael Tomasello for their editorial assistance.

REFERENCES

Barrett, M. (1983). The early acquisition and development of the meanings of action-related words. In T. Seiler & W. Wannenmacher (Eds.), *Concept development and the acquisition of word meaning* (pp. 39–67). Berlin: Springer.

Bates, E., Bretherton, I., & Snyder, L. (1988). *From first words to grammar: Individual differences and dissociable mechanisms.* New York: Cambridge University Press.

Berman, R. A. (1988). Word class distinctions in developing grammars. In Y. Levy, I. M. Schlesinger, & M. D. Braine (Eds.), *Categories and processes in language acquisition* (pp. 45–72). Hillsdale, NJ: Lawrence Erlbaum Associates.

Bloom, L. (1973). *One word at a time: The use of single word utterances before syntax.* The Hague, Netherlands: Mouton.

Bloom, L. (1991). *Language development from two to three* (pp. 1–85). New York: Cambridge University Press.

Bowerman, M. (1976). Semantic factors in the acquisition of rules for word use and sentence construction. In D. M. Morehead & A. E. Morehead (Eds.), *Normal and deficient child language* (pp. 99–179). Baltimore: University Park Press.

Bowerman, M. (1985). What shapes children's grammars? In D. Slobin (Ed.), *The crosslinguistic study of language acquisition* (Vol. 2, pp. 1257–1319). Hillsdale, NJ: Lawrence Erlbaum Associates.

Braine, M. D. (1976). Children's first word combinations. *Monographs of the Society for Research in Child Development, 41*(1, Serial No. 164).

Braine, M. D. (1988). Modeling the acquisition of linguistic structure. In Y. Levy, I. M. Schlesinger, & M. D. Braine (Eds.), *Categories and processes in language acquisition* (pp. 217–259). Hillsdale, NJ: Lawrence Erlbaum Associates.

Braunwald, S. R. (1978). Context, word and meaning: Toward a communicational analysis of lexical acquisition. In A. Lock (Ed.), *Action, gesture and symbol: The emergence of language* (pp. 485–527). New York: Academic Press.

Braunwald, S. R. (1989, April). *Interindividual differences in the lexical acquisition of two sisters.* Paper presented at the Biennial Meetings of the Society for Research in Child Development, Kansas City, KS.

Braunwald, S. R., & Brislin, R. (1979a). The diary method updated. In E. Ochs & B. Schieffelin (Eds.), *Developmental pragmatics* (pp. 21–42). New York: Academic Press.

Braunwald, S. R., & Brislin, R. (1979b). On being understood: The listener's contribution to the toddler's ability to communicate. In P. French (Ed.), *The development of meaning* (pp. 71–113). Japan: Bunka Hyoron.

Brown, R. (1973). *A first language: The early stages.* Cambridge, MA: Harvard University Press.

Bruner, J. (1990). *Acts of meaning.* Cambridge, MA: Harvard University Press.

Chomsky, N. (1988). *Language and problems of knowledge: The Managua lectures.* Cambridge, MA: MIT Press.

Clark, E. V. (1978). Strategies for communicating. *Child Development, 49*, 953–968.

Dromi, E. (1987). *Early lexical development.* New York: Cambridge University Press.

Dunn, J. (1988). *The beginnings of social understanding.* Cambridge, MA: Harvard University Press.

Edwards, D., & Goodwin, R. (1985). Action words and pragmatic function in early language. In S. A. Kuczaj & M. D. Barrett (Eds.), *The development of word meaning: Progress in cognitive development research* (pp. 257–272). New York: Springer-Verlag.

Fenson, L., Dale, P. S., Reznick, J. S., Thal, D., Bates, E., Hartung, J. P., Pethick, S., & Reilly, J. S. (1993). *MacArthur communicative development inventories: User's guide and technical manual.* San Diego, CA: Singular Publishing Group.

Gentner, D. (1978). On relational meaning: The acquisition of verb meaning. *Child Development, 49*, 988–998.

Gentner, D. (1982). Why nouns are learned before verbs: Linguistic relativity versus natural partitioning. In S. Kuczaj (Ed.), *Language development* (Vol. 2, pp. 301–334). Hillsdale, NJ: Lawrence Erlbaum Associates.

Golinkoff, R. M., Jacquet, R. C., & Hirsh-Pasek, K. (1991, April). *Lexical principles underlie the learning of verbs.* Paper presented at the Biennial Meetings of the Society for Research in Child Development, Seattle.

Huttenlocher, J., & Smiley, P. (1991, April). *Early words for movement.* Paper presented at the Biennial Meetings of the Society for Research in Child Development, Seattle.

Jackendoff, R. (1983). *Semantics and cognition.* Cambridge, MA: MIT Press.

Kuczaj, S. A. (1982). On the nature of syntactic development. In S. A. Kuczaj (Ed.), *Language development: Vol. 1. Syntax and semantics* (pp. 37–71). Hillsdale, NJ: Lawrence Erlbaum Associates.

Levy, Y. (1988). The nature of early language: Evidence from the development of Hebrew morphology. In Y. Levy, I. M. Schlesinger, & M. D. Braine (Eds.), *Categories and processes in language acquisition* (pp. 73–98). Hillsdale, NJ: Lawrence Erlbaum Associates.

Lieven, E., Pine, J., & Dresner Barnes, H. (1992). Individual differences in early vocabulary development: Redefining the referential-expressive distinction. *Journal of Child Language, 19*, 287–310.

Maratsos, M. (1988). The acquisition of formal word classes. In Y. Levy, I. M. Schlesinger, & M. D. Braine (Eds.), *Categories and processes in language acquisition* (pp. 31–44). Hillsdale, NJ: Lawrence Erlbaum Associates.

Maratsos, M. (1991). How the acquisition of nouns may be different from verbs. In N. A. Krasnegor, D. M. Rumbaugh, R. L. Schiefelbusch, & M. Studdert-Kennedy (Eds.), *Biological and behavioral determinants of language development* (pp. 67–88). Hillsdale, NJ: Lawrence Erlbaum Associates.

Naigles, L. (1990). Children use syntax to learn verb meanings. *Journal of Child Language, 17,* 357–374.

Nelson, K. (1973). Structure and strategy in learning to talk. *Monographs of the Society for Research in Child Development, 38*(1–2, Serial No. 149).

Nelson, K. (1991). Concepts and meaning in language development. In N. A. Krasnegor, D. M. Rumbaugh, R. L. Schiefelbusch, & M. Studdert-Kennedy (Eds.), *Biological and behavioral determinants of language development* (pp. 89–115). Hillsdale, NJ: Lawrence Erlbaum Associates.

Nelson, K. E. (1989). Strategies for first language teaching. In M. L. Rice & R. L. Schiefelbusch (Eds.), *The teachability of language* (pp. 263–310). Baltimore, MD: Paul H. Brookes.

Ninio, A. (1988). On formal grammatical categories in early child language. In Y. Levy, I. M. Schlesinger, & M. D. Braine (Eds.), *Categories and processes in language acquisition* (pp. 99–119). Hillsdale, NJ: Lawrence Erlbaum Associates.

Ninio, A., & Snow, C. E. (1988). Language acquisition through language use: The functional sources of children's early utterances. In Y. Levy, I. M. Schlesinger, & M. D. Braine (Eds.), *Categories and processes in language acquisition* (pp. 11–30). Hillsdale, NJ: Lawrence Erlbaum Associates.

Peters, A. (1983). *The units of language acquisition.* New York: Cambridge University Press.

Pine, J. M., & Lieven, E. V. (1990). Referential style at thirteen months: Why age-defined cross-sectional measures are inappropriate for the study of strategy differences in early language development. *Journal of Child Language, 17,* 625–621.

Pinker, S. (1989). *Learnability and cognition: The acquisition of argument structure.* Cambridge, MA: MIT Press.

Schlesinger, I. M. (1988). The origin of relational categories. In Y. Levy, I. M. Schlesinger, & M. D. Braine (Eds.), *Categories and processes in language acquisition* (pp. 121–178). Hillsdale, NJ: Lawrence Erlbaum Associates.

Scollon, R. (1973). *A real early stage: An unzippered condensation of a dissertation on child language* (Working Papers in Linguistics, Vol. 5, No. 6). Honolulu: University of Hawaii.

Smith, C., & Sachs, J. (1990). Cognition and the verb lexicon in early lexical development. *Applied Psycholinguistics, 11,* 409–424.

The MacArthur communicative development inventory: Words and sentences. (1993). San Diego: Singular Publishing Group.

Tomasello, M. (1992). *First verbs: A case study of early grammatical development.* New York: Cambridge University Press.

Tomasello, M., & Kruger, A. (1992). Joint attention on actions: Acquiring verbs in ostensive and non-ostensive contexts. *Journal of Child Language, 19,* 311–333.

Veneziano, E., Sinclair, H., & Berthoud, I. (1990). From one word to two words: Repetition patterns on the way to structured speech. *Journal of Child Language, 17,* 633–650.

Vygotsky, L. (1962). *Thought and language.* Cambridge, MA: MIT Press.

PART TWO

BASIC PRINCIPLES OF VERB LEARNING

CHAPTER FIVE

Pragmatic Contexts for Early Verb Learning

Michael Tomasello

Emory University

> *Language is a social art. In acquiring it we have to depend entirely on intersubjectively available cues as to what to say and when.*
> —Quine (1960)

The currently most popular approach to the study of lexical acquisition is the constraints approach. In this approach the basic problem of word learning is formulated in terms of Quine's (1960) dilemma of the indeterminacy of meaning. The child's problem, in this view, is analogous to the task of a linguist in a foreign culture who hears an unknown piece of language in an ill-defined communicatory context. The question is how the child or linguist can know which one of the infinitely many possible meanings of the unknown linguistic expression is the one the speaker intends. The answer given by constraints theorists invokes Chomsky's (1986) poverty of the stimulus argument: Because there is not enough information available to the child or linguist to limit the hypothesis space of potential meanings, there must be at work some form of a priori knowledge. This knowledge is most often characterized as constraints that rule out certain classes of hypotheses (Markman, 1989, 1992).

The constraints approach to lexical acquisition has not addressed itself to the question of verb learning, and in fact it is explicitly biased toward the acquisition of object labels. In Markman's model, the object label bias is embodied in the *whole object* constraint, which specifies for the nascent language learner that, in the absence of evidence to the contrary, a novel word is the name of a whole object and not, for example, an attribute, part, or activity in which it is engaged. The main piece of evidence for this view is that most children learning most of the world's languages have a pre-dominance of nouns in their early vocabularies (Gentner, 1982). In this view children learn to talk about other aspects of their experience only because a second constraint is also at work. The principle of *mutual exclusivity* specifies that any given object has one and only one appropriate label, so that if the child already knows a label for the object the adult is looking at then some other aspect of the object (e.g., its shape or color or activity) is likely to be the adult's intended referent.

The constraints view of lexical acquisition is currently being questioned on the basis of a number of empirical observations. First, much recent evidence casts doubt on the conceptual priority of object labels in early language, suggesting instead that children's early preference for nouns is very likely due to the nature of the language they are learning and the kinds of situations in which they hear that language used—with some discourse contexts actually favoring talk about actions (see Gopnik & Choi, this volume, and Tomasello, 1992a, for discussions). Second, a number of studies cast doubt on children's use of the principle of mutual exclusivity before their second birthdays (see Merriman, 1991; Mervis & Bertrand, 1993; Mervis, Golinkoff, & Bertrand, in press). On the basis of these and other findings, a number of lexical acquisition theorists have recently taken issue with the assumption of the a priori nature of word-learning constraints. Theorists such as Merriman (1991) and Golinkoff, Mervis, and Hirsh-Pasek (in press)— who more often designate what they study not as constraints but as word-learning principles—do not characterize children as operating with con-straints or principles from the outset but rather as learning general principles about words as they gain more experience with them. It is important to point out, however, that word-learning principles acquired as language de-velopment proceeds will not solve Quine's dilemma of how children first understand language.

Even if it turns out that these empirical problems are not as serious as they now seem, Markman's (1989, 1992) theory has two additional problems relevant to the issue of verb learning. First, the theory simply assumes, without explicit treatment, that children have an understanding of the so-cial-pragmatic dimensions of language. Thus, the theory does not address the question of how young children determine the object to which an adult refers if there are multiple objects in the immediate context without known names; presumably this is a common situation in the lives of young children with limited vocabularies. It must be the case in such situations that children are relying on their implicit understanding of specific social-pragmatic cues, such as adult gaze direction and pointing gestures. The omission of this dimension of the problem becomes much more troublesome and is not easily remedied in the case of verb learning. As demonstrated in this chapter, to learn novel verbs children must understand a number of complex and subtle social-pragmatic cues to adult intentions that go much beyond simple gaze following.

The second problem is that Markman's theory makes no provisions for precisely what the child is to do when mutual exclusivity overrides the whole object constraint. Thus, if the adult points to an object for which the child already has a name and uses a new piece of language, the child has no rule to use to decide among the many non-object aspects of the situation. With specific reference to the problem of verb learning, Golinkoff, Hirsh-Pasek, Mervis, Frawley, and Parillo (this volume) proposed that children may have a hierarchy of word types that they assume the adult to be using and that verbs (in the absence of evidence to the contrary) may be second in this hierarchy, behind object labels. This is a plausible hypothesis, although it is somewhat ad hoc and will become even more so if the hierarchy is expanded to cover all the word types young children learn—or even different types of verbs specifying different aspects of the same event.

The major alternative to the constraints or principles theory of lexical development is the social-pragmatic account (e.g., Bruner, 1983; Nelson, 1985, 1988; Tomasello, 1992b). In this account, the problem of word learning is posed in an entirely different way: The child's problem is to determine precisely what the adult is doing in a given situation and why she is doing it, including why she is making these odd noises. Language use is a social-communicative act, and the acquisition of words or other pieces of language is thus dependent most importantly on children's understanding of the actions of other persons because it is persons, not words, that engage in acts of linguistic reference. Children are able to begin acquiring language at a tender age because adults structure contexts for children in culturally specific ways and because children have the capacity to understand these contexts and adult action in them, in some form, before language acquisition begins (Tomasello, in press-b). The a priori knowledge that makes language possible in this view is thus not physical or linguistic knowledge but social knowledge, as Quine himself opined in the quote that introduced this chapter.

Although there is nothing explicit in the social-pragmatic approach to word learning that singles out object labels as particularly important or salient in early language acquisition (as, e.g., the whole object assumption), researchers with this focus have also been guilty of an almost exclusive concern with object labels—perhaps because they seem like the simplest case. For example, Tomasello and Farrar (1986a) found that young children learn object labels best when an adult follows their already established attention to an object; Baldwin (1991, 1993) found that when adults and children are looking at different objects as the adult utters a novel word, young children attach the object label not to the object on which they are focused but to the object on which the adult is focused; and Tomasello and Barton (in press) found that young children can use nonlinguistic cues to adult intentions (e.g., smiles and frowns) to infer which of a number of novel objects the adult intends to indicate (see also Akhtar, Dunham, & Dunham, 1991; Bruner, 1983; Ninio, 1980; and Snow & Goldfield, 1983). It is important to point out that all of these studies focused on how young children determine which one of the many possible objects in the immediate context an adult intends. The researchers simply assumed that children know what type of entity the adult is indicating (e.g., an object)—precisely the issue on which constraints theory is focused.

Because the two approaches focus on somewhat different aspects of the word learning process, it may plausibly be argued that the constraints approach and the social-pragmatic approach are complementary: Constraints direct the child's attention to the kinds of things to which an adult may be referring, and social-pragmatic information helps to direct attention to the specific one that is intended. Perhaps. But this happy complementarity cannot be the case if it turns out that neither the whole object nor mutual exclusivity constraint is empirically viable. Moreover, the constraints approach begins to seem much less plausible when we leave the domain of object labels and focus on other word types to which the whole object constraint does not apply, such as verbs. The social-pragmatic dimension that Markman assumes becomes much more prominent in children's acquisition of verbs, as this chapter shows. Young children hear their early verbs in a variety of very different pragmatic contexts, and how they learn in these contexts—as exemplified in the studies reported in this chapter—demonstrates the power of the social and social-cognitive skills children bring to the word-learning process. Although there is no empirical evidence at this time, it is possible that these skills are powerful enough to make the whole object constraint unnecessary or at least to suggest that it be reformulated in terms of the pragmatics of communication.

PROBLEMS OF VERB LEARNING[1]

The acquisition of verbs presents the child with a number of unique problems. Most important are the packaging problem and the pragmatics problem. Once the child has determined that the adult is referring to an action, there is nothing like a whole action constraint to help the child determine which aspects of the current experience are being indicated or "packaged"

---

[1]For purposes of simplicity, throughout this chapter I write of actions as the referents of verbs. Verbs can be used to refer to all kinds of processes and states as well. The crucial factor is that they always involve a sequence, even in the case of a state that remains the same over time (Langacker, 1987).

by a novel verb. Golinkoff et al. (this volume) have some interesting suggestions about the child's construction of action-based image schemas, but more is involved in verb learning than picking out a motion event. As Talmy (1985) and Gentner (1982) demonstrated, a verb may be defined in diverse ways, such as by the manner of motion (e.g., *to float*), by the instrument involved (e.g., *to hammer*), by the result achieved (e.g., *to empty*), by the action performed (e.g., *to wave*), and so forth. There are other semantic elements, such as the causative, that may or may not be a part of a verb's meaning, as illustrated by the contrasts between such pairs as *disappear* and *hide, die* and *kill,* and *fall* and *make fall* (cf. Bowerman, 1982). There are also some verb pairs that serve to depict the same event from a different perspective, such as *buy* and *sell, chase* and *flee,* and *lead* and *follow.* The packaging problem thus seems much more difficult in the case of verbs than in the case of object labels. It is almost as if there were another layer of choices to be made—involving the aspects or perspectives on an action event—than in the case of object labels, which seem to anchor themselves at the basic level (Mervis, 1987). This makes the simple hierarchy of choices proposed by Golinkoff et al. (this volume) a much more complex proposition than they have envisioned.

One part of the solution may be contained in Gleitman's theory of syntactic bootstrapping (Landau & Gleitman, 1985; Lederer, Gleitman, & Gleitman, this volume; Naigles, Fowler, & Helm, this volume), which proposes that syntactic cues in the linguistic context surrounding verbs also constrain possible word meanings. Thus, the child who hears "Big Bird is gorping Cookie Monster" will know that *gorp* is a transitive verb, whereas the child who hears "Big Bird is gorping" will know that the verb is intransitive (Naigles, 1990). This distinction requires that children know some important syntactic distinctions of the language they are learning before they learn verbs; Gleitman (1988) proposed that much syntactic structure is innate. Knowledge of syntax before word learning may underlie children's recognition of verbs as verbs by virtue of their argument structures. This may also provide a solution to the packaging problem, as more fine-grained distinctions among closely related verbs are made on the basis of the contrasting ranges of syntactic contexts in which different verbs participate.

While acknowledging that syntactic cues are very important in learning words of all types later in development, few theorists believe that syntactic bootstrapping can be the whole story of early verb learning, not even Gleitman in her most recent formulations (e.g., 1990, this volume). Two-year-old children simply show no evidence of being as syntactically sophisticated as they would need to be for Gleitman's theory to work. Children at this age produce many of their verbs in identical sets of syntactic contexts, indicating that they do not differentiate them syntactically in a fine-grained way. Moreover, although 2-year-olds may use syntactic cues to make global distinctions such as transitive-intransitive (the only distinction studied experimentally; Naigles, 1990), these cues will not help to distinguish the many individual verbs within these classes. To learn a new verb, therefore, young children must be relying to some degree on associating the novel verb they hear with some aspects of their nonlinguistic experience. And they can learn new verbs without the kinds of syntactic information Gleitman (1990) proposes, as evidenced both by naturalistic observations of Japanese children (Rispoli, this volume) and by experimental studies of children learning English verbs (Olguin & Tomasello, 1993). Precisely how children use their social and linguistic understanding to solve the packaging problem in learning verbs of different types is an issue to which I return in the concluding sections of this chapter.

The second nettlesome issue is that verbs are not used by adults very often in the ostensive paradigm that is considered canonical for noun learning: They do not very often simply name actions for the child. Rather, adults use verbs in a variety of pragmatic contexts, such as to regulate the child's behavior, to anticipate impending events, or to comment on completed events (Tomasello, 1992a). Because the actions and changes of state to which verbs refer are mostly transient, this means that, unlike the case of object labels, the referent situation in the case of verbs is often not perceptually available to the child when the word is uttered, nor can it be located by visual or other perceptual inspection of the immediate context. Thus, an adult who wants a child to perform certain actions may say, "Put it up there" or "Do you want to go?"; to encourage children to attend to upcoming action, an adult may say, "Watch me throw it" or "I'll wash it now"; to point out the results of an event, the adult may say, "You spilled it" or "I ate it all up." In none of these cases is the referent action perceptually available for the child continuously before, during, and after the word is said, the way that a referent object is available in the ostensive learning of object labels.

Related to this pragmatic difference between noun and verb learning contexts is the problem that the types of pragmatic contexts in which children must learn verbs are much more diverse than the contexts for nouns. The social-pragmatic information for noun learning is usually of the same type across all different kinds of concrete object labels. Many early object labels are learned by children as they follow an adult's pointing or eye gaze or some other cue to which object is intended, and the format is the same in all cases of this type—Brown's (1958) "original word game." Verb learning does not occur in a single canonical learning situation; verbs are used in situations of behavior or attention regulation that vary from context to context. If a child's father wants her to wipe her face he may hand her a cloth, if he wants her to pick up her toys he may gesture to the toy box (or the toys to be picked up), if he wants her to get into the car he may push her in that direction, or if he wants her to eat her peas he may hold them on a fork up to her mouth. The problem is that there is no single "original verb game" that may be applied across verb learning contexts. Thus, verb learning seems to demand from children some fairly sophisticated abilities to understand a very wide array of social-pragmatic cues for determining adults' semantic intentions.

Obviously, I can not resolve all of these issues in this chapter. What I can do is to report six studies of children's early verb learning that my associates and I conducted over the past several years. They are only a beginning. They do not address the packaging problem at all, as they all focus on transitive (causative) actions, and they do not help us to understand how children know that an action, rather than some other aspect of their experience, is currently being referenced. They do address problems associated with how young children zero in on the specific action referent intended by an adult uttering a novel verb, especially in non-ostensive contexts. The studies are reported here in six sections. The first reports a naturalistic study of the various pragmatic contexts in which western middle-class children hear their early verbs. The second reports a study of how children respond to adults' use of verbs in these different contexts. The third reports a study that compares children's verb learning in ostensive contexts (i.e., the verb is uttered as the action is ongoing) and non-ostensive contexts (i.e., the action is either impending or completed). The fourth and fifth sections focus on children's verb learning in the important and prevalent impending-action context; the study tests whether children need to know what action is impending, or if indeed they need to see an action at all, to learn a new verb. The sixth section reports a study investigating the social-pragmatic cues in the impending-action context that children may use to determine adult semantic intentions. I then return to the other problems of verb learning and discuss how they can be addressed by a social-pragmatic theory of lexical development.

STUDY 1: PRAGMATIC CONTEXTS IN WHICH CHILDREN HEAR VERBS USED

To address the question of how young children learn verbs, we must first find out something about the contexts in which they hear them. Adults name objects for beginning language learners mostly in ostensive contexts with the object visually present (Harris, Jones, & Grant, 1983). Using diary notes, Tomasello (1992a) made the inference that his child learned some verbs from non-ostensive models only (e.g., direct requests), but the data were retrospective. The contexts in which children hear their early verbs has not been investigated in any systematic way.

To address this issue, Tomasello and Kruger (1992, Study 1) videotaped 24 middle-class white children who had begun to produce language. Children were observed in dyadic interaction with their mothers on two occasions for 15 minutes each, once at 15 months of age and again at 21 months of age. The videotapes were transcribed and all utterances in which mothers used action verbs were extracted from the transcripts. Each maternal verb model was then coded as belonging to one of six mutually exclusive and exhaustive categories reflecting two dimensions. The first dimension had to do with the timing of the utterance of the verb relative to the child's experience of the action or change of state. There were three types: *impending:* The action described is about to take place (e.g., the mother announces her intention to perform an action, infers the child's intention to perform it, or requests the child to perform it, as in, "Now I'm going to roll it" or "Can you spin it?"); *ongoing:* The action being described takes place as the utterance is being made (e.g., "Look, the ball is rolling" or "You are sweeping it"); and *completed:* The action described took place in the immediate past in the current context (e.g., "You rolled it" or "I found it"). The second dimension concerned the person performing the action, that is, whether it was infant action or other action (i.e., action by mother or an object) that was being described. Coding each utterance for timing (three categories) and person (two categories) yielded six possible maternal verb models: impending infant, impending other, ongoing infant, ongoing other, completed infant, completed other. To assess intercoder reliability, five transcripts (21%) were recoded independently by a second team of assistants using these same six categories. A Cohen's kappa of .82 resulted.

The proportional frequency with which mothers used the six different verb model types is reported in Table 5.1. ANOVAs were used to analyze any differences among the types (there were no effects involving child age). The three timing categories were significantly different from one another in frequency: impending verbs were more frequent than either ongoing verbs or completed verbs ($p < .05$ in both cases), and ongoing verbs were more frequent than completed verbs ($p < .05$). More maternal verb models referred to infant actions than to other actions ($p < .05$). There was a significant interaction between these two variables, primarily due to the very high frequency of verb uses in the impending infant category, in which the frequency of verbs was over three times that in the next most frequent category.

The impending infant category (60% of the total) included two clearly discriminable types of utterance, mothers' direct requests for infant action (e.g., "Put the toy on the shelf") and mothers' anticipation of the infant's intention to act (e.g., "Oh, you're going to put it on the shelf"). Given previous findings on the effects of maternal directiveness on the acquisition of object labels (see Tomasello, 1988, for a review), we felt it necessary to repeat our analyses for these two subcategories separately. The same pattern of results was obtained, as maternal impending infant models were roughly

TABLE 5.1
Mean Proportion of Adult Verb Uses of Each Model Type in Study 1

	Person	
Timing	Infant	Other
Impending	.60*	.05
Ongoing	.18	.13
Completed	.03	.02

*Approximately half of these were requests of the infant, and half were anticipations of infant actions.

equally divided into these two subtypes, each of which was still reliably higher than any other category ($p < .05$).

Although this is obviously only one relatively small sample of children from one cultural group, the answer to the question of how these children heard their early verbs is clear: Almost 70% of the time they heard verbs in non-ostensive contexts, the majority of these being anticipations of or requests for child actions. Also, the context in which children were observed in this study should be one in which adults are, if anything, only minimally directive in their utterances to children. It is known, for example, that in multiple-child contexts (e.g., with a sibling or peer) adults use more directive utterances than when they are with one child (Barton & Tomasello, 1994), which should yield even more impending infant models for multiple-child contexts. If the non-quantitative ethnographic data are accurate, the same patterns may occur in other cultural groups in which a relatively high proportion of directives is used (Schieffelin & Ochs, 1986). Overall, then, the findings of this study confirm our intuitions that parents, even Western middle-class parents in a context in which they should be relatively non-directive, do not name actions for children as a matter of course. The next question is whether children learn verbs equally well in the many different pragmatic contexts in which they hear them used.

STUDY 2: CHILDREN'S RESPONSES TO VERBS IN DIFFERENT PRAGMATIC CONTEXTS

Tomasello and Kruger (1992) also coded children's responses to maternal utterances of different types; specifically, we coded whether children responded appropriately, either verbally or nonverbally, to the verb in the utterance (e.g., by performing the action or by making a verbal reply that could only be made if the verb were understood). An assessment of each child's productive verb vocabulary was also made for the 21-month age: We made a list of the verbs produced by the child as reported in a maternal interview and then added any additional verbs the child produced during the videotaped session. Thus verb vocabulary was simply the number of verbs (types) in the child's productive vocabulary as evidenced by the combination of these two sources at 21 months.

To evaluate the infants' responsiveness to the six maternal verb model types, proportions were calculated within each category, collapsing across age (due to small numbers in some cells). The mean proportions of maternal verb models that received an appropriate child response are presented in Table 5.2. Once again, the impending verb models received proportionally more responses than the other two timing models, and infant models received proportionally more responses than other models ($p < .05$).

Obviously, for reasons of pragmatics, a higher infant response rate may be expected when mothers directly request actions of their infants. That is to say, although the infant may comprehend the mother's verb equally well when she is labeling an ongoing action and when she is requesting an action, the child may be more likely to show a codable response when requested to act. Therefore, two additional analyses were conducted using the two subcategories of impending infant: direct requests and anticipations. All results were identical in both cases because the mean infant response rate in both of the subcategories was nearly identical to the response rate for the impending infant category as a whole (approximately 25–30% in all three cases). It would thus not seem to be the case that the impending infant category showed a distinct pragmatic bias. It is also useful to note that the preliminary analysis of verbal responses alone—which would not seem to be subject to the same pragmatic bias toward impending infant (i.e., verbal responses should be just as frequent to comments as to directives)—showed no differences among the verb model types.

A number of correlational analyses indicated that the impending infant context was more highly associated with children's verb vocabularies than were the other model types. Within joint attentional episodes, defined as mother and child both visually focused on the same object with child acknowledgment of that joint focus (usually by a look to the mother's face), impending infant models correlated at .45 ($p < .05$) with the child's verb

TABLE 5.2
Mean Proportion of Appropriate Responses for Each Model Type in Study 2

	Person	
Timing	*Infant*	*Other*
Impending	.30*	.21
Ongoing	.12	.10
Completed	.05	.05

*The same response rates held for requests and anticipations.

vocabulary at 21 months of age. This correlation, along with the analysis of children's responses to the different model types, is of course open to various causal interpretations. To become more certain about the various relations between the different pragmatic contexts and child verb learning, experimental manipulations are required. This is done in the four studies reported in the remainder of this chapter.

STUDY 3: CHILDREN'S VERB LEARNING IN DIFFERENT PRAGMATIC CONTEXTS

To investigate children's causal inferences about pragmatic contexts and verb learning, a lexical training study was conducted (Tomasello & Kruger, 1992, Study 2). Forty-eight children at 24 months of age served as subjects. Only children who had some productive language (as determined by parental interview at recruitment) participated. Parents were also asked about their children's knowledge of a number of verbs; no parent reported that their child knew the target verb, nor did any child produce it in a pretest.

Activities in the experimental session revolved around a toy parking garage with a variety of associated objects and activities. Each child played with a female experimenter (E) for 30 to 45 minutes. During a warm-up period, E demonstrated all the activities possible with the toys and garage, including the target action of placing a doll at the top of the ramp and pushing the button so that the doll rolled down into a hole. E always referred to the target action with the word *plunk*, used as a transitive verb. When the child seemed comfortable and engaged with the toy, the experimental session began.

Children were randomly assigned to one of three learning conditions. The sentences in which the target verb was modeled were identical in the three conditions, with two exceptions: The subject pronouns *I* and *you* were varied as appropriate to the situation within learning conditions, and the verb tense and aspects (*plunk, plunking, plunked*) were used differently as required across the learning conditions. Each child received 10 models appropriate to the learning condition, interspersed naturally within the experimental session. The three conditions were: *impending:* E set the doll at the top of the ramp and either announced her own impending action or invited the child to act (e.g., "Look, Jason, I'll plunk the man" or "Look, Jason, can you plunk it?"); *ongoing:* E commented on the target action as either she or the child was performing it (e.g., "Look, Jason, I'm plunking the man" or "Look, Jason, you're plunking it" as the doll began its descent down the ramp); *completed:* E commented on the action after either she or the child had just completed it (e.g., "Look, Jason, I plunked it" or "Look, Jason, you plunked the man"). Because at the end of the session the children participated in a comprehension task at the end of the session (i.e., they were handed a doll and asked to plunk it), four other (distractor) actions with dolls were performed and labeled during the experimental session, interspersed with the experimental models at E's discretion. This ensured that the child knew of other actions that could be performed with the dolls. Three to five times during the session, E would *wash, roll, drive*, and *fly* the man, giving an appropriate model each time (e.g., "Look, Jason, I can fly the man" or "Look, Jason, you're washing it").

An observer recorded all occasions during the experimental session that the child used the target word *plunk*; the sum of these uses for a given child was referred to as the child's *spontaneous production*. After all modeling of all verbs (target and distractor) was completed, each child participated in *elicited production* and *comprehension* tasks. To determine an elicited production score, E performed the target action with the doll and asked the child, "What am I doing? What am I doing to the man? What is the man doing?" Children received a score of 1 if they produced the target word *plunk* appropriately and a 0 if they did not. To test comprehension, E asked the children to perform each of the various actions (target and distractors) that had previously been performed with the doll. Each child was asked to perform the actions (fly, wash, roll, drive, and plunk) in random sequence such that the target word *plunk* was neither first nor last. In each case, E asked the child, "Can you ___ the man?" A score of 1 was given to a child who correctly performed the target action *plunk* and at least one of the distractor actions (to ensure discrimination); a 0 was given to subjects not meeting these criteria.

Because of overall low frequencies, spontaneous production and elicited production scores were combined into one production score for each child. Children in the impending condition learned to produce the target word more frequently than children in the other two groups ($p < .05$ in both cases, planned pairwise comparisons): The means were .63 for impending, .06 for ongoing, and .13 for completed. Table 5.3 presents the number of children producing the target word at least once, the number of children comprehending the target word and one distractor item, and the number of children showing any learning, either production or comprehension, as a

TABLE 5.3
Number of Children per Condition Producing, Comprehending,
or Showing Any Learning in Study 3

Condition	Production	Comprehension	Any Learning
Impending	5	13	13
Ongoing	2	7	7
Completed	3	13	13

function of learning condition. Chi-square analyses showed that for both comprehension and any learning, the impending and completed conditions had the greatest number of children learning the target verb, $p < .05$.

What is clear from this experimental study is that children are learning the new verb better in the impending action context than in the ongoing context; there is some evidence that they are learning better in the completed than in the ongoing context as well. The reason for this advantage is not addressed by the study, but the relatively poor performance of children in the ongoing condition may have to do with the joint attentional demands of the experimental situation. In all conditions, both the action and the word were new for the children. In the ongoing condition they were presented simultaneously. If children's attention was focused too strongly on the novel action, they may have ignored the adult saying the word to them; this possibility is likely, given the novel, relatively extended, and highly engaging action. In the non-ostensive learning conditions, on the other hand, children could focus on the action and word at separate moments, thus reducing the immediate processing demands. This may be especially important when the novel action or the novel word is especially engaging or difficult, as the action arguably was in this study.

STUDY 4: TWO MECHANISMS FOR VERB LEARNING IN THE IMPENDING ACTION CONTEXT

The three studies reported thus far have established that the impending action context is very common in the lives of western middle-class children, and it turns out to be a very facilitative context in which to learn verbs. There are at least two possible learning mechanisms that might underlie it. First, it may be that children hear the word *plunk* and have no idea of its meaning, but they then see an event which, for any of a number of reasons, they connect with the word *plunk*, heard a moment ago. Alternatively, children may only learn new verbs when they know from previous experience that an action is coming. That is to say, children may only learn the new verb after developing an expectation that when the toy man is set on the top of the ramp, the toy's descent through the hole and into the car follows; the action that has yet to happen is thus in some sense mentally present, in the form of an expectation, when the word is said. It may even be that in some cases children are able to attach the word to the expectation even if the action never actually occurs (see Study 5).

To test these hypotheses, forty 24-month-old children were recruited (Tomasello & Barton, in press, Study 1). Only children who knew some verbs but did not know the target verb (as determined by parental interview) were used as subjects. A set of giant waffle blocks was used to construct a play center with four action stations. The action stations were a curved chute to drop an object through, an automatic tape measure used to pull in a ring, a basket to hoist with a rope and pulley, and a curved platform to hit and to launch an object into the air. A set of four Sesame Street characters was used to perform the four actions. The target action was to "plunk" a character down the curved chute.

The design of the study was as follows. The model of the target verb *plunk* was manipulated along two dimensions: the timing of the language model relative to performing the action (impending vs. ongoing), and the predictability of the upcoming action (known vs. unknown). With regard to timing, in the impending condition, E held a character away from the action station, faced the child, and gave the language model, "I'm going to (or Can you) plunk Big Bird. I'm going to (or Can you) plunk him." E then did the action or let the child do it. In the ongoing condition, E gave the model, "I'm (You're) plunking Big Bird. I'm (You're) plunking him" as she or the child dropped the character into the chute. Thus, for each impending or ongoing model, E used the target verb twice and paired it with one demonstration of the target action. The second variable was whether, based on past experience, the child could predict the action to come next. This predictability variable was manipulated by setting up specific expectations with specific objects before and during the experimental models of the target verb. These two variables were then crossed to form four experimental conditions: impending-known, impending-unknown, ongoing-known, and ongoing-unknown. Children were randomly assigned to one of the four conditions.

The procedure was as follows. Subjects came to a psychology laboratory for two visits, during which they played with a female experimenter (E) for approximately 30 minutes. Each visit included an initial warm-up period, after which E began four rounds of action demonstrations and language models. A round began with a demonstration of each action station without any language models. During these demonstrations, E used neutral language (e.g., "Watch this!") or invited the child to do the action (e.g., said, "Can you do this?" demonstrated the action, and gave the child a chance to try). The order of the actions and characters was rotated as specified according to condition. In the unknown conditions, all characters were rotated through all action stations in a random fashion throughout the four rounds; thus, there was no way to know when E picked up a character what might be done with it. In the known conditions, Big Bird was always paired with plunking and never with any of the other actions, whereas the other characters were randomly paired with actions; over time it became apparent that when E picked up Big Bird the action would be plunking. Each round ended with the verb model appropriate for that condition, modeled twice in a row. Thus, at the end of the four rounds, a subject had received eight models of the target verb/target action pairs.

Following the completion of Round 4 on each day, children were allowed a few minutes of free play with the toys, after which elicited production and comprehension tests were conducted. For the children in the known condition, the elicited production task included E plunking Big Bird and asking, "What am I doing to Big Bird?" or "What's Big Bird doing?" In the unknown condition, E plunked up to three different characters, each time asking, "What am I doing to him?" Verbal responses were recorded by the observer as E went on to the comprehension test. If a child was unresponsive, the probe was repeated (up to 3 times) to encourage the child to answer. To test comprehension, E introduced a new character (Cookie Monster) and allowed the child to play with it for a few minutes. E then handed Cookie Monster to the child and asked, "Can you plunk Cookie Monster? Go plunk him." When the child performed one of the four possible actions, the observer recorded that response and testing ended.

The results of this experiment were clear (see Table 5.4). Children produced and comprehended the target verb equally well in all four conditions (chi-square tests all nonsignificant). Seven to 10 children in each condition showed some signs of learning in either production or comprehension. Testing at the end of the first day showed less learning overall, but the four groups were still essentially the same: Five to eight children in each condition showed some signs of learning (chi-square tests all nonsignificant). It is important to note that there was no advantage for the impending action context in this study, as there was in Study 3. The most likely reason for the difference between studies is that in Study 3, the target action was novel, exciting, and temporally extended, thus creating high attentional demands that needed coordination between word and action. In Study 4, the plunking action was similar but much quicker: The toy came through the pipe in less than a second, whereas the toy completed the action in almost 2 seconds in Study 3. The most plausible interpretation, then, is that the impending action and ongoing action contexts are equally facilitative of child verb learning, with one or the other perhaps better under certain conditions.

The findings with regard to the known-unknown variable were a surprise. Knowledge of the action that was impending was expected to make learning easier for the children. After all, the known condition had all of the features

TABLE 5.4
Number of Children per Condition Producing, Comprehending,
or Showing Any Learning in Study 4

Condition	Production	Comprehension	Any Learning
Impending-Unknown	6	9	10
Impending-Known	4	8	8
Ongoing-Known	4	6	7
Ongoing-Unknown	3	9	9

of the unknown condition plus the knowledge of the upcoming action. It is of course possible that our manipulation did not work and the children did not develop an expectation, but there were a variety of child behaviors that indicated their anticipation of what was to come (e.g., orienting to the place where the action would be coming). What this means is that not only can 24-month-old children learn verbs for impending actions in predictable circumstances, but they also can learn when they need to hold the word in mind until the action comes (or, said another way, to remember the word at the time of the action). It is still our hypothesis that this variable should be an important one, but perhaps it is only important at an earlier age, when children's information processing skills are less fully developed. In any case, in the next study we see that 24-month-olds are capable of learning verbs in a situation in which they never see the referent action.

STUDY 5: CHILDREN'S VERB LEARNING WITHOUT PERCEPTION OF A REFERENT ACTION

Forty-eight 24-month-old children served as subjects, 16 in each of two experimental conditions and 8 in each of two control conditions (Akhtar & Tomasello, 1993). Only children who produced at least five verbs and who did not know the target verb (as determined by parental interview) were invited to participate in the study. Four Sesame Street characters and four action props were used to perform four actions, with each character always associated with only one action and its associated prop. Throughout all phases of the study, action props and characters were kept in a canvas bag, extracted one at a time, and replaced before another was extracted. These action props and their associated actions included a tape measure used to pull a ring in which a character sat, a curved platform that catapulted a character into the air when hit on one side, a curved chute through which a character was dropped, and a plastic lid in which a character could be twirled. Each child heard the target verb *meek* used with one and only one action and character (e.g., Big Bird being catapulted). The action that served as the target verb was counterbalanced across learning conditions.

In a first pretraining period, each action was demonstrated for the child a total of 12 times with neutral language: "Watch what I can do to (character's name)," and the child was given the opportunity to perform the actions. The main purpose of these demonstrations was to familiarize children with the actions associated with specific characters and action props so that they would build an expectation of, for example, Big Bird's association with the catapult prop and its catapulting action. The four actions were demonstrated in two rounds of six demonstrations each, in random order.

In the experimental period in both experimental conditions, the target action prop (e.g., the catapult) was taken out of the bag as E presented the initial language model, "Now let's meek Big Bird! Let's meek him, okay? Let's meek him." In the referent condition, E found Big Bird in the bag and the target action was performed; E then went on to demonstrate the three nontarget actions with neutral language, so that they would be equally salient to the child in the comprehension testing. In the absent referent condition, E searched in the bag for the character and said, "Uh-oh, I can't find Big Bird. I can't find him." She then put away the target prop and proceeded to demonstrate the three nontarget actions with neutral language. The referent control condition included the same sequence of events as the referent condition, but the verb *meek* was never used—neutral language was used for all four actions. The absent referent control condition mirrored the absent referent condition but without the use of the target verb *meek.*

For the comprehension test, the four action props were set in front of the child in random order. The child was then handed a character not seen before (Cookie Monster) and was asked to show E how to "meek" Cookie Monster. After the child responded, the action props were repositioned, and the comprehension test was repeated. Two independent coders later reviewed 25% of the videotapes and achieved 89% agreement on which action was performed on the comprehension trials.

The nontarget action props were then removed from sight, and the elicited production test was conducted. This test consisted of E performing the target action a number of times and asking the child, "What am I doing? What am I doing to Cookie Monster?" If the child performed the action, E asked, "What are you doing?" All spontaneous and elicited productions of the target word during both the modeling and test phases were carefully examined to determine whether the word was used in reference to the target action. Thus, "meek" was considered an example of correct production only if the child uttered it while performing the action, about to perform the action, or watching E perform the action. Two independent coders reached 90% agreement on the classification of all productions of the target word in 25% of the videotapes.

The second column of Table 5.5 shows the number of subjects in each condition who performed the target action in the comprehension test. The control conditions were examined first to determine if choice of the target action was significantly different from the rate expected by chance alone (25%). They were not (binomial test, $p > .05$), as only one child performed the correct action. As these conditions did not differ from one another (Fisher exact probability = 0.50), they were combined to form one control group with $N = 16$ to serve as a baseline measure in the comprehension test. In contrast to the control condition, 8 of the 16 subjects in the referent condition performed the target action in the comprehension test (Fisher exact probability = 0.007). Moreover, 10 of the 16 subjects in the absent referent condition performed the target action in the comprehension test; this rate was

TABLE 5.5
Number of Children per Condition Producing, Comprehending,
or Showing Any Learning in Study 5

Condition	Production	Comprehension	Any Learning
Referent	7	8	9
Referent Control	0	0	0
Absent Referent	3	10	10
Absent Referent Control	0	1	1

also significantly higher than in the control condition (Fisher exact probability = 0.001). The two experimental conditions did not differ from one another (Fisher exact probability = 0.22), indicating that both were equally good contexts for learning to comprehend the new verb.

The number of children appropriately producing the novel verb is shown in the first column of Table 5.5. No child in the control conditions produced the new verb appropriately. Because performance was identical in the referent-control and absent referent-control conditions, these two conditions were again combined to serve as a baseline measure against which to compare the two experimental conditions. Seven of the 16 subjects in the referent conditions produced the novel verb appropriately. This frequency is significantly different from that found in the control condition (Fisher exact probability = 0.003). Only 3 of the 16 subjects in the absent referent condition produced the novel verb appropriately (versus control, Fisher exact probability = 0.11). However, although more than twice as many children produced the novel verb appropriately in the referent condition, the distributions of these frequencies in the two experimental conditions were not statistically different (Fisher exact probability = 0.10). (Note also that children in the referent condition had more opportunities to make appropriate productions; i.e., they saw the referent action three times after the first language models were given, whereas children in the absent referent condition did not see the referent again until the elicited production test.) The number of children showing any learning also did not differ between the two experimental groups (9 and 10), both of whom were above chance ($p < .05$).

To summarize, 24-month-old children do not need to have a perceptually present referent in order to learn a verb-to-action mapping. Thus, even in what could be considered the "ultimate" non-ostensive context, young children learned to comprehend (and a few learned to produce) a novel verb. These results show that even at a fairly early stage in lexical development, young children can actively use their experience to aid them in understanding the action an adult intends to indicate with a novel verb, even if they never see that action after the new verb is introduced.

STUDY 6: UNDERSTANDING ADULT INTENTIONS
IN THE IMPENDING ACTION CONTEXT

The results of Studies 4 and 5 demonstrate something of the robustness of children's verb learning abilities—2-year-olds can learn a novel verb when they anticipate the action that is coming, when they do not anticipate the action, and even when they never see the referent action at all. We still do not know, however, very much about precisely what cues of adult behavior children use to infer semantic intentions. One possibility is that the children do not use any such cues. In Studies 3–5, after the adult announced her intention to plunk the toy, she turned to the appropriate place and proceeded to perform the action (or to be frustrated in her attempts to perform the anticipated action). It may be, then, that the child is following the relatively simple procedure of assuming that the action immediately following the new word (either actual or anticipated) is its appropriate action referent. On the other hand, taking the social-pragmatic perspective on the situation, it may be that the children were actively monitoring the adult's intentions in the experimental situation to discover the intended referent of the new word. To decide between these two hypotheses, we designed a study in which the adult announced her intentions to act ("Let's plunk it") and then proceeded to perform two actions, one marked as accidental (i.e., "Whoops!" and a clumsy motion) and one as intentional (i.e., "There!" with a deliberate motion) (Tomasello & Barton, in press). By pairing these two types of action in each of the two possible temporal orders we can determine which cue is more powerful, the temporal contiguity of word and referent or the behavioral cues to adult intentions.

In this study sixteen 24-month-old children served as subjects. Only children who produced at least five verbs and who did not know the target verbs (as determined by parental interview) were invited to participate in the study. Two action props were used as stimuli: a crane and a merry-go-round. Each action prop was designed to support two distinct, novel actions. A set of toy characters was used to perform all actions with the props. The crane consisted of a wooden "T" mounted on a spring, with a clear plastic cup hung from it. The two actions assigned to this toy were to "hoist" and to "twang" the characters who were placed in the clear plastic cup. To hoist a character entailed putting it in the cup and pulling on the plastic ring until the cup was raised to the cross-arm; to twang a character entailed putting it in the cup and pushing or pulling on the middle of the cross-arm (where it was attached to the spring) to make the cross-arm and cup jiggle from the spring's action. The merry-go-round consisted of a modified 2-tiered lazy susan. The top tier had a 3-inch hole in the center, with a hinged platform immediately adjacent. The two actions assigned to this toy were to "plunk" and to "whirl" the characters who were placed on the platform. To plunk a character entailed tipping the hinged platform and causing the character to slide through the hole; to whirl a character entailed placing it on the platform and pushing the merry-go-round to make it spin.

The design of the study was as follows. Each child was taught two words, one associated with each toy. To model the target verbs, E paired a language model with a demonstration of the target action. For example, E said, "Watch. I'm going to hoist Big Bird. I'm going to hoist him." The target verb was always said twice in the language model. Following the language model, E used one of two modeling conditions to demonstrate the target action: intentional action followed by accidental action or accidental action followed by intentional action. In the intentional–accidental condition, E first performed the target action (e.g., hoisted the cup) and then performed the non-target action as an accidental action. To mark these two actions as intentional and accidental, E performed the two actions according to the following script: E says language model, "Let's ___ Big Bird. Let's ___ him"; E puts the character in place and says, "OK"; E performs the target actions and says, "There!"; and E does the nontarget action accidentally and says, "Whoops!" or "Uh-oh!" In the accidental–intentional condition, E reversed the order of actions performed, so that the accidental action was first and the intentional one was next. Each child participated in both conditions, learning one word in the intentional–accidental condition and the other word in the accidental–intentional condition (one with each toy). The assignment of target words, the order of conditions, and the order of toys were all counterbalanced.

Subjects came to a psychology laboratory for two 30-minute visits. At each visit, following an initial warm-up period with the characters, E introduced the first action prop, nonverbally demonstrating and encouraging the child to perform both actions. When the child had performed both actions at least two times, the modeling phase began. The modeling phase consisted of six pairings of the language models and action models. Thus, E gave the language model, said the target verb twice, and then performed the appropriate sequence of intentional and accidental actions. After the modeling phase with the first toy was complete, the toy was removed from sight and the second toy was introduced. The procedure for the second toy was the same as with the first: initial warm-up of its two actions and modeling of the six language–action pairs.

For comprehension testing, a new character was introduced and handed to the child. Then E asked the child to perform the target action of the first toy (e.g., "Can you go plunk Ernie?"). The prompt was repeated until the child performed one of the four possible actions with one of the toys. The observer recorded the child's first response (or pair of responses if, for example, the child hoisted then twanged in immediate sequence). The observer then introduced another new character and gave it to the child. The child was asked to perform the action associated with the second toy. Again the prompt was repeated until the child performed one of the four possible actions. The child's first response (or pair of responses) was recorded, and the session ended.

Results were straightforward (see Table 5.6). Across both days, children produced novel verbs only for intentional actions and equally in the two learning conditions (5 children in each condition). Under the assumption that subjects would be equally likely to produce the target verb for either the accidental or the intentional action, the 5 to 0 comparisons in each condition are unlikely to happen by chance (sign test, $p < .05$). In terms of comprehension, they also learned the two verbs equally well regardless of whether the intentional action immediately followed the announcement of an impending action or came after an interceding accidental action (6 and 10 children in the two conditions; all chi-squares nonsignificant). Only 2 children in each condition associated a novel verb with an accidental action, even when the accidental action immediately followed the announcement of an impending action. Comprehension of intentional and accidental actions in the intentional first condition did not differ (sign test, $p > .05$), but in the intentional last condition they did differ, 10 to 2 ($p < .05$).

The interpretation of these results is also relatively straightforward. Young children do not learn words in the impending action context by means of any simple rule such as "attach the new word to the next action performed by the speaker." They ignore the first action and associate the new word with the second action if the first action is marked as accidental. Children in this situation are clearly monitoring the actions of E, discriminating accidental from intentional actions, and associating the new word with intentional actions only. It is possible that the same effect might be found if there were an intermediate act that was seen as preparatory in a situation in which the child understood the relation of the preparatory to the consummatory act (e.g., arranging a toy's parts so that an action can be performed). Whether or not children rely on similar cues in other contexts that vary systematically from the one we studied, and whether they do so at an even earlier age, are questions for future research.

TABLE 5.6
Number of Children per Condition Producing, Comprehending,
or Showing Any Learning of the Intentionally Marked Verb in Study 6

Order	Production Intentional	Comprehension Intentional	Any Learning Intentional	Comprehension Accidental
Intentional Action First	5	6	7	2
Intentional Action Second	5	10	11	2

Note. The number of children selecting the accidental action in the comprehension test is included for comparison.

HOW TO LEARN A VERB

The series of experiments presented here demonstrates that early in their language development, western middle-class children are exposed to verbs mostly in non-ostensive contexts, that children have no trouble learning verbs in such contexts, that in the especially prevalent impending action context they can learn a verb whether or not they know what action is impending, and that they can learn a novel verb solely by understanding cues in the adult's behavior that provide information about the intended action. Although these findings are relevant to only a limited set of issues, I address some other questions that they raise, especially with respect to the relative merits of a constraints versus a social-pragmatic approach to lexical development. I do this in the context of what I conceive as the three major issues in the investigation of early verb learning: the problem of reference, the problem of kind of referent, and the problem of which referent.

The problem of reference is of course not unique to verbs but is the sine qua non of language acquisition of all types. How do young children know that the noise an adult currently is making is intended to refer to something, whereas other noises they make are not intended to refer? Golinkoff et al. (in press) identify reference as the first operating principle the child must master in language. They further specify that in order to understand an adult act of reference the child must understand something of the adult's intentions. This formulation is almost certainly correct, but it needs to be pushed one step further.

We know that at around 9 months of age infants begin to be able to determine adult intentions toward the environment in a variety of contexts. For example, infants follow adults' gazes (Scaife & Bruner, 1975), they social reference (Walden & Ogan, 1988), and they imitatively learn novel actions on objects (Meltzoff, 1988). Thus, before their first birthdays, infants are very good at determining something of adult intentions toward the environment. One way to view an act of reference is as a special kind of *social intention*, that is, as one person's intention that someone else attend to something in the environment. Following Gibson and Rader (1979), we may further view attention as intentional perception: Organisms attend to things that are relevant to their current intentional states. Therefore, we can say that to understand that an adult is referring to the rolling of a ball the child must understand that the adult intends for the child to intend to perceive the rolling as opposed to other things (Tomasello, Kruger, & Ratner, 1993). Children's early understanding of adult acts of reference may be seen as belonging to the same general class of competencies as their understanding of adult intentional action in general, but it adds an extra social-intersubjective dimension: children must comprehend an adult's intention toward their own intentional states. Although we do not understand the process very well at this point, we can at least say with some certainty that linguistic reference is a thoroughly social or social-cognitive act, the understanding of which allows a child to enter with an adult into the states of joint attentional focus that provide the bedrock of language acquisition (Tomasello, in press-a).

Given an understanding of the adult's intention to refer, the second problem is that the child must determine to what aspect of the environment the adult intends to refer. This is of course the major problem that Markman's (1989, 1992) constraints theory was designed to solve. With specific reference to the problem of verb learning, the constraints account posits that upon hearing an unknown word in the presence of an object for which the name is known, a child will search for some other aspect of the experiential event to attach to the new word. Golinkoff et al.'s (this volume) proposal is a preference hierarchy in which children assume first that a new word is being used to refer to an object but with other evidence (e.g., knowledge of the name of the object engaging in an action) they move to the second level of the hierarchy, actions. Again I can only say that this approach seems ad hoc at best, as we need to extend the hierarchy to adjectives, prepositions, and a whole host of other word types—not to mention different verb types. It is also true that if the child has innate knowledge of syntax prior to word learning (Gleitman, 1990), various syntactic cues in a novel utterance may help the child determine the type of referent involved. Again, I plead implausibility, for children in the beginning phases of word learning show no evidence of having knowledge of such things, except for the ability to discriminate transitive from intransitive frames in a preferential-looking paradigm at age 2 (Naigles, 1990).

To get a handle on the issue of what kind of referent we must first reorient our thinking about early cognition. It is important to conceptualize the child's early cognition not solely in terms of objects and their properties, as many theories do, but rather in terms of event structures, with objects being no more prominent in the child's conception of the world than the activities and events in which they are embedded (see Piaget, 1952; Mandler, 1993; Nelson, 1985). Mandler (1993) in particular, building on theories of cognitive linguistics, gave us a very specific account of how infants come to construct event-based image schemas early in their cognition. Tomasello (1992a) discovered some very specific event schemas underlying his daughter's early verbs, and Golinkoff et al. (this volume) provided a very interesting discussion of the role of event-based image schemas in early verb learning. With such a view of early cognition, we do not need to think of the child as synthesizing events out of more elementary cognitive elements such as objects and relations. Events are as basic and developmentally primary as objects, and thus there is no cognitive reason that the child should focus first on either objects or actions.

It is also possible, of course, that social-pragmatic factors are involved in children's identification of the kind of entity to which the adult is referring with a novel piece of language. There may be some behavioral cues on the part of adults to signal that they are talking about an event and not an object; for example, they may point to objects but perform some iconic gesture for actions. Analyses of adult gestures, however, do not find such differential specificity (Schnur & Shatz, 1984). More likely, the salience of actions in pragmatic and discourse contexts affects verb learning. Thus, if a novel action is performed by a well-known object or person in a well-known context, the pragmatic inference that the new aspect of the situation—the novel action—is the referent of the adult's new piece of language may be more likely. This may or may not involve the child's knowing the names of the objects involved. For example, one could imagine a situation in which an adult and child are interacting with a novel object for some time before the adult spins it and says "It's spinning" or "You spin it." We can imagine that in such a context the child understands that the adult is naming the new happening in the environment because adults talk about new and interesting, not old and boring, things. If the adult had wanted to name the object she or he would have done so when it was first introduced. Such an understanding could occur independently of the child's knowledge of a name for the object, the -*ing* ending, and, possibly, the child's understanding that the word *it* is used for objects previously established in the discourse. Also, the script knowledge a child possesses in particular contexts may facilitate understanding of adult intentions, especially if the adult uses a requestive intonation and the child has learned that this intonation is associated with the adult's desire that the child perform some action.

Related to the issue of how the child knows that an adult is referring to an action is the problem of how the child knows the aspect of the action to which the adult is referring, a.k.a. the packaging problem. This is a very difficult problem that we have not begun to solve. The classic constraints approach has simply not addressed this issue. Gleitman (1990, this volume) supposed that the child's innate knowledge of syntax is at work, in combination with the way specific verbs are used in adult language, but I believe that this cannot be the whole answer. There may be some child predispositions (e.g., that the causal outcome of events are especially salient; Behrend, 1990; Forbes & Farrar, in press; Tomasello, 1992a), but these cannot help with all types of verbs. It is also hard to imagine specific nonlinguistic information that would help children to decide from which perspective a verb depicted an action or whether it was a causative verb. All of these sources of information and biases may be useful in some manner to young children, but in addition I believe we must once again invoke discourse and linguistic factors. The key, I believe, is in two types of linguistic contrast.[2]

---

[2] This is not the place to get into differences in these two formulations, but Clark's (1988) conception of contrast as a pragmatic principle (e.g., "If Mom had meant to refer to that she would have used that word which we have used together before") is what is intended here.

First, children build up their verb vocabularies gradually. Any new verb is potentially related conceptually and semantically to known verbs. For example, my daughter learned the word *give* and then a variety of other words, such as *share* and *have* and *use* and *take*, for which there was much similarity in the overt situations in which they were used (i.e., object transfer among people). One possibility, therefore, is that the child learns to comprehend verbs designating different aspects of some generic situation by contrasting them with her preexisting knowledge of the verb for the generic situation and any other verbs she knows in the same conceptual domain (Tomasello, Mannle, & Werdenschlag, 1988). This gradual buildup of the verbs in a semantic field was seen in the diary study reported by Tomasello (1992a). It is also important to point out in this context that children do not accomplish this feat easily. In that diary study, for example, there were many early packaging mistakes, such as using the words *clean* and *cook* not as change-of-state words referring to objects going from dirty to clean or uncooked to cooked but rather as a designation of the characteristic actions involved: wiping with a cloth and stirring in a pot. For this subject *fixing* was simply hammering something, and to *hold* something only meant that she wanted possession of it in some manner. Presumably the use of these expressions in discourse, coupled with feedback from adults, helps children to fine tune their initial childlike uses into more adultlike uses.

A second sense of contrast also seems to be important in helping children to discern precisely to which aspects of events adults are referring with novel verbs. Children may rely to some degree on their knowledge of other words in the sentence and their knowledge of what is happening in the situation to identify through a process of elimination the aspect of the event that the verb is meant to depict. Thus, in such sentences as Talmy's (1985) famous "The bottle floated into the cave," and "The bottle entered the cave, floating," a knowledge of all the nonverb words in the sentence—especially the word *into*—and of the event being described is a big help in determining the aspects of the event that the verb was intended to indicate. This could be accomplished without the kinds of innate syntactic knowledge that Gleitman (1990) assumes in her theory of syntactic bootstrapping. All that is needed is knowledge of words and their meanings.

Finally, the third issue in early verb learning is the issue of which referent. Given a knowledge of reference and that the reference is to an action, to which action is the adult referring? Constraints theory may have nothing to say to explain the results of the last two studies reported in this chapter because in both cases children needed to pick out one action referent from among other potential action referents, none of which they had names for. Thus, none of the currently proposed constraints or principles could help children to determine the adult's intended action referent. We are just beginning to identify some of the social-pragmatic cues that children use in such situations. In ostensive contexts, presumably the salience of actions, both perceptually and in the discourse context, is of prime importance. In non-ostensive contexts, a variety of things may be at work. First, when the adult is requesting a behavior of the child, nonlinguistic cues to their desires are typically present at the same time (e.g., pulling the child to the car while telling her, "Come on"). When the adult is anticipating a child action, the action is often one the child can predict that the adult is interested in from the context. In other cases, such as in the third and sixth studies reported here, the child discerns the adult's intentions by continuing to monitor the behavior after the new word is said. When the adult is speaking about completed actions, as in some conditions of the third study, the child presumably has some understanding of the action that led to the results and some assumption that the adult is talking about this action. Also of importance in many of these situations are signs of the adult's affective or intentional state, as in the sixth study in which the adult engaged in behaviors that signaled her satisfaction or dissatisfaction that she had fulfilled her intention. Other similar cues may in some contexts be signs of preparation, surprise, satisfaction, disappointment, and so forth—all coupled with knowledge of the kinds of things in which adults might be interested in particular social and discourse contexts.

It is clear that to account fully for children's early word learning, including verb learning, we need to combine something of the social-pragmatic and principles or constraints approaches. But we must be clear about how to do this, and how not to do it. There are certainly some aspects of word learning that the social-pragmatic approach takes for granted. For example, children form categories and generalize them based on taxonomic principles—generalization and categorization are basic characteristics of the human cognitive system, and, in fact, of the cognitive systems of many animal species (Roitblat, 1987). A principle like mutual exclusivity, contrast, or novel-name-nameless-category may be an important part of lexical development as well, although how early in development it is useful to the child is an issue that is currently being debated (e.g., Mervis & Bertrand, 1993; Mervis et al., in press). There are also other word-learning principles involving such things as the bases of children's extensions of words to new referents that are clearly operative as well. My specific proposals about constraints or principles are thus only two: that we abandon the whole object constraint in its current form and recognize the cognitive complementarity of objects and actions, and that we recognize that word learning principles are a posteriori, not a priori, and that the bedrock on which the initial stages of language acquisition are built is children's understanding of the intentional actions of other persons, including their understanding of adults' social actions, such as making linguistic reference to their shared world.

In terms of the whole object assumption I can only say that the empirical evidence is not being kind at this point. Almost all children learn some non-object words in their early vocabularies (Nelson, 1973), and some children have a predominance of such words in their early vocabularies (Gopnik, 1982)—in fact, in some languages most children have a predominance of nonobject words in their early vocabularies (Gopnik & Choi, this volume). In some languages children learn verbs with very little reference to objects in the situation (Rispoli, this volume), and many of children's early nouns are for fairly abstract objects such as "breakfast" and "the park" (Nelson, Hampson, & Shaw, 1993). Finally, children at an early age can be trained to learn action words as easily as object words (Tomasello & Farrar, 1986b). The statistical preference for nouns in early language discovered by Gentner (1982) is most likely due not to a basic conceptual or linguistic bias but rather to pragmatic and discourse factors involving the importance of objects in children's interactions with adults (see Bridges, 1986; Gillis, 1990; Gold-field, 1990; Gopnik & Choi, this volume). Although it is certainly likely that children have some perceptual bias toward whole objects rather than their parts or properties, the actions that people perform on objects, or in which objects participate, are not subordinate to the whole object in this way. Events and actions are just as important in children's conception of the world as are concrete whole objects.

With respect to the a posteriori nature of word learning principles, I can only say that the framers of the basic issues involved in the problem of reference were the philosophers Wittgenstein (1953) and Quine (1960), both of whom were adamant that language is based in large part on the vagaries of human convention, which differ from culture to culture. I take from their expositions that the foundation of language acquisition is not a set of general cognitive or linguistic principles but rather children's specific social-pragmatic understandings of what adults are attempting to do in particular situations—how adults are trying to manipulate their attention. It is this kind of understanding that makes possible the human use of linguistic symbols, as opposed to the other kinds of communicatory signals used by nonhuman mammals, because symbols presuppose an intersubjective dimension (Bates, 1979; Tomasello, in press-a). This is not to say that children never learn general principles about the way adults use words or that children do not use their knowledge of some aspects of language to help them to learn other aspects. They surely do both of these things, and both Markman (1992) and Golinkoff et al. (in press) have specified how they may do so. The argument is simply that these sources of information are not necessary for word learning, they are probably not available in the initial stages of language acquisition, and when they are used by children they are used totally in the service of their attempts to understand the pragmatic intentions of those around them.

THE IMPORTANCE OF STUDYING VERB LEARNING

In concluding this chapter I ask the following question: What would a theory of lexical acquisition look like if we took as the paradigmatic case of word learning not object label learning but verb learning? My answer to this question focuses on three sets of factors.

First, our characterization of the cognitive processes that underlie early words must be much richer than it has been previously in our excessive concern with the perceptual and functional features of objects. Verbs involve event structures that of necessity unfold over time, can be construed from a number of different perspectives, and involve different aspects of the perceptual event. Moreover, many if not most of children's early verbs involve intentional human action, which in some theories provides for the functional understanding of objects (Nelson, 1985). In all, there are many different kinds of verbs involving complex spatial relations, complex human intentions, complex groups of objects, and complex sequencing of events (Smiley & Huttenlocher, this volume; Tomasello, 1992b) that would seem to have no parallel in the conceptualization of objects. An appreciation of this dimension of infant cognition (as in Golinkoff et al., this volume; Mandler, 1993; Tomasello, 1992a) thus considerably broadens our appreciation of the cognitive bases of early language.

Second, our characterization of the social-cognitive processes underlying early word learning must be much richer as well. In the acquisition of object labels, such things as pointing and gaze direction seem so utterly transparent that the issue of where the adult's attention is focused seems a trivial problem. It is not, of course, and this becomes clear as we study what children have to do to acquire verbs from the naturally occurring, often non-ostensive contexts involving adult requests, intention checks, and so on. In these contexts children must not only tune into gaze and pointing direction but also actively monitor adults' intentions over time as they engage in activities or request that children do so. It is important to emphasize that these non-ostensive contexts are not strange or infrequent learning contexts in the lives of beginning language learners. Indeed, one can argue that it is the ostensive learning context that is strange and infrequent outside of psychological experiments and the homes of western, middle-class parents who intentionally teach their children new words because they are concerned that they have large vocabularies early in development (Schieffelin & Ochs, 1986). A strong argument can in fact be made that children learning their words within the natural flow of human action and social intercourse, rather than in mini-linguistics lessons, is the norm for all children in some cultures, for some children in all cultures, and, perhaps, for all children in all cultures when learning some types of words (e.g., articles, prepositions, and verbs). In addition, social-pragmatic factors of early verb learning may be different in the case of different types of verbs. For example, many of my daughter's early verbs for distinctive actions such as sweeping, waving, swinging, and crying were learned in ostensive contexts as the adult named the child's ongoing distinctive action (Tomasello, 1992a). Many of her verbs for changes of state (e.g., *give, put,* and *make*), on the other hand, were used in non-ostensive contexts in which the adult asked the child to achieve a certain result in her action. Once again the investigation of verbs leads to a much richer conceptualization of the process.

Finally, a focus on verb learning forces researchers to pay more attention to linguistic context, both in the sense of the pragmatics of contrast and in the sense of surrounding language in the discourse context. Gleitman (1990, this volume) has been arguing this for several years, but only recently have researchers seriously begun to investigate the proposal empirically, leading to the discovery that argument structure plays a much less important role in the verbs Japanese-speaking children are exposed to (Rispoli, this volume) and studies of the use of argument structure in the verb learning of children with language-learning problems (Naigles et al., this volume). It is also clear that children's reliance on linguistic contrast and linguistic information in the modeled sentence undoubtedly becomes greater as they acquire more language, although this is not something that has been studied systematically. An understanding of children's early verbs as lexical items is an important element in understanding the transition to early grammatical competence (Bloom, 1991; Tomasello, 1992a).

A systematic consideration of the unique problems presented by verb learning is essential if we are to understand the full range of children's word learning capabilities and how they fit into the process of language acquisition as a whole. In future research we must not only apply our knowledge of general principles of object label learning to verbs—to force them into this framework—but also apply knowledge we have gained from the study of verb learning to the case of object label learning. If we do this, we will discover a much wider array of word-learning processes than we have used in the study of object label learning. At some point we will have to move on to other word types as well, which will presumably lead to even more comprehensive theories of how children acquire the linguistic conventions of those around them.

ACKNOWLEDGMENTS

Portions of this research were supported by a grant from the Spencer Foundation. Thanks to Bill Merriman, Carolyn Mervis, Nameera Akhtar, and Malinda Carpenter for helpful comments on an earlier version of the manuscript.

REFERENCES

Akhtar, N., Dunham, F., & Dunham, P. (1991). Directive interactions and early vocabulary development: The role of joint attentional focus. *Journal of Child Language, 18*, 41–50.

Akhtar, N., & Tomasello, M. (1993). *Twenty-four month old children learn words for absent referents.* Manuscript submitted for publication.

Baldwin, D. (1991). Infants' contribution to the achievement of joint reference. *Child Development, 62*, 875–890.

Baldwin, D. (1993). Infants' ability to consult the speaker for clues to word reference. *Journal of Child Language, 20*, 395–418.

Barton, M., & Tomasello, M. (1994). The rest of the family: The role of fathers and siblings in early language development. In C. Galloway & B. Richards (Eds.), *Language addressed of children.* Cambridge, England: Cambridge University Press.

Bates, E. (1979). *The emergence of symbols: Cognition and communication in infancy.* New York: Academic Press.

Behrend, D. (1990). The development of verb concepts: Children's use of verbs to label novel and familiar events. *Child Development, 61*, 681–696.

Bloom, L. (1991). *Language development from two to three.* New York: Cambridge University Press.

Bowerman, M. (1982). Reorganizational processes in lexical and syntactic development. In L. Gleitman & E. Wanner (Eds.), *Language acquisition: The state of the art* (pp. 319–346). Cambridge, England: Cambridge University Press.

Bridges, A. (1986). Actions and things: What adults talk about to one year olds. In S. Kuczaj & M. Barrett (Eds.), *The development of word meaning* (pp. 287–311). New York: Springer-Verlag.

Brown, R. (1958). How shall a thing be called? *Psychological Review, 65*, 14–21.

Bruner, J. (1983). *Child's talk.* New York: Norton.

Chomsky, N. (1986). *Knowledge of language.* Berlin: Praeger.

Clark, E. (1988). On the logic of contrast. *Journal of Child Language, 15*, 317–336.

Forbes, J., & Farrar, J. (in press). Children's initial assumptions about the meaning of novel motion verbs: Biased and conservative? *Cognitive Development.*

Gentner, D. (1982). Why nouns are learned before verbs: Linguistic relativity versus natural partitioning. In S. Kuczaj (Ed.), *Language development* (Vol. 2, pp. 301–334). Hillsdale, NJ: Lawrence Erlbaum Associates.

Gibson, E., & Rader, N. (1979). Attention: The perceiver as performer. In G. Hale & M. Lewis (Eds.), *Attention and cognitive development* (pp. 1–21). New York: Plenum.

Gillis, S. (1990, July). *Why nouns before verbs? Cognitive structure and use provide an answer.* Paper presented at the meeting of the International Association for the Study of Child Language, Budapest.

Gleitman, L. (1988, October). *Syntactic bootstrapping.* Address given at the Boston University Conference on Language Development, Boston, MA.

Gleitman, L. (1990). The structural sources of verb meaning. *Language Acquisition, 1*, 3–55.

Goldfield, B. (1990, May). *Maternal input and the child's acquisition of nouns and verbs.* Paper presented at the Seventh International Conference on Infant Studies, Montreal.

Golinkoff, R., Mervis, C., & Hirsh-Pasek, K. (in press). Early object labels: The case for lexical principles. *Journal of Child Language.*

Gopnik, A. (1982). Words and plans: Early language and the development of intelligent action. *Journal of Child Language, 9*, 303–318.

Harris, M., Jones, D., & Grant, J. (1983). The nonverbal context of mothers' speech to infants. *First Language, 10*, 21–31.

Landau, B., & Gleitman, L. (1985). *Language and experience: Evidence from the blind child.* Cambridge, MA: Harvard University Press.

Langacker, R. (1987). Nouns and verbs. *Language, 63*, 53–94.

Mandler, J. (1992). How to build a baby II: Conceptual primitives. *Psychological Review, 99*, 587–604.

Markman, E. (1989). *Categorization and naming in children.* Cambridge, MA: MIT Press.

Markman, E. (1992). Constraints on word learning: Speculations about their nature, origins, and word specificity. In M. Gunnar & M. Maratsos (Eds.), *Modularity and constraints in language and cognition.* Hillsdale, NJ: Lawrence Erlbaum Associates.

Meltzoff, A. (1988). Infant imitation and memory: Nine-month-olds in immediate and deferred tests. *Child Development, 59*, 217–225.

Merriman, W. (1991). The mutual exclusivity bias in children's word learning: A reply to Woodward and Markman. *Developmental Review, 11*, 164–191.

Mervis, C. (1987). Child basic categories and early lexical development. In U. Neisser (Ed.), *Concepts and conceptual development* (pp. 201–233). New York: Cambridge University Press.

Mervis, C., & Bertrand, J. (1993). *Acquisition of the novel name–nameless category (N3C) principle.* Manuscript submitted for publication.

Mervis, C., Golinkoff, R., & Bertrand, J. (in press). Two-year-olds readily learn multiple labels for the same basic level category. *Child Development.*

Naigles, L. (1990). Children use syntax to learn verb meanings. *Journal of Child Language, 17*, 357–374.

Nelson, K. (1973). Structure and strategy in learning to talk. *Monographs of the Society for Research in Child Development, 38*(1–2, Serial No. 149).

Nelson, K. (1985). *Making sense: The acquisition of shared meaning.* New York: Academic Press.

Nelson, K. (1988). Constraints on word learning? *Cognitive Development, 3*, 221–246.

Nelson, K., Hampson, J., & Shaw, L. (1993). Nouns in early lexicons: Evidence, explanations, implications. *Journal of Child Language, 20*, 61–84.

Ninio, A. (1980). Ostensive definition in vocabulary teaching. *Journal of Child Language, 7*, 565–574.

Olguin, R., & Tomasello, M. (1993). Two-year-olds do not have a grammatical category of verb. *Cognitive Development, 8*, 245–272.

Piaget, J. (1952). *Origins of intelligence in children.* New York: Norton.

Quine, W. (1960). *Word and object.* Cambridge, MA: Harvard University Press.

Roitblat, H. (1987). *Introduction to comparative cognition.* San Francisco: Freeman.

Scaife, M., & Bruner, J. (1975). The capacity for joint visual attention in the infant. *Nature, 253*, 255–266.

Schieffelin, B., & Ochs, E. (1986). *Language socialization across cultures.* New York: Cambridge University Press.

Schnur, E., & Shatz, M. (1984). The role of maternal gesturing in conversations with one-year-olds. *Journal of Child Language, 11*, 29–42.

Snow, C., & Goldfield, B. (1983). Turn the page please: Situation specific language acquisition. *Journal of Child Language, 10*, 551–570.

Talmy, L. (1985). Lexicalization patterns: Semantic structure in lexical forms. In T. Shopen (Ed.), *Language typology and syntactic description* (Vol. 3, pp. 57–139). Cambridge, England: Cambridge University Press.

Tomasello, M. (1988). The role of joint attention in early language development. *Language Sciences, 11*, 69–88.

Tomasello, M. (1992a). *First verbs: A case study of early grammatical development.* Cambridge, England: Cambridge University Press.

Tomasello, M. (1992b). The social bases of language acquisition. *Social Development, 1*, 67–87.

Tomasello, M. (in press-a). The cultural roots of language. In B. Velichkovsky & D. Rumbaugh (Eds.), *Naturally human: Origins and destiny of language*. Princeton, NJ: Princeton University Press.

Tomasello, M. (in press-b). Joint attention as social cognition. In C. Moore & P. Dunham (Eds.), *Joint attention: Its origins and role in development*. Hillsdale, NJ: Lawrence Erlbaum Associates.

Tomasello, M., & Barton, M. (in press). Acquiring words in non-ostensive contexts. *Developmental Psychology.*

Tomasello, M., & Farrar, J. (1986a). Joint attention and early language. *Child Development, 57,* 1454–1463.

Tomasello, M., & Farrar, J. (1986b). Object permanence and relational words: A lexical training study. *Journal of Child Language, 13,* 495–505.

Tomasello, M., & Kruger, A. (1992). Acquiring verbs in ostensive and non-ostensive contexts. *Journal of Child Language, 19,* 311–333.

Tomasello, M., Kruger, A., & Ratner, H. (1994). Cultural learning. *Behavioral and Brain Sciences, 16,* 495–552.

Tomasello, M., Mannle, S., & Werdenschlag, L. (1988). The effect of previously learned words on the child's acquisition of words for similar referents. *Journal of Child Language, 15,* 505–515.

Walden, T., & Ogan, T. (1988). The development of social referencing. *Child Development, 59,* 1230–1240.

Wittgenstein, L. (1953). *Philosophical investigations*. New York: Macmillan.

CHAPTER SIX

Children's Disposition to Map New Words Onto New Referents

William E. Merriman
John Marazita
Lorna Jarvis
Kent State University

Children tend to map new words onto aspects of the world that they cannot already name rather than onto ones that they can. This behavior has both applied and theoretical significance. Although children may be able to determine a new term's reference from cues such as speaker gaze or word morphology, these may not always be sufficient. For example, a toddler who hears, "There is something wrong with the antenna" from a person who is fiddling with the rabbit ears on top of a television may not be able to tell from the speaker's behavior whether *antenna* refers to the television or its aerial. If a label for the television is already known, the tot may decide that the antenna is the referent. Thus, the mapping tendency is relevant to how youngsters solve ambiguity problems that must arise at least occasionally. The theoretical significance of the tendency is that it fits with the view that abstract principles guide the acquisition of word meaning.

We examine the disposition for nouns and verbs, which are the only form classes that have been investigated. Although much more is known about the noun case, one commonality is that the mapping effect for both changes during early childhood.

NOUNS

Children who are 2½ years or older behave differently from younger children when they must decide whether a novel noun refers to something that they can already name or to something unfamiliar. We call the tendency to select unfamiliars the *disambiguation effect*, following Merriman and Bowman (1989), who characterized it as one of four possible consequences of the *Mutual Exclusivity bias*, the inclination to accept only one name for something (see also Markman, 1987, 1989).

Children Who Are 2½ Years Old or Older

There are two tests of noun disambiguation. In the unopposed test, subjects must find the referent of an unfamiliar label in a set that contains at least one object that they can name and at least one that they cannot. Typically, a pair of objects is presented (e.g., a shoe and a painter's palette). The disambiguation effect occurs if unfamiliar objects are selected more often than chance, that is, if children tend to avoid overlap between a novel and a familiar label. The effect is considered unopposed because other factors that might influence selections are not set against it. In opposed tests, such a conflict is engineered.

Unopposed Tests

Youngsters between the ages of 2½ and 6 years have shown a strong unopposed effect for common nouns (Au & Glusman, 1990, three studies; Golinkoff, Hirsh-Pasek, Baduini, & Lavallee, 1985; Golinkoff, Hirsh-Pasek, Bailey, & Wenger, 1992; Hutchinson, 1986; Markman & Wachtel, 1988; Merriman & Bowman, 1989, Study 1; Merriman & Schuster, 1991). For example, the average rate of unfamiliar item selection shown by 4-year-olds in the five studies that have included this age group is .95. Markman and Wachtel (1988), Merriman and Schuster (1991), and Golinkoff et al. (1992) also reported that selection rates for no-word control groups, in which children were simply asked to pick objects, were either at or below chance, indicating that disambiguation is not an artifact of novelty preference.

The research has been quite narrow. We do not know whether the effect would be found for proper, mass, or collective nouns. For example, no one has examined whether preschoolers would decide that *Larry* is more likely to be the name of a stranger than it is to be another name for their friend Pete. Even the research on common nouns has been limited to a certain type of referent, a whole object, and has only used the singular noun form.

In five of six cross-sectional studies, a significant increase has been noted in the size of the effect from age 2 to 4 years, or over part of this range (Hutchinson, 1986; Merriman & Bowman, 1989, three studies; Merriman & Schuster, 1991; Vincent-Smith, Bricker, & Bricker, 1974). The exception is Vincent-Smith et al. (1974), who noted a nonsignificant increase over a very short age range (7 months). Four-year-olds tend to select unfamiliar objects on every trial, whereas children who are younger than 2½ years merely select them more often than familiar objects. Adults show a ceiling-level selection rate (Au & Glusman, 1990; Golinkoff et al., 1992).

Opposed Tests

A new name may be mapped onto something that children can already name if some factor favors doing so. The following disambiguation-opposing forces have been examined: the Whole Object bias, token novelty, name similarity, object atypicality, and linguistic cues.

In five studies by Markman and Wachtel (1988), 3- and 4-year-olds were repeatedly shown an object, told an unfamiliar name for it, and tested for whether they thought the term referred to the object itself or to some attribute that they could not already label (the object's substance in three studies and one of its parts in the other two). When the object itself was unfamiliar, youngsters tended to map the name to it. This behavior is consistent with the *Whole Object bias* (WO), which is the disposition to map a count noun onto an object rather than onto something else. If the children already knew a name for the object, they tended to map the novel label onto an unfamiliar attribute. For example, when told that a metal pair of tongs was "pewter," they usually interpreted the word as a name for a pair of tongs, whereas when the name was introduced for a metal cup, they usually took it to be a name for a kind of metal. The latter tendency was far from perfect, however (average rate = .74). Thus, the WO bias blocked the disambiguation effect on a minority of trials.

A study by Markman, Horton, and McLanahan (1980) can also be interpreted as one in which the disambiguation effect was attenuated by conflict with both the WO bias and grammatical cues. Children heard a novel count noun used in the plural (e.g., "These are fims") for a set consisting of several examples of each of two familiar types of objects (e.g., ones they had just learned to call zavs and tids). The word interpretation that is compatible with WO and the semantics of the term's sentence frame (i.e., "These are ___s") is superordinate class noun (i.e., a fim as a name for a zav or a tid), which counters the disambiguation effect. Seventeen-year-olds made this interpretation on nearly every trial, but 8- to 14-year-olds reacted about half the time as if the singular form of the trained word designated the combined set, not an individual member (i.e., as if *fim* were a collective noun akin to *herd*), thus preserving the disambiguation effect.

We (Merriman & Bowman, 1989; Merriman & Schuster, 1991) found that token novelty has a small impact on the noun mapping of 2½- to 4-year-olds. That is, when unfamiliar objects were examined and later paired with novel tokens of familiar types (i.e., things that could be named but had not been examined), the youngsters still tended to map novel labels to the unfamiliar types, but the rates of such mapping were slightly lower than when token novelty was not manipulated. The decrement was a nonsignificant .04 in one study (Merriman & Bowman, 1989) and a significant .07 in the other (Merriman & Schuster, 1991).

Merriman and Schuster (1991) also found that 4-year-olds were more likely to map a word that sounded like the name for a familiar object onto that object rather than an unfamiliar one, even though a group of agemates had judged such test words to be incorrect names for the familiar objects (e.g., that *glower* was not a correct name for a flower). Name similarity also affected mapping on trials in which children had to choose between atypical and typical familiar objects. The youngsters most likely judged the test words to be mispronunciations of the familiar labels and selected what they believed were the intended referents. After selecting a familiar kind, they sometimes uttered its real name as if to correct the experimenter. If this explanation is valid, then name similarity did not actually reduce the disambiguation effect since two words were not mapped to the same thing. However, it is also possible that a similar-sounding name was occasionally identified as a new label but mapped to the familiar object because name similarity was treated as a weak cue for semantic similarity. Such an exception would be helpful for other tasks, such as learning how grammatical morphemes modulate word meaning (e.g., how meaning changes from *car* to *cars*). If this process occurred, then name similarity did reduce the disambiguation effect.

Four-year-olds' disambiguation effect was found to be weaker when familiar objects were atypical rather than typical (Merriman & Schuster, 1991). For example, an unfamiliar kind of pump was selected over a car as the referent of *bunty* less often when the car had some unusual features (e.g., an elevated body) than when it was very ordinary looking. Although reduced, disambiguation was greater than chance and greater than the no-word control group's corresponding tendency. Typicality also influenced children's decisions regarding which of two familiar objects was the referent of a novel name; they selected atypicals more often than typicals. The no-word control group made no such differentiation.

The older the child, the less likely he or she is to map a novel name onto an untagged entity when this mapping conflicts with a reliable linguistic cue. Also, the more explicit the cue, the more likely it is that younger children will rely on it. In Markman et al.'s (1980) study, 17-year-olds but not younger children consistently interpreted one name as including the referents of the two others when syntactic information indicated that each designated a class (e.g., "These are fims"); however, all subjects made the correct interpretation when given explicit class inclusion information (e.g., "Zavs and tids are kinds of fims"). Likewise, Au (1990; Au & Laframboise, 1990; Au & Markman, 1987) found that adults learned a new color name from linguistic contrast (e.g., "This is zav, not red," said of a mauve patch), but that 3- to 5-year-olds only did so when the negated term was the one that they thought was correct (e.g., "This is zav, not gray," said of a mauve patch). Au and Glusman (1990) reported that 4- and 5-year-olds do not show a disambiguation effect when an object label is from a different language than the name for the familiar object.

Explanations

The set of possible explanations for these phenomena is embarrassingly rich. We consider six principles that have been cited in accounts of disambiguation: *Contrast, Cooperation, Mutual Exclusivity* (ME), *Lexical Gap-Filling* (LGF), *Novel-Name-for-Nameless-Category* (N3C), and *Feeling of Novelty* (FN). Each of these principles may be valid; that is, children may hold all of these proposed beliefs about word meaning. However, the principles differ in their degree of sufficiency and in the number of phenomena that they can explain, and they sometimes conflict with one another.

Contrast. According to Clark (1983), children believe that no two words mean exactly the same thing. This belief alone cannot generate the disambiguation effect. A child who must decide whether a palette or a cup is a zav, for example, would not necessarily be directed away from the cup because *zav* can differ in meaning from *cup* and still refer to a cup. The high rate of unfamiliar object choices in the unopposed disambiguation test is incompatible with a model in which random selection is made from the set of all possible unique meanings. Some other principle(s) must be posited to explain why unique interpretations that exclude familiar referents are favored over ones that do not.

The account would be insufficient even if it were supplemented with the Whole Object (WO) bias; many object name interpretations that are not synonymous with *cup* but include cup in their extensions are possible.

Cooperation. According to Gathercole (1989), the disambiguation effect may derive from Grice's (1975) Cooperation principle that ". . . if a speaker chooses something other than a readily available means for encoding a message, he or she must mean something other than what is usually encoded by the word that has not been used, unless he or she elaborates otherwise" (Gathercole, 1989, p. 694). This principle is basically a pragmatic casting of Contrast and thus is as insufficient. Meaning differences do not strictly imply reference differences.

ME. This expectation cannot, by itself, explain unopposed disambiguation either; there is nothing to prevent a novel property of the familiar object from taking the novel name. However, addition of the WO principle makes for a satisfactory account. That is, children 2½ years and older may map *zav* onto a palette rather than a cup because they assume that count nouns designate objects and that object labels are mutually exclusive.

Both principles should be considered default expectations, that is, assumptions that are made when little information is available. Because children need to learn count nouns that do not designate whole objects (e.g., part names) as well as pairs of count nouns that are not mutually exclusive (e.g., synonyms and hyponyms), they must have some willingness to abandon default values when contradictory evidence is encountered.

The results obtained with the opposed disambiguation paradigm are compatible with the default ME-plus-WO account. The studies by Markman and her colleagues (Markman et al., 1980; Markman & Wachtel, 1988) show that youngsters abandon one of these assumptions when they conflict and that children who are more than 7 years old at least relinquish ME when an inclusion relation is very clearly specified in input. Research with paradigms other than disambiguation (e.g., whether interpretation of a familiar word will be corrected in response to hearing a new word for one of its referents) show that children as young as 3 years old give up ME when contradictory linguistic cues are presented (Gelman, Wilcox, & Clark, 1989; Merriman, 1986; Merriman & Bowman, 1989).

The weak impact of token novelty on disambiguation (Merriman & Bowman, 1989; Merriman & Schuster, 1991) can be attributed to a conflict between ME and the Feeling of Novelty (FN) principle—the expectation that novel words will be introduced for things that feel new (Merriman, Marazita, & Jarvis, 1993a)—with ME winning out most of the time. Alternatively, children's attraction to novel tokens may simply distract them on a few disambiguation trials.

The attenuating effect of name similarity (Merriman & Schuster, 1991) may derive from children's judgments that the names were mispronunciations, as already noted, and/or from their treatment of sound similarity as a cue for semantic similarity that conflicts with ME.

Regarding the object typicality effect, because children are less certain that a familiar name applies to an atypical than to a typical exemplar, they may be less certain that choosing an atypical as the referent of a novel name violates ME. This explanation implies that on the trials when atypicals were chosen over unfamiliars, the children must have corrected their belief that a familiar name applied to the atypical; otherwise, they would have been in violation of ME. Merriman and Schuster (1991) did not assess such corrections, although 4-year-olds have been observed to make them in other studies (Merriman, 1986; Merriman & Bowman, 1989, two studies). Alternatively, children may learn from experience that ME is more likely to be violated with atypicals than with typicals. New subordinate names tend to be introduced more frequently for atypical than for typical examples of familiar names (Anglin, 1977). Although the evidence does not distinguish between these possibilities, we can at least rule out the claim that 4-year-olds maximize ME in situations in which no evidence directly contradicts it. Maximizers would select unfamiliars over atypicals on every trial because the latter have the greater probability of being referents of familiar names.

The following developmental claims should be added to this account: Older children have a stronger tendency than younger ones (a) to maintain ME in a default situation, and (b) to respond appropriately to cues that reliably contradict ME. The rationale for (b) is that older children have had more experience with which to learn the implications of these cues. Three reasons support (a). First, because younger children are more easily distracted and more impulsive than older ones, they will maintain ME less consistently in a default situation (e.g., unopposed disambiguation). Second, older children have had more opportunity to learn that ME tends to be maintained in a default situation. Finally, older children's greater conscious access to their own knowledge states (Perner, 1991; Wellman, 1990) should support their tendency to maintain ME in a default situation. Specifically, their realization that they already know a name for an object should lead them to avoid mapping other words onto it.

Evidence for the last claim comes from Merriman and Schuster's (1991) finding that 4-year-olds who acknowledged the unfamiliarity of a novel noun (e.g., said, "No" when asked, "Do you know what a zav is?") showed a more consistent unopposed disambiguation effect than their peers and were also more likely to justify their selections by citing the name they knew for the familiar object. For example, when asked to say why they picked a ducting tube rather than a key as a pilson, they said, "Because this is a key," pointing to the key, rather than describe something novel about the ducting tube.

LGF. Clark (1983, 1987) has also hypothesized that children are motivated to fill lexical gaps, that is, to find words for whatever untagged categories are salient to them. Unopposed disambiguation can be explained in terms of this motivation, on the assumption that most of the unfamiliar objects in the studies were salient (Merriman & Bowman, 1989). Disambiguation can also be explained in terms of an expectation that lexical gaps will be filled; that is, LGF need not be a motivation.

Similar to our treatment of ME, LGF should be made a default expectation and be supplemented with the WO bias. This allows the child to give up LGF when other evidence contradicts it and prevents a child from mapping the novel name onto a salient, untagged property of a familiar object.

LGF should be translated, "If an instance of an untagged category is perceived, seek (or expect to hear) a name for it," and not as, "If a novel name is introduced, seek (or expect to see) an instance of an untagged category." The latter is essentially a different wording of ME; seeking untagged categories necessarily means rejecting any tagged categories one should discover.

LGF should be strengthened by adding an anti-homophone bias to it: "If an instance of an untagged category is perceived, seek (or at least expect to hear) a novel name for it." That is, a 4-year-old would probably not accept that a painter's palette is a dog, for example, although we know of no studies testing this. The child may accept homophones that occur in novel syntactic frames (e.g., a painter's palette might be a give), although they would probably be less receptive to these than to completely novel words (e.g., if asked whether a painter's palette was a give or a tukey, they might favor the latter, unless they guessed that giving was somehow involved in the use of palettes). Again, no studies have been conducted.

Clark (1987) argued against an anti-homophone bias on the grounds that young children know many homophones. However, it would not be impossible to learn them if the bias were an overrideable default (just as learning synonyms and hyponyms is possible with a default ME bias). Moreover, most child homophones cannot be used in the same syntactic frames (e.g., *two* and *too*). (See Walley, 1993, for a review of child homophony research.)

Although LGF and ME are different principles, one can see how both may be learned from the experience of hearing many new words for entities that cannot already be named rather than for ones that can.

The opposed disambiguation results can be characterized in terms of LGF, rather than ME, although perhaps not as plausibly. For example, Markman and Wachtel's (1988) finding that 3- and 4-year-olds tend to map a new noun onto an untagged property of an already-tagged object rather than onto the object itself can be explained in terms of a disposition to seek or expect names for salient categories (in this case, a property category). This explanation assumes that the untagged property was salient to the children and thus name-expectant before the test word was introduced. If the property only became salient when the tagged object was rejected, then ME is the only principle behind the effect.

The two principles can be differentiated experimentally. The three potential consequences of ME other than disambiguation that were outlined by Merriman and Bowman (1989)—rejecting a new name that has been introduced for the referent of a familiar name, correcting a familiar name after hearing a new name used for one of its referents, and restricting the generalization of familiar names to keep them from overlapping—are not logical consequences of LGF. That is, these effects maintain ME but do not function to secure names for untagged categories. There is ample evidence for the correction and restriction effects in children who are 2½ years or older; the only study to examine the rejection effect in this age range found little evidence for it (Merriman, 1991).

The evidence for ME should not be interpreted as evidence against LGF. One can hold both beliefs without contradiction, both can be abstracted from observations of how objects tend to be named, and both may be at work in children's mapping. The problem is that there is presently no evidence for LGF that cannot also be explained by ME. Tasks that would be affected by LGF but not ME can be given to children, but no one has done this. Perhaps the simplest test would be to ask children whether a novel name applied to an unfamiliar type of object.

Some might find support for LGF in Clark's (1987) observation that youngsters often overgeneralize morpho-semantic regularities to create forms that fill lexical gaps (e.g., call a gardener "plant-man") but abandon these once conventional equivalents are introduced (e.g., once they learn *gardener*). However, this phenomenon could be explained without positing LGF.

N3C. Golinkoff et al. (1992) proposed the novel-name-for-nameless-category principle (N3C) as an alternative to Contrast and ME:

> N3C states only that novel names will be mapped onto unnamed categories. That is, in the presence of an unnamed and a named object, the child will affix the novel name to the unnamed object. N3C differs from the previously proposed explanations in the situation in which only named objects are present. Unlike Contrast, N3C does not require that the child eschew synonymy. Unlike ME, N3C does not require that objects have only one name. (Golinkoff et al., 1992, p. 2)

If N3C is not equivalent to ME, then it is either equivalent to LGF or is a very narrow principle that essentially restates the disambiguation effect as an expectation. The latter would be rather odd because it would mean that children have no mapping expectations when only named objects are present or only unnamed ones are; they just have them for mixed sets. Golinkoff et al. reject LGF, however, on the grounds that it presupposes Contrast, which they disavow, and that it is untestable. But default LGF does not presuppose Contrast; one can seek or expect a novel name for an untagged category but be willing to accept exact synonymy under certain circumstances. Regarding LGF's testability, we have already described a way to test it as well as a "homophonophobic" form of it.

The passage from Golinkoff et al. makes clear that N3C must also be supplemented by the WO bias (which Golinkoff et al., 1992, refer to as the Object Scope principle). Without WO, there is nothing to prevent the nameless category to which the novel name is to be mapped from being an attribute category.

FN. Preschoolers' disambiguation may also be influenced by the Feeling of Novelty principle (FN), the expectation that new names will map onto physical entities that feel new. This principle differs from the others in that it is not couched in terms of the nameability of a candidate referent. How novel an object feels depends on its type and token novelty. When the latter is held constant, unfamiliar types (i.e., stimuli that cannot be named) tend to feel more novel than familiar types. Thus, the FN principle generates the unopposed disambiguation effect, just as ME, LGF, and N3C do. (Of course, all four need to be supplemented by WO.) Also, since atypical instances of familiar types should feel more novel than typical instances, FN accounts for the typicality effects documented by Merriman and Schuster (1991).

FN yields several predictions that the other principles do not. When type novelty is held constant (e.g., when two stimuli are either both nameable or both unnameable), a new word should be assigned to the more novel token. Merriman and Bowman (1989, Experiment 1) confirmed this prediction for two unnameable objects.

When the token of an unfamiliar type is preexposed and the token of a familiar type is not, FN implies that the disambiguation effect will be reduced and possibly reversed, because both type and token novelty determine how novel a stimulus feels. As already noted, preexposure of the unfamiliar object reduces the disambiguation effect for 3- and 4-year-olds, but not by much. The small impact of preexposure is open to at least two interpretations. One possibility is that when FN conflicts with the nameability principle(s) (e.g., ME), children tend to base their decisions on the latter. A second is that the feeling of novelty that an object evokes in this age group is primarily based on type novelty, not token novelty. The plausibility of the latter is called into question by preschoolers' excellent object recognition memory (Brown & Scott, 1971), a skill that requires ignoring how familiar or novel a type feels and focusing on the feeling of familiarity or novelty evoked by a token.

All of the noun evidence for FN is open to an alternative explanation. Children may not expect novel names to map onto objects that feel new; rather, their greater attraction to novel than to familiar tokens may merely disrupt their disambiguation performance on occasion. Support for this idea can be found in Merriman and Schuster's (1991) report that children in no-word control conditions were more likely to select novel than preexposed tokens of unfamiliar types when these were pitted against novel tokens of familiar types (31% vs. 15% of trials). However, because our verb data favor FN over this alternative explanation, we explicate the principle further. Because unfamiliar types tend to evoke feelings of novelty and familiar types tend to evoke feelings of familiarity, children can abstract both the FN and ME principles from hearing novel words used more often for unfamiliar than for familiar types.

Three factors favor the more rapid acquisition of FN than ME. First, things are monitored from birth for how novel or familiar they feel, as is evident from neonatal habituation and dishabituation, whereas children may need to become rather facile at retrieving object names before they monitor object nameability consistently enough to notice that one name tends not to extend to the referent of another. Note that we are not claiming that when infants monitor novelty they realize what they are doing. An object's degree of novelty is assumed to register immediately with the infant in the same way that static perceptual attributes such as color and shape do. See Metcalfe (1993) for a distributed memory model of how an item's degree of novelty could register automatically and for a discussion of the value of novelty monitoring to the cognitive system. Because the felt novelty of a stimulus would be a more available cue than its nameability, especially for young children, the former's association with the felt novelty of a name might be learned more readily.

Second, ME may be difficult to learn because it involves a negated element (i.e., "One name tends not to overlap with another"). Hearst (1991) has built a strong case for the claim that because nonoccurrences are less salient than occurrences, relations involving a negated element are more difficult to learn than ones that only involve positive elements. If novelty is experienced as something that a stimulus has, rather than as merely the absence of familiarity, then FN is an association between positive elements.

Finally, FN may be rather easy to learn because it is essentially an association between identical attributes, namely, the felt novelty of a stimulus and the felt novelty of its name. Such associations may be easier to learn than ones between different attributes. Rescorla (1980) showed that second-order Pavlovian conditioning (learning that one CS predicts another CS, which predicts a US) proceeds more rapidly when the CS's are similar. However, it can also be argued that although ME does not associate identical attributes, it seems quite natural for children to compare labels, that is, to notice that a name in input differs from the name known for a particular object.

On the other hand, two factors favor ME over FN. First, because it is not restricted to novel names, ME has broader applicability than FN. That is, not only do new names tend not to map onto the referents of other names, familiar names tend not to either. The ME expectation may be bolstered by a child's noticing that many pairs of semantically related familiar names (e.g., *turkey* and *chicken*) do not overlap or from the reception of corrective feedback involving such pairs (e.g., "That's not a chicken; that's a turkey"). Thus, once children begin to monitor object nameability reliably, they have more opportunity to learn ME than FN. Second, FN may not be supported in the very earliest stages of word learning in which children acquire names for many objects that have been familiar for quite some time. New names might only tend to be introduced for objects that feel new once labels for the most familiar objects in the environment have been learned. Because of these conflicting factors, it is difficult to predict how the relative strength of FN and ME changes over development.

FN can be decomposed into two subprinciples, analogous to the difference between ME and LGF. One is, "If a stimulus feels quite novel, seek or expect for it a name that feels novel," and the other, "If a name feels novel, seek or expect for it a stimulus that feels novel." However, if one is learned from experience, it is quite likely that the other is too.

The introduction of the FN principle forces a redefinition of acceptable evidence for the ME, LGF, and N3C principles. That is, in the writings of Merriman, Markman, and colleagues, the basic contention has been that ME can be demonstrated by showing that children are less likely to map a new name onto something when they already know a name for it than when they do not. However, the FN principle describes a way in which such behavior may occur without the child ever considering nameability: Children may reject novel names for objects that they can already name, not because they can already name them, but because such objects feel familiar. So the ante is upped a bit; it must be shown that children consider nameability in the process before the ME, LGF, or N3C principles can be accepted.

Many philosophers of language have noted the problem that lies at the heart of the previous paragraph's discussion, namely, the referential opacity of propositional attitudes. That is, phrases that designate the same entity cannot necessarily be interchanged as objects of the same stated attitude. A girl may expect that the man in front of her is going to sing, for example, but not expect that Mickey Rooney is going to sing, even if the man in front of her is Mickey Rooney. Although it may be said that the child in some sense believes that Mickey Rooney is going to sing, she does not believe it in the sense that most people would give to the sentence, "The child believes Mickey Rooney is going to sing." Similarly, most people interpret statements of the ME, LGF, and N3C principles as presupposing that a physical entity's nameability is considered in the process of deciding whether a particular name applies to it. (Note that it is not correct to consider the one sense of the three principles as explicit knowledge and the other as implicit. Both are implicit; neither presupposes that children have any representation of their own lexical decision making, whether this process involves encoding nameability or not.)

FN can be distinguished experimentally from ME. Of the three potential consequences of ME other than disambiguation—new name rejection, familiar name correction, and familiar name restriction—only the first can be explained by FN (the referent doesn't feel new, so the new name is rejected). The effects that involved familiar names are not covered by FN because this principle describes an expectation about new names. Thus, there is evidence for ME that cannot be attributed to FN. As already noted, there is also evidence for FN that cannot be attributed to ME (i.e., the effects of token preexposure on novel name mapping), although it can be explained in terms of attraction to novel tokens.

One criticism of FN is that the feeling of novelty that a stimulus evokes cannot be directly assessed, whereas measuring nameability is a simple matter of asking a subject what something is called. However, many useful theoretical constructs are not directly observable (e.g., the memory trace). The utility of FN lies in the general prediction that it yields, namely, that any procedure that alters the perceived novelty of a stimulus (e.g., presenting a familiar object in an unexpected setting) will alter the disambiguation effect for that stimulus accordingly.

Summary

Children who are 2½ years old or older show a strong unopposed disambiguation effect when test words are count nouns and the choices are objects. The size of the effect increases after age 2 and approaches ceiling around the fourth birthday. The tendency to prefer unfamiliar over familiar objects can be reduced by placing it in conflict with other sources of lexical information (e.g., linguistic specification of an inclusion relation). The claims that children have WO and ME default expectations and that the latter becomes stronger and more accessible to reflection during the preschool years provide a sufficient account of these data. However, other default principles may also support children's tendency to map nouns onto unfamiliar rather than familiar objects, namely, LGF and FN. Although there is no evidence for LGF that cannot also be accounted for by ME, the critical experiments have not been performed (i.e., LGF yields unique predictions). On the other hand, children have been observed to behave in ways that fit FN but are beyond the scope of ME. Unfortunately, these FN-compatible data can be explained without positing FN, that is, in terms of the attractiveness of novel tokens. Some factors should promote the more rapid acquisition of FN than ME, but other factors should have the opposite effect, making it difficult to predict which principle emerges earlier and how the principles change over the course of development.

Children Who Are 24 +/− 6 Months Old

Children who have just turned two, or who are just about to, show a weak noun disambiguation effect. Some lexical principle(s) are implicated; that is, the children's behavior is not merely a consequence of novelty preference. However, the data do not allow us to pinpoint the operative principles. In contrast to the case for older children, a firm conclusion cannot be drawn about whether 2-year-olds have an ME bias.

Unopposed Tests

In four investigations that have used a two-choice procedure (unfamiliar versus familiar objects), 22- to 25-month-olds' rates of unfamiliar object selection have ranged from .60 to .76 (average = .68) (Hutchinson, 1986; Merriman & Bowman, 1989, Study 1; Merriman & Schuster, 1991; Vincent-Smith et al., 1974). These rates are significantly different from chance in only some of the studies. Hutchinson (1986) assessed late 1-year-olds with both a two- and a four-choice test (three unfamiliars versus one familiar). With four choices, children's rate of selecting unfamiliars (.77) was no different from chance (.75). The author speculated that the children selected randomly because "there was no clear right answer" (p. 53). Two-and-a-half- and 3-year-olds' selection rates were near ceiling in this task, however.

In Merriman and Schuster's (1991) experiment, young 2-year-olds' rate of mapping nouns onto unfamiliar objects was significantly greater than their rate of selecting such objects in response to no-word control instructions (.68 vs. .43, respectively). This finding failed to support Merriman and Bowman's (1989) proposal that toddlers' disambiguation effect for object names is an artifact of novelty preference. The operation of some abstract lexical principle(s) is implicated. Hutchinson's (1986) results also support this conclusion; she used no-word control performance to eliminate suspect object pairs from her analyses.

In a recent chapter, Markman (1992) briefly described a series of studies (Markman & Wasow, in preparation) in which children were shown a familiar object and were asked to find the referent of a novel noun. Babies as young as 15 months bypassed the familiar object and searched for an unfamiliar one. Markman argued that because an unfamiliar object was not in view when the label was presented, the search behavior cannot be explained in terms of LGF or N3C, which are claims about what is expected or desired when an unfamiliar object is encountered. Although the results are compatible with both FN and ME, it is not clear that bypassing a familiar object implies either. That is, the children may have behaved this way simply because they did not know whether the familiar object was the referent of the new name; being uncertain, they looked further.

Two-year-olds are much less likely than 4-year-olds to acknowledge their unfamiliarity with a novel noun (Merriman & Bowman, 1989, two studies; Merriman & Schuster, 1991). When asked whether they know what a cardle is, for example, they tend to say yes (45% of trials) or not respond at all (40%). Also in contrast to older children, toddlers who tend to admit their ignorance of a new name (or at least not to say they know it) do not show a stronger disambiguation effect than their agemates.

Opposed Tests

Four factors have been examined for their power to reduce toddlers' tendency to map novel nouns onto unfamiliar objects; token novelty, object atypicality, name similarity, and subsyllabic preexposure. Token novelty has a much stronger impact on 2-year-olds' performance than it does on older children's (Merriman & Bowman, 1989; Merriman & Schuster, 1991). Merriman and Bowman (1989, Study 1) reported that 24-month-olds selected novel tokens of familiar types of objects more than twice as often as familiar tokens of unfamiliar types as the referents of novel nouns (e.g., children chose an ordinary cup that they had not seen before over a binder clip that they had just played with as the referent of *binder clip*). Although token novelty was not quite as potent in two subsequent studies (Merriman & Bowman, 1989, Study 2; Merriman & Schuster, 1991), it was strong enough to erase the disambiguation effect. In contrast to the strong age differences found regarding token novelty, Merriman and Schuster (1991) found that object atypicality and name similarity affected 2-year-olds' mapping of novel nouns in the same way as these variables affected the mapping of 4-year-olds but to a lesser degree.

The effect of subsyllabic priming on name mapping has also been examined (Merriman & Marazita, 1994). Most syllables consist of two parts, onset (i.e., the portion from the beginning of the syllable up to but not including the vowel) and rime (i.e., the remaining part). For example, /b/- and -/at/ are the respective onset and rime for /bat/ (Treiman, 1988). We hypothesized that if these components of a novel word were preexposed, children's processing of the label would be facilitated. That is, they would be able to establish and maintain a phonological representation of the word in working memory more readily. This would allow them to devote more attentional resources to the other steps in solving the disambiguation problem, such as that of comparing the representation of this label to the label retrieved for the familiar object. In Study 1, sixteen 24-month-olds heard a story in which an onset and rime were repeated. On four trials these components primed the test word, and on four it did not. For example, one story was, "This is *l*ittle *Pat* *L*ovey. *L*ittle *Pat* *s*at on *L*arry the *l*azy *c*at. . ."); the test word was either *lat* or *wog*, and the choice objects were a spoon and a painter's palette. As predicted, unfamiliar objects were selected significantly more often when the word was primed (e.g., *lat*) than when it was not (e.g., *wog*) (73% vs. 50%). Study 2 was identical except that the familiar objects' names sounded like one of the test words (e.g., *lat* could be mapped to either a hat or an unfamiliar object). The predicted effect was obtained—64% and 37% selection of the unfamiliar object after hearing primed and unprimed words, respectively. There was also a replication of Merriman and Schuster's (1991) name similarity effect: The tendency to select unfamiliar objects was weaker in Study 1 than Study 2 (50% vs. 61%). Study 3 replicated Study 2 with a between-subjects design (16 per group)—61% versus 35% selection of the unfamiliar object after hearing primed and unprimed words. A third group, who heard stories without sound repetition, selected unfamiliar objects at an intermediate rate (47%), suggesting that encoding similar-sounding words facilitates the subsequent encoding of new terms that sound like these words, but impedes this process for new terms that sound different.

Explanations

Although the Contrast (Clark, 1983) and Cooperation (Gathercole, 1989; Grice, 1975) principles are just as inadequate as accounts of toddlers' weak disambiguation effect as they are of preschoolers' strong one, the data do not allow us to decide which of the other four principles—ME, LGF, N3C, or FN—are operative. For the older children, we argued that there was evidence for ME that could not be attributed to the other principles—familiar name correction in response to a new name and mutual restriction of familiar name extensions. A third phenomenon, rejection of a new name that is introduced for a familiar name's referent, cannot be attributed to LGF or N3C but is covered by FN. No one has demonstrated either of the familiar name effects in 24-month-olds, although there have not been that many attempts.

In Studies 2 and 3 of Merriman and Bowman (1989), the introduction of a new name for an atypical referent of a familiar name made people who were 2½-year-olds or older less likely to accept the familiar name for the object, but young 2-year-olds were not affected by this manipulation. Moreover, when they were asked to select referents of first one familiar noun and then another (e.g., *car* and *truck*), the younger children were as likely to select overlapping as nonoverlapping sets. In contrast, 2½-year-olds and older children selected fewer overlapping than nonoverlapping sets.

Woodward and Markman (1991) suggested that 24-month-olds' failure to show the correction effect may reflect their not having learned the new label that had been introduced for the familiar name's referent. However, several training and naturalistic studies have reported that 1½- to 2-year-olds show near-ceiling level rates of maintaining their use of familiar names for objects immediately after acquiring new labels for them (e.g., they continue to accept a bus as a referent of *car* after learning that it is called "bus") (Banigan & Mervis, 1988; Mervis, 1984; Rescorla, 1976; Taylor & Gelman, 1989, Experiment 2 and 3).

Regarding the failure of the 2-year-olds in Merriman and Bowman's (1989) studies to mutually restrict the extensions of familiar names, Woodward and Markman (1991) argued that subjects may have believed that the names were mutually exclusive but may not have been sure which name was appropriate for which test item and may not have remembered which item they had already chosen. Merriman (1991) countered that even if children had some uncertainty and forgetting, a desire to avoid overlap should have caused them to select fewer referents for the second name tested than for the first. They did not, even though they selected well over 50% of the relevant items as referents of the first name.

It is possible that performance deficits such as forgetting, confusion, and distractibility prevent 2-year-olds from showing their ME bias in the familiar name paradigms. Also, the objects used may have fit 2-year-olds' representations of familiar names too well for an ME bias to have changed their minds about the acceptability of these labels. Even in older children, the ME bias does not correct beliefs that familiar names apply to typical instances (e.g., telling them that a yellow dump truck is a jegger does not make them less likely to judge that it is a truck; Merriman & Bowman, 1989). Lastly, 2-year-olds may just be very reluctant to give up a belief that a familiar name applies to something.

Regarding new name rejection, Mervis (1984) reported that in mother–toddler free play, when a new name was introduced for something that the child called by an incorrect name (e.g., *bank* for what he or she called "ball"), the youngster often made the object function as though it were still a referent of the incorrect name (e.g., rolled it) or uttered the incorrect name. Children were less likely to act this way when their attention was drawn to a distinctive object property (e.g., the slot in the bank). The toddlers' reactions seem like name rejections, but this is disputable: They may have only intended to convey their belief that the familiar name was what they would call the object. The rich interpretation of their utterance could be "and it's a ball," for example.

In a follow-up study (Banigan & Mervis, 1988), 24-month-olds learned a new name for something they could already label (e.g., *unicorn* for what they called "horse") more readily when a distinctive property was highlighted (e.g., the animal's horn) than when one was not. Children in the latter condition may not have rejected the name, however; it may simply be easier to learn associations that involve distinctive elements than ones that do not (Jacoby & Craik, 1979). The LGF explanation for this finding is that highlighting properties made an untagged category salient (e.g., horses with horns) and thus promoted learning. Furthermore, because the correct test objects were not identical to the training objects, it is not clear whether the condition differences reflect learning or the scope of generalization. Taylor and Gelman (1988, 1989) reported that when a new name was introduced for something 24-month-olds could already label, most learned the label but extended it to only a subset of the old name's referents. Finally, if the children in the no-highlighting condition did reject the name, either FN or ME can account for this.

Liittschwager and Markman (1991) reported a study in which 24-month-olds acquired first and second labels for objects with equal ease. However, in a follow-up in which two words (either two first or two second labels) were trained, fewer subjects acquired the second than the first labels. The authors suggested that toddlers fall back on the ME assumption when processing demands increase. In a third study, 16-month-olds had trouble learning second but not first labels when taught only a single new word. These results are as open as those of Banigan and Mervis (1988) to the alternative FN- and LGF-based interpretations.

Merriman, Marazita, and Jarvis (1993a) showed four groups of 24-month-olds a one-minute film in which a novel name was used for an unfamiliar object and then showed a second film in which either a second novel name was used for the same object (ME Violation), pronouns were used for the same object (ME Violation–Control), a second novel name was used for a new unfamiliar object (ME Maintenance), or pronouns were used for the new unfamiliar object (ME Maintenance–Control). There were no differences between the groups in how they attended to the critical events in the second film; that is, they were no more likely to attend to the violation than to the maintenance of ME. They were not even more likely to attend to naming than to pronominal reference. This null effect is difficult to interpret. Violation of the ME expectation, which is also a violation of FN in this case, should have been surprising if children had either of these expectations. However, it could be argued that, by the LGF principle, the events of the ME Maintenance condition were particularly informative. It is possible that the effects of these principles on attention canceled each other out.

Merriman et al. (1993) found that the children in the ME Maintenance condition learned the second label better and generalized it more accurately than those who heard this label used for the same object as the first label. This finding can be reconciled with Liittschwager and Markman's (1991) results by assuming that overlap between a second label and a barely familiar first label taxes processing capacity more than overlap between a second label and an overlearned first label. FN- and LGF-based accounts of this result can also be constructed.

Finally, what of our recent evidence (Merriman & Marazita, 1994) that subsyllabic preexposure moderates the disambiguation effect? If one accepts our explanation that such preexposure reduces the processing resources required to develop and maintain a phonological representation of the novel word in working memory, then little light is shed on which of the four principles—ME, LGF, N3C, or FN—is operative. Children could well use the additional resources at their disposal to apply any one of the principles more consistently.

Summary

The unopposed disambiguation effect of children who are about 24 months old is rather weak and can be obliterated by opposing it with token novelty, object atypicality, and name similarity. The impact of token novelty is greater for this age group than for older children, but that of the other two factors is lesser. The effect can be enhanced or diminished by preexposing a rime and onset that either comprise the test word or do not. Toddlers have been observed to reject second labels on occasion, and when their processing capacity is taxed, they do not learn second labels as easily as first ones. Unfortunately, these findings do not allow us to rule ME, FN, LGF, or N3C in or out.

VERBS

Because there have been no published studies of ME-relevant phenomena with verbs (although see Golinkoff, Hirsh-Pasek, Mervis, Frawley, & Parillo, this volume), we now shift from reviewing old research to presenting new data. Both an unopposed and a token novelty-opposed disambiguation effect for action words was assessed in 4-year-olds (Study 1) and 2-year-olds (Study 3). Both age groups showed a significant though moderate tendency to map novel verbs onto unnameable rather than nameable actions. The results of Study 2 suggested that 4-year-olds' disambiguation effect is stronger for object than for action words. In Study 4, a proposal for why 2-year-olds showed the effect for self-focused actions (e.g., cranking the arm vs. running) but not for object-focused ones (e.g., rolling fingers on a door vs. opening it) in Study 3 was tested.

Four-Year-Olds

A full report of Studies 1 and 2 can be found in Merriman, Marazita, and Jarvis (1993b). In the first experiment, 4-year-olds were asked to decide which of two simple actions, one they could name and one they could not, was the referent of a novel verb. The second experiment examined this age group's disambiguation of object names in a paradigm that matched the one used in Study 1 on several methodological dimensions.

Study 1

Our test for action names had the same structure as the one we have employed for object names. Twelve pairs of 5–10-second videotaped actions were used. Six portrayed different actions on objects, and the other six presented self-focused actions in which the agent was the patient (see Table 6.1). Object- and self-focused action are typically described by transitive and intransitive verbs, respectively. The tapes were selected on the basis of a pilot study in which 2- and 4-year-olds were asked to name filmed actions.

Each 4-year-old (N = 32) sat across from two color monitors which sat atop two adjacent VCRs. Three tasks were administered: preexposure, disambiguation, and naming. In the first, the child watched a tape showing six unfamiliar actions (three object-focused and three self-focused); the tape was presented three times. This experience was intended to reduce the token novelty of half of the unfamiliar actions to be presented in the next task.

Instructions for disambiguation varied according to condition. The children in the Novel Word group were told, "I'm going to show you two videos. On one of these TVs you'll see a man jeggering [or whatever the first test word was]. Now watch this one [one of the actions from a pair in Table 6.1

TABLE 6.1
The Familiar–Unfamiliar Action Pairs in Study 1

Familiar Action	Unfamiliar Action
Self-Focused	
Man runs back and forth twice	Man whirls forearm in horizontal plane in front of him
Man cries	Man wiggles lips repeatedly
Man sleeps lying down	Man moves legs together and apart repeatedly
Man sits down once	Man repeatedly puffs up one cheek then the other
Woman sings	Woman crosses legs once
Woman jumps up and down repeatedly	Woman leans back while turning in circle twice
Object-Focused	
Man washes door with rag	Man repeatedly turns scraper over against door
Man kicks three balls one at a time	Man repeatedly shuffles three balls around on palm
Man picks up spoon once	Man hits down on end of spoon making it catapult off chair
Man opens door once	Man repeatedly rolls fingers on door
Woman drinks orange juice from glass	Woman repeatedly bobs fist in glass of orange juice
Woman cuts paper with scissors	Woman makes several holes in paper with hole puncher

was presented on the left monitor]. Now watch this one [the other action of the pair was shown on the other monitor]. Now I'm going to show you both at the same time [the two actions were presented simultaneously]." As the films came on, each child was asked, "Can you point to the one of the man jeggering?" If the actions were object-focused, the request mentioned the patient (e.g., "Can you point to the one of the man jeggering the door?"). The format of the remaining eleven trials was the same except that different actions and nonce verbs were used and each trial began with the child being asked whether he or she knew the verb to be tested (e.g., "Do you know what cardling is?").

The children in the No Word group viewed the films in the same manner but were not asked to identify the referents of unfamiliar verbs or to say whether they knew these verbs. During the phase in which two actions were presented simultaneously, they were told, "I want you to pick one of these. Which one do you think it is?" This condition was included to assess children's preference for one kind of film over another.

The naming task was only given to the Novel Word group. All actions from the disambiguation test were presented one at a time and the children were asked to name each one.

Results of the last procedure were used to eliminate, on a child-by-child basis, those disambiguation trials that had not truly pitted a familiar action against an unfamiliar action. Any trial that contained an unfamiliar action that was named or a familiar one that was not named by a specific verb was dropped from analyses. The data from two children were completely excluded because the children named nearly every action. For the remaining children, an average of 4.1 of the 12 trials was eliminated. We decided not to eliminate cases in which an unfamiliar action was named by one of the following pro-verbs (see Clark, 1983): *move, go, put, make*, or *do*. These general terms were considered akin to broad superordinate object labels such as *animal* or *toy*, which Au and Glusman (1990) showed do not alter 4-year-olds' disambiguation (e.g., a novel name will be mapped onto an unfamiliar animal rather than a dog even though the former can be called "animal"). Moreover, no human action is so unfamiliar that it cannot be described by one of these general words.

Both instruction and token novelty of the unfamiliar action affected children's selections, $ps < .01$ (see top section of Table 6.2). The Novel Word group chose an unfamiliar action more often than the No Word group (66% vs. 45% of trials). Only the former's rate of selecting unfamiliar actions differed significantly from chance. This rate was essentially the same for self-focused (67%) and object-focused (65%) actions.

Seventeen percent of trials involved unfamiliar actions that were labeled with pro-verbs on the posttest. When these were excluded from analysis, the disambiguation effect was slightly smaller (62% vs. 66%), indicating that

TABLE 6.2
Percentage of Trials in Which an Unfamiliar Stimulus
Was Selected in Studies 1 and 2

Study/Context	Gender	Instruction	Token Novelty of Unfamiliar Action	
			High	Low
1	Girls	Novel word	77	63
		No word	48	42
	Boys	Novel word	76	48
		No word	53	37
2/Action	Girls	Novel word	85	92
		No word	32	23
	Boys	Novel word	79	72
		No word	50	54
2/Static	Girls	Novel word	93	79
		No word	21	23
	Boys	Novel word	92	90
		No word	33	42

Note. Because familiar actions were never preexposed, token novelty was high on all trials.

our estimate of the size of this effect was not reduced by including such trials.

In both instruction conditions, an unfamiliar action that had high token novelty was chosen more often than a preexposed one (64% vs. 48% of trials). Thus, 4-year-olds' tendency to maintain ME between verbs was attenuated by making the token of an unfamiliar action less novel than the token of a familiar action. This manipulation also reduced the No Word group's rate of selecting unfamiliar actions.

The impact of action preexposure was related to how children in the Novel Word group performed on the posttest. Those who generated the fewest specific verbs for the 24 actions were influenced by token novelty more than those who came up with the most, $r(12) = -.58$, $p < .05$. The 7 children who generated the fewest verbs selected a novel token of an unfamiliar action on 84% of trials but selected a preexposed one on only 37%. In contrast, the corresponding figures for the other children were 71% and 72%, respectively. Those with larger verb vocabularies may be less susceptible to token novelty variation than those with smaller ones.

The disambiguation effect for action words was weaker than the one that 4-year-olds have shown for object names. In five studies of this age group (Au & Glusman, 1990, 3 studies; Merriman & Bowman, 1989, Study 1; Merriman & Schuster, 1991), the average rate of unfamiliar object selection on unopposed trials was .95; the comparable rate in the current study was only .77. If .95 is taken to be the value of the population mean for object names, then .77 is significantly lower, $t(13) = 3.18$, $p < .01$. Likewise, the rate for trials in which token novelty opposed selection of the unfamiliar action (.55) is much lower than that reported in the object studies (i.e., Merriman & Bowman, 1989, reported rates of .90 or more in three studies, and Merriman & Schuster, 1991, reported a rate of .77). The children in the Novel Word group were more strongly affected by token novelty, their rate having been reduced by 22 points, than the children in the noun studies were, where reductions ranged from 4 to 7 points.

When asked whether they knew the test verbs, 6 children in the Novel Word group said, "No" on at least 10 of 11 trials, 5 said, "Yes," and 3 responded inconsistently. The 2 children whose data were excluded also said, "No" on every trial. These proportions are comparable to those obtained for unfamiliar nouns (Merriman & Bowman, 1989, two studies; Merriman & Schuster, 1991). The correlation between number of "No" responses and size of the disambiguation effect was not significant, $r(12) = .32$, $p > .10$. This contrasts with the significant positive correlation found in object-name studies (Merriman & Bowman, 1989, Study 1; Merriman & Schuster, 1991). However, the test of the correlation for verbs has weak statistical power due to the small sample size; in fact, the correlation is not significantly different from the .61 and .65 values obtained in the noun studies. Thus, it is not clear whether 4-year-olds' disambiguation effect and tendency to acknowledge name unfamiliarity are more strongly related for object than for action names.

Study 2

The problem with comparing results to those obtained for object names is that there are many differences other than type of word and referent. The use of videotapes in Study 1 was unique, and the syntax of the test question (e.g., "Can you point to the one of the man jeggering?") was more complex than has been used with nouns (e.g., "Can you point to the jegger?"). Also, whereas some children in Study 1 may have mistakenly mapped the test verbs onto objects in the films (although this was not likely), those in the object studies were prevented from making the analogous error of mapping the test nouns onto actions because the referents were stationary.

In Study 2, we examined two object name variants of Study 1. For the Action Context condition (N = 32), twelve pairs of 5–10-second videotapes were created, showing an adult performing a familiar action on a familiar and an unfamiliar object. For example, one pair consisted of a man patting a spoon and a man patting a staple extractor. The Study 1 procedure was used except that the new videotapes replaced the old ones, the test question contained a novel noun, rather than verb (e.g., "Can you point to the one of the man patting the biff?"), and in the posttest, children were asked to name objects, not actions. In the Static Context condition, a stationary object was presented on each of the two video monitors, one familiar and the other not, and instructions were worded very simply (e.g., "Can you point to the biff?").

An average of 2.25 of 12 trials were eliminated based on the same posttest naming criteria as were used in Study 1. Only instruction (Novel vs. No Word) and Instruction × Gender had significant effects on unfamiliar object selections (see Table 6.2). The Novel Word group chose objects that they could not already name over ones that they could on 85% of trials, a rate significantly greater than chance, $p < .001$. The corresponding percentage for the No Word group was 34. The selections of the Novel Word group were not significantly affected by either context or token novelty. Both the substantial disambiguation effect and the nonsignificant effect of token novelty are comparable in size to those obtained in previous noun studies, suggesting that these effects are not appreciably altered by mode of presentation (i.e., videotape).

Regarding the Instruction × Gender interaction, in the Novel Word condition, boys selected unfamiliar objects nearly as often as girls did (83% vs. 87% of trials, respectively), but in the No Word condition, boys chose such objects more often than girls did (45% vs. 27%). Why only the girls preferred objects that they could name over ones that were unfamiliar is not obvious. Of more importance is our finding that the object name disambiguation effect did not vary according to gender.

The lack of an effect of context suggests that children's tendency to map new nouns onto new kinds of objects was not affected by action embedding or by question complexity. Because there were no significant effects or interactions involving context, the data were combined and compared to the data from Study 1. Significant effects of instruction and token novelty were obtained, as were three significant interactions: Study × Instruction, Study × Token Novelty, and Gender × Instruction. Consistent with our comparison of the results of the first study to those that have been obtained for objects, the disambiguation effect was found to be smaller for actions than for objects. Simple effects tests indicated that the difference between the Novel Word conditions of the two experiments (.85 vs. .66) was significant, but the difference between the No Word conditions (.34 vs. .48) was not. Also, the tendency to select unfamiliar stimuli was significantly reduced by preexposure in the case of actions but not in the case of objects.

Although the Gender × Instruction interaction was significant, it only accounted for 4% of the variance. Gender differences in the No Word condition were largely responsible. In the Novel Word condition, boys and girls selected unfamiliar stimuli on 73% and 79% of trials, whereas in the No Word condition, the corresponding percentages were 34 and 45.

When children in the Static Context condition were asked whether they knew the unfamiliar nouns, 8 said, "No" on at least 11 of 12 trials, 4 said, "Yes," and 4 responded inconsistently. In the Action Context condition, these response patterns were shown by 8, 3, and 5 children, respectively. These distributions are comparable to both those found for the unfamiliar verbs in Study 1 and those reported in previous noun studies.

The correlation between number of "No" responses and size of the disambiguation effect was significant in the Action Context condition ($r(14) = .43$, $p < .05$, one-tailed) but not in the Static Context condition ($r(14) = .10$, $p > .10$). Given the small sample sizes, little should be made of this inconsistency: The difference between the two r values is not statistically significant. Combining the Z-transformed r values of this study with those obtained in two other noun studies ($r = .65$ in Merriman & Schuster, 1991, and $r = .61$ in Merriman & Bowman, 1989, Experiment 1) yields an average r of .47, which is not significantly different from the r value of .32 obtained for the verbs in Study 1.

General Discussion

The results of Study 2 suggest that the weak disambiguation effect shown by the 4-year-olds in Study 1 reflects some difference between the way action and object names are processed or represented, rather than some methodological idiosyncrasy of Study 1. Because current theoretical accounts of lexical principles have ignored verbs, no account predicts the difference we found. Therefore, a two-factor explanation that is primarily intended as a framework for further research is sketched here.

The first factor is a hypothesized weaker ME bias for action than for object words. The set of acceptable labels for any object tends to be hierarchically organized (e.g., *vehicle–car–Bonneville*), and the basic level term (e.g., *car*) has cognitive primacy (Mervis & Rosch, 1981). If a child does not know basic-level labels for all objects in an array, he or she can fairly safely assume (in the absence of contradictory evidence) that a new name will be a basic-level label for one of the unnameable objects. If the child does know basic-level labels for all the candidate objects, he or she can still assume ME at the subordinate level. Au and Glusman (1990) have documented that preschoolers map a new name onto a breed of dog that cannot already be named rather than onto a familiar breed, for example, but they allow the name to overlap with *dog*.

In contrast, action names have a mostly non-hierarchical structure (Huttenlocher & Lui, 1979) and consequently lack a basic level. Because even a simple action involves several components (e.g., agent, intention, direction, manner of movement, instrument, patient, and result) and may well be part of a coordinated series of actions (e.g., pouring is part of shampooing), several verbs can often be mapped onto it, each emphasizing a different subset of components or a different part of the series. According to Gentner (1982), children find verbs difficult to learn for this very reason: There are too many ways to interpret them. Thus, it is not that safe a bet that a new verb will designate an action that cannot already be named rather than one that can. For example, the act of chopping off a chicken's head with an ax can be labeled as "___-s the chicken," with any of the following filling the blank: *murder, kill, execute, abuse, attack, harm, hurt, destroy, chop(-s) up, axe, cut, decapitate, slaughter, slice, split, strike, swing(-s) at, affect, process,* or *prepare*. Although some of these verbs are hierarchically related (e.g., murdering is a kind of killing), most are not (e.g., one can swing at something without cutting it and cut it without swinging at it). Moreover, the pairs that are hierarchically related tend not to be part of the same hierarchy.

A related argument is that noun disambiguation is supported by the Whole Object bias (Markman & Wachtel, 1988), which keeps a novel word from being mapped onto an unnamed aspect of a familiar object (e.g., an unfamiliar part). There is no analogous whole action bias for novel verbs; indeed, Behrend (1990) has documented great variability in the components conveyed by the different verbs that preschoolers know (e.g., *swing*, manner; *clean*, result; *saw*, instrument). Thus, a child who knows only a result-emphasizing verb for a particular action (e.g., *clean* for someone wiping a countertop) may decide that a novel verb (e.g., *wipe*) emphasizes the manner of this familiar action.

Our claim is that children learn that in situations in which no explicit information about the relation between two verbs is received (i.e., default situations), new verbs are only somewhat more likely to be used for actions that cannot be named than for ones that can be named. In contrast, they learn that the differential likelihood of these two kinds of uses of a novel noun is much greater.

A second factor is needed to explain why token preexposure works against the disambiguation effect and why this countervalence is stronger for actions than for objects. We propose that some 4-year-olds abide by the FN principle for action words. The results of Study 1 suggest that FN greatly influenced the action-word mapping of approximately half of these children, whereas ME governed that of the others. The selections of the former group were strongly influenced by token novelty, whereas those of the other children were not affected by it at all. The youngsters who disregarded token novelty also tended to have larger verb vocabularies than did the ones who were swayed by it. We posit FN for the first group, rather than hypothesize that they were just extremely attracted to novel tokens, because the token preexposure effect for this group was so much greater than in the No Word condition.

In Study 2, as well as in previous object studies, token novelty had little impact. There are at least two ways of handling this result. First, those who rely on FN for action words may switch to ME for object words. A child may need to have a certain amount of experience with the words in a particular semantic domain (e.g., action words) before learning that new labels tend to designate unnameable rather than nameable members of that domain. Because action words are learned more slowly than object words (Gentner, 1982), and because the covariation between referent nameability and name novelty may be stronger for objects than actions, the switch to ME may occur later for actions. This proposal is supported by two findings: the strong impact of token novelty on 2-year-olds' object disambiguation (Merriman & Bowman, 1989; Merriman & Schuster, 1991) and the negative correlation in Study 1 between the number of actions 4-year-olds could name and their sensitivity to token novelty. Because of their limited experience, 2-year-olds should rely on FN in all domains. Four-year-olds who have larger verb vocabularies than their agemates may have had more opportunity to detect covariation between action nameability and verb novelty.

An alternative hypothesis is that 4-year-olds who rely on FN in action-word mapping also use it to direct their selection of object-word referents, but type novelty is a much larger component than token novelty of how novel an object feels than it is of how novel an action feels. This proposal explains the larger disambiguation effect for objects than actions and explains why the effect for objects is less affected by token preexposure. One problem, however, is that 4-year-olds have excellent object recognition memory (Brown & Scott, 1971), a skill that requires ignoring how familiar or novel a type feels and focusing on the feeling of familiarity or novelty evoked by a token. This evidence suggests that token novelty ought to influence how novel an object feels to the FN-guided group. However, it does not necessarily rule out the possibility of type novelty making a much greater contribution to their feelings of novelty.

New types of action may not strike children as much more novel than familiar types. Because there are only so many body parts and so many ways of moving them, and because youngsters are quite familiar with the ways their bodies can move, no movement may seem very new. Children may well have performed some of the unnameable actions from Study 1 themselves, or they may have seen others perform them. In contrast, there are innumerable potential object parts and ways of combining them into an object; in fact, any object could be used as a component of a larger thing. Moreover, children may find many parts and configurations to be foreign.

We can decide between these alternatives by examining intercorrelations between the token novelty effects for nouns and verbs—if these were strong, the second alternative would be supported. Also, the second alternative implies that attention and memory phenomena that are known to be affected by item distinctiveness (e.g., the von Restorf effect, release from proactive interference) would be stronger for unfamiliar types of objects than for unfamiliar types of actions.

Of course, this is all very speculative. We do not even have direct evidence that it is the ME rather than the LGF or N3C principle that underlies the moderate disambiguation tendencies that 4-year-olds show for action verbs. Study 1 only establishes that these tendencies are not an artifact of novelty preference and that they are not greatly affected by whether actions are object- or self-focused. Study 2 provides evidence that these tendencies are weaker than those for nouns.

Two-Year-Olds

Two investigations of young 2-year-olds' disambiguation of novel action words were conducted. The results were quite different from those obtained for 4-year-olds (Study 1).

Study 3

We administered the procedures of Study 1 to 23- to 26-month-olds (N = 32). The data from three children in the Novel Word group were dropped because they did not name actions in the posttest. An average of 4.62 trials of the remaining subjects in that group were excluded from analyses because an unfamiliar action was named or a familiar action was not named by a specific verb.

An analysis of variance of the disambiguation results revealed a robust Instruction (Novel vs. No Word) × Action Type (Self- vs. Object-Focused) interaction, $p < .005$ (see Table 6.3). The Novel Word group selected unfamiliar self-focused actions (69% of trials) significantly more often than the No Word group (45%), but the difference in their selection percentages for object-focused actions was not significant and was in the opposite direction (36 and 54, respectively). The Novel Word group's response patterns for self-focused actions were significantly different from chance, but the response patterns for object-focused ones were not. Action preexposure had no impact on either the Novel Word or No Word group.

The results generally contrast with those obtained from the 4-year-olds in Study 1 as well as from 2-year-olds in object studies. Regarding the latter, the unopposed effect for self-focused actions was as strong as that for objects, but the token-novelty-opposed one was stronger (Merriman & Bowman, 1989; Merriman & Schuster, 1991). The unopposed effect for object-focused actions was much weaker than that which is typically found for objects, but the token-novelty-opposed effect was comparable. The lack of a significant effect of token preexposure in the current study stands in marked contrast to the strong effect of this variable in the noun studies.

Regarding age differences, 2-year-olds' performance depended greatly on action type, but 4-year-olds' responses in Study 1 did not. Also, whereas token novelty affected 2-year-olds' noun but not verb mappings, the opposite was true for 4-year-olds.

When asked whether they knew the unfamiliar verbs, the 2-year-olds were less likely to say "No" and more likely either to say "Yes" or not to respond than the 4-year-olds of Study 1 were. The 2-year-olds' rates of "Yes-," "No-," and non-response, counting the three excluded subjects, were .55, .26, and .19, respectively. (Nodding or shaking the head were scored as "Yes" and "No" responses, respectively.) The corresponding rates for the

TABLE 6.3
Percentage of Trials in Which an Unfamiliar Action Was Selected in Study 3

| | Action Type by Token Novelty of Unfamiliar Action | | | |
| | Object-Focused | | Self-Focused | |
Condition	High	Low	High	Low
Word	37	35	68*	69*
No Word	45	61	55	36

Note. Because no familiar actions were preexposed, token novelty was high on all trials.
*$p < .05$, two-tailed.

4-year-olds of Study 1, counting the two excluded subjects, were .45, .55, and .00. The age-related increase in the tendency to admit one's ignorance of an unfamiliar word has also been found in the noun studies. In addition, the toddlers in Study 3 were less consistent in their replies than were the older children. Only 8 gave the same response to at least 9 of 11 questions, whereas 14 of the 4-year-olds did so.

The toddlers' inconsistency as well as their rates of "No-" and non-response were unique to the current study. In the object studies (Merriman & Bowman, 1989; Merriman & Schuster, 1991), 2-year-olds were as consistent as 4-year-olds in their responses to name familiarity questions. Also, their rates of "No" response were lower (average = .13, range = .06 to .20) and their rates of non-response higher (average = .49, range = .28 to .67) than in the current study.

The 2-year-olds' tendency to acknowledge the unfamiliarity of the test verbs was not correlated with the overall size of their disambiguation effect, $r(11) = .20$, $p > .10$. However, a significant correlation was obtained for self-focused actions, $r(11) = .59$, $p < .05$, but not for object-focused ones, $r(11) = -.23$, $p > .10$. The results for self-focused actions do not match those that have been obtained with objects (Merriman & Bowman, 1989; Merriman & Schuster, 1991).

Study 4

We hypothesized that the action type effect may have been caused by 2-year-olds' detection of greater sound similarity of the test sentences to their own descriptions of object-focused actions than to those of self-focused ones. That is, the action type effect was suspected to be an instance of the similarity effect reported by Merriman and Schuster (1991) for object names. In Study 3, the sentences for object-focused actions always included a direct object. For example, a child was shown a man opening a door and a man rolling his fingers on a door and was asked to point to "the man who is glarving the door." The child's own description of the familiar object-focused action may have included the same direct object (e.g., he or she may have encoded it as "he is opening the door"). The element shared by the test sentence and the child's encoding of the familiar object-focused action (e.g., ". . . the door") may have promoted the mapping of the test phrase onto the familiar action. In contrast, the sentences for self-focused actions lacked a direct object (i.e., the sentences were intransitive) and thus could not share an element with the child's descriptions. In short, children may have judged that "glarving the door" sounded more like "opening the door" than that "jeggering" sounded like "crying."

In Study 4, we compared 2-year-olds' responses to questions that contained direct objects (e.g., "Can you point to the one of the man clowing a nail?") to their responses to questions that did not (e.g., "Can you point to the one of the man clowing?"). We also developed pairs of self-focused actions that involved the same affected body part (e.g., a man opening and closing his eyes and a man crossing and uncrossing his eyes). This made it possible to vary whether or not a direct object was mentioned in questions about both object- and self-focused actions (e.g., "Can you point to the one of the man baving [his eyes]?").

Forty-eight 2-year-olds were given the same three kinds of tasks as in Study 3, namely preexposure, disambiguation, and naming. In the preexposure task, films of every familiar and unfamiliar action were presented one time to familiarize subjects with the actions rather than to create token novelty opposition as in Study 3. The disambiguation task consisted of eight unfamiliar-familiar action pairs (see Table 6.4) and four familiar-familiar action pairs. The latter four were included to warm up children to the task of selecting action referents for verbs and to keep them on task. For half of both kinds of pairs, the patient was the self; for the others, it was an object. The naming task was unchanged.

Children were assigned to one of three conditions: Novel Word–Direct Object, Novel Word–No Direct Object, and No Word. On each trial of the disambiguation task, children in the first condition were told that they would see a man doing something to an object or body part (e.g., "On one of these T.V.'s you'll see a man firshing paper"). They were asked whether they knew the test verb (e.g., "Do you know what firshing is?") and were then shown both actions in the pair (e.g., "Look what he is doing to the paper [pointing to the monitor on the left]. Now look what he is doing to the paper [pointing to the other monitor]"). The actions were then presented simultaneously, and the children had to indicate which one was the referent of the test verb (e.g., "Can you point to the one of the man firshing the paper?"). These test questions always contained a direct object (e.g., paper). For unfamiliar–familiar trials, the test verb was a nonsense word (e.g., *firshing*). For familiar–familiar trials, it was the conventional name for one of the actions presented (e.g., *throwing*). The task began with two familiar–familiar trials. The other two pairs of this type were presented on the fifth and eighth trials.

Children in the No Direct Object condition were given the same instructions except that the verbs were intransitive. For example, they were told, "On one of these T.V.'s you'll see a man firshing . . . Do you know what firshing is . . . ? Look what he is doing. . . . Now look what he is doing. . . . Can you point to the one of the man firshing?"

Children in the No Word condition received the same instructions as the children in the No Direct Object condition except that they were merely asked to pick a film on each trial. They were never asked questions about nor given information about unfamiliar verbs.

TABLE 6.4
The Familiar-Unfamiliar Action Pairs Used in Study 4

Familiar	*Unfamiliar*
Object-Focused Actions	
Man cutting paper with a scissors	Man punching holes in paper
Man kicking balls	Man shuffling balls around on his palm
Man picking up a spoon	Man hitting down on the end of a spoon so that it flies off a chair
Man pounding a nail with a hammer	Man turning a scraper over on top of a nail
Self-Focused Actions	
Man washing his hand with a rag	Man tracing his hand with a pizza cutter
Man combing his hair	Man grasping different parts of his hair with ice tongs
Man waving goodbye	Man rotating his arm in a broad circle in the horizontal plane in front of his chest
Man opening and closing his eyes	Man crossing and uncrossing his eyes

One unanticipated result in this study was that many children behaved shyly and were reluctant to talk. The experimenters were not as adept as those who had administered Study 3 in making the children feel at ease. Although all responded to requests to point to videos, half did not name actions in the posttest. Also, rate of non-response to name unfamiliarity questions (e.g., "Do you know what firshing is?") was fairly high (.52), and many of those who answered these questions did so nonverbally (i.e., by nodding or shaking their heads).

After eliminating the data from those who did not name actions in the posttest as well as the data of the few others who overextended names to most of the unfamiliar actions, only 6 children in the Direct Object condition and 9 in the No Direct Object condition remained. These two groups showed nearly identical tendencies; that is, there was no evidence that children were more likely to map a novel verb to a familiar action when the test question contained a direct object than when it did not. In both conditions, the disambiguation effect was somewhat stronger for self-focused actions than for object-focused actions. The children's rates of selecting unfamiliar object- and self-focused actions in the Direct Object condition were .58 and .67, respectively. The corresponding rates for children in the No Direct Object condition were .56 and .66. When the data from the two conditions were pooled, the effect of action type was not significant, $t(14) < 1$.

Because of the small number of retained subjects, the analysis had very weak statistical power. For this reason, we analyzed the selection rates of all the children in the Novel Word groups. For those who named actions in the posttest, we used the corrected rates (i.e., we eliminated the cases in which they named unfamiliars or failed to name familiars). For the others, we used the uncorrected rates.

These data were quite similar to those of the smaller sample. In the Direct Object condition, the rates of selecting unfamiliar object- and self-focused actions were .57 and .70, respectively. The rates in the No Direct Object condition were .52 and .66. There was no evidence that the children's disambiguation effect was attenuated when the referring phrase contained a direct object. When the data were pooled, the rate for self-focused actions was not significantly higher than that for object-focused actions, $t(31) = 1.24$, $p > .10$. However, only the selection rate for self-focused actions was significantly greater than chance ($t(31) = 2.96$, $p < .01$; for object-focused actions, $t(31) = .73$, $p > .10$). Also, only the rate for self-focused actions was significantly greater than that of the No Word group (.49), $t(46) = 1.97$, one-tailed $p < .05$. The Novel and No Word conditions did not differ with respect to object-focused actions, $t(46) = 1.26$, one-tailed $p > .10$. The No Word group's selection rate for unfamiliar object-focused actions was .42.

When asked whether they knew the unfamiliar verbs, the 2-year-olds' rates of responding affirmatively, negatively, or not at all were .30, .18, and .52, respectively. This pattern fits with that which has been observed in object name disambiguation studies but contrasts with the pattern of Study 3. Children's rate of "No" responses did not correlate with the size of their disambiguation effect for either object- or self-focused actions ($rs = .01$ and $-.09$, respectively). This result also converges with that found for object names but not with that for the action names in Study 3.

General Discussion

Two-year-olds tended to map a novel verb onto an unfamiliar rather than a familiar self-focused action, whether the verb was intransitive (Studies 3 & 4) or took a body part name as a direct object (Study 4). They did not show this effect for either transitive or intransitive verbs for object-focused actions, however.

In Study 3, the tendency to acknowledge the unfamiliarity of novel verbs correlated with the disambiguation effect for self-focused actions but not for object-focused actions. This pattern was not replicated in Study 4, but many of the individual scores on both variables may have been unreliable due to children's reluctance to respond to both verb familiarity questions and posttest naming instructions. Greater difficulty warming up to the lab situation may explain the higher rate of non-response in this study as well as in past noun studies. In this light, the consistent finding of no correlation between acknowledgment of name unfamiliarity and the size of the disambiguation effect in the noun studies is seen as less than compelling evidence for the null hypothesis.

We were unable to establish why 2-year-olds show the disambiguation effect for self-focused but not object-focused actions. The results of Study 4 did not support the hypothesis that differential sound similarity between test sentences and children's own descriptions of actions was responsible. One possibility is that object-focused actions are more difficult for toddlers to compare than self-focused ones are. The former can be conceptualized as more complex relations because unlike the latter, the agent differs from the patient. An alternative hypothesis is that toddlers are reluctant to map a novel verb to a novel object-focused action if they perceive the action as having had little impact on the patient. Self-focused actions always have substantial impact on their patients; because the agent is the patient, the action cannot be performed without transforming the patient. In contrast, some of our novel object-focused actions altered the patients very little (e.g., turning a scraper over and over on a nail). Although every object can be assigned a basic level name, not every action is lexicalized below the pro-verb level (e.g., there is no specific verb that fits the frame, "He is ___-ing the doll" to label making a doll raise one arm). Two-year-olds may judge lexicalization to be likely only when a patient is strongly affected.

We concluded from the results of Studies 1 and 2 that 4-year-olds have a stronger expectation that novel nouns map onto untagged objects than that novel verbs map onto untagged actions. The results of Studies 3 and 4 suggest that a similar claim cannot be made for 2-year-olds. Their verb disambiguation effect for self-focused actions was just as strong as the noun disambiguation effects that children of this age show for objects. It may be that from 2 to 4 years of age, children experience more violations of ME involving novel and familiar names for self-focused actions than involving novel and familiar names for objects in default contexts (i.e., ones in which the relation between the words is not explicitly marked).

The lack of effect of token preexposure in Study 3 was very surprising, in view of the substantial effect that this manipulation has on toddlers' object-word mapping. Future research should assess the following conjectures: First, comparing two simultaneously presented actions taxes 2-year-olds' processing resources, but comparing two objects does not. Second, preexposure not only reduces the FN that a stimulus evokes but also reduces the processing capacity needed to encode the stimulus when it is presented at a later time. Therefore, the two effects of preexposure offset one another in action-word disambiguation, but only the effect on FN has an impact on object-word disambiguation.

CONCLUSIONS

Much research needs to be done before the roles of nameability and novelty in youngsters' decisions about the referent of an unfamiliar noun or verb can be established. The case in which the word is a novel count noun and the choices are an unfamiliar and a familiar object has received the most attention. Young 2-year-olds show a moderate though reliable preference for the unfamiliar object, and the strength of this so-called disambiguation effect increases with age, nearing ceiling by age 4. Several factors can weaken or even reverse the effect, however, factors such as preexposure to the unfamiliar object, atypicality of the familiar object, and sound similarity between the noun and the name for the familiar object.

The noun results for children who are 2½ years or older can be explained by claiming that youngsters assume that a novel count noun designates a whole object and does not overlap with other nouns (i.e., by default WO and ME principles). Other lexical principles, such as the expectation that new words map onto referents that feel new (FN), may also play a role, but definitive evidence is lacking.

The lexical beliefs that underlie the noun mapping of young 2-year-olds have yet to be pinpointed, although it has been shown that their choices are not simply a matter of preference for novelty. Unlike the older children, there is no clear-cut evidence that toddlers have an ME bias.

Very little is known about children's verb mapping. In Study 1, 4-year-olds showed a disambiguation effect for words for both self- and object-focused actions. Comparison of results to those of previous noun studies and of Study 2 suggested that the verb effect is weaker than the noun effect but more strongly affected by token novelty. Four-year-olds' ME assumption was hypothesized to be weaker for action than for object words, owing to the children observing ME violations in default situations involving action words more often than ones involving object words. It was also proposed that for 4-year-olds, verb mapping is primarily influenced by FN but that when mapping nouns, they either switch to ME or rely on a feeling of novelty that is much more strongly influenced by type than by token repetition.

Two-year-olds tended to map novel verbs onto unfamiliar rather than familiar self-focused actions but showed no familiarity preference among object-focused actions (Studies 3 and 4). The results of Study 4 did not support the hypothesis that sound similarity between test sentences and children's own descriptions of actions explains why the disambiguation effect was restricted to self-focused actions. Future research should address two other hypotheses: that the greater complexity of object-focused actions make them more difficult than self-focused actions for toddlers to compare and that toddlers do not expect actions that have little impact on a patient to be lexicalized.

Even though several investigations have found 2-year-olds' noun mapping to be strongly affected by token preexposure, the children's verb mapping in Study 3 was not affected by this manipulation. Future research should consider whether this difference is explicable in terms of action comparison requiring greater processing resources than object comparison and in terms of token preexposure causing both a reduction in the FN that a stimulus evokes and in the processing resources needed to encode it.

REFERENCES

Anglin, J. M. (1977). *Word, object, and conceptual development*. New York: Norton.

Au, T. K. (1990). Children's use of information in word learning. *Journal of Child Language, 17*, 393–416.

Au, T. K., & Glusman, M. (1990). The principle of mutual exclusivity in word learning: To honor or not to honor? *Child Development, 61*, 1474–1491.

Au, T. K., & Laframboise, D. E. (1990). Linguistic contrast as corrective feedback in color name acquisition. *Child Development, 61*, 1808–1823.

Au, T. K., & Markman, E. M. (1987). Acquiring word meanings via linguistic contrast. *Cognitive Development, 2*, 217–236.

Banigan, R. L., & Mervis, C. B. (1988). Role of adult input in young children's category evolution: 2. An experimental study. *Journal of Child Language, 15*, 493–504.

Behrend, D. A. (1990). The development of verb concepts: Children's use of verbs to label familiar and novel events. *Child Development, 61*, 681–696.

Brown, A. L., & Scott, M. S. (1971). Recognition memory for pictures in preschool children. *Journal of Experimental Child Psychology, 11*, 401–412.

Clark, E. V. (1983). Meanings and concepts. In J. H. Flavell & E. M. Markman (Eds.), P. H. Mussen (Series Ed.), *Handbook of child psychology: Vol. 3. Cognitive development* (pp. 787–840). New York: Wiley.

Clark, E. V. (1987). The principle of contrast: A constraint on language acquisition. In B. MacWhinney (Ed.), *Mechanisms of language acquisition* (pp. 1–34). Hillsdale, NJ: Lawrence Erlbaum Associates.

Gathercole, V. C. (1989). Contrast: A semantic constraint? *Journal of Child Language, 16*, 685–702.

Gelman, S. A., Wilcox, S. A., & Clark, E. V. (1989). Conceptual and lexical hierarchies in young children. *Cognitive Development, 4*, 309–326.

Gentner, D. (1982). Why nouns are learned before verbs: Linguistic relativity vs. natural partitioning. In S. A. Kuczaj, II (Ed.), *Language development: Syntax and semantics* (pp. 301–334). Hillsdale, NJ: Lawrence Erlbaum Associates.

Golinkoff, R. M., Hirsh-Pasek, K., Baduini, C., & Lavallee, A. (1985, October). *What's in a word? The young child's predisposition to use lexical contrast*. Paper presented at the Boston University Conference on Language Development, Boston, MA.

Golinkoff, R. M., Hirsh-Pasek, K., Bailey, L., & Wenger, N. (1992). Young children and adults use lexical principles to learn new nouns. *Developmental Psychology, 28*, 99–108.

Grice, H. P. (1975). Logic and conversation. In P. Cole & J. L. Morgan (Eds.), *Syntax and semantics: Vol. 3. Speech acts* (pp. 41–58). New York: Academic Press.

Hearst, E. (1991). Psychology and nothing. *American Scientist, 79*, 432–443.

Hutchinson, J. E. (1986). Children's sensitivity to the contrastive use of object category terms. *Papers and Reports on Child Language Development, 25,* 49–55.

Huttenlocher, J., & Lui, F. (1979). The semantic organization of some simple nouns and verbs. *Journal of Verbal Learning and Verbal Behavior, 18,* 141–162.

Jacoby, L. L., & Craik, F. I. M. (1979). Effects of elaboration of processing at encoding: Trace distinctiveness and recovery of initial context. In L. S. Cermak & F. I. M. Craik (Eds.), *Levels of processing in human memory* (pp. 1–22). Hillsdale, NJ: Lawrence Erlbaum Associates.

Liittschwager, J. C., & Markman, E. M. (1991, April). *Mutual exclusivity as a default assumption in second label learning.* Paper presented at the biennial meeting of the Society for Research in Child Development, Seattle, WA.

Markman, E. M. (1987). How children constrain the possible meanings of words. In U. Neisser (Ed.), *Concepts and conceptual development: Ecological and intellectual factors in categorization* (pp. 255–287). Cambridge, England: Cambridge University Press.

Markman, E. M. (1989). *Categorization and naming in children: Problems of induction.* Cambridge, MA: The MIT Press.

Markman, E. M. (1992). Constraints on word learning: Speculations about their nature, origins, and domain specificity. In M. R. Gunnar & M. P. Maratsos (Eds.), *Modularity and constraints in language and cognition: Minnesota symposium on child psychology* (Vol. 20, pp. 59–101). Hillsdale, NJ: Lawrence Erlbaum Associates.

Markman, E. M., Horton, M. S., & McLanahan, A. G. (1980). Classes and collections: Principles of organization in the learning of hierarchical relations. *Cognition, 8,* 227–242.

Markman, E. M., & Wachtel, G. F. (1988). Children's use of mutual exclusivity to constrain the meanings of words. *Cognitive Psychology, 20,* 121–157.

Markman, E. M., & Wasow, J. (in preparation). *Very young children's use of the mutual exclusivity principle to guide their interpretation of words.* Stanford University, Palo Alto, CA.

Merriman, W. E. (1986). Some reasons for the occurrence and eventual correction of children's naming errors. *Child Development, 57,* 942–952.

Merriman, W. E. (1991). The mutual exclusivity bias in children's word learning: A reply to Woodward and Markman. *Developmental Review, 11,* 164–191.

Merriman, W. E., & Bowman, L. L. (1989). The mutual exclusivity bias in children's word learning. *Monographs of the Society for Research in Child Development, 54* (3–4, Serial No. 220).

Merriman, W. E., & Marazita, J. (1994). *The effect of processing similar-sounding words on two-year-olds' fast mapping.* Paper presented at the Boston University Conference on Language Development, Boston, MA.

Merriman, W. E., Marazita, J., & Jarvis, L. H. (1993a). *On learning two names for the same thing: The impact of mutual exclusivity violation on two-year-olds' attention and learning.* Paper presented at the biennial meeting of the Society for Research in Child Development, New Orleans, LA.

Merriman, W. E., Marazita, J., & Jarvis, L. H. (1993b). Four-year-olds' disambiguation of action and object word reference. *Journal of Experimental Child Psychology, 56,* 412–430.

Merriman, W. E., & Schuster, J. M. (1991). Young children's disambiguation of object name reference. *Child Development, 62,* 1288–1301.

Mervis, C. B. (1984). Early lexical development: The contributions of mother and child. In C. Sophian (Ed.), *Origins of cognitive skills* (pp. 339–370). Hillsdale, NJ: Lawrence Erlbaum Associates.

Mervis, C. B., & Rosch, E. H. (1981). Categorization of natural objects. In M. R. Rosenzweig & L. W. Porter (Eds.), *Annual Review of Psychology* (Vol. 32, pp. 89–115). Palo Alto, CA: Annual Reviews.

Metcalfe, J. (1993). Novelty monitoring, metacognition, and control in CHARM: Implications for Korsakoff amnesia. *Psychological Review, 100,* 3–22.

Perner, J. (1991). *Understanding the representational mind.* Cambridge, MA: MIT Press.

Rescorla, R. A. (1980). *Pavlovian second-order conditioning: Studies in associative learning.* Hillsdale, NJ: Lawrence Erlbaum Associates.

Taylor, M., & Gelman, S. A. (1988). Adjectives and nouns: Children's strategies for learning new words. *Child Development, 59,* 411–419.

Taylor, M., & Gelman, S. A. (1989). Incorporating new words into the lexicon: Preliminary evidence for language hierarchies in two-year-olds. *Child Development, 60,* 625–636.

Treiman, R. (1988). The internal structure of the syllable. In G. Carlson & M. Tanenhaus (Eds.), *Linguistic structure in language processing* (pp. 27–52). Dordrecht: Reidel.

Vincent-Smith, L., Bricker, D., & Bricker, W. (1974). Acquisition of receptive vocabulary in the toddler-age child. *Child Development, 45,* 189–193.

Walley, A. C. (1993). The role of vocabulary development in children's spoken word recognition and segmentation ability. *Developmental Review, 13,* 286–350.

Wellman, H. M. (1990). *The child's theory of mind.* Cambridge, MA: MIT Press.

Woodward, A. L., & Markman, E. M. (1990). Constraints on learning as default assumptions: Comments on Merriman and Bowman's "The mutual exclusivity bias in children's word learning." *Developmental Review, 14,* 57–77.

CHAPTER SEVEN

Lexical Principles Can Be Extended to the Acquisition of Verbs

Roberta Michnick Golinkoff
University of Delaware

Kathy Hirsh-Pasek
Temple University

Carolyn B. Mervis
Emory University

William B. Frawley
Maria Parillo
University of Delaware

> *As important as nouns are, . . . there has been the repeated finding that the verb is the real hero in determining what children learn about language structure. . . . Verbs . . . reflect conceptual development (and) the semantics of the verbs that children learn have a mediating effect on language learning.*
>
> —Bloom (1978, pp. 1–2)

As Bloom's statement indicates, the study of the acquisition of verbs brings us closer to understanding the origins of grammar. The combinatorial requirements of verbal argument structure, coupled with the requisite inflectional morphology, demand that the learner have some command of the grammatical system if verbs are to be used productively. Yet even before focusing on the acquisition of verbs per se, there are a number of issues to consider. What is a verb? How do children identify a novel word as a verb? When does the child have the syntactic category "verb" as opposed to the simpler, nonformal category of "action word"? How does perceptual–cognitive development contribute to verb learning? How do children know which aspect of an event (in the case of motion events, for example) the verb labels? That these are not simple questions to answer is obvious. Not only are the questions surrounding verb learning very complex, but the methodology required to study them has often plagued researchers.[1] For example, many verbs describe dynamic events. Until recent methodological innovations made possible by the use of videotape, research in early lexical acquisition was greatly biased against studying verbs and toward the study of nouns and the representation of static relations (Golinkoff, Hirsh-Pasek, Cauley, & Gordon, 1987).

Nonetheless, the field's emphasis on nouns has had its advantages and was strategically sensible for a number of reasons. First and foremost, nouns are the most prevalent class of words in early language acquisition in a wide variety of languages (Gentner, 1982, 1988; Nelson, 1973; but see Bloom, Tinker, & Margulis, in press; Nelson, Hampson, & Shaw, 1993). Second, the class "noun" maps to "concrete object" (in addition to other entities both material and nonmaterial) in all the world's languages (Maratsos, 1991). Third, the field's interest in nouns dovetailed with wide interest in conceptual development (e.g., Rosch, Mervis, Gray, Johnson, & Boyes-Braem, 1976). Fourth, and most pertinent to the present chapter, there has been a recent spate of research on principles of lexical acquisition (e.g., see Clark, 1983a, 1983b; Markman, 1989; Merriman & Bowman, 1989; Waxman & Kosowski, 1990) that were mostly designed with nouns in mind. Guided by these principles, children move certain hypotheses about the meaning of nouns to the top of the stack, as it were. These principles have the effect of making noun acquisition tractable.

This chapter extends work on the principles of noun learning to the acquisition of verbs. We argue that verb learning requires four components: scene analysis (an ability to perceptually analyze observed events into meaning components), semantic analysis (an ability to recognize how a language conflates these meaning components into its verbs), syntactic analysis (particularly, an ability to utilize information found in a verb's subcategorization frames to narrow the verb's meaning further[2]), and last, a set of word learning principles (derived by the child from observing how words work) that enable verb learning to proceed efficiently. We first define the construct "verb" and the concepts verbs encode. Following this, and drawing heavily on Mandler (1992), we consider whether the categories of meaning linguists have posited overlap with the way in which infants analyze events. Because Gleitman (this volume) and Naigles (this volume) discuss in depth how children use syntax to narrow verb meaning, we do not concentrate on syntactic analysis. The bulk of the chapter is devoted to extending the developmental lexical principles framework (Golinkoff, Mervis, & Hirsh-Pasek, 1994) to the acqui-

---

[1]Not all researchers were daunted, however, as a few in-depth studies of verb acquisition indicate (Bloom, Lightbown, & Hood, 1975; Huttenlocher, Smiley, & Charney, 1983; Landau & Gleitman, 1985; Pinker, 1989; Tomasello, 1992).

[2]See Pinker (1989) for another perspective on how children form what he calls *narrow range lexical classes*.

sition of action labels (i.e., verbs). These principles enable children to avoid many blind alleys in mapping novel verbs to their nonlinguistic representations of the world's events.

WHAT IS A VERB?

A purely syntactic method for defining verbs is that any verb can be seen as "something that takes a subject or object" (Frawley, 1992, p. 141). The verb not only *takes* these things but may also change in form depending on properties of the subject or object. For example, number, animacy, definiteness, and person of the subject or object can trigger morphological marking on the verb. Other syntactic tests for verbhood are passivization or dativization, pro-verb substitution, certain deletion patterns, and theory-specific criteria (e.g., verb movement in Chomsky's [1981] government-binding syntax).

Frawley also defined "verb" from a semantic perspective as a word that "encodes *events*: A cover term for states or conditions of existence, . . . processes or unfoldings, . . . and actions or executed processes" (p. 141). Thus, a verb is a description of a relation that occurs over time. For example, compare the verb *arrive* with its noun form *arrival.* Both words describe someone or something's final state; only the verb form, however, "retains access to the states leading to the result" (p. 144).

Frawley discussed the differences between four types of verbs: states, acts, causes, and motion. The difference between acts and states is that stative events (such as "costs" or "likes") are internally uniform and do not imply a series of substates. Something costs a certain amount today and that same amount tomorrow—no temporal change or dynamism is implied. Acts such as "prices" or "runs," on the other hand, imply that a sequence of events occurred and unfolded over time. In "Harry priced the book," the active verb *to price* implies that a series of component events took place to come up with the final price. Frawley described a number of tests to distinguish between active and stative verbs; for example, only actives can be used in the progressive. Causatives are verbs that express a relationship between two events—a prior event results in or gives rise to a subsequent event. Thus, in "Maria forced Bill to write a book," an antecedent–consequence relationship is being described. Motion events for Frawley entail "*displacement* of some entity, or positional change" (p. 171). Because children's earliest verbs are most often of the motion variety (e.g., *ride, go,* etc.; Bloom, Lightbown, & Hood, 1975), and because motion verbs incorporate discussion of causation and acts, we focus on that category.

In order to describe motion events, Frawley critically synthesized the work of a number of linguists (notably Jackendoff, 1983; Talmy, 1985) to derive a list of eight semantic factors that bear on displacement. The first of these is *theme* (or what Talmy, 1985, called *figure*), the displaced entity the event is about. The next two are *source* and *goal*. Source captures the origin of the motion, whereas goal captures the destination of the motion event. *Path*, or the trajectory the theme or figure takes in the event, is frequently encoded in English with separate prepositions such as *along* or *across*; in other languages, such as Korean, path is conflated—incorporated—within the verb (Choi & Bowerman, 1992). The *location* or fixed site of a motion event is expressed in English most often as a separate form. The *cause* of the motion is encoded in some languages in a separate form but in some languages is conflated within the verb itself. For example, in English the verb *feed* can be glossed as "cause to eat," but there is no such causal conflation for *drink*, as in, *"I drank the baby." The factor of *conveyance* captures the means by which the event is carried out, as in the distinction between "go by vehicle" or "go by foot"—a distinction explicitly marked, for example, in verbs in Polish, German, and many other Indo-European languages. The last factor, *manner* of motion, encodes such things as the speed and intensity of the motion. Talmy (1985) noted that many languages conflate manner within the verb (as in the distinction between "*knock* on the door" and "*hammer* on the door").

Are such characteristics and distinctions psychologically meaningful for the infant learning to use verbs, or are they simply dimensions linguists have abstracted from observation of adult verb usage? In answering in the affirmative, Mandler (1992) attempted to forge a link between semantic factors such as those proposed by Talmy (1985, 1988) and Jackendoff (1990) and what infants bring to the language learning task. We now turn to that work.

HOW DO INFANTS ANALYZE SCENES?

Mandler (1992) developed a theory of both the origin of children's meaning representations and the role of these representations in language acquisition. She borrowed heavily from the work of the cognitive linguists (e.g., Johnson, 1987; Lakoff, 1987; Talmy, 1985) to speculate on the form and content of infants' evolving representations of the world. Because Mandler's theory is important for our claim that children must be able to analyze events into a discrete set of meaning components in order to learn verbs, we describe Mandler's views in some detail.

For infants to get from perception to conceptualization and thence to language, they go through three levels. In the first level, infants interpret the world through perceptual analysis, largely inaccessible for conscious reflection. However, during the first six months of life, infants begin to convert this information into a recoded form—into global, rather than differentiated, meanings that later serve as the basis of concepts. For example, as Mandler noted, sometimes perceptual analysis involves comparing two objects; this comparison may lead the infant to discover that they are the same kind of object. These recodings (redescriptions in Karmiloff-Smith's [1992] terms) of perceptual phenomena are not useful to the infant for language until they become what Mandler called a non-verbal "vocabulary of meanings . . . from which the concepts are composed" (p. 590). Such a vocabulary is attained only at the second level, intermediate between the perceptual analysis of the first level and the linguistic meaning of the third level. The units of the second level are *image-schemas* (Johnson, 1987), or arrangements of conceptual primitives, rooted in the infant's spatial analysis of the world. These form the basis for linguistic meaning, which arises at level 3.

Image-schemas, which play a central role in Mandler's theory, are defined as "dynamic analog representations of spatial relations and movements in space" (Mandler, 1992, p. 591). They are not yet propositional in form and do not consist of discrete symbols. Instead, they are continuous, under-specified representations of transpiring events—hence primitives. They include concepts similar or in some cases identical to those linguists have posited for verbs: path, up-down, animacy, causality, agency, containment, and support. Although image-schemas are universal, the language(s) children acquire express them in different ways.

Mandler reviewed the sparse literature presently available on first-year infants' knowledge of these concepts. For example, *caused motion* (as distinct from self-motion), one of the image-schemas that infants develop, is represented by Mandler as shown here:

A

Caused Motion　　

She explained: "A vector toward object A, with another vector leaving the point" (p. 595); in other words, an object (e.g., a ball) moving in some direction impacts on something else (e.g., a toy car), starting that object on a course. Each vector is associated with a trajectory or path, represented as a straight line. The straight line is simply the default condition; a path can be more complex. Thus, caused motion requires, minimally, a *scene* where an object, A, is acted on from without (i.e., the first vector) and then produces its own vector with onset at 0. Crucially, caused motion requires spatial and temporal continuity of the trajectories: The second trajectory must begin when the first one ends (or changes direction). Leslie (1988) found that even 4-month-old infants respond to events with this structure differently from similar events with a spatial or temporal pause between vectors. Thus, young infants appear to be analyzing the spatial continuities between moving objects. In more recent work on the perception of causation, Cohen and Oakes (1993) demonstrated that 6-month-olds analyze events by noting the perceptual characteristics of the elements in the events. By 10 months, however, infants have moved to "Mandler-type" image-schemas in which they distinguish between caused motion and two different forms of noncaused motion.

Four- and 7-month-old children also appear to have developed an image-schema for *agency* as shown by infants' surprise when a hand that approaches an object fails to make contact with the object but the object moves anyway (Leslie, 1982). Golinkoff (1975, 1981) and Golinkoff and Kerr (1978) showed that by 14 months infants function with the concept of agency in the face of other perceptual changes. For example, in Golinkoff (1975), infants repeatedly saw a film of the same event: two people, one of whom pushed the other repeatedly across the screen. Then the event changed in one of two ways. Infants showed significantly more visual attention when the characters changed their roles (agent vs. patient of the action) than when they simply changed their relative positions (and therefore the direction of the action) on the screen but maintained the same role relations. Thus, not only do infants appear to have image-schemas for caused motion and agency, but the finer ability to discriminate between events in which agency is reversed rather than simply spatially reoriented (see also Cohen & Oakes, 1993).

HOW DO INFANTS MAP THE PRODUCT
OF THEIR SCENE ANALYSES (IMAGE-SCHEMAS)
INTO LINGUISTIC MEANINGS AT LEVEL 3?

If infants are eventually to acquire verbs for motion events, regardless of their particular language, they must be capable of mapping their knowledge of the spatial relations captured by image-schemas onto language. Thus, at the third level, children have to figure out how the particular language(s) around them express the perceptually derived, image-schematic relations of Level 2 (e.g., for motion, notions such as self-motion versus caused motion, agency, location, etc.). Using the image-schema of containment as an example, Mandler (1992) wrote:

> The distinction between *in* and *on* is not a perceptual one. The perceptual system makes many fine gradations where languages tend to make categorical distinctions [which are often binary]. Languages vary as to where they make these cuts, and the child must learn from listening to the language. But the hypothesis I am operating under is that however the cuts are made, they will

be interpreted within the framework of the underlying meanings represented by nonverbal image-schemas. That is, some of the work required to map spatial knowledge onto language has already been accomplished by the time language acquisition begins. Children do not have to consider countless variations in meaning suggested by the infinite variety of perceptual displays with which they are confronted; meaningful partitions have already taken place. . . . What remains for children is to discover how their language expresses these partitions. (p. 599)

Mandler's approach helps us to understand why children start to talk in the first place and why language acquisition does not take place more quickly. Children may start to talk because they want to talk about the important relational information contained in their image-schemas. Bloom (in press) argued that infants learn language in order to express the contents of their minds—the functions of regulation and instrumental gain are secondary. Bloom's principle of *discrepancy* states that as the contents of mind become increasingly discrepant from the data of perception (in Mandlerese read this as, "as children construct image-schemas"), children need language (i.e., a propositional code) to express themselves effectively. Thus, Mandler's theory gives Bloom's children the contents they want to discuss.[3]

Why does language production not take place earlier, say, in the first year of life? It appears that children must first construct their image-schemas in order to have the meanings upon which language is built. In addition, infants must learn how their particular language maps image-schemas onto language. For example, in English there are separate morphemes for the discrete image-schemas of containment and support: *in* and *on*, respectively. However, in Korean there are separate morphemes (in the form of verbs) for whether something is *on* tightly or loosely, or is *on* the head or the body. Although one might expect Korean children to express these more complicated notions later than their American counterparts who have only two words to learn (viz., "on" and "in"), they do not appear to (Choi & Bowerman, 1992). This means that the first year of life, when language comprehension exceeds language production, must be a critical time for the infant to sort out these things. Since image-schemas, as described by Mandler, do not contain the details of "on the head" versus "on the body," it must be the case that the infant realizes that these events are treated differently by noting that they are labeled by different phonological forms. As Brown (1958) pointed out, noting a difference in reference spurs the child to note a difference in meaning.

Mandler's discussion of image-schemas illustrates how infants may lay the meaning foundation upon which verbs are built. Although considerable additional research is needed to validate Mandler's claims, we have treated

---

[3]See Tomasello (1992) for an image-schematic approach to verb acquisition.

the theory in some detail because it provides a needed link between the infant's perceptual–cognitive development and the ability to learn verbs (see Tomasello, 1992, for a case study of the image-schemas underlying early verbs). It has also helped to highlight how the analysis of scenes is insufficient for verb learning because children must also discern how their particular language carves up the scene. Furthermore, although both scene analysis and semantic analysis take us at least halfway to understanding verb learning, the child must also observe how particular verbs are morphosyntactically encoded. Finally, the child must construct the lexical principles described in the following pages to make the mapping between meanings and language possible in the first place and efficient in the second. However, the exact relation between Mandler's levels and the lexical principles described here remains unclear. One possibility is that word learning principles mediate or intervene in the transition between levels 2 and 3, in which case they have a causal role in the transition. A weaker position is that they oversee or guide the transition: Rather than serving as algorithms that produce a determinate result, they serve as heuristics that elevate some choices for mappings between meanings and forms to the top of the stack.

THE DEVELOPMENTAL LEXICAL PRINCIPLES FRAMEWORK

Principles (sometimes referred to as biases or constraints) in part explain how children appear to avoid the Quinean (1960) conundrum of entertaining an infinite number of possibilities for what a novel word might mean. Some of these principles address the issue of the intension of word meanings; others address the issue of extension, namely, which objects (or events) the child denotes with a word. The origin of these principles and the ways in which they function are sources of debate. Indeed, some researchers question their necessity altogether (e.g., Bloom, 1993; Nelson, 1988). For instance, Bloom et al. (in press) argued that lexical principles are the invention of researchers who describe the data rather than the child who is acquiring the lexicon (see also Bloom, 1993). However, this position begs the question of how children determine the meanings of words without considering a myriad of hypotheses, even if they can focus on what the speaker appears to be talking about (Bloom et al.'s principle of *relevance*). Other challenges to the existence of these principles are sometimes based in the belief that the principles must be all-or-none in character (Nelson, 1988). To counter this argument, Merriman and Bowman (1989) discussed the default nature of these principles. Thus, unlike the principles of G-B syntax (Chomsky, 1981), which (purportedly) tightly constrain the acquisition of syntax, lexical principles are more biologically feasible because of their flexibility (Lieberman, 1991). In addition,

Waxman (1989) countered the view that these principles are unable to accommodate to individual differences (cf. Nelson, 1988).

By now a number of lexical principles have been posited, and research to validate these principles and their predictions proceeds apace (e.g., Golinkoff, Hirsh-Pasek, Bailey, & Wenger, 1992; Landau, Smith, & Jones, 1992; Markman & Hutchinson, 1984; Merriman & Bowman, 1989; Waxman & Kosowski, 1990). Golinkoff et al. (1994) attempted to organize this literature to choose between competing principles. They proposed a developmental lexical principles framework to explain the acquisition of object labels during the first two years of life. This framework is a two-tiered sequence (see Fig. 7.1), with the principles of the second tier building on and refining the principles of the first tier. The principles function not as infallible rules but rather like problem-solving heuristics (Glass, Holyoak, & Santa, 1979). Just as people do not always entertain all the relevant data when facing a new problem or evaluate all the logically possible alternatives (see Wason & Johnson-Laird, 1972), so lexical principles work to narrow the search space (i.e., as a heuristic) rather than to determine the outcome (i.e., as an algorithm). As in problem solving, where certain solutions are at the top of the stack and available for quick use, the principles that guide word learning keep the child on track, evaluating only a small set of probable

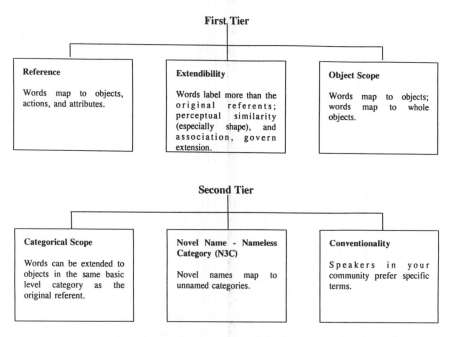

FIG. 7.1. Six lexical principles posited by Golinkoff, Mervis, and Hirsh-Pasek (1994) for the acquisition of object labels.

alternatives. Thus, lexical principles sometimes are violated and sometimes result in errors but more often than not enable rapid word learning.

Golinkoff et al.'s (1994) developmental lexical principles framework has three clear advantages over prior discussions of word learning principles that do not couch the principles in a developmental perspective. First, taking a broad look at lexical development, rather than at one or two aspects, allows principles that were previously presupposed to emerge clearly. For example, various proposals have been made about the criteria children use for noun extension (e.g., Markman & Hutchinson's [1984] taxonomic assumption; Landau, Smith, & Jones' [1988] shape bias). However, both these principles presuppose that children realize that a term can be extended at all. Golinkoff et al. (1994) called this more basic realization (which is seen around the end of the first year of life) the principle of *extendibility*. This principle captures the knowledge that first, a term can apply to more than the original exemplar or exemplars someone else has labeled for the child and second, that extension should occur on the basis of perceptual similarity (especially shape) or associative link. A principle of the second tier, *categorical scope*, then narrows the application of the principle of extendibility by specifying that extension should occur to referents in the same basic-level category as the original referent.

Second, when principles are organized in a developmental framework, explanations emerge for such standard observations as noncategorical overextensions. For example, an explanation for unusual object label extensions (such as on thematic grounds) is that the child has only the principle of extendibility and not the principle of categorical scope. Unusual extensions may thus result from the child's failure to realize that extension occurs only on the basis of membership in the same basic-level taxonomic category.

The third advantage of the developmental lexical principles approach is that the principles are designed to work *in light of* the linguistic and nonlinguistic input and not *despite* the input. That is, this perspective calls for cooperation, rather than competition, between grammar and meaning. For example, to learn a novel verb the child must determine which word in a sentence is the verb. Lexical principles can only indirectly assist in this discovery. By the age of 2½, English-speaking children appear able to utilize phrase structure and morphological cues (such as the inflectional morphemes -*ed* and -*ing*) to predict whether a novel word is a noun or a verb (Golinkoff, Diznoff, Yasik, & Hirsh-Pasek, 1992). By the age of 3 (if not earlier), children are able to use syllable number as a cue to whether a novel term is a noun or a verb (Cassidy & Kelly, 1991). On average, at least in English, verbs have a smaller number of syllables than do nouns (Cassidy & Kelly, 1991). There may even be prosodic cues parents inadvertently provide to signal the form class of a novel word. For example, parents appear to introduce novel nouns by placing them in the final position in the utterance on a pitch peak with an elongated vowel (e.g., Fernald & Mazzie, 1991)—even when parents speak Turkish, in which nouns in final position violate the language's canonical word order (Aslin, 1992). Perhaps research will reveal that when novel verbs are introduced they, too, receive some different, equally unique treatment. For example, verbs are consistently used in parental speech prior to the event they describe (Tomasello & Kruger, 1992).

In sum, the developmental lexical principles framework unpackages previously proposed principles by exposing the presuppositions they contain. The unified approach of this framework also provides explanations for common phenomena in lexical acquisition, such as overextensions. Further, this framework emphasizes the child's use of linguistic and nonlinguistic input to construct the principles and to supplement their functioning. Lexical principles help reduce the burden of word learning by bringing certain hypotheses about what a novel term might mean to the top of the stack.

CAN THE DEVELOPMENTAL LEXICAL PRINCIPLES FRAMEWORK WORK FOR VERB ACQUISITION?

Because verbs appear later than nouns in lexical acquisition, some researchers argue that verbs are semantically (let alone syntactically) more complex than nouns. By implication, then, lexical principles are even more important for verb than noun learning. Gentner (1981, 1982), for example, argues that verbs encode a wider range of meanings than do nouns and that verbs are at a disadvantage for acquisition because they label ephemeral events instead of palpable, consistent objects (her *natural partitions* hypothesis). On the other hand, it is easy to come up with counters to this position, such as the fact that nouns have their own semantically relevant subproperties, like rigidity, animacy, and so on (Frawley, 1992). Regardless of the relative complexity of nouns vis-à-vis verbs, what matters for acquisition is that both classes have semantically relevant subproperties. Principles of lexical acquisition increase the likelihood that children will consider certain of these subproperties more relevant than others in determining the meaning of a novel term.

The question that remains is whether principles of lexical acquisition originally conceived with the learning of nouns in mind will transfer readily to verbs. One possibility is that only a poor Procrustean fit will result from this effort. Yet another possibility is that some principles will readily transfer to verb learning, whereas others will need to be abandoned. Obviously the best outcome would be if the developmental lexical principles framework readily transferred to verbs. As Golinkoff et al. (1994) argued, if a totally different set of principles is required for the acquisition of tokens in each word class, the number of such principles and their possible interactions will be enormous. If the principles readily transfer to verbs, they gain in power and efficiency as they extend their predictions to yet another open class.

THE DEVELOPMENTAL LEXICAL PRINCIPLES FRAMEWORK

Principles of the First Tier: Reference, Extendibility, and Object Scope

The first tier of principles, estimated to be operating by the end of the first year of life, captures the piecemeal, one-at-a-time character of early lexical acquisition. Although these principles are sufficient to permit word learning to occur, none of them assists the child in acquiring new words with ease. These principles are, however, foundational to the process of lexical acquisition. Next we present the principles sequentially, although any allusions to the age of appearance of these principles, or indeed to their order of appearance within a tier, should be taken as only tentative. It should also be recognized that because verbs appear later than nouns in sentence production, the timetable for the appearance of these principles for verbs may be somewhat later than for nouns.

The Principle of Reference. Logically, the principle on which all others rest is reference. As Brown (1958) wrote, "The use of language to make reference is the central language function which is prerequisite to all else" (p. 7). It states that words can be mapped onto the child's representations of objects, actions, or attributes in the environment. Even before reference emerges, however, it may be expected that words have some special salience for the infant above and beyond music or tones accompanying novel objects. New research by Waxman and Balaban (1992) suggests that 9-month-old infants distinguish between a word and a tone: Only the former prompts infants to form a category when presented with a variety of pictures of animals. This research and other preliminary work by Echols (1991) and Baldwin and Markman (1989) appears to indicate that words have special status for the infant even in the first year of life (but see Roberts & Jacob, 1992).

Some researchers have claimed that reference is innate (e.g., Macnamara, 1982). Golinkoff et al. (1994) claim, to the contrary, that reference has its origins in prelinguistic communication, during which period infants learn to interpret the referential gestures of others (e.g., points) and to produce such gestures themselves. This is not to claim, however, that referential gestures are equivalent to linguistic elements used referentially. Linguistic reference entails a degree of specificity not found in all-purpose referential gestures (such as pointing) that cross ontological boundaries (Petitto, 1993).

For an observer to judge that a child is using a term referentially, it must be clear that the word is in a symbolic or "stands for" relationship with the concept it represents rather than merely an indexical or "goes with" relationship. That is, the word must be used in ways that convince the observer that it is not just an associate of the referent. For example, a term may be said to be used referentially if it is used in the absence of any instrumental goal, in the absence of the referent itself, and to label multiple exemplars. However, all researchers do not necessarily agree with these criteria. Thus, diagnosing when reference has occurred is a matter of some dispute (Harris, Barrett, Jones, & Brookes, 1988). Furthermore, reference may occur even if children do not engage in these behaviors, despite our inability to diagnose it unequivocally.

The principle of reference was originally formulated to include action words, object words, and attribute words. The child must know that just as labels can be used to refer to objects, labels can be used to refer to actions. As with nouns, it may be the case that the earliest verbs children use in both comprehension and production are context-bound and often embedded in a particular routine (Benedict, 1979; Dromi, 1987; Smith & Sachs, 1990). For example, a parent may say, "Blow your nose," and the child will wrinkle up her nose and make a blowing sound, even though she may not understand "blow" in any other context.

The principle of reference is necessary but not sufficient for verb learning, however. The child must know that names for actions can be extended to actions that they have not previously heard labeled. For example, if the only time the child seems to understand the verb *blow* is when it is used in the phrase *blow your nose*, the word *blow* may not have attained symbolic status for the child (i.e., whether it has an intension in addition to reference or extension). Only when *blow* is recognized outside of that specific routine can we conclude that reference has occurred. Using a term (noun or verb) for more than just the original exemplar or exemplars previously labeled for the child is made possible by the next principle, the principle of extendibility.

The Principle of Extendibility. For the class of object labels, the principle of extendibility is that a word can be used to label referents that someone else has not previously labeled. If children knew only that people used words to make reference, word learning would proceed very slowly indeed. There is nothing in the principle of reference that states that a word can label more than the original referent. There is some evidence that at an early point in lexical development many infants do not extend words to referents other than those which they have previously heard labeled (see Dromi, 1987; Harris et al., 1988). The criteria for extension under the principle of extendibility are similarity to the original referent or common thematic relation. Shape is the most common basis for extension, although smell, taste, sound, and texture are also bases for extension (Clark, 1983b). Thus, the basis for novel label extension is purposely left somewhat vague because similarity can be defined in any number of ways. A principle of the second tier—categorical scope—refines the basis for the extension of object labels to membership in the same basic-level class.

The principle of extendibility transfers readily to the acquisition of labels for actions. A label learned for an action, like a label learned for an object, must be used to label more than just the original exemplar. This by itself is an important insight because it represents the power of language to categorize nonidentical events. Choi and Bowerman (1992), citing data collected from Bowerman's two daughters and other diarists, claimed that children's earliest spatial words (such as *up* and *down* as shortened forms of verbs like *stand up* and *sit down*) spread readily to new uses. Korean children also seem to extend their early verbs rapidly beyond their original contexts of use, although Korean children do not start out with these disembodied spatial words because Korean treats path (which such words represent) differently than does English. Originally, as Choi and Bowerman pointed out, such particles (e.g., *up*) are used to comment on or request motion in different circumstances; only later are these particles used to comment on states. Nonetheless, that children have the ability to extend such particles of verbs or action words to new situations implies that children are capable of abstracting the shape of the main event (as Pinker, 1989, calls it). Yet the "shape" of an event is different from that of objects, for which shape refers to a persistent, palpable object contour. For actions, shape lasts only as long as the event and refers to the overall configuration of the action. To say that the child abstracts the shape of the main event is to say that the child constructs an image-schema of it (Mandler, 1992); this allows the infant to lose the detail of each individual event (i.e., to "bleach" it) and to represent a class of events with a single representation. Thus, if a child uses the word *fall* to comment on his or her own fall, the fall of an object, and the fall of a pet, the child is indicating that he or she has abstracted the idea that *fall* captures the concept of downward motion. The particular individual or object doing the falling (the Figure) is not a part of the verb's meaning for the English-speaking child.

Take, for example, the action labeled by the verb *dance*. Presumably the child can form a concept of "dance" even before hearing a label, given that dancing involves fairly rapid movement of the legs, either in a single location or along a path. To test the hypothesis that infants rely on event shapes for extendibility, point lights could be placed on joints and actors filmed as they carry out dancing in the dark (see Soken & Pick, 1992, for evidence that young infants can process such point light displays). The action of dancing could then be pitted against, say, the action of waving or the action of running (also both displayed in point lights) in the preferential looking paradigm used by Golinkoff et al. (1987) with real actions. If infants rely on the shape of an action, when they are asked to "Find dancing!" they should watch the point light display for dancing significantly more than the point light display for waving. Waving differs significantly from dancing in manner of motion, but running resembles the manner of motion seen in dancing. Running and dancing differ in that dancing does not involve a goal, whereas running often does. Thus, children should more often confuse running with dancing than waving with dancing. In fact, one of the author's sons (M. Pasek at age 3.5) was convinced that running in place was an example of dancing. Thus, younger children should make errors, confusing dancing with running, whereas older children should be fooled less often. Moreover, a reliance on the shape of the event may also lead to infants failing to see dancing when it in fact has occurred. Older infants should find it easier to pull out the invariants of the dancing action even if they are embedded in some amount of action noise, such as the action of sitting both preceding and following the dancing.[4]

On this albeit tentatively offered event–shape view, nonstandard extensions of verbs occur for two reasons: children's desire to fill a lexical gap for which they do not have the correct verb (e.g., Bowerman's daughter saying "open" instead of "separate" when two frisbees are stuck together; Choi & Bowerman, 1992) and children's failure to recognize which semantic elements are conflated in the verb so that they extend only on the basis of the overall shape of the main event. As an example of the latter, the English-speaking child may use the verb *fall* when *drop* is needed (as in, "I falled the book"), failing to note that *fall* does not conflate cause in its meaning. This formulation of extendibility for action words predicts that young children show extension errors for verbs whose main events differ only by perspective. For example, verbs such as *give* and *take* apply to situations that look exactly the same but reverse participants. They even take the same arguments—both verbs take agents, patients, and objects. As Gleitman (1990) argued,

> I think the problem is that words don't describe events *simpliciter*. If that's all words did, we wouldn't have to talk. We could just point to what's happening, grunting all the while. But instead, or in addition, the verbs seem to describe specific perspectives taken on those events by the speaker, perspectives that are not "in the events" in any direct way . . . since verbs represent not only events but the intents, beliefs, and perspective of the

---

[4]Another way to test the shape claim is to ask children to sort events with and without a label. Only in the presence of a label should children be concerned about selecting items that share the same overall configuration. The parallel to this work has been done with objects by Landau et al. (1988). Although children form object categories on a number of bases in the absence of a label, once they are offered a label they switch to the criterion of shape.

speakers on those events, the meanings of the verbs can't be extracted solely by observing the events. (p. 17)

In other words, attending to the main event of the action is not enough; the child must go beyond a single element of the scene labeled by the verb (e.g., the shape or configuration of the event) to discern the semantic elements entailed in the verb. The argument presented previously does make empirical predictions: It predicts that early verb errors should differ from later verb errors in that relatively more early errors will be with verbs such as *give* and *take*, or *come* and *go*, verbs that differ primarily on perspective but share manner of action and path. Later errors will usually be based on the child's failure to discern a key semantic component entailed in the verb (Pinker, 1989).

Next we review evidence that young children operate with the principle of extendibility in comprehension before any verb production. Research has established that the comprehension of a lexical item often precedes its production (see Golinkoff et al., 1987). Thus, by implication, extension of verb meanings must first be seen in comprehension as well. Smith and Sachs (1990) gave mothers of children between 12 and 19 months of age a detailed questionnaire that required mothers to evaluate how their children comprehended and produced verbs. For example, mothers were asked, "Would your child understand, 'give Nana a cup'?" to see if the verb *give* was understood outside of specific, highly practiced routines. Smith and Sachs found that mothers reported that children between 16 and 19 months comprehended 33.75 verbs. However, only 12.50 of these verbs were considered to be contextually flexible, by which Smith and Sachs meant that the verbs were comprehended outside of specific routines. Perhaps extension is underestimated by mothers; their judgments of comprehension may be confounded with their judgments of their children's willingness to comply with these requests. It may be that until researchers avail themselves of the preferential-looking paradigm or other comprehension methods that do not tax young children and permit the portrayal of dynamic events, underestimates of children's early verb extension will result.

A number of studies show the early extension of verbs in comprehension. Hirsh-Pasek and Golinkoff (1991, 1993, 1994) used the preferential-looking paradigm (Golinkoff et al., 1987), in which infants show comprehension by watching one of two simultaneously presented video events accompanied by a linguistic stimulus. Would infants at about 14 months of age recognize that language maps to complex events? The experimenters created pairs of videotaped events that involved one adult on each screen performing presumably familiar actions (e.g., kissing, tickling) on unlikely objects. A linguistic stimulus that accompanied these events described only one of the displays (see Fig. 7.2). The dependent variable in this paradigm is visual fixation time: Does the infant watch the screen matching the linguistic stimulus more than

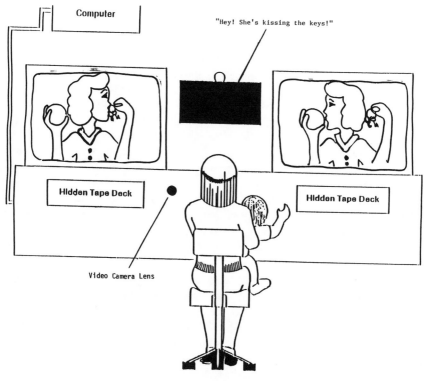

FIG. 7.2. A pair of stimuli presented by Hirsh-Pasek and Golinkoff (1991) to test infants' sensitivity to constituent structure.

the screen that does not match? For example, on one screen, infants saw a woman kissing some keys and holding a ball in the foreground. On the other screen, they saw a woman kissing a ball and dangling the keys in the foreground. The linguistic stimulus was, "Where's she kissing the keys?" (or its reverse, "Where's she kissing the ball?" in the counterbalanced condition). Three outcomes were possible: Either children could watch the event with the keys being kissed, indicating that they interpreted the verb phrase as a unit; or they could watch the event with the keys dangling in the foreground (if they paid attention only to the last word); or they could watch both events equally because both contained *she's, kissing,* and *keys.* Results indicated that infants watched the matching event significantly more than the nonmatching event. This suggests that infants understood the verbs used on the tapes and interpreted the verb phrases in which these verbs occurred (i.e., they could distinguish between "kissing the ball" and "kissing the keys"). Thus, results from a paradigm that does not require infants to do more than look at the screen matching the linguistic stimulus suggest that infants may indeed extend action words in comprehension months before they produce them.

This assertion is further supported by a study by Golinkoff et al. (1987) with infants a few months older, also conducted with the preferential-looking paradigm. Golinkoff et al. found that 17-month-old infants showed compre-hension of a set of eight common action words. For example, infants saw a woman dancing on one screen and a woman waving on the other and were asked, "Where's she dancing?" In response to the linguistic stimulus, they watched the screen showing dancing significantly more than the screen showing waving. With these common action verbs, children with very limited production vocabularies (some as few as two nouns) showed extension in comprehension.

Thus, the limited data suggest that infants can understand some verbs when used outside the original context of acquisition by about 17 months of age, and perhaps as early as 14 months of age. In order to extend the name of an action, even in comprehension, it seems that children would have to have formed some concept of the action, presumably based on the shape of the main event. When the second tier principle of categorical scope comes on-line, children focus on uncovering the semantic components the verb conflates (e.g., causation, manner). Errors based on how the main event looks diminish. The parallel with the operation of the principle of extendi-bility for nouns is exact. Although children extending object labels often appear to be extending on the basis of common category membership they are really extending only on the basis of the object's shape. Shape often—although not always—is one of the cues to common basic-level category membership. It is only when children construct the principle of categorical scope that they truly extend object labels on the basis of category member-ship. We are making the identical argument for verbs: Initial extension is based on perception, that is, how the main event of the verb appears. Later extension (i.e., after the child has constructed the principle of categorical scope) is based on the semantic components entailed in the verb. Not sur-prisingly, given children's level of linguistic skill, attention to the meaning components entailed in verbs requires some linguistic experience.

Although older children are more concerned with the presence of the semantic components required of that particular verb before they extend, rather than the shape of the main event per se, shape continues to be important, especially when few syntactic frames are provided to allow the child to uncover a verb's entailed semantic components. In a study with 34-month-olds, Golinkoff, Jacquet, and Hirsh-Pasek (1993) showed that chil-dren extend a newly learned verb to another agent performing the same action after only a single exposure to the original token and minimal linguistic input. As Fig. 7.3 shows, subjects must have made this judgment based on the overall shape of the main event, which they saw in a two-dimensional

FIG. 7.3. Stimuli from the experiment by Golinkoff, Jacquet, and Hirsh-Pasek (1993).

drawing. So, for example, Big Bird was in the same position as Cookie Monster and was performing the same novel action that Cookie Monster had performed on an earlier trial. Having pointed to the picture of Big Bird doing a novel action in answer to the question, "Where's glorping?" children were then able on the next trial to point to another character glorping—even in the presence of another unnamed, novel action. This result suggests that toddlers are able to extend a novel action word to another exemplar on the basis of the shape of the event, after only a single exposure of a two-dimensional representation of the novel action.

Figure 7.4 shows the two principles discussed thus far. The principle of reference allows children to recognize that people use words to refer to

First Tier

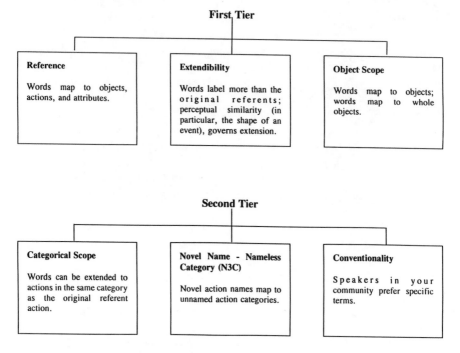

| **Reference** | **Extendibility** | **Object Scope** |
| Words map to objects, actions, and attributes. | Words label more than the original referents; perceptual similarity (in particular, the shape of an event), governs extension. | Words map to objects; words map to whole objects. |

Second Tier

| **Categorical Scope** | **Novel Name - Nameless Category (N3C)** | **Conventionality** |
| Words can be extended to actions in the same category as the original referent action. | Novel action names map to unnamed action categories. | Speakers in your community prefer specific terms. |

FIG. 7.4. The six lexical principles as they apply to the acquisition of action labels.

objects and actions (and attributes). The principle of extension, which may appear at the same time as reference, allows children to extend their object and action labels to exemplars other than the original on the basis of shared shape.

The Principle of Object Scope. Object scope effectively reduces confusion about the likely referent of a novel word. The principle of object scope has two parts. First, it states that words label objects. Thus, if a child hears a word while observing an unnamed object involved in a novel event, the child is biased to assume that the term labels the object, not the event. Data for this claim come from a study by Echols (1992) in which infants (0;9 and 1;2) were shown one of two displays accompanied by the same linguistic message. Either a novel object was seen undergoing three different motions (viz., a straight movement across a plane, a wave-like movement, or an angular movement), or three different objects were seen undergoing the same motion (viz., the wave-like movement). Infants were also divided into groups depending on whether or not they heard a label ("That's a danu") as they watched these events. At test, infants in both conditions were shown the same stimuli: An old object undergoing a novel motion and a novel object undergoing an old motion. The outcome was as predicted by object scope. The older infants who had heard a label, *danu* (whether in the consistent motion or the consistent object condition), watched the novel object/old motion combination more than the old object/new motion combination. This result suggests that by 1;2, infants are predisposed to connect a label with an object rather than the object's motion.

How does object scope help the infant learn verbs, given that it superficially appears to obstruct verb learning? Just as there is a hierarchy for the aspects (e.g., shape, size, color, material) of an object young children prefer that a novel name label (see Xu, 1991), there may be a hierarchy to determine the element of an event that gets named when neither the object nor the action already has a name. As object scope predicts, a novel term is first taken as the name for the object; only if the object is named is it taken for the motion or action of the object. Tests of such a hypothesis are similar to Echols' (1992) procedures, except that known (and previously named) objects and actions must also be included in the events infants are shown. If object scope is in force, names for actions will be learned faster if a previously named object is seen undergoing a novel motion than if an unnamed object is seen undergoing a novel motion. In this latter case, the infant may attempt to connect the new motion name with the object rather than the action. Recall that object scope is a first tier principle; as children become more sensitive to syntactic markers for verbs in the second year of life, the strict hierarchy (i.e., affix labels first to objects, then to actions) suggested here may not always be observed.

The second part of object scope states that words refer to a whole object as opposed to its parts or attributes. Macnamara (1982) was the first to enunciate this principle when he noted that in the presence of a word, infants "automatically take the word as applying to the object as a whole" (p. 190). Object scope, therefore, predicts that labels for whole objects will predominate in children's early vocabularies—and they do (see Mervis, 1990). Additional evidence of the preponderance of nouns that label whole objects is found in Nelson (1973), who gathered data on children's first 10, 30, and 50 productive vocabulary items. At each point (as an examination of the Appendices from that monograph reveals), the majority of the words in children's lexicons were object labels, and the vast majority were labels for whole objects.

Infants may possess a corollary of this second part of object scope for verbs, which Golinkoff, Jacquet, and Hirsh-Pasek (1993) have called *action scope*. Just as object scope predicts that children learn names for whole objects before they learn the names for parts (Mervis, 1983), action scope predicts that children assume that a novel action word labels a larger rather than a smaller action. This claim follows from Mandler's (1992) conceptualization of image-schemas, which themselves are whole bleached events. Thus, the body parts with which actions are performed or the types of objects (within the animate or inanimate class) that undergo action are not relevant to the formation of image-schemas, most of which are binary, rough, analogic representations of spatial knowledge.

Evidence for the claim that infants learn particular distinctions somewhat later than broader distinctions comes from Choi and Bowerman's (1992) work on Korean motion verbs—although they would probably not interpret their findings in the same way that we do. In contrast to English, Korean makes many distinctions for the ground of the event "put on" (as in clothes). There is a separate verb for putting clothes on legs, clothes on the head, and clothes on the trunk of the body, whereas English has only one verb. Although these verbs all seem to emerge at around the same time in production, and not much later than other verbs, if action scope for verbs is correct, children should err in comprehension by attempting to apply these verbs more broadly than they actually do, perhaps accepting the verb for "put on the legs" just as readily for a situation in which something is being put on the head or on the body. This prediction can be tested with the preferential-looking paradigm (Golinkoff et al., 1987).

Saliency also supports action scope, although the measurement and definition of salience is very slippery. As Fisher, Hall, Rakowitz, and Gleitman (1994) observed, "For verb interpretation, salience considerations also arise to narrow the learner's space of conjectures. It may well be more natural to interpret an observed action as 'walking' than as 'successive leg movement,' 'muscle-twitching,' etc." (p. 7, ms.). Presumably a young child is predisposed to pay attention to a whole action rather than a part of the action. If this is true, experimental studies should show that if an event is labeled, the child will be more likely to treat it as a totality than if it is not labeled. Other than a study by Forbes and Farrar (1993), tests of this hypothesis have not yet been conducted. Forbes and Farrar (1993) taught children a novel name for a novel action and then changed the action in various ways. A control group saw the same actions without labels. One dimension of action changed by the researchers was *continuity*: The original event started, stopped, and then resumed. When children were asked if the altered action was of the same type as the original action, the children who had been given a label generalized significantly more than those who had not received a label. This result supports the claim that children may be more likely to see an event as a unit when they hear a label than when they do not. Action scope, then, helps children limit their hypotheses about the part of the witnessed event that the verb is labeling by encouraging children to select the most salient aspect of the event as the referent for the novel verb.

Summary of the First Tier Principles. The principles of reference, extendibility, and object scope constitute the first tier of the developmental lexical principles framework. These principles enable children's word learning to get off the ground but new words are not yet acquired with ease. For both object and action labels, these principles are in place by the end of the first year of life, manifested most often in comprehension. Production at this time has a very deliberate look, with the child producing at most one to two new words every few weeks. The principles of the second tier further refine the word-learning process and allow the child to speed up lexical acquisition.

Seen in light of Mandler's (1992) image-schemas, the principles of the first tier appear to be greatly influenced by cognitive development. In order to recognize that words can refer to objects and events (i.e., the principle of reference), the child first needs to form representations of objects and events. By the end of the first year of life, as work by Spelke (1990), Leslie (1988), and Baillargeon (1993) attests, infants know a good deal about the permanence and solidity of objects and the kinds of events in which they can engage. The principle of extendibility is a natural outgrowth of image-schema formation because, for extension to occur, the infant must categorize a new token as a like kind. However, children judge "like kind" differently at this age than they do at a later age. Initially, the child is guided mainly by the overall shape of the main event, paying relatively less attention to the specific semantic components entailed by the verb. For more advanced language-learners, extensions are increasingly guided by the verb's entailed semantic components. Further, nouns are acquired before verbs because, on the principle of object scope, a novel term used to label a novel event is interpreted as labeling an unnamed object in that event before the unnamed action. Action scope, a parallel to the second part of object scope, predicts that children attempt to affix a novel event label to the whole event as opposed to some part of the event.

Although originally developed for the acquisition of object labels, the principles of the first tier apply directly to the acquisition of event labels (i.e., verbs). We next examine whether the second tier principles transfer as easily to verbs as do the first tier principles.

Principles of the Second Tier: Categorical Scope, Novel Name–Nameless Category (N3C), and Conventionality[5]

The second tier of principles further constrains the basis for object and event label extension (categorical scope), helps children readily map new words to objects and events in the environment (novel name–nameless category or N3C), and encourages children to adopt conventional names for objects and events (conventionality; Clark, 1983). These more advanced principles enable the dramatic increase in vocabulary that begins in the middle of the second year of life.

---

[5]See Merriman (this volume) for alternatives to these principles.

Categorical Scope. The principle of categorical scope builds on an important insight first captured by Markman and Hutchinson (1984) in their taxonomic assumption, namely, that words label categories (see also Waxman and Kosowski, 1990, for a related principle called the *noun-category bias*). Although this basic insight was retained, the principle of categorical scope (Golinkoff, Shuff-Bailey, Olguin, & Ruan, 1993) was devised to speak more precisely to the nature of the categories labeled by object words. The principle of categorical scope states that an object label may be extended to objects other than the original referent that are in the same basic-level category as that referent. Thus, object-label extension occurs to objects the child perceives to be of like kind as the original. Although the judgment of "like kind" can be based on perceptual similarity (such as shape), "like kind" is more than that—objects in the same basic-level category require the same program of motor movements and the shortest names, relative to terms at either the sub- or superordinate level of the concept hierarchy (Rosch et al., 1976). Because label extension for objects is said to be at the basic level (see Golinkoff et al., 1993, for empirical support for this claim), categorical scope is more specific than the taxonomic assumption (Markman & Hutchinson, 1984). The taxonomic assumption is more similar to our principle of extendibility because it allows extension on the basis of any number of perceptual similarities and at any level of the concept hierarchy.

Categorical scope for verbs must guide the child to extend action labels to actions in the same category as the original referent, or else the power of language to classify non-identical events is lost. We stop short, however, of claiming that a verb labels a basic-level category of events because it is unclear that actions and their names can be organized into a hierarchy. Categorical scope for verbs states that action labels are extended to other actions that appear to require the same semantic components as the original action. Thus, extension under categorical scope (unlike under extendibility) is less dependent upon the way the action appears and more upon the child's recognition of the presence of additional semantic components conflated in the verb. Thus, the errors predicted to occur during extendibility are different from those predicted to occur under categorical scope. In fact, the errors predicted under categorical scope are a subset of those that occur under the principle of extendibility. As the child becomes more aware of the semantic components that are conflated in the verb and can keep these components in mind, errors are more likely to be a result of the child's noting all but one of the semantic components entailed in the verb. Choi and Bowerman (1992) provided an excellent example, reporting that one of the Korean children they studied used the verb *ollita* [cause to go up] incorrectly, to mean "putting [something] away regardless of directionality" (that is, up or down). Choi and Bowerman argued that the child does this because he fails to realize that the element path is included in the verb.

Path in Korean is conflated within transitive verbs, unlike in English, where path (up, down, on, etc.) is typically marked outside the verb (regardless of whether it is transitive or intransitive) with adverbial particles. Pinker (1989) reached much the same conclusion after a review of the literature on children's verb substitution errors. He concluded that children's initial representations of verb meaning sometimes fail to include all the relevant semantic distinctions encoded by the verb.

How do children come to recognize the semantic components a verb contains? The first datum children can rely on is their perception of the events they observe, as previous discussions of image-schemas in this paper have described. As Gleitman (1990, this volume) and her colleagues (Hirsh-Pasek & Golinkoff, 1994; Hirsh-Pasek, Naigles, Golinkoff, Gleitman, & Gleitman, 1988; Landau & Gleitman, 1985; Naigles, this volume) have noted, verbal meaning cannot come only through observation of the world's events; the form of language itself acts like a zoom lens, giving perspective on the main event. This process, known as *syntactic bootstrapping* (Landau & Gleitman, 1985), occurs when the child attends to the syntactic frames in which the verb is used. With children's observation of the verb's main event and their ability to link event components into semantic components, syntactic bootstrapping gives children refined information about the meaning of the verb. The frames tell the listener, as Pinker (1994) put it, "whether to focus on one actor or another, one affected entity or another, the cause or the effect" (p. 22). Thus, the child must already know some language to make sense of the data available in these frames. For this reason, more advanced verb usages (e.g., a verb appearing in different kinds of alternations, such as the passive or dative, etc.) depends on the child's sensitivity to the syntactic structures in which a verb is found. According to Pinker (1989), on the other hand, observations of the situations in which particular verbs are used drives the child's discovery of additional semantic components entailed in the verb, semantic components that do or do not license the verb's participation in various alternations. This debate aside, however, the principle of categorical scope allows the child to analyze instances of a particular action word's usages to discover the semantic components entailed. Because this process requires some amount of linguistic experience, it occurs mainly in the second tier. Although children's verb usages are influenced by their native language in the first tier as well (see Choi & Bowerman, 1992, for a strong statement of this case), early extensions (under the principle of extendibility) are based more on an event's appearance rather than on its entailed semantic components.

Is there evidence that children can use the frames in which a verb appears to help narrow down its meaning? Research using the preferential-looking paradigm (Golinkoff et al., 1987), showed that by 2 to 2½ years of age, children are sensitive to the implications for meaning of different verb frames (e.g., Hirsh-Pasek & Golinkoff, 1994; Hirsh-Pasek et al., 1988; Naigles, 1990). For example, children hearing a verb in a transitive sentence frame such as, "Oh, see Big Bird glorping Cookie Monster!" are likely to watch a causal event in which Big Bird is making Cookie Monster do something more than a noncausal event in which Big Bird and Cookie Monster are performing a novel action together. The opposite result occurs when children hear an intransitive sentence such as, "Oh, see Big Bird is glorping with Cookie Monster!" Hearing this sentence, children watch the noncausal event more than the causal event (Hirsh-Pasek et al., 1988). Thus, studies such as this look at the effect of syntactic frames on the child's interpretation of verb meaning. Other studies (reviewed next) do the opposite: They manipulate event components while presenting a novel verb in a single syntactic frame to investigate children's construal of the meaning of a novel verb. Both types of studies are important for understanding how children who have the categorical scope principle attempt to narrow down the possible meanings of novel verbs.

The first study of this latter type was conducted by Behrend (1990), who taught 3-year-old children novel verbs for novel events seen on videotape. When the original actions were altered by changing either the result, manner, or instrument used, extension was inhibited more if the result and nature of the action changed than if the instrument changed. On our analysis, two reasons may account for this finding. First, changes in the result and nature of the action change the shape of the event, whereas changes in the instrument do not. Even though these children were old enough to have the principle of categorical scope, without a sufficient corpus of sentences containing the verb children have little to go on other than the shape of the main event. Second, changes in the result and nature of the action may substantially change the meaning of the event, whereas a change in the instrument employed to carry out the action would change its meaning less. For example, the action of sweeping (i.e., a horizontal movement of the hands with an instrument) with the end result of either a pile of something or the dispersement of something, may arguably still be sweeping if done with a broom, the customary instrument, or a large piece of cardboard, a novel instrument. This study suggests, then, that a hierarchy may exist among the eight semantic components encoded in verbs discussed earlier in the chapter, some of which may be more crucial for the meaning of a verb than others.[6]

Forbes and Farrar (1993) performed a similar experiment with 3-year-olds, 7-year-olds, and adults. They manipulated causative agent, continuity, direction, or instrument to see what changes most inhibit extension. Results indicated that the youngest children were less likely to extend a verb after any type of change than were either of the other two age groups. This in

---

[6]An older study by Gentner (1978) with known verbs also found evidence for a hierarchy of semantic components, with manner being more salient than change of state. Thus, 5- to 7-year-olds seemed to know the meaning of verbs like *beat* or *shake* sooner than a verb like *mix*, which requires the end result that two or more substances be interleaved.

itself is an interesting finding because it suggests that young children are more conservative in their extensions, perhaps requiring more exposures to both the main event and the verb in more syntactic frames before they are willing to consider altered events as exemplars. In addition, subjects extended differentially depending on the aspect of the event that was changed. A change in causation inhibited extension the most. That is, when the agent who caused the event himself was now made to cause the event by someone else, subjects were least likely to agree that this action should be called by the same name. For example, in the target event, a person seen kneeling in a shopping cart used a shovel to paddle away; in the causative agent change, another person pushed the cart while the kneeling person used the shovel. By reducing their extension in the face of causation changes, children showed sensitivity to a key component of verb meaning, perhaps on analogy with verbs such as *die* (non-causal death) and *kill* (caused to die) or *fall* (non-caused downward movement) and *drop* (caused to move downward). On the other hand, changes in continuity of the event (i.e., whether it started and stopped) or a change in direction (e.g., performed at a 45° rotation) inhibited extension much less. Once again, there is a suggestion of a hierarchy of semantic components for verbs. Causation is crucial for defining events; continuity and direction are less important. This outcome is consistent with Mandler (1992), who required a different image-schema for caused and self-motion but not for continuity and direction changes. In addition, our framework predicts an interaction with age such that children much younger than those tested by Forbes and Farrar (1993) should be less likely to generalize a novel action name to actions that changed continuity and direction and more likely to generalize to actions that altered causation—given the same overall shape of the main event. Under extendibility, the shape of the event matters more than the semantic components; under categorical scope, the semantic components matter more than shape.

In sum, the principle of categorical scope states that extension is governed by the presence of the semantic components entailed in the verb. Although this claim does not imply that the child will not make errors of verb extension, the nature of their extension errors will be different than those when the child had only the principle of extendibility. Research to evaluate this claim has not yet been conducted; research that manipulates the syntactic frames in which verbs appear or the semantic components seen in subsequent exemplars is just beginning.

Novel Name–Nameless Category (N3C). This principle states that novel terms map to previously unnamed objects. Thus, when presented with a set of objects, some of which have a name and some of which do not, N3C predicts that the child will map the new word to a whole object (based upon the principle of object scope) without a name. For example, Golinkoff,

Hirsh-Pasek, Bailey, and Wenger (1992) tested whether 31-month-olds would assume that a new term mapped to an unnamed object if the connection between the new term and new object was not explicitly pointed out to them. Subjects were shown 4 objects on each of 12 trials, of which one or two were unfamiliar (e.g., a plastic tube for the bottom of a chair leg). Subjects were asked, in counterbalanced order, to give the experimenter either a known or an unknown object (e.g., "May I have the glorp?"). Children picked the novel object in response to the novel word whether they were asked for the original (78%) or another token (69%). Thus, without any explicit directive to do so, children mapped the novel object to the novel noun, as predicted by N3C. Mervis and Bertrand (1993) obtained similar results in a study with children younger than 24 months old.

There is no logical reason why this principle must be limited to object names. N3C can be more broadly construed as predicting that a novel term will map to a previously unnamed object or action or even attribute. This formulation, however, begs the question of how a child knows the form class of a novel term. By the time N3C is constructed as part of the second tier of principles, children are sensitive to syntactic cues for form class (Golinkoff, Diznoff, Yasik, & Hirsh-Pasek, 1992; Golinkoff, Mennuti, Lengle, & Hermon, 1992; Golinkoff et al., 1994; Taylor & Gelman, 1988; Valian, 1986). In addition, describing the object scope principle, we posited the existence of a hierarchy for the child's interpretation of a novel term's meaning. A novel term is first taken to be a label for an unnamed object label and then as a label for an unnamed action.

Golinkoff, Jacquet, and Hirsh-Pasek (1993) examined whether N3C operates in verb acquisition as it does in noun acquisition. Using virtually the same paradigm as that used in the Golinkoff, Hirsh-Pasek, Bailey, and Wenger (1992) study, Golinkoff, Jacquet, and Hirsh-Pasek (1993) presented children who were almost 3 years old with colored drawings of familiar and novel actions performed by Sesame Street characters. It was ascertained first that children knew the names of the supposedly familiar actions by asking them to point to one of three choices of pictured actions. On test trials in counterbalanced order, the experimenter asked each child to point to one familiar and one novel action out of a group of four pictures. Children had no difficulty pointing to already-named actions, as in "Where's running?" When asked to select the referent of a novel term (e.g., "where's glorping?"), children picked a previously unnamed action an average of 83% of the time, despite the fact that no explicit link between the novel term and the unnamed action was made by the experimenter. Thus, children appeared to assume that the action without a name was being named when the experimenter used a novel action term. This is what N3C predicts—rapid mapping of a novel term to the unnamed action.

This finding follows from the predictions of an N3C principle expanded to incorporate at least nouns and verbs. In order to acquire many new vocabulary items as quickly as the data suggest children do in the end of the second year of life (see Carey, 1978), children need a principle such as N3C to allow them to map new terms to new referents rapidly. On the other hand, to decide that a new term is a verb (or a noun) requires that the child be able to exploit some of the available cues to form-class membership. As argued in Golinkoff et al. (1994), by the time N3C emerges in the second tier of principles, children can effectively capitalize on this aspect of the linguistic input.

Conventionality. According to Clark (1983a, 1983b, 1988), conventionality is the assumption that "for certain meanings, there is a conventional form that speakers expect to be used in the language community" (Clark, 1988, p. 319). This principle seems equally applicable to acquisition for any open class word. In order to be understood by their linguistic community, children must use the term expected by their group. Thus, idiosyncratic uses of verbs understood only within the family are eventually supplanted by canonical verbs used in the wider linguistic community. For example, "lawning the grass," used by the first author's son for "mowing the grass," was eventually replaced by the standard form. Evidence from diary studies (or the CHILDES database) should yield further examples of unconventional verbs that are eventually preempted by conventional ones.

Summary of the Principles of the Second Tier. The principle of categorical scope allows children to extend verbs on the basis of shared semantic components. The N3C principle has children fast-mapping (Carey & Bartlett, 1978) novel terms to unnamed actions. Finally, the conventionality principle motivates children to try to get their names for objects and events in line with the names others around them use.

Compared to the principles of the first tier, which piggyback on perceptual–cognitive development, the principles of the second tier are language-specific in origin and emerge from the child's experiences with language. For example, the categorical scope principle is rooted in the child's ability to use information in the syntactic frames that surround the verbs they hear (see Gleitman, this volume); without this ability, the child could not discern the semantic components conflated within the verb. The application of the N3C principle is also prompted by a linguistic stimulus. In the Golinkoff, Diznoff, Yasik, & Hirsh-Pasek (1992) experiment, when asked to select a novel action in the condition where it was not asked for by name (e.g., "Show me someone doing something"), children randomly selected an action from among the four present. However, if an action was asked for by a novel name (e.g., "Show me someone daxing"), children systematically selected the unnamed action. Conventionality seems quintessentially linguistic because the child takes a perfectly serviceable name that is understood by the immediate family and shelves it in favor of the common name used by others.

OVERALL SUMMARY AND CONCLUSIONS

The purpose of this chapter has been to examine the possibility that infants begin the task of verb learning guided by a set of principles that ease their task. The discussion of this perspective was preceded by a discussion of the construct "verb" and a characterization of the syntactic and semantic characteristics of that word class. The emphasis in this discussion was on motion verbs—the class of verbs children use most often in their early language. Eight semantic factors that characterize motion verbs were identified, factors that are sometimes incorporated into the verb and sometimes encoded in separate morphemes, depending on the language. The link between these semantic elements and the kinds of primitive meanings infants construct from viewing events was discussed, drawing heavily on Mandler (1992). The meanings infants create from observing events, in the form of image-schemas, are the necessary substrate for verb learning. That is, having discriminated notions like path and causality from the flux and flow of events, infants arrive at the doorstep of language learning prepared to determine how their particular language maps onto these primitives.

We introduced the developmental lexical principles framework (Golinkoff et al., 1994), which contains a set of six lexical principles originally created to explain the acquisition of object labels. This framework describes how young children acquire these principles (some new and some previously proposed in the literature, e.g., Clark, 1983a, 1983b) in two tiers, as a result of their experience with observing how words work. We expanded this framework to include verbs and discussed a number of ways in which these extensions can be put to empirical test.

Now that this exercise has been completed, an evaluation of our efforts is in order. The first question is: When these principles are reworked to include verbs, are they variants of the same principles or do they become different principles? The second question is whether the positing of a set of principles for word learning helps us to understand the process of word learning. In particular, does such an approach suggest new research?

Question 1. Do the Lexical Principles Originally Posited for the Learning of Object Labels Work for the Learning of Action Labels?
The answer is yes. For all the principles originally proposed, there was ready transfer to the learning of action labels. The principle of reference, for example, was originally formulated to include action labels. To learn verbs,

children must be willing to hook up actions with action names. Yet reference, as foundational as it is for word learning, is still too unconstrained a principle to permit rapid word learning. A principle of the second tier, N3C, builds on the basic insight behind reference and allows word learning to occur with ease. N3C states that novel names are mapped to unnamed referents. By the time the child has N3C, the child may be able to distinguish between novel names and novel words from other form classes (see Waxman & Kosowski, 1990, for a demonstration that at 25 months of age children respond differently to novel adjectives than to novel nouns in a label extension task). Thus, using linguistic and nonlinguistic information, the child can map novel action names to actions.

The basic insight of the principle of extendibility (i.e., a word can be used to label more than exemplars previously labeled for the child) was retained for verbs as was the basis for extension, namely, the shape or the overall gestalt of the main event. Just as the child operates with a kind of gross similarity metric for the earliest extension of object labels, the child uses the overall gestalt of the main event for the extension of action labels. However, focusing on only gross perceptual similarity does not allow the child to use the verb (or noun) correctly. As Pinker (1989) wrote, "verb meanings do not correspond to speakers' conceptual categories for kinds of events or states" (p. 107). Rather, to use verbs in the particular syntactic alternations (e.g., the dative) in which they may appear, the child must discern the components of a verb's semantic structure. By the time children have the principles of the second tier, they are much more sensitive to the syntax of their language than they were earlier, and they can use language like a zoom lens (Gleitman, 1990) to help them tease out a verb's semantic structure. Thus, categorical scope for verbs refines the basis for the extension of verbs in much the same way that categorical scope for nouns refines the basis for the extension of object labels.

The first part of the principle of object scope (i.e., a novel term applies to an object in a novel event) was allowed to stand. We posited that object scope helps children learn new verbs because if the objects involved in the event are already labeled, the child should try to attach the new term to the action before trying to attach it to anything else. Thus, we proposed a hierarchy of novel word assignment to word classes: object then action. The second part of object scope, which states that a novel object label applies to the whole object and not to its parts or attributes, was changed to action scope to accommodate verbs. That is, the child operates as if the verb labels a larger rather than a smaller aspect of the action. For both action and object labels, then, the child appears to be drawn to perceptual salience in attempting to form "hookups" between novel terms and their referents. If the child were not guided by salience, the number of hypotheses to be considered for the meaning of a new term (either noun or verb) would be enormous, as every tiny facet of an object or an event would be a potential referent for a new term.

In order to have some mechanism to allow children to correct their word learning errors and adopt canonical rather than idiosyncratic terms, Clark's (1983a, 1983b) principle of conventionality was incorporated into the developmental lexical principles framework. Conventionality works just as well for verbs as it does for nouns, encouraging the child to drop alternative words when conventional ones already exist.

Question 2. Does a Principles-Based Approach to Verb Learning Suggest New Research? The answer to this second question is also yes, and some of the early research this perspective has generated was reviewed in this chapter. There are at least four ways in which lexical principles motivate new kinds of studies of verb learning. First, by examining the acquisition of verbs through the lens of a principles approach, principles that were previously presupposed in the literature (such as reference and extendibility) become available for study. Second, as we reviewed each principle we made testable predictions about how it operates. For example, we claimed that object scope biased the child to interpret a novel label as the name for a novel object before they interpreted it as the name for the novel action in which the object was engaged. Third, we have claimed that children will function differently prior to the construction of a principle than after they have constructed it. This claim can best be evaluated in longitudinal research designs. The same child should function differently in the same word-learning situation before and after they have a particular principle. Mervis and Bertrand (1993) conducted such a study in the domain of noun learning, focusing on the N3C principle. They asked 32 children (age 1;4– 1;7) to indicate a known and an unknown object (e.g., "Is there a nup?"). All the children were able to select the known objects. However, only the children who had had a vocabulary spurt according to maternal report consistently selected the unknown object (this is evidence for the possession of the N3C principle). The two groups of children did not differ in age. Mervis and Bertrand monitored the vocabulary acquisition of the 16 children who had been unable to use the N3C principle. Once these children had attained a vocabulary spurt, they were retested using a different set of objects. This time, the children were successful at selecting the unknown objects and at extending the novel word to another appropriate referent. Last, research on how children derive the principles for word learning is an interesting research front in its own right.

To conclude, the answer to the two questions posed above is yes. It appears that lexical principles originally proposed for object labels do help explain the acquisition of action labels. The essence of each principle was retained despite a few changes in the formulation of some of the principles to accommodate the differences in word class. It also appears that these principles can spur us to consider a host of new research questions. Thus, the developmental lexical principles framework can serve as a heuristic for researchers interested in addressing the next hurdle in language acquisition, namely, verb learning.

ACKNOWLEDGMENTS

We wish to thank the editors of this volume for their very helpful comments on this chapter and Lois Bloom and Lila Gleitman for valuable discussions of these issues. The research conducted by Golinkoff and Hirsh-Pasek was supported by grants to them from NICHD (HD19568, 5964); to Golinkoff from the John Guggenheim Memorial Foundation, the James McKeen Cattell Sabbatical Fund, the University of Delaware Biomedical Funds, and a UDRF grant from the University of Delaware; and to Hirsh-Pasek from the Pew Foundation and Temple University Biomedical Funds. Mervis was supported by a grant from NICHD (HD27042).

REFERENCES

Aslin, R. N. (1992). Segmentation of fluent speech into words: Learning models and the role of maternal input. In B. de Boysson-Bardies, S. Schonen, P. Jusczyk, P. MacNeilage, & J. Morton (Eds.), *Developmental neurocognition: Speech and face processing in the first year of life* (pp. 305–316). Dordrecht: Kluwer Academic Publishers.

Baillargeon, R. (1993). The object concept revisited: New directions. In C. E. Granrud (Ed.), *Visual perception and cognition in infancy: Carnegie Mellon symposia on cognition.* Hillsdale, NJ: Lawrence Erlbaum Associates.

Baldwin, D. A., & Markman, E. M. (1989). Establishing word-object relations: A first step. *Child Development, 60,* 381–389.

Behrend, D. A. (1990). Constraints and development: A reply to Nelson (1988). *Cognitive Development, 5,* 313–330.

Benedict, H. (1979). Early lexical development: Comprehension and production. *Journal of Child Language, 6,* 183–200.

Bloom, L. (1978). *The semantics of verbs in child language.* Paper presented at the meeting of the Eastern Psychological Association, New York.

Bloom, L. (1993, Winter). Word learning. *SRCD Newsletter,* pp. 1, 9, 13.

Bloom, L. (in press). Meaning and expression. In W. Overton (Ed.), *The nature and ontogenesis of meaning.* Norwood, NJ: Ablex.

Bloom, L., Lightbown, P., & Hood, L. (1975). Structure and variation in child language. *Monographs of the Society for Research in Child Development, 40* (2, Serial No. 160).

Bloom, L., Tinker, E., & Margulis, C. (in press). The words children learn. *Cognitive Development.*

Brown, R. (1958). *Words and things.* Glencoe, IL: The Free Press.

Carey, S. (1978). The child is a word learner. In M. Halle, J. Bresnan, & G. Miller (Eds.), *Linguistic theory and psychological reality* (pp. 264–293). Cambridge, MA: MIT Press.

Carey, S., & Bartlett, E. (1978). Acquiring a single new word. *Papers and Reports on Child Language Development, 15,* 17–29.

Cassidy, K. W., & Kelly, M. H. (1991). Phonological information for grammatical category assignments. *Journal of Memory and Language, 30,* 348–369.

Choi, S., & Bowerman, M. (1992). Learning to express motion events in English and Korean: The influence of language specific lexicalization patterns. In B. Levin & S. Pinker (Eds.), *Lexical and conceptual semantics* (pp. 83–121). Cambridge, MA: Blackwell.

Chomsky, N. (1981). *Lectures on government and binding.* Dordrecht: Foris.

Clark, E. V. (1983a). Convention and contrast in acquiring the lexicon. In T. B. Seiler & W. Wannenmacher (Eds.), *Concept development and the development of word meaning* (pp. 67–89). Berlin: Springer-Verlag.

Clark, E. V. (1983b). Meanings and concepts. In J. H. Flavell & E. M. Markman (Eds.), *Handbook of child psychology: Vol. III. Cognitive development* (pp. 787–840). (Gen. ed. P. Mussen). New York: Wiley.

Clark, E. V. (1988). On the logic of contrast. *Journal of Child Language, 15,* 317–337.

Cohen, L. B., & Oakes, L. M. (1973). How infants perceive a simple causal event. *Developmental Psychology, 29,* 421–433.

Dromi, E. (1987). *Early lexical development.* Cambridge, England: Cambridge University Press.

Echols, C. H. (1991, April). *Infants' attention to objects and consistency in linguistic and non-linguistic contexts.* Paper presented at the Biennial Meetings of the Society for Research in Child Development, Seattle.

Echols, C. H. (1992, May). *Developmental changes in attention to labeled events during the transition to language.* Paper presented at the International Conference on Infancy Studies, Miami, FL.

Fernald, A., & Mazzie, C. (1991). Prosody and focus in speech to infants and adults. *Developmental Psychology, 27,* 209–221.

Fisher, C., Hall, G., Rakowitz, S., & Gleitman, L. R. (1994). When it is better to receive than to give: Syntactic and conceptual constraints on vocabulary growth. *Lingua, 92,* 333–375.

Forbes, J. N., & Farrar, M. J. (1993). Children's initial assumptions about the meaning of novel motion verbs: Biased and conservative? *Cognitive Development, 8,* 273–290.

Frawley, W. (1992). *Linguistic semantics.* Hillsdale, NJ: Lawrence Erlbaum Associates.

Gentner, D. (1978). On relational meaning: The acquisition of verb meaning. *Child Development, 49,* 988–998.

Gentner, D. (1981). Some interesting differences between verbs and nouns. *Cognition and Brain Theory, 4,* 161–178.

Gentner, D. (1982). Why nouns are learned before verbs: Linguistic relativity versus natural partitioning. In S. A. Kuczaj, II (Ed.), *Language development: Vol. 2. Language, thought, and culture.* Hillsdale, NJ: Lawrence Erlbaum Associates.

Gentner, D. (1988, October). *Cognitive and linguistic determinism: Object reference and relational reference.* Paper presented at the Boston University Conference on Language Development, Boston, MA.

Glass, A. L., Holyoak, K. J., & Santa, J. L. (1979). *Cognition.* Reading, MA: Addison-Wesley.

Gleitman, L. (1990). Structural sources of verb meaning. *Language Acquisition, 1,* 3–55.

Golinkoff, R. M. (1975). Semantic development in infants: The concepts of agent and recipient. *Merrill-Palmer Quarterly, 21,* 181–193.

Golinkoff, R. M. (1981). The case for semantic relations: Evidence from the verbal and nonverbal domains. *Journal of Child Language, 78,* 413–438.

Golinkoff, R. M., Diznoff, J., Yasik, A., & Hirsh-Pasek, K. (1992, May). *How children identify nouns versus verbs.* Paper presented at the International Conference on Infant Studies, Miami, FL.

Golinkoff, R. M., Hirsh-Pasek, K., Bailey, L., & Wenger, N. (1992). Young children and adults use lexical principles to learn new nouns. *Developmental Psychology, 28,* 99–108.

Golinkoff, R. M., Hirsh-Pasek, K., Cauley, K. M., & Gordon, L. (1987). The eyes have it: Lexical and syntactic comprehension in a new paradigm. *Journal of Child Language, 14*, 23–46.

Golinkoff, R. M., Jacquet, R., & Hirsh-Pasek, K. (1993). *Lexical principles underlie verb learning.* Unpublished manuscript.

Golinkoff, R. M., & Kerr, J. L. (1978). Infants' perceptions of semantically defined action role changes in filmed events. *Merrill-Palmer Quarterly, 24*, 53–61.

Golinkoff, R. M., Mennuti, T., Lengle, C., & Hermon, G. (1992, May). *Is "glorpy" a noun or an adjective?: Identifying the part of speech of a novel word.* Paper presented at the International Conference on Infant Studies, Miami, FL.

Golinkoff, R. M., Mervis, C., & Hirsh-Pasek, K. (1994). Early object labels: The case for lexical principles. *Journal of Child Language, 21*, 125–155.

Golinkoff, R. M., Shuff-Bailey, M., Olguin, R., & Ruan, W. (1993). *Young children extend novel words at the basic level: Evidence for the principle of categorical scope.* Unpublished manuscript.

Harris, M. B., Barrett, M., Jones, D., & Brookes, S. (1988). Linguistic input and early word mappings. *Journal of Child Language, 15*, 77–94.

Hirsh-Pasek, K., & Golinkoff, R. M. (1991). Language comprehension: A new look at some old themes. In N. Krasnegor, D. Rumbaugh, M. Studdert-Kennedy, & R. Schiefelbusch (Eds.), *Biological and behavioral aspects of language acquisition* (pp. 301–320). Hillsdale, NJ: Lawrence Erlbaum Associates.

Hirsh-Pasek, K., & Golinkoff, R. M. (1993). Skeletal supports for grammatical learning: What the infant brings to the language learning task. In C. K. Rovee-Collier & L. P. Lipsitt (Eds.), *Advances in infancy research* (Vol. 8, pp. 299–338). Norwood, NJ: Ablex.

Hirsh-Pasek, K., & Golinkoff, R. M. (1994). *The origins of grammar: Evidence from early language comprehension.* Unpublished manuscript, Temple University, Philadelphia.

Hirsh-Pasek, K., Naigles, L., Golinkoff, R. M., Gleitman, L. R., & Gleitman, H. (1988, October). *Syntactic bootstrapping: Evidence from comprehension.* Paper presented at the Boston University Conference on Language Development, Boston, MA.

Huttenlocher, J., Smiley, P., & Charney, R. (1983). Emergence of action categories in the child: Evidence from verb meanings. *Psychological Review, 90*, 72–93.

Jackendoff, R. (1983). *Semantics and cognition.* Cambridge, MA: MIT Press.

Jackendoff, R. S. (1990). *Semantic structures.* Cambridge, MA: MIT Press.

Johnson, M. (1987). *The body in the mind: The bodily basis of meaning, imagination, and reasoning.* Chicago: University of Chicago Press.

Karmiloff-Smith, A. (1992). *Beyond modularity: A developmental perspective on cognitive science.* Cambridge, MA: MIT Press.

Lakoff, G. (1987). *Women, fire, and dangerous things: What categories reveal about the mind.* Chicago: University of Chicago Press.

Landau, B., & Gleitman, L. R. (1985). *Language and experience.* Cambridge, MA: Harvard University Press.

Landau, B., Smith, L. B., & Jones, S. S. (1988). The importance of shape in early lexical learning. *Cognitive Development, 3*, 299–321.

Leslie, A. (1982). The perception of causality in infants. *Perception, 11*, 173–186.

Leslie, A. (1988). The necessity of illusion: Perception and thought in infancy. In L. Weiskrantz (Ed.), *Thought without language* (pp. 185–210). Oxford, England: Clarendon.

Lieberman, P. (1991). *Uniquely human.* Cambridge, MA: Harvard University Press.

Macnamara, J. (1982). *Names for things.* Cambridge, MA: MIT Press.

Mandler, J. M. (1992). How to build a baby: II. Conceptual primitives. *Psychological Review, 99*, 587–604.

Maratsos, M. (1991). How the acquisition of nouns may be different from that of verbs. In A. Krasnegor, D. M. Rumbaugh, R. L. Schiefelbusch, & M. Studdert-Kennedy (Eds.), *Biological and behavioral determinants of language development* (pp. 67–88). Hillsdale, NJ: Lawrence Erlbaum Associates.

Markman, E. M. (1989). *Categorization and naming in children.* Cambridge, MA: MIT Press.

Markman, E. M., & Hutchinson, J. E. (1984). Children's sensitivity to constraints on word meaning: Taxonomic vs. thematic relations. *Cognitive Psychology, 16,* 1–27.

Merriman, W. E., & Bowman, L. (1989). The mutual exclusivity bias in children's word learning. *Monographs of the Society for Research in Child Development, 54*(3–4, Serial No. 220).

Mervis, C. B. (1983). Acquisition of a lexicon. *Contemporary Educational Psychology, 8,* 210–236.

Mervis, C. B. (1990). Early conceptual development of children with Down syndrome. In D. Ciochetti & M. Beeghly (Eds.), *Children with Down syndrome: A developmental perspective* (pp. 252–301). Cambridge, England: Cambridge University Press.

Mervis, C. M., & Bertrand, J. (1993). Acquisition of early object labels: The roles of operating principles and input. In A. P. Kaiser & D. B. Gray (Eds.), *Enhancing children's communication: Research foundations for interventions* (Vol. 2, pp. 287–316). Baltimore, MD: Brookes.

Naigles, L. (1990). Children use syntax to learn verb meanings. *Journal of Child Language, 17,* 357–374.

Nelson, K. (1973). Structure and strategy in learning to talk. *Monographs of the Society for Research in Child Development, 38*(1–2, Serial No. 149).

Nelson, K. (1988). Constraints on word learning? *Cognitive Development, 3,* 221–246.

Nelson, K., Hampson, J., & Shaw, L. (1993). Nouns in early lexicons: Evidence, explanations and implications. *Journal of Child Language, 20,* 61–84.

Petitto, L. (1992). Modularity and constraints in early lexical acquisition: Evidence from children's early language and gesture. In M. R. Gunnar & M. Maratsos (Eds.), *Modularity and constraints in language and cognition: The Minnesota Symposia on Child Psychology* (Vol. 25, pp. 25–58). Hillsdale, NJ: Lawrence Erlbaum Associates.

Pinker, S. (1989). *Learnability and cognition: The acquisition of argument structure.* Cambridge, MA: MIT Press.

Pinker, S. (in press). How could a child use verb syntax to learn verb semantics? *Lingua.*

Quine, W. V. O. (1960). *Word and object.* Cambridge, England: Cambridge University Press.

Roberts, K., & Jacob, M. (1992). Linguistic versus attentional influences on nonlinguistic categorization in 15-month-old infants. *Cognitive Development, 6,* 355–375.

Rosch, E., Mervis, C. B., Gray, W. D., Johnson, D. M., & Boyes-Braem, P. (1976). Basic objects in natural categories. *Cognitive Psychology, 8,* 382–439.

Smith, C. A., & Sachs, J. (1990). Cognition and the verb lexicon in early lexical development. *Applied Psycholinguistics, 11,* 409–424.

Soken, N. H., & Pick, A. D. (1992). Intermodal perception of happy and angry expressive behaviors by seven-month-old infants. *Child Development, 63,* 787–795.

Spelke, E. S. (1990). Principles of object perception. *Cognitive Science, 14,* 29–56.

Talmy, L. (1985). Lexicalization patterns: Semantic structure in lexical forms. In T. Shopen (Ed.), *Language typology and syntactic description: Vol. III. Grammatical categories and the lexicon.* New York: Cambridge University Press.

Talmy, L. (1988). Force dynamics in language and cognition. *Cognitive Science, 12,* 49–100.

Taylor, M., & Gelman, S. A. (1988). Adjectives and nouns: Children's strategies for learning new words. *Child Development, 59,* 411–419.

Tomasello, M. (1992). *First verbs: A case study of early grammatical development.* Cambridge, England: Cambridge University Press.

Tomasello, M., & Kruger, A. C. (1992). Joint attention on actions: Acquiring verbs in ostensive and non-ostensive contexts. *Journal of Child Language, 19,* 311–333.

Valian, V. (1986). Syntactic categories in the speech of young children. *Developmental Psychology, 22,* 562–579.

Wason, P. C., & Johnson-Laird, P. N. (1972). *Psychology of reasoning.* Cambridge, MA: Harvard University Press.

Waxman, S. R. (1989). Linking language and conceptual development: Linguistic cues and the construction of conceptual hierarchies. *The Genetic Epistemologist, XVII,* 13–20.

Waxman, S. R., & Balaban, M. T. (1992, May). *The influence of words vs. tones on 9-month-old infants' object categorization.* Paper presented at the International Conference on Infant Studies, Miami, FL.

Waxman, S. R., & Kosowski, T. D. (1990). Nouns mark category relations: Toddlers' and preschoolers' word-learning biases. *Child Development, 61,* 1461–1490.

Xu, F. (1991), *A hierarchy of preferences in the fast mapping of word learning.* Unpublished manuscript.

CHAPTER EIGHT

The Dual Category Problem in the Acquisition of Action Words

Katherine Nelson

City University of New York Graduate Center

The acquisition of verbs requires that children engage in both a semantic and a syntactic analysis of forms used in discourse. The grammatical category problem has been viewed from both directions, and it is probably fair to say that the current consensus is that children must engage in a semantic analysis, proposing as an initial hypothesis that verbs are forms denoting actions (Bates & MacWhinney, 1989; Pinker, 1984). This proposal can be tested in terms of forms that refer to actions but that may be used as either noun or verb in sentences in ordinary discourse. If the child encounters action words used in sentence positions reserved for nouns and with noun syntax the child's hypothesis that action = verb is contradicted. It is an important fact of English grammar that many such verbs exist, including a large number that very young children hear, learn, know, and use. How the child handles such data is the question explored here.

In this chapter I first document the facts about these verb/nouns and then report on the use of some of the problematic types by parents and by young children. I conclude with a discussion of the implications of these findings for understanding children's acquisition of meanings and grammatical categories.

THE VERB/NOUN PROBLEM

Most discussions of lexical assignment to grammatical category proceed as though the issue were straightforward: Words for objects are assigned to the noun class, those for actions to the verb class, and these assignments are then generalized to less clear cases on the basis of both semantic and syntactic characteristics. But action words that can be either verb or noun may pose difficult problems for the child and hence for the theory. This general problem has received almost no focused discussion in the literature.

As is well known, English is a language in which grammatical relations are primarily realized through word order rather than through grammatical particles identifying the role of words in sentences. But verb morphology indicating tense and aspect and agreement with the subject person and number may provide a key to the identification of a verb in an otherwise ambiguous string. For example:

(1) John is calling to Daddy
(2) John calls to Daddy
(3) They call to Daddy
(4) John's call to Daddy

Here, -*ing* indicates that the first use is a verb and -*s* that the second *call*[1] is a verb, whereas the possessive -*s* on *John* indicates that the fourth use is a noun. Although the citation form *call* is the same for both noun (4) and verb (3), position in the sentence and verb morphology generally serve to differentiate the two uses. However, there are also many instances, as in (3) and (4), in which there is no difference between a noun form and a verb form in actual utterances. This occurs in both imperative ("Call daddy") and question constructions ("D'you wanta call Daddy?") with the verb form, which is the same as the noun in "Give Daddy a call." For an adult, of course, *call* is not ambiguous but is recognizable by the structure of the sentence. The question is whether the same is true for a child beginning to acquire syntax and semantics simultaneously.

The standard assumption in theories of children's word acquisition is that one word has one meaning; the child's problem is to identify that meaning on the basis of reference. In the case of forms that are both verb and noun, there may be one meaning (e.g., referring to an action), disjoint meanings (e.g., referring to an object and an action), or some overlap. These possibilities are considered in more detail later in this chapter. The point here is that the standard assumption is not justified for a large class of words that children learn and use.

Standard assumptions also include the recognition that reference may be ambiguous, and a means of resolving ambiguity has been attributed to the child in the form of principles. In particular, children are held to favor object reference when hearing a new word (Markman, 1989). In a related discussion,

---

[1]Citation forms of the words are italicized; quotations or examples are given in quotation marks.

Gentner (1982, 1988) provides an extensive analysis of why children may learn nouns rather than verbs in early language. A brief consideration of this claim is relevant here because it implies that children prefer (all?) nouns over verbs; thus, words that could be either might be assigned a noun function.

Gentner (1988) invoked three types of simplicity to support the claim that nouns are simpler than verbs and thus easier for the child to learn. These are:

1. Nouns are less conceptually opaque. This seems to be true (to the extent that intuitions are reliable) for object and person classes but not necessarily for other types of common nouns. For example, is *kiss* as a noun less opaque than *kiss* as a verb? Is the concept *morning* less opaque than the concept *jump*?

2. Nouns are less polysemic than verbs. This claim is based on the fact that dictionaries tend to list many more meanings for verbs than nouns (Gentner, 1988). However, when a word has both noun and verb forms, the noun may be just as or even more polysemous than the verb; *kiss*, for example, has three meanings for the noun and two for the verb in Webster's (1974) *New World Dictionary* (see other examples following). It seems that the claim that nouns are less polysemic than verbs applies only, if at all, to the prototypic object, animal, and people names and to prototypical verbs. Polysemy that crosses word class divisions may be particularly troublesome for the child who is trying to acquire semantics and grammar at the same time.

3. Nouns are less "linguistically defined" than verbs (Gentner, 1988). According to this proposal, verbs conflate different aspects of a scene in different languages: English conflates the manner of motion with the verb (e.g., "floating") whereas Spanish conflates the direction, leaving manner to be specified separately. In contrast to these differences in the aspects of the observable world that are incorporated into verb meanings in different languages, nouns are not so linguistically dependent, according to Gentner (1982): "Any language is overwhelmingly likely to parse the perceptual bits that we refer to as 'bottle' into one cohesive object . . . a language is constrained by the nature of the perceptual world to make coherent lexicalizations of objects. . . . This fixity does not obtain for verbs" (p. 323). Of course, this observation applies only to nouns that refer to objects. Noun forms of dual category words may be just as linguistically variable as the verb forms.

These considerations support the conclusion that nouns are simpler than verbs, but only if the claim applies primarily to first-order nouns (Lyons, 1977) that are names of object, person, and animal classes and not to the wide class of words that can play noun roles. In particular, they do not apply to forms that denote actions or events in both noun and verb functions. Therefore we would not expect them to influence whether a child learns an action word as noun, verb, neither, or both.

FREQUENCY OF DUAL CATEGORIES

The relative frequency of nouns, verbs, and dual category terms in the language that children hear might be expected to influence the child's assignment of category. If children do not hear dual category words used—if parents avoid using ambiguous forms or use them only in one categorical function—then the existence of such forms in the adult language would not be a problem for child learners. Nelson, Hampson, and Kessler Shaw (1992) analyzed the nouns in children's early (20-month) vocabulary, focusing on those nouns that were not used to reference basic concrete object classes. In the course of this analysis, based on a vocabulary checklist completed by parents (Bates, Bretherton, Shore, & Snyder, 1984), it was discovered that most of the words categorized as verbs (or action words) can also be used as nouns. Specifically, of 101 verbs listed under the heading "actions, activities, games, and verbs," 70 (70%) also have noun meanings. Some of the meanings are the same for both verb and noun (e.g., *kiss*), others are essentially homonyms (e.g., *park*), and some of the noun uses are probably not familiar to young children (e.g., *play, finish*). (A few words primarily used in noun form in reference to objects, such as *button*, can also be used as action verbs, but they were not the focus of this analysis.) A large number of these words appeared to be familiar in both forms in everyday parent–child talk, and they were included in the analysis of children's learning of nouns on the basis of evidence in the transcripts of parent–child talk that they were used as such by parents.

Among the words identified in that study were six verbs chosen as the focus of the analyses in the later sections of this chapter: *call, drink, help, hug, kiss,* and *walk*. An important characteristic of these particular verbs is that their noun forms do not refer to concrete objects, whereas other verb/nouns do refer in their noun form to objects (e.g., *button, comb*). Thus, if actions imply verbs and objects imply nouns in early language acquisition, the words considered here should be categorized as verbs in the child language. Are they?

Recognition of this problem raises the question of how pervasive and general it is and whether children experience it as a problem. Several attempts to assess these issues are reported here. They involve frequency in the adult language, salience of categorical assignment for adults, maternal uses of these forms, child uses, and discourse constraints. Each of these is considered in turn.

Frequency of Dual Categories in Adult English

Many writers have described the child's problem in acquiring grammar as similar to the linguist's in discovering the structure of the grammar of a particular language. If we take the analogous stance of the child as a budding lexicographer, one who is attempting to tease out the meanings of words by observing their uses in discourse, we discover that the child faces many ambiguities in assigning words to word classes. As one lexicographer has outlined the problems for English:

> parts of speech can seldom be recognized by formal appearance. . . . Consider a shape like *out*. It is a preposition in *out the window*, a noun in *the catcher made an out*, a verb in *truth will out*, an adjective in the *batter is out*, probably an adverb in *carried out to sea*, and like almost all words, it can be used as an interjection. That is, *out* as form can be almost anything; one can determine its part of speech only on the basis of use, and even this device has limits. . . . Consider 'They went walking'; . . . is *walking* a noun, some sort of complement? If we now add a phrase so that the sentence becomes 'They went walking down the highway,' the word that formerly looked verbal or nominal seems to be some sort of modifier, although whether adjectival or adverbial might pose a good question." (Laird, 1974, p. xxviii)

If children encounter words that can be either verbs or nouns and base their categorical decisions on probability, do they assign these words as nouns or verbs? It is often stated (following Gentner's [1982] analysis) that the preponderance of nouns in early vocabularies cannot be accounted for in terms of their frequency in the language. Gentner's (1982) explanation of the preponderance of nouns in child language, specifically the claim that nouns are simpler than verbs, was motivated in part by this observation. Indeed, if one counts tokens in spoken language, nouns are not a great deal more frequent than verbs; this is to be expected, given that sentences are constructed in terms of verb-argument structures in which the verb-to-noun phrase ratio ranges from 1:1 to 1:3, with pronouns or complex noun phrases (including gerunds and nominal clauses) rather than common nouns very frequently serving in the NP role.

Frequency of Types. If we consider types rather than tokens, it is clear that there are many more nouns than verbs in the adult language as well as in the child language. In the analysis of children's vocabularies based on the checklist we found 70% of the words were nouns and 19% were verbs, a ratio of about 3.5:1 (Nelson et al., 1992). By 20 months, according to mothers' documentation of children's vocabularies, children had learned more of the nouns (about 30%) than the verbs (about 25%), making the ratio of nouns learned to verbs learned 4:1.

How does this compare with the ratio in adult language? To determine the relative frequency of nouns and verbs and of dual category forms in the language as a whole, dictionary entries were sampled.[2] Approximately 1 out of every 30 pages (i.e., approximately 1 out of every 30 entries) were sampled. All noun entries on each sampled page were tabulated, with the exceptions that proper nouns, simple variants of a single form, and types that were simple derivations of verb types such as those constructed from -ity or -tion (unless the resulting form was a common form with a clear and distinct meaning) were eliminated. The result of these exclusions was a conservative count of nouns. All verbs were counted without exception. If a single citation form was listed as both noun and verb it was counted separately, and forms were distinguished as to whether they were given as nouns first or as verbs first, an indication of the basic form from which the other derived.

In this count there were a total of 1,059 nouns and 270 verbs, for a ratio of about 4:1, about the same as that in the child language count noted previously. However, it is of considerable interest that 11% of all entries were dual category (12% of all forms, i.e., Ns, Vs, N/V, and V/N). Over half of the verbs (53%) were cited also as nouns, and most (64%) of these were secondary to nouns. In comparison to the 53% of verb forms that were also nouns, only 14% of the cited nouns were also cited as verbs, and almost two thirds of these were cited as nouns first. When forms that are cited only as nouns or only as verbs were considered, the ratio of noun to verb is far higher than for the total sample—about 7 to 1—and much higher than most estimates of child language.

Thus it seems clear that noun types strongly predominate over verb types in the adult English language, to a larger extent even than they do in child language. It must be noted that this is primarily because many very complex and abstract entities are realized as nouns in the adult language. The common object names so prevalent in early child language are a very small proportion of the nouns cited in the count reported here. As has been pointed out previously, however, common object names are not the majority even for the 211 nouns among the 500 most common words in English; fewer than 50% of these common nouns are concrete object names (Nelson, 1991). The words examined in this chapter are thus representative of frequently encountered nouns and verbs.

DEFINITIONS AND SENTENCE USES OF FOCAL WORDS

The surveys just described suggested that children hear and learn many of these grammatically ambiguous words. Further analyses were designed to

---

[2]Both Webster's *New World Dictionary of the American Language* (1974; see Laird, 1974) and Webster's *Ninth New Collegiate Dictionary* (1984) were used for this purpose.

discover whether individual words have one dominant form or use in discourse, which could simplify the child's assignment problem.

Dictionary Definitions

Dictionary definitions from Webster's (1974) *New World Dictionary* were checked for the six terms examined here. In all cases, the verb meanings were given first, and all terms were polysemous to a greater or lesser degree in both noun and verb forms. The major meanings and degree of polysemy for all terms are summarized as follows.

Call. There are two main entries for *call* as an intransitive verb with six subentries for the first meaning (variations on "to speak in a loud distinct voice"), two main entries for the transitive verb with numerous subentries, and 11 combining forms (e.g., *call forth, call it a day* and *call it quits*). There are 10 entries for *call* as a noun (beginning with "an act of calling"), and six of the meanings are directly related to the verb forms. This word is thus homonymous between noun and verb but also polysemous within each grammatical type; some of these meanings overlap, and others do not.

Drink. The primary meaning of the transitive verb is "to take (liquid) into the mouth and swallow it"; the verb also has an intransitive corollary. *Drink* has a total of nine specific verb senses and four related senses of the noun form.

Help. There are four major transitive verb meanings (with minor differentiations) for this word, two intransitive meanings, and three noun meanings. The primary meaning, "to make things easier or better for (a person); aid; assist" was close to the definitions given by adults (see section following). Both the verb and noun meanings of *help* are more abstract and general than for the other words examined here.

Hug. This word also has transitive (4) and intransitive (1) verb meanings followed by the noun meaning (3). The primary meaning is given as "to put the arms around and hold closely"; the noun is specified as "a close, affectionate embrace."

Kiss. The first meaning for the transitive verb is defined in terms of the noun (the third meaning): "to give a kiss to (a person or thing)." The noun is defined as "a touch or caress with the lips."

Walk. This is the most definitionally complex of the words considered here. There are (in order) 7 definitions for the intransitive verb, 8 for the transitive verb, and 16 for the noun. The first definition, "To go along or move about on foot at a moderate pace," is followed by specifications of the action. The noun is defined first as "the act of walking" and second as "a period or course of walking."

Dictionary definitions have confirmed that all of these words are polysemous as both verbs and nouns, and all have some overlapping meanings as nouns and verbs. All are given priority as verbs.

Adult Definitions and Sentences
Using Ambiguous Words

To explore the dominance of form class of the words in focus for ordinary speakers, I carried out a small survey of their use in sentences and definitions. Eleven graduate students in psychology and philosophy, with no special background in child language or linguistics, responded in class to the request for sentences and definitions using the terms in question. Two additional words were included on the list as distractors—*pet* and *food*. It was assumed (incorrectly) that *pet* would be interpreted as a noun referring to a category of animals, and correctly that *food* would be interpreted as a superordinate. Students first wrote sentences containing each word (in the following order: *call, help, pet, drink, food, walk, kiss, hug*) in response to the brief instructions: "On this sheet write a short sentence using each of the following words."

After completing this task they were given a second sheet with the same words in the same order and asked to give definitions following the instructions:

> Please write in the spaces below the best concise definition you can for each of the words listed. If more than one definition occurs to you, record each in the order in which it occurred. The form of the definitions is not the focus of this analysis; record any information that seems critical to you regarding the meaning of the term in common usage. You should take no more than one to two minutes for each definition.

Sentences and definitions were collected from all participants.

The results of the sentence task verified that each of the words was viewed as either a noun or verb, although they varied considerably in the degree of bias toward one or the other form. For example, *call* elicited nine sentences using it as a verb and two as a noun, whereas the reverse was true for *help* (see Table 8.1). *Call* and *drink* were used primarily as verbs, *help* and *hug* were used predominately as nouns, and *kiss* and *walk* elicited each about equally. There does not seem to be any obvious explanation for this result.

The column "Inflected V" in Table 8.1 shows that all but 5 of the 32 verb uses in these sentences were in their citation forms, without inflections, a surprising result given the assumption that verb morphology is a useful

TABLE 8.1
Forms Used in Sentences (N = 11)

	Verb	Inflected V	Noun
Call	9	1	2
Drink	9	1	2
Help	2	0	9
Hug	2	1	9
Kiss	6	1	5
Walk	4	1	7

guide to verb class. None of these words used as a noun carried any inflection (plural or possessive) although with the exception of *call* and *help* they were almost invariably used with *a*.

Definitions given by these subjects varied more in terms of referring to either verb or noun, as shown in Table 8.2. Because on this task many subjects gave two or more definitions for each word, the numbers are in terms of definitions, not subjects. Because more than one meaning is available within a form class, especially for *call, drive*, and *walk*, numbers may exceed the total number of subjects within a cell.

It can be seen from Table 8.2 that the patterns do not map directly from definitions to sentences. On this task *help, hug*, and *kiss* drew equal numbers of both types, whereas *call* and *walk* elicited more verbal definitions. Note particularly the discrepant asymmetry for *drink*, which elicited almost twice as many noun definitions, although it was predominately used as a verb in sentences.

Both tasks revealed that adults have readily available both noun and verb forms for the words under examination here and that the verbs are used in sentences in their citation (i.e., non-inflected) form. That is, if these results are indicative of common uses, children may hear the words used in both grammatical contexts in the same form. Neither the dictionary survey nor this adult use survey suggested that the words in question have one dominant grammatical function.

TABLE 8.2
Definitions by Form Class (N = 11)

	Verb	Noun
Call	17	3
Drink	7	13
Help	9	8
Hug	7	7
Kiss	6	5
Walk	11	6

IMPLICATIONS FOR CHILD LANGUAGE LEARNING

What are the implications of the findings described thus far for verb learning? The most striking result of the survey of dictionary form types is that over half of the verbs sampled share their citation form with a related noun. This fact has not been widely recognized as a problem for children learning the language, and it may be thought that it does not apply particularly to child language. As noted previously, however, the great majority of the action verbs surveyed by Nelson et al. (1992) could also be used as nouns. Some of these referred to both action and object, as, for example, *hammer, brush,* or *bump* or to different entities entirely, as, for example, *park* (the car) and (walk in the) *park.* Others refer to action or the result of action in both noun and verb forms: *cut,* (diaper) *change, ride, drive.* It is the latter class of verbs that may theoretically pose the most problems for children beginning to acquire the semantics and syntax of their language. Before considering evidence from language in use by parents and children, let us speculate further as to how children might solve the problem posed by these words, according to some current theoretical assumptions.

1. (a) One clear prediction made by most theorists is the one form/one function principle that is claimed to be used by children in acquiring both lexicon and grammar (Clark, 1987; Pinker, 1984; Slobin, 1973). According to this principle, a given word should be assigned as either a noun or a verb but not both and should be given one distinct meaning. (b) Alternatively, if for some reason the child recognizes a distinction between the forms (e.g., on the basis of use in different discourse contexts), the child might assign the form to two classes with distinctive reference. That is, the forms would somehow be viewed as distinct, possibly on the basis of their morphology.

2. The prediction from semantic bootstrapping (Bates & MacWhinney, 1989; Pinker, 1984) and related hypotheses would be that the child assigns these words as verbs on the basis of their action reference. Recognizing the centrality of verbs to grammar and sentence construction as well as the semantics of actions, children should be disposed to assign words that can be used in reference to action preferentially as verbs.

3. (a) The prediction from syntactic bootstrapping (Landau & Gleitman, 1985) and related positions would depend upon the salience of morphological and function markers in parental speech. Thus, one issue raised is how frequent and salient verb marking is on these forms in parental speech to children. (b) Alternatively, if children have identified the noun class and recognized its typical determiner marking (*a, the*) early in the second year (see Macnamara, 1982), then these grammatical functors might be more salient to children and thus lead to the classification of the words as nouns.

4. (a) If (all) nouns are simpler than verbs (Gentner, 1982; see previous discussion) then children should assign words preferentially as nouns. (b) In contrast, if they have recognized the object–noun relation, they might avoid assigning any nonobject word to the noun class in early language.[3]

5. The simplest hypothesis is that children always follow the frequency of use in parental language, using words as verbs or nouns depending on the predominant use by parents.

Although the preponderance of current thinking seems to support the expectation that children should assign these anomalous forms as verbs, not nouns, there are also reasons (1b, 3b, 4a, 5) to support the prediction that they might assign them as nouns. In addition, it is possible that there are differences among the words in their assignments, and these need to be explained.

Different Verb/Noun Types

One clear difference among the terms is in the type of reference involved in the noun use. A common type of dual category is the action/object type. This type was the focus of Macnamara's (1982) analysis.

Macnamara's Analysis. Macnamara (1982) considered the problem of words that were used as both noun and verb, and in this connection he reported his son Kieran's uses of terms for both action and object. On one occasion he taught Kieran (at 17;27) a new word (*comb*) in an action-object context and found that Kieran used the word for both object and action. However, this was unusual. In general Kieran kept action words and object words separate. He had difficulty, for example, shifting the word *shave* from his first use for a razor to the action of shaving. When the action and object were not associated in an event, however, the same word was readily learned for both (see the discussion of *bite* in a later section).

Macnamara further analyzed uses by Sarah (Brown, 1973) of words that could be both noun or verb and reported, "In no case was there any evidence of her adopting adult flexibility—using the same word of an object and of an activity—before the 30th session when she was almost 2½ years old" (p. 125). Although Macnamara refers to adult flexibility in terms of the use of the same words as both noun and verb, he obscures the fact that for many of the dual-category words in Sarah's vocabulary the noun actually denotes an action or an event and not an object (e.g., *dance, ride, walk*).

On the basis of his analysis of his son's vocabulary, Macnamara concluded that "noun" is "inductively based on the concept object word—object being

---

[3]This hypothesis, however, is not supported by the data presented in Nelson et al. (1992).

that which calls for a sortal term" (p. 126). However, lists of his son Kieran's "common names" (i.e., nouns) include terms such as *bath, name, noise,* and *work,* which are clearly not objects by his own definition ("things you can pick up or bump into" (p. viii). Moreover, in this listing of Kieran's early vocabulary there is another category, "action descriptions," which includes words such as *drink* and *rain.* Macnamara notes with respect to *rain* that he cannot tell whether Kieran used it to refer to both the action and the "object" (sic). Did Kieran ever apply the word *drink* in contexts where "I want a drink" would be the correct gloss, thus suggesting that it should fall into the "common name" category? Single word usage makes these kinds of assignments fundamentally ambiguous. Furthermore, the words listed imply that the conclusion that nouns refer to sortals is more circular than Macnamara apparently recognized. It is not obvious that sortals include events, auditory stimuli, activities, abstract entities, or substances, as those cited did, except by some further act of stipulation.

More important in the present context is the problem that words that are used interchangeably as nouns and verbs referring to the same action or used interchangeably within the same event present the child with a difficult semantic/syntactic problem with multiple possible solutions, as previously discussed. Macnamara's analysis indicates that children may tend to assign words to only one class initially, but it does not speak clearly to the other possible solutions outlined. Indeed, his tendency to lump together all kinds of nouns regardless of their conceptual content obscures the real problems posed by nonobject nouns and words that serve two functions for which the semantics are not clearly distinct.

Semantic Distinctions Between Types. Among the many verb/noun forms, there are differences, particularly in the semantics of the nouns involved, that may influence the child's decisions. Consider the types classified in Table 8.3. This classification suggests a number of dimensions that might make the differentiation of meanings of the noun and verb forms of the word easier or more difficult. For example, differentiating between an action and an object should be maximally easy, and Macnamara's noting of his son's acquisition of *comb* for both suggests that this might be correct. Even more distinct is a single polysemous form that refers to unrelated actions and objects or nonobjects, such as *park* (the car) and (walk in the) *park* or *turn* (the handle) and (take your) *turn.* On the other hand, those words that refer to the same easily observed action in both forms should be more difficult to differentiate; that is, the use would be more confusable to the child on syntactic grounds, but more consistent semantically. This is the case for *kiss* and *hug,* for example. These considerations suggest that there are different degrees of polysemy involved, from highly distinct meanings to virtually the same meaning in both forms.

TABLE 8.3
Dual-Category Types

Type	Example
Action/Object	*hammer, brush* (often an instrument of the action)
Action/Related Object	*bite* (of food)
Action/Substance	*drink* (reference ambiguous as to substance, substance in object, or action)
Action/Unrelated Entity	*park* car/*park* (place); *turn* handle/ *turn* (sequence)
Action/Result	*change* (diaper)
Action/Action	*hug, kiss* (action is same in both N and V function)
Action (Abstract)/ Action (Abstract)	*help* (differs from *hug* in degree of abstractness or generality of the action involved; *help* is situationally defined not in terms of a specific action as is *hug*)
Action1/Action2	*call* (to someone), (phone) *call*
Action/Event	*walk* (event involves action)

The six terms in the following analyses can be ordered on this dimension in terms of distinctness of meaning between the two functions as follows:

$$walk > call^4 > help > drink > hug > kiss.$$

This order is motivated by the following considerations. *Walk* (as documented previously) has many specific meanings, but the most commonly used noun form with children is that of the extended event "go for a walk," which involves the action of walking but much more in the form of participants, places, times, and so on. *Call* also has many specific and diverse meanings as both noun and verb. "Call Daddy" may mean to get Daddy's attention by uttering his name in a loud voice, or it may mean to pretend to call him on the phone. The latter overlaps in meaning with the most common noun form used with children (see discussion following) and produced by our adult sample, namely "make a (phone) call." *Drink*, as previously noted, also has many specific meanings in the adult language. For children, however, its meanings as noun and verb overlap in terms of action, event, and object or substance. When Mother says, "What kind of a drink do you want?" or "What do you want to drink?" the referential meaning of the two uses is virtually indistinguishable. Yet the action of drinking is distinguishable from the substance to be drunk. *Help* is difficult to classify because its reference is abstract, nonspecific, and context-dependent. However, the noun and verb meanings overlap almost entirely. "Do you

---

[4]*Call* in its most common uses (i.e., name, shout) is infrequently nominalized; the noun form is most often used in reference to a phone call, for which verb and noun are virtually indistinguishable. Thus, the distinctiveness of this word will vary depending on the meanings invoked.

want some help?" and "Let me help you" have the same implications in the same situation. *Hug* and *Kiss* are both most specific and least polysemous with the greatest overlap in noun and verb forms. "Kiss me" and "Give me a kiss" implicate precisely the same action, and the same is true for *hug*. The only variation in either case is who is the giver and who the recipient of the action.

The implication of these considerations is that if semantic and pragmatic overlap aids understanding of either or both forms, then one order of acquisition would be expected, whereas if distinctiveness of noun and verb meanings helps, then the opposite ordering would be expected.

MATERNAL AND CHILD USES
OF DUAL CATEGORY TERMS

As the definitions presented previously imply, one might expect differences among the words in focus here with respect to their use by parents with young children. The analysis here is based on the identification of all uses of these terms by 12 mother–child dyads videotaped in their homes.[5] There were 8 girls and 4 boys in the sample. They each participated in five taping sessions of 30 minutes each when the children were 13, 16 (2 sessions), 18, and 20 months; all but the second 16-month session were divided equally into play and food (usually lunch) contexts. Play sessions included playing with a specific set of toys provided by the experimenter.

All uses of the six terms by either mother or child across sessions (a total of 30 hours of taping) were identified and classified as noun, verb, or unclassifiable on the basis of use. The latter constituted a small portion of maternal uses for each verb, including some words or constructions in which the use was not clear.

Maternal Uses

The total uses of each term by mothers within each category and by children is shown in Table 8.4. It can be seen from this table that mothers used the words frequently in the recorded sessions. Although the ratios of verbs to nouns vary from .58 (for *kiss*) to 5.88 (for *call*), all of the words were used by mothers some of the time as both verb and noun.

The inclusion of verb morphology in parental uses of these words provides evidence of the availability of syntactic information to children, from which they might be able to infer category assignment. This information is indicated in Table 8.5. It can be seen from this table that, with the exception

---

[5]The data were collected for the dissertation research of June Hampson (Hampson, 1989). See Nelson, Hampson, and Kessler Shaw (1992) for further details.

TABLE 8.4
Frequency of Maternal and Child Uses of Terms

	Maternal Uses						Child Uses
	Vi	Vt	Total Vs	N	%N	Total	
Call	15	85	100	17	14%	117	1
Drink	9	49	58	44	42%	105	22
Help	21	64	85	19	18%	107	4
Hug	—	26	26	22	45%	49	5
Kiss	8	17	25	43	61%	70	1
Walk	25	—	25	11	31%	36	3

Note. Vi = intransitive verb; Vt = transitive verb; N = noun.

of *call,* fewer than half of the verb tokens were used with morphological endings or in infinitive form. Indeed, the infinitive may be perceived simply as the citation or single noun form, especially in the common "gonna" and "wanna" uses. *Wanna* particularly may be confusable with *want a* (compare "D'you wanna call" and "d'you want a call"). If the infinitive form is discarded from the analysis, the percentages of verb morphology reduce to 50%, 17%, 8%, and 8% for *call, drink, help,* and *hug,* respectively (the values for *kiss* and *walk* remain as shown in the table).

Although these values are highly variable, they are somewhat surprising, given the general assumption that verb morphology may aid the child in identifying new verb forms. Here, where the forms are ambiguous, morphology is absent much of the time. (Recall that the same was true of the sentences provided by adult subjects.) Most nouns of these types are preceded by "a" or "some" or an adjective (e.g., *phone, little*). There are very few plurals except for some *kisses* and *hugs.* Thus, the main clue to category assignment for either verb or noun must reside in position in the sentence or in semantics.

TABLE 8.5
Use of Verb Morphology With Selected Words

	Total Vs	-s	to	past	-ing	Total morph	% morph
Call	100	0	28	22	28	78	78
Drink	58	1	16	2	7	26	45
Help	85	4	19	2	1	26	31
Kiss	25	0	2	1	1	4	16
Hug	26	0	0	0	10	10	38
Walk	25	0	0	5	4	9	36

Child Uses

The number of child uses of these terms over the 13- to 20-month observation sessions, shown also in Table 8.4, was too small to submit to further analysis, with the exception of the word *drink*. Children in this sample always used *drink* either as a single word (9) or in a verb context (12), except for one ambiguous noun use. On the face of it, a connection among use of a word, its noun or verb use by mother, and its semantic overlap as outlined above is not apparent. The only suggestion of some relation is the almost total lack of child use of the word *kiss*, which was identified as most similar in noun and verb forms. The special case of *kiss* will be considered further after additional child data is reviewed.

Although few uses of these words were observed in the taping sessions, all were used productively by the 20-month assessment by a significant number of children in both the 12-child subgroup and in the larger sample of 45 children from which this group was drawn. Frequency of parental indication of productive use of the words is shown in Table 8.6.

Because of the infrequent uses by children in the sample observed, additional data were sought. For this purpose, for each word we considered citations in Tomasello's (1992) data and occurrences in the data from the child Emily from 21 to 36 months (Nelson, 1989).[6] Use as noun, verb, or single word, as well as morphology and functor were tabulated. Because Tomasello focused only on verb uses, his data are summarized first.

Tomasello's Data. Tomasello lists no entries for *call,* and one entry for *called:* "Dana called me Lauren" (19.26), glossed as "Dana told T to call Lauren." The gloss indicates some confusion as to the use of the word *call* for communicating or for naming—not surprising, given its polysemous nature and frequent use for both meanings.

Drink (and sometimes *drinking*) was used as a single word to comment on own or other's action at 18–19 months. All 11 combinations of either *drink* or *drinking* cited between 19 and 23 months are plausibly verbs, with the possible exception of "pick that coffee up drink" (21.06).

Help was observed in single-word use from 16 months, for example in asking for help with her chair (18.25). The use in combination from 18 to 21 months appears to be verb-like ("help me") with the exception of "help . . . more help" at 19.27. Tomasello notes that parental use was primarily in terms of "Do you need help?" (i.e., as a noun) or as a single word in mock fear when playing a chase game.

---

[6]Transcripts of parent–child talk of ten 24-month-old children observed in caretaking situations (Lucariello & Nelson, 1986) were also examined, but the occurrence of the words was too infrequent to be informative.

TABLE 8.6
Frequency of Use of Words at 20-Month Assessment

| | # Children Producing Word | |
	Subsample (N = 12)	Full sample (N = 45)
Call	3	15
Drink	6	22
Help	6	16
Hug	5	21
Kiss	6	23
Walk	8	23

For *hug*, only one use was cited, at 20.16: "Hug Fred real good." *Kiss* was used as a single word at 19 to 20 months to ask to kiss people. One combination is cited: "Kiss Grover" at 19.30. Thus, the only evidence is that these uses were as verbs.

Walk was used twice in combinations at 19 and 20 months: "Walking here funny" and "Fred walking pillow." No citations for the simple form *walk* are given.

In summary, then, there was evidence that Tomasello's daughter learned and used each of these terms, and in each case the use seemed to be solely as a verb. All these terms are relatively late acquisitions, coming in after the first phase of verb learning. However, it should be borne in mind that due to the nature of the diary data and the focus on verbs and verb constructions, Tomasello may have overlooked an occasional noun use.

Emily's Verb/Noun Uses. Transcripts of pre-bed dialogue between Emily and her parents and of pre-sleep monologues were obtained over a 16-month period when Emily was between 21 and 36 months (see Nelson, 1989, for details). These transcripts were searched for all occasions of child use of the terms examined here, whether in dialogue or monologue. These uses are tabulated in Table 8.7.

Several comments may be noted regarding Emily's uses of the different terms over time. First, all but *kiss* and possibly *hug* were used predominately if not exclusively as verbs. The use was identified primarily on the basis of word order—little verb morphology was recorded at any age. If we take the first age period (21 to 23 months) as indicative of early language use, we find that *drink* was the only word in the list that was used at all frequently, and it was used to express her desire for a drink before bed (e.g., "I drink," "Emmy drink," "Need drink"). It was used as well during this period in her crib narratives about events (e.g., "drink p-water"). In contrast, *kiss* was observed only twice during the first 6 months (both as nouns) but became frequent in the bedtime routine during the third period (27 to 29 months).

TABLE 8.7
Uses of Terms by Emily, 21–36 Months

Age[1]	Verb	Verb+ ed	Verb+ ing	Other Verb Morphology[2]	Total Verbs	Noun	Noun+ Morphology[3]	Total Nouns	Total
Call									
1	2				2				2
2		1		2					3
3		1	1						2
4									
5	1	1							2
Total	3	3	1	2	9	0	0	0	9
Drink									
1	8	1			9	1?		1?	10
2									
3				1					1
4									
5									
Total	8	1	0	1	10	1?	0	1?	11
Help									
1	1				1				1
2	1				1				1
3	2				2				2
4									
5									
Total	4	0	0	0	4	0	0	0	4
Hug									
1									
2									
3									
4									
5						3		3	3
Total	0	0	0	0	0	3	0	3	3
Kiss									
1							1	1	1
2							1	1	1
3							1	8	9	9
4	2				2	8	2	10	12
5	10				10	5		5	15
Total	12	0	0	0	12	16	10	26	38

(Continued)

TABLE 8.7
(Continued)

Age^1	Verb	Verb+ed	Verb+ing	Other Verb Morphology²	Total Verbs	Noun	Noun+ Morphology³	Total Nouns	Total
Walk									
1									
2				1	1				1
3	1		1		2				2
4									
5	2	7	2		11				11
Total	3	7	3	1	14	0	0	0	14

[1] Age in months: 1 = 21–23; 2 = 24–26; 3 = 27–29; 4 = 30–32; 5 = 33–36.
[2] Other verb morphemes including *to*.
[3] Noun morphemes: plural, possessive.

Note that it was first used as a noun and subsequently as a verb ("kiss me"). This suggests that Emily first assigned the word as a noun and only later began to use it flexibly as both. *Hug* was used very little at any age, but when used it was as a noun.

The conclusion to be drawn from these relatively few data points from child use must be very tentative. On the one hand, it appears that most children most of the time assign these action words exclusively as verbs, regardless of parents' frequent use of them as nouns. On the other hand, it appears that *kiss* and possibly *hug* may be exceptions; this accords with the fact that noun use is most frequent by parents for *kiss* (see Table 8.4). This finding suggests that semantics may not always be the determining factor in a word's assignment to a grammatical category. But the fact that Emily's uses of *kiss* were confined to the noun function for several months before verb use was observed suggests that the one form–one function principle may indeed be operative, even when semantics is overruled.

Evidence From Mother–Child Discourse

Examination of the discourse context in which the terms are used by parents may clarify the evidence that children use to infer meaning and assign grammatical category. Toward this end, four words used frequently in the transcripts from the 12 children reported in Table 8.4 are examined further: *call*, observed in use only once by a child in that sample; *drink*, observed most frequently; *kiss*, observed most frequently as a noun by Emily; and *bite*. The latter word has not been the focus of analysis thus far, but it contrasts with the others in an important and interesting way.

First, consider the form *bite*. This word has not been considered thus far because it differs from the others analyzed here in the relation of its noun form to the verb. The verb is clearly a specific, concrete action involving the mouth and specifically the teeth. In contrast, the noun, as used by parents, refers to small pieces of diverse objects, specifically bits of food. These bits are not typically the result of biting but rather are offered by spoon or hand accompanied by such expressions as "Give me a bite," "That's mommy's bite," "D'you want a bite?", and "A little bite." In other words, the reference is clear—a small food object—and the form is unambiguously a noun. Unlike *kiss, drink,* and *call,* for *bite* mothers did not alternate the noun and verb forms in the same discourse context, although they did use the verb as well as the noun (about 8:1 noun to verb). The verb was used also in food contexts but to direct action, as in, "bite it," or in play contexts with other objects, as in, "don't bite it."

Although the verb and noun forms are related, they are used in quite distinct contexts for quite distinct references. Not surprisingly, children used the term fairly frequently (15 uses in the study) and either as a single word or as a noun. Although the dictionary gives priority to use as a verb, for children priority is clearly in the direction of the noun, both syntactically and semantically. This is not the case for the other forms considered here and in the previous sections.

In the transcripts of parent–child talk for the 12 dyads in the longitudinal study, *call* was used by mothers 117 times (see Table 8.4). The vast majority of uses were in verb form (85% transitive) in the context of symbolic play with the toy telephone provided by the experimenter for every play session (together with other toys and books). Parents engaged their children in telephone play with such invitations as "D'you wanna call someone?" However, it is important to note two exceptions to these observations. First, a considerable minority of uses in the phone context were nouns (17, or 14%), as in, "Phone call for Susy." Second, 22 of the 100 verb uses (22%) came in the context of naming books or individuals (11), labeling objects (10), or communicating with someone in person (1), rather than in the act of telephoning. Altogether, these represent a restricted range of meanings compared to those listed in the dictionary, but they are probably representative of parent–child talk at this age. On the other hand, the balance among meanings is probably skewed by the availability of the toy telephone in the observational sessions.

A few recurrent phrases characterized most of the talk between mothers and their children around the telephone. For example, the following phrases occurred across dyads and ages: "D/you wanna call X?" (12 times); "Who/re you calling?" (9); "Who're you gonna call?" (6); and "Who's (was) calling?" (8). Variations on these formulas constituted much of the rest of the talk. Alternation between noun and verb within the same segment of play was frequent, as in the following examples:

Calling Susie
Call for Susie
Calling Susie

Who's calling
Phone call for Susie

You're gonna make a call?
Who should we call?
Call for Joe, call for Joe

As can be seen in Table 8.5, about half of the verbs were in the citation form *call*, as of course were the nouns. For this simple uninflected form the verb to noun ratio was about 3:1.

Only one use of *call* by a child in this sample was observed, in the form "Goin call Daddy." By all counts, children use this verb relatively infrequently, although 15 of 45 mothers indicated on the checklist that their children produced it by 20 months (see Table 8.6). Also, children responded to parental talk about calling in the phone situation, and when asked what something was called, children responded appropriately. The fact that so many uses of *call*, and particularly noun uses, were observed in these transcripts is probably attributable to the presence of the toy phone. However, it seems likely that children hear parents talk about phone calls, both real and pretend, frequently in everyday discourse. Confusion between the verb and noun used in the phone context may be compounded by the use of *call* for other forms of communicating ("call Daddy") and for referring to the names of things ("what's it called?"). It remains a problem for future research to determine whether in fact children recognize the latter meanings as attached to the same form as the former. That is, it may be that two forms are identified (identical for the adult user, but not for the child) and eventually attached to two different functions.

Emily's uses (see Table 8.7) included phone calls ("call up Carl"), communication ("they called their mother"), and naming/attribution ("I call my bed red . . . that's what Emily calls it"; "do not call me Emmy"). All three types were distributed in her talk from 23 months to 35 months; thus, the same form apparently did have different meanings synchronically for Emily.

Drink was used in much more contextually bounded ways than *call*, always for real or play food and drink contexts in which drinking a liquid, usually from a cup, was the topic of the discourse. As shown in Table 8.4, mothers often used *drink* as a noun (42% of the time), usually in a construction such as, "Do you want a drink?" Another frequent expression was "Drink X," with water, milk, tea, coffee, what, something, it, or that as X. Possible confusion in the analysis of verb and noun was possible in con-

structions such as "have to drink," "has a drink," "something to drink."
Mothers also alternated between noun and verb, as in the following:

M: Would you like . . . should I bring a drink?
C: No.
M: Are you gonna drink water from your bottle? Or should I?
C: No.
M: D'you want a drink?

However, children always used the word either as a single word or as a
verb (e.g., "drink coffee" in the pretense situation).

In the case of *drink* it was possible to compare the mothers' dominant
use of the word as both noun and verb (4 mothers) or as predominately
verb (7 mothers) to their children's use of the word. No relation was found.
Of 5 children who used the word, 2 had mothers in the first group, 3 in the
second. Of 6 children who did not, 2 had mothers in the first group, 4 in
the second. (One pair did not use the word at all in their recorded discourse.)

It seems probable that the clear relevance of the word *drink* to everyday
activities made its use salient and interpretable to the child in both forms.
That it was used by children almost exclusively as a verb despite its alternation in function by parents certainly implies a semantic analysis basis for
assignment to grammatical class. However, that conclusion does not hold
for *kiss*. As shown in Table 8.4, *kiss* was used by mothers 61% of the time
as a noun, most frequently in the "give X a kiss" format. As a verb, it was
usually of the "kiss me" or "kiss X" form. Almost always, the word was used
in discourse about the child's actions, most frequently with dolls or soft
animal-like toys. Although more than half of the children in full sample were
credited with the word, only one use was observed in the taped sessions.

Given its relatively frequent use by mothers, and its clear reference to a
specific action, why was it not observed more often? (Note in Table 8.6 that
6 of the children in the observation sample were credited by their mothers
with productive use of *kiss*.) Obviously there are a number of possible
explanations. One is that children did not perceive a discourse function for
their own use, although they readily interpreted the parents'. When parents
urged kissing, the appropriate response was an action, not a word. Thus,
children may know the word and use it on occasion (as mothers recorded
on the vocabulary checklist), but they may have little use for it in most
discourse situations where parents use it. It seems possible that children
were cautious in assigning the word as a noun or verb because the concrete
action was salient to the child, but the mothers used the word more as a
noun than as a verb. It should also be noted that mothers often used the
plural form, *kisses*, and quantified it (e.g., "two kisses"), which may have

made the noun use more salient. The verb form was almost never used with verb inflections. Recall from Table 8.5 that verb inflections were relatively infrequent for all the verbs in use here.

The data from Emily, who began to use the term frequently rather late in the observation sessions as she engaged her parents in the "one more kiss" delaying tactic before bed, may be informative with respect to the one form–one function principle and its relation to the child's semantic analysis. In line with our observation of frequent parental use of the form as a noun, we see in Table 8.7 that Emily's first uses were also as a noun. Only late in the game did she begin to use the form as both verb and noun. This is a case in which frequency of use in a grammatical category might override the semantic analysis even in the early stages, so that the one form–one function principle rules out the most obvious semantically based assignment.

In summary, then, examination of use of the terms in discourse may reveal the specific basis for children's inferences regarding meaning and grammatical category. As revealed here, *bite* is used in contexts for which both object reference and grammatical function determine its assignment as a noun. Its more usual verb function in the adult language is overshadowed, and as long as children hold to the one form–one function principle it does not emerge. *Drink*, like *bite*, is used in event activity contexts that make its pragmatic role clear, although its grammatical function in adult speech varies. Presumably the action component of *drink* is sufficiently salient to the child, who achieves a personal goal by means of such action, that the action-verb assignment emerges. In contrast, the action component of *kiss*, which would seem to be among the most salient of all the verbs, is overridden in its use as a noun. Recall that the dictionary, although giving priority to the verb function of *kiss*, defined that function in terms of the noun ("to give a kiss"). Not only is the kiss referred to in noun form, but it is commonly included in the phrase "give X" and is often used in plural form. Giving kisses, then, is treated by adults as analogous to giving objects, and children have much experience in playing the "Give me the X" game. Thus, their interpretation of *kiss* as a noun, despite its obvious action reference, seems reasonable. Of course, as noted, children seem to use the term sparingly if at all in the early months, although they readily interpret its use by others.

Finally, consider polysemous *call*, used for both noun and verb functions in the phone call event and for a number of distinguishable meanings in other contexts. Although the children engaged in the phone call play, they did not use the term during the game (with one exception). It is not easy to determine whether children interpreted other uses of *call* in their intended meanings; nor can we say for certain that Emily's varied uses of the term were more than rote formulas.

How children deal with polysemy has generally not been the focus of attention. It is possible that children recognize the single form and are confused by the apparent distinguishable meanings. On the other hand, it may be that a single form in different pragmatic contexts is not recognized as such. This topic clearly deserves more attention.

SUMMARY AND CONCLUSIONS

The purpose of this chapter has been to consider the implications for child language learning of a major group of words in English that are ambiguous with respect to grammatical category assignment. It is clear from the data presented that both verb and noun functions of these words are salient in both adult and child discourse contexts. It was assumed that such words might pose problems for children both semantically and grammatically. How does a child interpret a word referring to an action as "an X"? How do children settle on a grammatical category assignment—if they do—when a word is used alternatively as "an X" and "to X"? Does grammar, semantics, frequency of maternal use, or clarity of discourse context determine its assignment? Do children obey the one form–one function principle in the face of alternating uses by parents? If so, which function do they choose? Does overlap of meaning for the two functions help or hinder acquisition? Does distinctness of meaning suggest two forms for two functions?

A group of six verbs were chosen as representative of the class of words that might pose problems for children. All were reported by mothers to be learned and used at 20 months by many of the 45 children surveyed in a longitudinal study. All were cited in the dictionary as both verbs and nouns, with verbs as the primary citation. All were given both verb and noun meanings and were used in sentences in both forms by a group of adults. All were used as both verbs and nouns in discourse with children by mothers in a longitudinal study.

Except for *drink*, there were too few observations of child uses in the longitudinal study to provide relevant information about children's semantic and syntactic inferences. When these data were supplemented with observations from Tomasello's study of his daughter and with uses by the child Emily, a somewhat fuller picture emerged. Together, these findings allow some preliminary conclusions about the predictions outlined earlier.

The expectation that children would preferentially assign words as nouns is clearly falsified. Most uses of these words in multiword contexts were as verbs.

For most forms, most children seemed to obey the one form–one function principle in production, a principle that has often been proposed for many different levels of analysis. However, children also apparently interpreted the uses by parents in both functions appropriately. Moreover, there were occasional productions even in the data from early uses suggesting that this principle was not inviolate (e.g., Emily's "need drink"). Perhaps most telling is the evidence from Olguin and Tomasello's (1993) experiment, which showed that all the 2-year-old children used novel words as nouns at least once, although the words were modeled only as referring to actions. Nonetheless, as might be predicted by most theorists, children appeared to focus on the semantics of the term for assignment to grammatical class for most of the words, using action words in verb contexts. This outcome supports the semantic bootstrapping hypothesis.

In contrast, however, both *kiss* and *bite* (and possibly *hug*) were used initially as nouns rather than verbs. Two different explanations seem plausible for this outcome. *Bite* was used as a noun by mothers 80% of the time, and it was used in discourse contexts in which the noun referred to (pieces of) objects. Thus, both the semantics and syntax in the discourse context pulled for noun usage, despite the intuition that in the adult language the primary meaning of *bite* is verbal (as the dictionary indicates). *Kiss* was also primarily used by mothers as a noun, although its reference to a specific action was the same in both verb and noun contexts and parents used the functions alternatively in the same discourse context. Most of the children sampled did not use the word in the contexts observed (although the parents of 6 asserted that their child used it productively), possibly suggesting confusion as to its grammatical function. Observation of Emily's uses indicated that it was initially assigned as a noun. It is speculated that the pragmatics of the familiar "give X" game when applied to the action of kissing induced the child to interpret the action as a kind of object and thus accept its usage as a noun.

Two considerations emerge from this study that argue against a straightforward syntactic bootstrapping (or distributional analysis) solution. First, parental uses of the words as both nouns and verbs provide the child with ambiguous evidence. Second, when the words were used as verbs, they were used most often in the citation form without inflection, thus being indistinguishable from noun use in terms of form. This is one of the most surprising outcomes of the study, given the common assumption that the child's analysis of morphology contributes importantly to the construction of grammatical classes. If the observations here are representative, it appears that for English speakers of simple sentences in here-and-now contexts (which are typical with very young children), verb morphology is largely absent and thus is not available for the child's analysis.

The analysis of different types of dual category words, classified in Table 8.3, was set forth to suggest that relations between meanings of the verb and noun may differentially affect the child's acquisition of the term. The implications of this analysis could not be adequately tested against the restricted data examined, but there was some indication that distinctness of reference might disambiguate the forms. When the two functions are sufficiently distinct (as with *bite*), both uses may be interpreted appropriately in comprehension, although one form may be chosen for production on the basis of its salient discourse function.

Thus, to fully explain the child's acquisition of the grammatical functions of these words, it is necessary to look to their functions in discourse. Discourse analysis indicates that each form is subject to specific contextual effects based on sentential frames and discourse uses in familiar events. When parents say "give a ___," children may recognize the "gift" as a noun, although conceptually it is an action, based on inferences from prior experience with the giving frame, in which the gift is in fact an object and thus labeled by a noun.

The most general conclusion emerging from this study is that both general and specific factors underlie the child's analysis of ambiguous forms. As expected on the basis of prior work, children prefer one function for one form, and in the early stages of verb acquisition they tend to rely on a conceptual analysis of the event (Tomasello, 1992) and use action-referring words in verb contexts. However, specific parental models (as with *kiss*) may override such preferences. Children appear to be quite flexible in their adaptiveness to uses in different grammatical functions even without such models (Olguin & Tomasello, 1993). Although there was little evidence on which a child could base a distributional analysis of grammatical class for these words, such analysis may emerge a bit later in development than the period explored here.

All in all, the data seem to fit with and even go beyond Tomasello's (1992) verb island hypothesis to suggest a *word island hypothesis*. That is, at the outset of grammatical construction the child may view each word independently in terms of its semantics and sentential frames. From this perspective, it cannot be claimed that children assign *bite* or *kiss* as nouns, contradicting their emerging semantically based noun and verb classes, which refer to objects and actions respectively. Rather, these (and other similar words) are treated as having independently specified sentential and semantic frames. Such treatment is not then an exception to the child's rules, because the rules themselves are not at this point well formulated but are still in the process of formation. When formulated the rules will necessarily take into account the action-word-as-noun subset, which, as has been documented here, is neither anomalous nor unusual in everyday English use.

Whether or not this speculation is correct, this category of words clearly has the potential to shed light on many issues in semantic and syntactic development, and further study of the acquisition of words of these types is clearly warranted. The actual acquisition principles that emerge from unclear cases of this kind are likely to be more revealing of children's strategies and structures than are the clear cases of object referents so beloved by contemporary theorists.

REFERENCES

Bates, E., Bretherton, I., Shore, C., & Snyder, L. (1984). *Early language inventory. Part I: Vocabulary checklist.* University of California at San Diego.

Bates, E., & MacWhinney, B. (1989). Functionalism and the competition model. In B. MacWhinney & E. Bates (Eds.), *The cross-linguistic study of sentence processing* (pp. 3–73). Cambridge, England: Cambridge University Press.

Brown, R. (1973). *A first language: The early stages.* Cambridge, MA: Harvard University Press.

Clark, E. V. (1987). The principle of contrast: A constraint on language acquisition. In B. MacWhinney (Ed.), *Mechanisms of language acquisition* (pp. 1–34). Hillsdale, NJ: Lawrence Erlbaum Associates.

Gentner, D. (1982). Why nouns are learned before verbs: Linguistic relativity versus natural partitioning. In S. A. Kuczaj (Ed.), *Language development: Vol. 2. Language, thought, and culture* (pp. 301–334). Hillsdale, NJ: Lawrence Erlbaum Associates.

Gentner, D. (1988, October). *Cognitive and linguistic determinism: Object reference and relational reference.* Paper presented at the Boston University Conference on Language Development. Boston, MA.

Hampson, J. (1989). *Elements of style: Maternal and child contributions to the expressive and referential styles of language acquisition.* Unpublished doctoral dissertation, City University of New York Graduate Center.

Laird, C. (1974). Language and the dictionary. In D. B. Guralnik (Ed.), *Webster's New World Dictionary of the American Language* (pp. xv–xxx). Cleveland: William Collins & World.

Landau, B., & Gleitman, L. (1985). *Language and experience: Evidence from the blind child.* Cambridge, MA: Harvard University Press.

Lucariello, J., & Nelson, K. (1986). Context effects on lexical specificity in maternal and child discourse. *Journal of Child Language, 13,* 507–522.

Lyons, J. (1977). *Semantics.* Cambridge, England: Cambridge University Press.

Macnamara, J. (1982). *Names for things.* Cambridge, MA: MIT Press.

Markman, E. M. (1989). *Categorization and naming in children.* Cambridge, MA: MIT Press.

Nelson, K. (Ed.). (1989). *Narratives from the crib.* Cambridge, MA: Harvard University Press.

Nelson, K. (1991). The matter of time: Interdependencies between language and thought in development. In S. A. Gelman & J. P. Byrnes (Eds.), *Perspectives on language and thought: Interrelations in development* (pp. 278–318). New York: Cambridge University Press.

Nelson, K., Hampson, J., & Kessler Shaw, L. (1992). Nouns in early lexicons: Evidence, explanations, and implications. *Journal of Child Language, 19,* 1–24.

Olguin, R., & Tomasello, M. (1993). Twenty-five-month-old children do not have a grammatical category of verb. *Cognitive Development, 8,* 245–272.

Pinker, S. (1984). *Language learnability and language development.* Cambridge, MA: Harvard University Press.

Slobin, D. I. (1973). Cognitive prerequisites for the development of grammar. In C. A. Ferguson & D. I. Slobin (Eds.), *Studies of child language development* (pp. 175–208). New York: Springer.

Tomasello, M. (1992). *First verbs: A case study of early grammatical development.* New York: Cambridge University Press.

Webster's New World Dictionary of the American Language (1974). Springfield, MA: Merriam.

Webster's Ninth New Collegiate Dictionary (1984). Springfield, MA: Merriam.

CHAPTER NINE

Processes Involved in the Initial Mapping of Verb Meanings

Douglas A. Behrend
University of Arkansas

It is customary to begin a chapter with some introductory remarks designed to convince the reader that the chapter addresses an important set of issues that demand the reader's close attention. This is especially true when the topic being addressed in some way represents a new topic or new approach to an old topic, as was the case when the acquisition of verb meanings became a topic of focused inquiry during the 1980s. However, given that this volume exists, I no longer need to convince readers of the importance of studying children's acquisition of verbs and their meanings, and that is good news. This topic has clearly found a niche in the field of language acquisition and, more broadly, in developmental psychology.

If I do not need to convince readers that verb acquisition is an important area of inquiry, what do I need to do in this chapter? My plan is to discuss children's acquisition of verb meanings in terms of three broad categories of learning processes that researchers agree are fundamental components involved in verb acquisition. The processes I discuss work independently and interactively to produce the patterns of word learning that have been observed when children are asked to make some determination of meaning after minimal experience with a verb, perhaps just a single exposure. These processes are classified as *child-driven, environment-driven*, and *language-driven*.

Child-driven processes are any preexisting perceptual, cognitive, or specifically linguistic strategies or constraints that the child brings to the verb learning context. Though there is controversy over the existence and nature of these child-driven processes (e.g., Behrend, 1990b; Golinkoff, Hirsh-Pasek, Bailey, & Wenger, 1992; Kuczaj, 1990; Markman, 1989; Nelson, 1988), the child is certainly not a verb learning tabula rasa, and inclusion of these child-driven processes is certainly merited. Although this chapter necessarily touches upon child-driven processes for word-learning in general, I focus on those processes that may have specific importance for verb learning, such as children's biases to attend to particular aspects of events.

Environment-driven processes involve at least two types of information that verb learners can exploit. First, there is the basic pattern of verbal and nonverbal input that children receive from other language users. I include under this heading basic factors such as the frequency, timing, and variability of both verb usage itself and the nonverbal cues to meaning that occur in the world, but I exclude grammatical cues to meaning (see following section on language-driven processes). Second, the characteristics of the real-world referents of verbs—actions and events—must also be analyzed. As Tomasello (this volume; Tomasello & Kruger, 1992) emphasized, events, unlike objects, are usually unavailable for continued inspection after they have been labeled by a verb. Many events labeled by verbs also have several distinct components that can be denoted in a verb meaning. These characteristics of events may have important implications for verb learning.

The language-driven processes also fall into two categories. First, there is the general issue of differences in the semantic organizations of verbs and nouns (e.g., Huttenlocher & Lui, 1979). I argue that these differences are related to differences in the patterns of noun and verb acquisition. Also, these organizational differences may affect the degree to which word-learning strategies that are beneficial for noun learning can be beneficial for verb learning. Second, there is the issue of syntactic bootstrapping (Landau & Gleitman, 1985). As the chapters in this volume attest, evidence is beginning to accumulate that children employ information from the syntactic context in which a novel verb is used to aid them in their mapping of its meaning. In this chapter, I construe the bootstrapping metaphor a bit more broadly than is typical (see also Shatz, 1988) and summarize my recent research that investigates children's use during the initial mapping of verb meanings of the helpful but only roughly accurate information carried by English verb inflections. This research indicates that children may use linguistic cues to meaning in a heuristic, nondeterministic way in order to make a reasonably narrow first interpretation of a verb meaning.

It should be clear that this attempt to categorize language acquisition processes into three neat boxes is somewhat artificial. After all, both children and languages exist in the environment, so why not just count these processes all as environment-driven processes? Why is frequency of occurrence an environment-driven process and not a language-driven process? Doesn't the semantic organization of verbs simply reflect the organization of events in the world? It is useful to make such distinctions for the following reasons. First, the separation of the language-driven process from the environment-driven processes allows for a role of the structure of language per se rather than simply the rate or manner in which these structures are presented to language learners. Recent cross-linguistic research has shown the need for between-language comparisons of verb learning (e.g., Gopnik & Choi, 1990). Second (and more broadly), categorizing language-learning processes in this manner facilitates the efforts of verb acquisition researchers by providing a logical framework in which to develop research designs. That is, by making the assumption that there are three separate and at least somewhat disso-ciable sets of processes that contributes to verb learning, researchers can systematically manipulate the variables that tap these processes in order to investigate their relative effects on verb learning. I demonstrate some variants of this approach in this chapter.

Finally, I conclude the chapter by arguing that before a unified theory of semantic development is achieved, it is necessary to understand the nature and contributions of all three of the processes described here and the degree to which these processes contribute differently to noun and verb acquisition. Using dynamical systems theory (e.g., Thelen & Ulrich, 1991) as a general framework, I argue that the same set of variables (or parameters, in systems theory terms) contribute to both kinds of acquisition but that different settings of the parameters differentially optimize noun and verb learning. This more inclusive framework should facilitate the manner in which the work of verb researchers and noun researchers can inform each other as we move toward the same goal: a unified theory of semantic development.

CHILD-DRIVEN PROCESSES

I am on record elsewhere (Behrend, 1990b) as accepting the existence of some set of child-driven processes that serve to constrain the set of hypothe-ses a child considers as the meaning or referent of a word. Most of these processes have been proposed and studied within the domain of the acqui-sition of object words, but many can be applied to action words as well (e.g., Golinkoff, Hirsh-Pasek, Mervis, Frawley, & Parillo, this volume; Mer-riman, Marazita, & Jarvis, this volume). These processes are best construed as default assumptions or expectations that can be overridden by experience (Behrend, 1989, 1990a; Markman, 1989; Merriman & Bowman, 1989).

A common process that has been proposed along these lines is that a child first assumes that a novel word refers to a class of objects (e.g., Markman & Hutchinson, 1984; Waxman & Gelman, 1986). Several individuals have made the argument that such an assumption is detrimental to the acquisition of verbs and other types of words (e.g., Nelson, 1988; Kuczaj, 1990). However, the assumption is perfectly consistent with the usual pattern of development in which verb acquisition lags considerably behind noun acquisition for most children (Bates, Bretherton, & Snyder, 1988; Gentner, 1982; Goldin-Meadow, Seligman, & Gelman, 1976; Nelson, 1973; but see Gopnik & Choi, 1991). Words that do not match these initial defaults should necessarily enter the vocabulary later and at a slower rate than nouns in a basic hypothesis-testing (Markman, 1989) or connectionist (MacWhinney, 1987) model of word learning.

The longitudinal data of Bates et al. (1988) is germane to this issue. Bates et al. found that 13-month-old children varied widely in referential capability, as measured by the proportion of common nouns in receptive and productive vocabularies. In addition, the proportion of nouns in productive vocabulary was correlated positively with overall vocabulary size in both comprehension and production. Thus, more referential children were more precocious in language development overall, and the ability to use object words was one of the few variables that correlated with measures of both expressive and receptive language (see also Nelson, 1973).

More importantly, Bates et al. (1988) found that the proportion of nouns in the children's vocabularies at 13 months was predictive of overall open class vocabulary at 20 months of age. Furthermore, the proportion of verbs in the 20-month vocabularies was most strongly associated with overall reported vocabulary at that age. Although this pattern of results seems to suggest a correlation between "nouniness" at 13 months and "verbiness" at 20 months, Bates et al. (1988) failed to find such a correlation. Rather, whereas acquiring verbs is apparently "the thing to do" in language development at 20 months, early referential precocity does not simply predict acquisition of verbs at 20 months, but rather it predicts overall open class vocabulary development. Thus, a child who was adept at noun learning at 13 months was not only a good verb learner at 20 months but had learned many more nouns and adjectives as well. One way to interpret these findings is to assume that the children who were able to learn nouns most quickly were able to use their relatively larger vocabulary as a richer source of comparison and contrast when new words were presented, thus enabling them to acquire a range of vocabulary items, including verbs (see Behrend, 1990b, for a similar argument regarding the mapping of novel words).

Knowing how quickly verbs are acquired or even knowing when a child recognizes that a novel word is a verb is not enough for us to describe verb acquisition in detail. Once a child recognizes that a novel word is a verb that labels some ongoing event, what is the child to think that the verb means? It has been pointed out by many (Behrend, 1990a; Clark, 1983; Huttenlocher, Smiley, & Charney, 1983) that verbs often include several different components of events in their meanings, ranging from the concrete attributes of actions, results, and instruments to the abstract attributes of causality and intentionality. Thus, when a child is exposed to a novel verb for the first time, the indeterminacy of the word's reference can be even more baffling than it is for object words. Exposure to multiple exemplars (an environment-driven process) and syntactic cues (a language-driven process) can help to reduce the indeterminacy, but the child may have some predilections or biases that lead him or her to make particular interpretations of the verb. In this chapter, I focus on how children make a particular distinction: whether a word is an action verb or result verb.

An action verb denotes the physical movement or manner of action of an agent without specifying the result that the movement achieves, whereas a result verb denotes the outcome of an event without specifying the movement or action that produced the result (Behrend, 1990a). A useful rule of thumb for distinguishing these two types of verbs (for which I am indebted to Bill Merriman for suggesting) is the following: Consider that you are shown a still picture of an event immediately after the event has ended (e.g., a glass of water after someone poured water into the glass). A verb is a result verb if a question about the event that uses that verb can be answered confidently, either in the affirmative or negative (e.g., "Did someone fill it?" "Did someone spill it?"). A question that uses an action verb can only be answered with uncertainty or a shrug of the shoulders (e.g., "Did someone pour?"; see Behrend, 1990a, for a more detailed account).

There are at least two ways to study preferences for action verbs versus result verbs: to look at children's acquisition and spontaneous use of action verbs and result verbs or to investigate children's mapping preferences during verb training experiments. The findings from these studies do not always lead to the same conclusions. When children are asked to choose between an action verb or a result verb to label a familiar event, children tend to use the action verb more frequently (Behrend, 1990a; Gentner, 1978; Gropen, Pinker, Hollander, & Goldberg, 1991). Naturalistic studies have also tended to show that action verbs enter children's vocabularies somewhat earlier and with greater frequency than result verbs (Behrend, 1992; Bloom, Lifter, & Hafitz, 1980; Huttenlocher et al., 1983). However, there are exceptions to this finding (Tomasello, 1992), and the discrepancy in frequency between these types of verbs does not endure for long (Behrend, 1992).

One potential explanation for this pattern stems from young children's attentional preferences when observing simple events. Golinkoff and Kerr (1978) and Robertson and Suci (1980) studied children's differential attention to actors playing different semantic roles in a filmed event. Golinkoff and Kerr (1978) showed that 16- and 24-months-olds were able to detect replacements of both the agents and recipients of actions in these films. However, Robertson and Suci (1980) showed that 17- to 20-month-olds were more likely to dishabituate to the occlusion of an agent than of a recipient if that occlusion occurred during or after the action. Even given that result verbs characterize patients rather than recipients, if children of this age range are more likely to attend to agents rather than recipients once actions have commenced, it should not be too surprising if action verbs show some advantage in early vocabularies.

The picture becomes somewhat cloudy, however, when children's initial mapping of verb meanings are studied. In these studies, children are typically taught a nonsense verb that is used to label an event that has both a clear manner of action and a clear result (and perhaps instruments, causal mechanisms, etc., as well). Children are then asked if they would use the newly taught verb as a label for events in which either the action or result differs from the events used to teach the verb. Studies by Behrend (1989, 1990a) showed that children had a preference for interpreting these novel verbs as result verbs, as indicated by 3- to 5-year-olds' unwillingness to extend them to events having new results. Forbes and Farrar (1993) and Kelly and Rice (1991) found comparable results using similar but not identical procedures and stimuli.

On the other hand, recent work by Gropen (1989, cited by Pinker, 1989) and by Fisher (personal communication) does not replicate this result. Gropen's data echo the manner of action over end state preference originally documented by Gentner (1978), whereas Fisher's subjects showed no preference for either manner of action or results. Pinker (1989) noted that manner of action and change of end state were confounded in the Gropen (1989) study, and Fisher's findings may have been affected by manipulation of the syntactic frame in which the verbs were presented. However, recent work by Behrend, Harris, and Cartwright (in press) that used stimuli with result and action changes rated a priori as equally different from training events found smaller and not always significant result verb preferences. As is always true with studies of young children's word learning, small differences in procedures and stimuli can produce important differences in findings.

Regardless of the actual strength of the result verb bias in novel verb learning, it is clear is that the pattern of results from spontaneous labeling and initial mappings of verbs do not run fully in parallel. In terms of child-driven processes, one possibility is that despite the greater salience of agents and actions in attentional tasks while language is not present, once the task becomes a word-learning task due to the introduction of a novel word, children rely less on basic attention or cognitive preferences and rely instead on learning procedures that are more specific to language. Such an explanation is consistent with findings from studies in which children have a preference to group objects together thematically when told to find two of the same kind but to group objects taxonomically when told to find the referents of a noun (Markman & Hutchinson, 1984; Waxman & Gelman, 1986; see also Bauer & Mandler, 1989, for a slightly different perspective). Thus, it appears that children may implement different learning strategies in the presence versus absence of language. Surprisingly, few verb learning studies have included a no-word control condition to assess children's performance in the absence of language, even though such conditions are important controls. In addition, I argued elsewhere (Behrend, 1990a) that the lack of parallel between labeling and word learning studies may reflect the semantic organization of verbs. I take up this issue in more detail in the following section.

ENVIRONMENT-DRIVEN PROCESSES

In this section I address two specific issues. First, does the pattern of adult usage of verbs, in very broad terms, have any impact on the types of verbs that are acquired by children or the rate of verb acquisition? Second, I investigate and discuss how children may use multiple exemplars of events to isolate the crucial semantic components of novel verbs. Although children's initial mappings may reflect default assumptions about verb meaning, these initial mappings must be modifiable and refinable on the basis of additional experience if children are to master the full range of conventional verb meanings.

One of the commonsense explanations for any pattern of language acquisition appeals to word frequency either in the language as a whole or in the input that the child receives from primary caregivers. After all, children are imitative creatures, and the more they hear certain words or constructions, the earlier or more frequently they ought to use them. Although frequency of occurrence may have some impact on early word choice (Harris, Barrett, Jones, & Brookes, 1988; Schwartz & Terrell, 1983), frequency explanations of acquisition patterns are usually erroneous or incomplete. Huttenlocher, Smiley, and Ratner (1984) found no relationship between parental verb frequency and the types of verbs uttered first by their children. Behrend (1990a) found that children actually used the least frequent types of verbs—instrument verbs—most frequently as labels for familiar events for which there was an appropriate instrument verb label (e.g., saying "hammering" rather than "pounding" or "sawing" rather than "cutting"). Frequency may have played some role, however, because the youngest children in this study, 3-year-olds, used fewer instrument verbs than older children or adults.

A recent study by Fu, Gelman, and Behrend (1992) sheds some additional light on this issue. Fourteen- and 20-month-olds were observed interacting with a parent in a quasi-naturalistic environment with a set of toys designed to elicit a wide range of object, action, and attribute words. The number of nouns, verbs, and adjectives that each parent used within the interactive setting was then correlated with children's production and comprehension both during the session and with checklist measures of lexical development.

The pattern of results was somewhat surprising. Significant negative correlations were found between the number of verbs used by parents during the interaction and their children's reported verb vocabulary. Conversely, parental noun use correlated positively with reported verb vocabulary. These data suggest that parents who used fewer verbs and more nouns had children with larger verb vocabularies during their second year.

There are two possible explanations for these surprising results. A first and uninteresting one is that there was something about the interactive setting that encouraged parents to respond in a particular, biased way and these correlations are simply an artifact of the setting. Nothing about the interactive setting suggests that this occurred. A more interesting possibility is that the findings reflect the operation of a type of bootstrapping. Recall that the syntactic bootstrapping hypothesis claims that children exploit the grammatical context in which a word occurs to help them determine a word's meaning (Landau & Gleitman, 1985; Naigles, 1990). It follows from this hypothesis that children who hear a word in a variety of syntactic contexts will be able to make a more accurate mapping of the verb's meaning. Before this conclusion can be made more confidently, however, some additional analyses need to be conducted. First, if syntactic bootstrapping is occurring, then parents should use individual verbs in a variety of argument structures, and this could be directly measured. More generally, there should also be a low verb token–noun type ratio. That is, taken across a large set of utterances, parents should be using a relatively small set of verbs with a larger number of nouns. These analyses are currently underway.

This first environment-driven process focuses on how children use multiple tokens of a verb type during acquisition. A second crucial question deals with how children use a variety of exemplars of the event to which a verb refers, rather than exemplars of the verb itself, when learning a new verb. It should be obvious that despite children's awesome fast-mapping capabilities, true verb learning probably takes place in most cases across a number of verb–event pairings. The typical word-learning study, however, usually pairs a word to only a small set of referents (occasionally only one) a few times before the key learning or extension questions are asked. Although studies that use such procedures indicate what children think a word means upon a first exposure to the word, they cannot tell us how flexible these original mappings are. Most word learning constraints or biases will be wrong at least some of the time, and it would clearly serve the child well to be able to alter these mappings in the face of evidence that contradicts their initial biases. A study that I conducted speaks directly to this issue (Behrend, 1989). Recall that Behrend (1990a) found that 3- to 5-year-olds and adults showed a result verb bias in their interpretation of a novel verb. That is, when asked to extend a newly learned verb to additional events in which either the result, action, or instrument was different from the events used to teach the verbs, subjects were least willing to extend that verb to events in which the result had been changed. Action changes were second in importance, and instrument changes were least likely to affect subjects' extension of the novel verb to new exemplars.

To test the flexibility of these mappings, Behrend (1989) systematically varied the events used to teach the verbs. Each subject was taught six verbs. During the training events, either the instrument, action, or result was varied across the events. Thus, subjects learned two verbs in which one event component varied during training. For example, subjects saw a person reaching over a cup on a table with a large metal bike lock and pulling the lock back towards her along the table to slide the cup toward her, flip over the cup, or drag the cup on its side to make it squeak. As in the other studies, subjects were then asked to extend the newly learned verbs to four test events. One test event was identical to one of the three training events, whereas in the other test events, either the instrument, action, or result was novel. Thus, for the example above, the subjects saw a fourth result in the result change test event.

It was predicted that subjects would use a novel verb to label an event in which the component that was varied during training was changed during testing (e.g., subjects should be more willing to accept a new result after having viewed three different results rather than three different instruments or actions labeled by the same verb). The results are summarized in Fig. 9.1. A set of orthogonal planned comparisons showed that although the predicted effect was not observed for instrument changes, perhaps because these changes are rarely important to begin with (Behrend, 1990a), it was significant for the action changes, $F(1, 35) = 61.2$, $p < .001$, and result changes, $F(1, 35) = 7.17$, $p < .01$. Thus, any biases the subjects had regarding the novel verb's meaning were influenced to some degree by exposure to three nonidentical exemplars of an event labeled by the same verb. A three-way interaction involving age further showed that these effects were more pronounced in the 5-year-old and adult groups than in the 3-year-old group.

Perhaps the most interesting finding from the study can be seen in the middle panel of Fig. 9.1. When results were varied in training, subjects were extremely unlikely to accept the action change test events. This data point was significantly smaller (Tukey multiple comparison test, $p < .05$) than the other eight data points in Fig. 9.1. Apparently, when subjects' default preference to make a result verb mapping was contradicted by the observational input, they switched to the action as the component of the event that was most specifically marked in the meaning of the novel verb. This finding suggests the possibility of some sort of ordering or default rule hierarchy such as those that have been proposed to account for a variety of human, animal, and machine learning (Holland, Holyoak, Nisbett, & Thagard, 1986; Jackendoff, 1983).

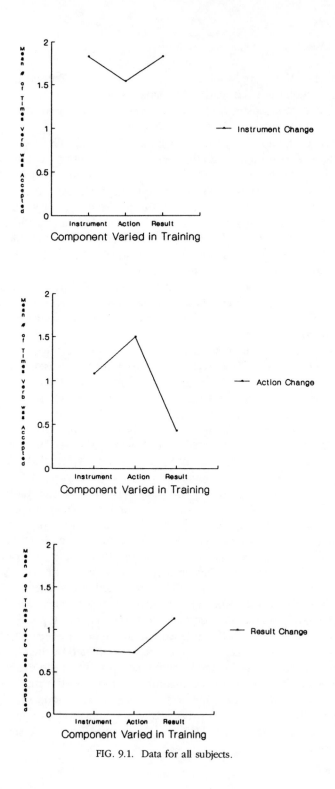

FIG. 9.1. Data for all subjects.

This study also suggests an issue that, to my knowledge, has yet to be addressed regarding verbs and their underlying concepts. When children's object concept learning is studied, one question that is frequently asked is whether children are performing exemplar-based learning or whether they are abstracting some sort of representation of the central tendencies of exemplars, such as a prototype (e.g., Kemler Nelson, 1983; Rosch, 1978; Ward & Scott, 1987). In other words, do children simply store the examples of the real world referents of the words they hear, and make the "best" example the basis for their category learning, or do they base their learning not on a real example but upon some amalgam of all the examples of a given category they have seen. Although exemplar-based learning and probabilistic learning are not mutually exclusive (e.g., Smith & Medin, 1981), this question has important implications for learning and changes in learning during early childhood (Kemler Nelson, 1983).

Although early studies suggested that children generally move from being holistic to analytic learners, there is currently a debate in the literature regarding when and if children make this shift as well as a discussion of exactly what it means to be a holistic or analytic processor (Kemler Nelson, 1983, 1988, 1990; Ward, 1990; Ward & Scott, 1987; Ward, Vela, & Hass, 1990). I do not wish to enter this controversy or to make some determination here as to what type of learners preschool children are. The point I make is that studying how children acquire verb concepts on the basis of multiple exposures to concept exemplars may shed light on this issue and more generally add to our understanding of the concepts that underlie verb meanings. For example, an implicit assumption that I (and others) have made while studying initial mapping of verb meanings is that children focus during learning on one component of an event either preferentially or to the exclusion of other components. That is, if a child thinks a verb is a result verb, then they treat the result as a criterial attribute (Kemler Nelson, 1990; Smith & Medin, 1981) when generalizing that verb to new exemplars. Clearly, however, many verbs include result and action (and instrument, causality, etc.) information in their meanings, and treating one component as criterial may interface with complete learning (i.e., believing that *mopping* only labels events involving a mop).

In order to investigate the holistic versus analytic learning issue regarding verb concepts, it is necessary to adapt one of the typical object concept learning experiments (Kemler Nelson, 1983; Ward & Scott, 1987) for use with verb concepts. That is, subjects would be taught a novel verb concept by being exposed to a variety of exemplars that differ along several dimensions. The stimulus set could be constructed in such a way that generalization trials test whether children form a prototype of the concept (e.g., generalize to a modal exemplar that they have never seen), use one attribute as criterial (e.g., generalize only when the result is the same), or simply store exemplars (e.g., generalize only to instances very similar to training stimuli). Such a study would show how children treat multiple exemplars of verb referents and in the process would illustrate similarities and/or differences between verb and noun concept learning.

A word of caution is necessary here. It is conceivable that subjects in a verb learning study of this nature simply may not accept such a wide variety of exemplars as instances of a particular verb. Several subjects in Behrend's (1989) study were somewhat reticent to accept three training events with different results as examples of the same novel verb. This tendency might be indicative of children's bias to interpret verb meanings as having a criterial attribute as opposed to their tendency to base object concepts on family resemblances made up of a variety of attributes. This is only anecdotal evidence, but it points to a potentially important difference in the acquisition of noun and verb meanings.

LANGUAGE-DRIVEN PROCESSES

The final set of processes that contribute to verb learning fall under the general heading of language-driven. Not being a Whorfian, I do not make the argument that the local language a child is learning indelibly shapes conceptual structure. However, positing the existence of language-driven processes necessitates some degree of linguistic relativity. That is, if verb learning is to any extent driven by language, then children learning different languages may show different learning patterns that are embedded within some broad constraints as to how human languages lexicalize verbs (Talmy, 1985). Some such differences have been documented (e.g., Gopnik & Choi, 1990).

Disclaimers made, I turn to the question of the semantic organization of verbs in English and related languages. Most theoretical accounts of the semantic organization of the verb lexicon claim that verbs are organized in semantic fields (e.g., Miller & Johnson-Laird, 1976; Talmy, 1985). A semantic field includes a large set of verbs that share some basic component of meaning, such as possession, movement, or perception. One characteristic of this structure is that they tend to be organized in a matrix fashion rather than in the hierarchical category structure into which object concepts nicely fall. The important consequence of a matrix organization is that verbs within one semantic field may share as many meaning components (the core concept excepted, of course) with verbs in another semantic field as they share with verbs in their own semantic field. This type of organization contrasts sharply with the hierarchical organization of nouns, in which different hierarchies represent different ontological categories and in which members of a particular branch of the hierarchical structure, by necessity of implication, share many meaning components.

Psycholinguistic studies have supported this theoretical claim. Word sorting studies have shown that when adults are asked to sort verbs into groups that "go together," they tend to group them in broad semantic categories (Miller, 1972) and that their organization is consistent over multiple sortings (Graesser, Hopkinson, & Schmid, 1987). This latter study showed that, in fact, adults' semantic network of verbs is less hierarchical and more matrix-like than their noun networks. This matrix organization ought to have consequences on some psycholinguistic tasks, and there is some data to support the contention that nouns and verbs are organized differently. Huttenlocher and Lui (1979) showed that two common effects seen in standard memory tasks—clustering in recall and release from proactive inhibition—were less pronounced when verbs were the stimulus words than when nouns were the stimulus words. Given that these effects are hypothesized to be a function of the hierarchical taxonomic organization of noun concepts, the matrix organization of verbs predicts the weakening of the effects.

Behrend (1990a) also argued that this difference in semantic organization may help to explain some discrepancies between findings from studies of children's spontaneous use of verbs and studies of children's initial mapping of verb meanings. Whereas these two kinds of studies of children's acquisition of object terms produce converging results (i.e., whole objects at more or less the basic level), Behrend found that children frequently used instrument verbs during spontaneous labeling but rarely showed a bias to interpret a novel verb as an instrument verb. It was argued that use of instrument verbs during spontaneous labeling reflected communicative pressure to use the most specific verb available whereas learning preferences reflected overall frequency of a verb type in the language, which served to maximize the correctness of the default hypothesis. Although basic-level terms in object hierarchies maximize both of these pressures by optimizing both within-category similarity and between-category differences, the matrix organization of verbs leads to differential responding in labeling and learning tasks. There is a clear need for more studies of the organization of children's verb lexicons.

The language-driven process that has received more attention is the manner in which the syntactic context or contexts in which novel words are used affects children's acquisition of those words. This process has been dubbed *syntactic bootstrapping* (Gleitman, 1991; Landau & Gleitman, 1985). Several chapters in this volume detail the theoretical basis and summarize empirical support for syntactic bootstrapping for verb acquisition. It is important to recognize that the syntactic bootstrapping hypothesis was not entirely a creation of verb researchers. Now-classic studies showed how small changes in sentence structure affect a child's interpretation of a novel word as a common noun versus a proper name (Katz, Baker, & MacNamara, 1974) or as a noun versus an adjective (Brown, 1958; Taylor & Gelman, 1988).

Given the action versus result interpretation of novel verbs, it seemed sensible to look for some syntactic cue that might clue children in to what type of verb they were hearing. Whereas other syntactic bootstrapping work has looked almost exclusively to argument structure as the determinant of a verb's meaning, it seemed that simple verb inflections may give children cues to the result/action distinction. Studies of English-speaking children's early use of verb inflections suggest that children initially apply the progressive *-ing* inflection to verbs denoting events that include durative actions and the past *-ed* inflection to verbs denoting completive events with clear results (Bloom, Lifter, & Hafitz, 1980). Antinucci and Miller (1976) showed an analogous pattern of findings for children learning Italian. Experimental studies also suggested that children may use the past, progressive, and imperfective inflections differentially to label events differing in lexical aspect in both French (Bronckart & Sinclair, 1972) and English (McShane & Whittaker, 1988).

These studies demonstrate a type of *semantic bootstrapping* (Pinker, 1984). That is, children apparently use the semantic content of a verb to guide their application of inflections to that verb. The obvious reciprocal question is whether children use these inflections to help them make action versus result interpretations of a novel verb that is used to label events that are both durative and completive. If they use these inflections, then children should be more likely to make an action verb interpretation when they hear the *-ing* ending and more likely to make a result verb interpretation when they hear the *-ed* ending.

Three studies that tested this hypothesis were performed by Behrend et al. (in press). Three-year-old, 5-year-old, and adult subjects learned a series of four verbs in the procedure developed by Behrend (1989, 1990a). In the first study each child was assigned randomly to one of three conditions. Subjects in the progressive condition heard all verb presentations with the *-ing* ending (e.g., "Watch, she is stiping"), subjects in the past condition heard all verb presentations with the *-ed* inflection (e.g., "Watch, she stiped that time"), and subjects in the neutral condition heard all verb presentations with a null inflection (e.g., "Watch her stipe"). After two presentations of the novel verb used to label a novel event in which an adult performed a physical action with an instrument to produce a clear result, subjects were then asked if they would use the newly learned verb to label four additional events. The test question was always asked with the inflection used during training. One event was identical to the training events, whereas the other three events varied either the instrument, action, or result from the training events.

A two-way interaction between condition and test event change was predicted. More specifically, it was predicted that subjects in the progressive condition would be more likely to make action verb than result verb interpretations and subjects in the past condition would be more likely to do the opposite. As predicted, subjects in the progressive condition were somewhat less likely to extend the novel verbs to action changes (an average of 22% of all trials) than result changes ($M = 25\%$), and past condition subjects were less likely to extend the novel verbs to result changes ($M = 27\%$) than to action changes ($M = 31\%$), but the interaction was not statistically significant. Also of interest was the lack of a result verb bias shown by subjects in this study. A second study was then conducted in which the learning paradigm was pared down to include just the elements of the design that were relevant to the specific interaction described previously. Thus, the neutral condition and instrument change event were dropped. In addition, a training event was added for each verb to give the children additional exposure to the syntax.

Although this strategy was scientifically sound and utterly sensible, the study did not produce the desired interaction or even the desired direction of the effect. An important difference in the results of this study compared to the first study was that subjects were less likely, overall, to accept the novel verb as a label for the test events. Subjects accepted the novel verb so rarely (11% of trials with a change in the event) that it appeared that many were simply rejecting the verb for test events that differed in any way from the training events. Including the instrument change test event (the event most likely to elicit extension of the novel verb) in previous studies may have had the serendipitous effect of indicating to the child that it was acceptable to extend the novel verbs to events that were different from the training events.

These two studies tested children from 3 to 5 years old as well as adults. Most studies of syntactic bootstrapping have found their effects in children from 18 months to 3 years of age. Although age did not interact significantly with inflections in these two studies, Behrend and Harris (1991) analyzed the responses of just the 3-year-olds in light of these earlier findings. Figure 9.2 displays the combined data from the 3-year-olds in both studies. When these data are analyzed, the interaction is in the predicted direction and is marginally significant, $F(1, 26) = 3.08$, $p = .08$. This analysis, although post hoc in nature, was consistent enough with both the original hypotheses and other bootstrapping work to motivate a third study.

There was still one more possible reason why the desired effect was weak or nonexistent in the first two studies. The between-subjects design of the studies exposed subjects to one and only one verb inflection. The rationale for employing this procedure was to obtain as much data as possible per subject per verb inflection and to avoid contaminating subjects in each condition by exposing them to verbs in other syntactic contexts. The first rationale was clearly sensible, but the second may have been somewhat misguided. By exposing subjects to one and only one inflection, the design inadvertently made it difficult for subjects to use the inflection diagnostically

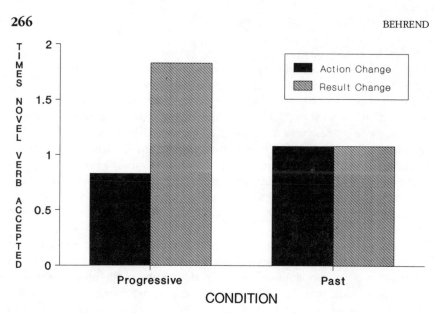

FIG. 9.2.   Condition × Test Change interaction for the 3-year-olds.

or contrastively to help them map the novel verb meanings. In other words, given that these inflections are only probabilistic and imperfect cues to verb meaning (in fact, they mark tense and aspect, not meaning), how could a child recruit this linguistic device if it did not vary across stimulus verbs?

With this in mind, a third study was conducted (Behrend & Harris, 1992). Each subject learned six novel verbs, three presented with the -*ing* inflection and three with the -*ed* inflection. The inflections alternated with each verb that was taught, with half of the subjects hearing -*ing* on the first verb and half hearing -*ed* on the first verb. Finally, given that the predicted effect was most strongly observed in the 3-year-olds in the first two studies, 16 children from 34 to 40 months of age were tested.

The findings were striking. Figure 9.3 shows the data relevant to the predicted verb ending by test event change interaction. When subjects heard the -*ing* ending they were less likely to accept the novel verb as a label for the action change test events than for the result change test events. In contrast, when subjects heard the -*ed* ending they were less likely to accept the novel verb as a label for the result change than for the action change test events. The interaction was significant, $F(1, 14) = 9.04$, $p < .01$.

If it was the change to a within-subjects design that enabled children to use the inflections as diagnostic cues to verb meaning, then it follows that the predicted effect should have been strongest after exposure to both inflections. In order to test this hypothesis, an analysis was conducted that divided responses to the six verbs into three sets of verb pairs based on the order in which the verbs were taught. That is, responses to the first pair, middle pair, and final pair of verbs were compared. An analysis that included

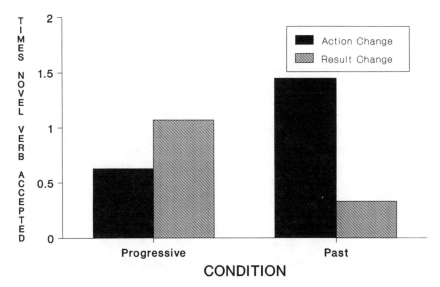

FIG. 9.3. Condition × Test Change interaction, within subjects.

verb pair as a within-subjects factor produced a three-way interaction between inflection, test event change, and verb pair, $F(2, 28) = 16.7$, $p < .01$.
Subjects applied the novel verb equally to the result and action changes for
the first verb pair regardless of inflection but applied the verbs to the second
and third verb pairs in a pattern conforming to the overall two-way interaction. This unique finding confirmed that the decision to perform a within-
subjects design was a good one and illustrates the need to enable subjects
to use syntactic information in a diagnostic manner.

This study illustrates a type of syntactic bootstrapping that is somewhat
more broad in its construal of what qualifies as a bootstrap. Syntactic bootstrapping studies (Gleitman, 1991; Naigles, 1990) have by and large focused
on subcategorization frames and argument structures as the primary determinants of a verb's meaning. There is strong support for this view, as adults
group verbs that participate in the same syntactic alternations and subcategorizations frames (Fisher, Gleitman, & Gleitman, 1991). Verb inflections,
on the other hand, encode tense and aspect in English and do not truly
reflect verb semantics. However, the aspectual distinction marked by these
inflections is probabilistically correlated with the action verb/result verb
distinction.

When speaking of children's bootstrapping using verb inflections, the
construal of bootstrapping is similar to that proposed by Shatz (1988). Shatz
(1988) conceptualized bootstrapping as a set of procedure or mechanisms
that enable children to use their incomplete linguistic knowledge to help
them acquire additional linguistic competence. Although Shatz does not

explicitly discuss the type of bootstrapping illustrated by the Behrend and Harris (1991, 1992) studies, it appears that these findings fit nicely into Shatz' conceptualization. In other words, using verb inflections as a bootstrap to the meaning of a novel verb may be more akin to a learning heuristic or strategy: a quick and easy way to make some initial determination of what a novel verb means. As is the case with all heuristics, the speed with which a determination can be made is gained by sacrificing some accuracy. Similar points have been made with regard to children's biases in fast-mapping nouns: The biases must ultimately be wrong on at least some occasions, but the biases allow children a toehold in language from which they may bootstrap themselves into greater competency.

CONCLUSIONS AND COMMENTS

In this chapter, I have proposed three general categories of processes that contribute to children's learning of verb meanings, focusing especially on the initial mapping of these meanings. Although I have separated these processes under the headings of child-driven, environment-driven, and language-driven processes, it should be clear that this trichotomy is somewhat artificial. These three processes do not operate in vacuums, separated and isolated from one another. Rather, they interact in ways that can produce both consistencies and inconsistencies in patterns of early verb learning, and the fact that they interact necessitated the need to include some discussion about each process in each of the major divisions of this chapter.

How may these interactions be described in a way that will advance our knowledge of verb acquisition and semantic development in general? Perhaps the most useful theoretical framework for describing and investigating these sets of variables is that of *dynamical systems theory.* With its origins in the physical and biological sciences, dynamical systems theory has been applied as a framework to study developmental phenomena that take nonlinear and, often, unpredictable developmental trajectories, such as infant motor development (e.g., Thelen, 1989; Thelen & Ulrich, 1991). Semantic development, with its bursts, pauses, and shifts in focus, seems to qualify as one of these difficult-to-predict phenomena (see also van Geert, 1991). Briefly, systems theory as applied to development postulates that different levels (stages, milestones, etc.) of development operate as *attractor states* to which the organism is naturally drawn. The achievement of any attractor state can be influenced, affected, or prevented by any of a number of *control parameters.* The control parameters for any attractor state operate in such a way that the unique interaction between them moves the child through *phase shifts* between attractor states. Thus, the relevant properties of the language, environment, and child are control parameters that contribute to the attractor state of fast-mapping of novel words (perhaps after a phase shift from basic referential abilities).

The application of a dynamical systems approach to any developmental issue involves several steps (see Thelen & Ulrich, 1991, for a more complete account). First, a longitudinal approach is needed in order to describe accurately the developmental trajectory of the outcome variable of interest, in this case the acquisition and composition of the lexicon. Fortunately, there is now ample longitudinal data available on both general lexical development (e.g., Benedict, 1979; Goldin-Meadow et al., 1976) and the acquisition of verbs per se (Behrend, 1992; Tomasello, 1992). Inspection of these data should reveal points of transition or instability (e.g., the vocabulary burst or a shift from learning object words to learning a variety of words) at which the investigator should look for variables that may qualify as the control parameters for the transition. Once such variables have been identified, then experimental work may be conducted in which these variables are systematically manipulated during points of transition, as systems theory hypothesizes that the system is especially sensitive to changes in the control parameters at transitions. Of course, it is unethical to manipulate control parameters on-line (e.g., by limiting children to exposure to only certain sentence structures), so investigators must be clever enough to design short-term experimental procedures in which the variables of interest may be changed in such a way to have a short-term impact on children's word learning. This approach characterizes experiments that have manipulated or controlled environmental variables such as joint attention (Tomasello & Farrar, 1986) and exposure to exemplars (Behrend, 1989), language variables such as grammar (Naigles, 1990) and morphology (Taylor & Gelman, 1988), and child variables such as familiarity with words that contrast with a new word to be learned (Merriman, 1986).

This outline of a systems theory approach to lexical acquisition is, at this point, only a useful analogy and illustrative of how it may be possible to develop a theory of semantic development that not only encompasses all the types of processes described in this chapter but that also encompasses the acquisition of all types of words. In systems theory terms, although the same parameters are involved in both noun and verb learning, it is almost certainly the case that the optimal values of the control parameters for noun learning are not the same values that optimize verb learning. Differences in the optimal learning contexts and applicability of lexical principles for learning nouns and verbs (e.g., Golinkoff et al., this volume; Tomasello & Kruger, 1992) are illustrative of the need for an approach that at once acknowledges the importance of a unique set of factors for all areas of semantic development and simultaneously acknowledges that what's good for learning "goose" is not necessarily what's good for learning "to gander." Dynamical systems theory—if not in itself, then at least in spirit—seems to fit this bill very well.

The work summarized in this chapter and this volume makes several things abundantly clear. First, the study of children's acquisition of verb meanings is an important and, still, fairly wide open area of inquiry. Second, there are several aspects of verb learning that make it unique and distinct from noun learning, and understanding these distinctions is a crucial goal of verb development researchers. Third, rather than allowing these distinctions to separate those who study verb concept development from those who study noun concept development, the distinctions should motivate us to develop a broad, inclusive theory of semantic development in which both noun and verb learning can be satisfactorily explained. Dynamical systems theory was offered as one possible framework for such a theory, but the type of theory that is developed is less important than the ability of that theory to unite the existing body of literature and guide future investigations of these issues.

REFERENCES

Antinucci, F., & Miller, R. (1976). How children talk about what happened. *Journal of Child Language, 3,* 169–189.

Bates, E., Bretherton, I., & Snyder, L. (1988). *From first words to grammar: Individual differences and dissociable mechanisms.* Cambridge, England: Cambridge University Press.

Bauer, P. J., & Mandler, J. M. (1989). Taxonomies and triads: Conceptual organization in one- to two-year-olds. *Cognitive Psychology, 21,* 156–184.

Behrend, D. A. (1989). Default values in verb frames: Cognitive biases for learning verb meaning. *Proceeding of the 11th annual meeting of the Cognitive Science Society* (pp. 252–258). Hillsdale, NJ: Lawrence Erlbaum Associates.

Behrend, D. A. (1990a). Constraints and development: A reply to Nelson. *Cognitive Development, 5,* 313–330.

Behrend, D. A. (1990b). The development of verb concepts: Children's use of verbs to label familiar and novel events. *Child Development, 61,* 681–696.

Behrend, D. A. (1992). *Beyond natural partitioning: The development of the verb lexicon.* Unpublished manuscript, University of Arkansas, Fayetteville.

Behrend, D. A., & Harris, L. L. (1991, April). *In search of syntactic bootstrapping: Verb endings and the initial mapping of verb meanings.* Paper presented at the Biennial Meetings of the Society for Research in Child Development, Seattle.

Behrend, D. A., Harris, L. L., & Cartwright, K. B. (in press). Morphological cues to verb meaning: Verb inflections and the initial mapping of verb meanings. *Journal of Child Language.*

Benedict, H. (1979). Early lexical development: Comprehension and production. *Journal of Child Language, 6,* 183–200.

Bloom, L., Lifter, K., & Hafitz, J. (1980). Semantics of verbs and the development of verb inflection in child language. *Language, 56,* 386–412.

Bronckart, J. P., & Sinclair, H. (1972). Tense, time, and aspect. *Cognition, 2,* 107–130.

Brown, R. (1958). How shall a thing be called? *Psychological Review, 65,* 14–21.

Clark, E. V. (1983). Meanings and concepts. In J. H. Flavell & E. M. Markman (Eds.), *Handbook of Child Psychology* (Vol. 3, pp. 787–840). New York: Wiley.

Fisher, C., Gleitman, H., & Gleitman, L. R. (1991). On the semantic content of subcategorization frames. *Cognitive Psychology, 23,* 331–392.

Forbes, J. N., & Farrar, M. J. (1993). Children's initial assumptions about the meaning of novel motion verbs: Biased and conservative? *Cognitive Development, 8,* 273–290.

Fu, P., Gelman, S. A., & Behrend, D. A. (1992, April). *Preponderance of nouns in children's early vocabulary: An examination of the role of linguistic and non-linguistic input.* Paper presented at the Conference on Human Development, Atlanta.

Gentner, D. (1978). On relational meaning: The acquisition of verb meaning. *Child Development, 49,* 988–998.

Gentner, D. (1982). Why nouns are learned before verbs: Linguistic relativity vs. natural partitioning. In S. A. Kuczaj (Ed.), *Language development: Language, culture, and cognition* (pp. 313–335). Hillsdale, NJ: Lawrence Erlbaum Associates.

Gleitman, L. (1991). The structural sources of verb meanings. *Language Acquisition, 1,* 3–56.

Goldin-Meadow, S., Seligman, M. E. P., & Gelman, R. (1976). Language in the two-year-old. *Cognition, 4,* 189–202.

Golinkoff, R. M., Hirsh-Pasek, K., Bailey, L. M., & Wenger, N. R. (1992). Young children and adults use lexical principles to learn new nouns. *Developmental Psychology, 28,* 99–108.

Golinkoff, R. M., & Kerr, J. L. (1978). Infants' perception of semantically defined action role changes in filmed events. *Merrill-Palmer Quarterly, 24,* 53–61.

Gopnik, A., & Choi, S. (1990). Do language differences lead to cognitive differences?: A cross-linguistic study of semantic and cognitive development. *First Language, 10,* 199–216.

Graesser, A. C., Hopkinson, D., & Schmid, C. (1987). Differences in interconcept organization between nouns and verbs. *Journal of Memory and Language, 26,* 242–253.

Gropen, J., Pinker, S., Hollander, M., & Goldberg, R. (1991). Syntax and semantics in the acquisition of locative verbs. *Journal of Child Language, 18,* 115–151.

Harris, M., Barrett, M. D., Jones, D., & Brookes, S. (1988). Linguistic input and early word meaning. *Journal of Child Language, 15,* 77–94.

Holland, J. H., Holyoak, K. J., Nisbett, R. E., & Thagard, P. R. (1986). *Induction.* Cambridge, MA: MIT Press.

Huttenlocher, J., & Lui, F. (1979). The semantic organization of some simple nouns and verbs. *Journal of Verbal Learning and Verbal Behavior, 18,* 141–162.

Huttenlocher, J., Smiley, P., & Charney, R. (1983). The emergence of action categories in the child: Evidence from verb meanings. *Psychological Review, 90,* 72–93.

Huttenlocher, J., Smiley, P., & Ratner, H. (1983). What do word meanings reveal about conceptual development. In T. R. Seiler & W. Wannenmacher (Eds.), *Conceptual development and the development of word meaning* (pp. 84–102). Berlin: Springer-Verlag.

Jackendoff, R. (1983). *Semantics and cognition.* Cambridge, MA: MIT Press.

Katz, N., Baker, E., & Macnamara, J. (1974). What's in a name? A study of how children learn common and proper names. *Child Development, 45,* 469–473.

Kelly, D. J., & Rice, M. L. (1991). *The effect of verb content on children's initial referential selections.* Paper presented at the Biennial Meetings of the Society for Research in Child Development, Seattle.

Kemler Nelson, D. G. (1983). Holistic and analytic modes in perceptual and cognitive development. In T. Tighe & B. E. Shepp (Eds.), *Perception, cognition, and development: Interactional analyses* (pp. 77–102). Hillsdale, NJ: Lawrence Erlbaum Associates.

Kemler Nelson, D. G. (1988). When category learning is holistic: A reply to Ward & Scott. *Memory & Cognition, 16,* 79–84.

Kemler Nelson, D. G. (1990). When experimental findings conflict with everyday observations: Reflections on children's category learning. *Child Development, 61,* 606–610.

Kuczaj, S. A. (1990). Constraining constraint theories. *Cognitive Development, 5,* 341–344.

Landau, B., & Gleitman, L. R. (1985). *Language and experience.* Cambridge, MA: Harvard University Press.

MacWhinney, B. (1987). The competition model. In B. MacWhinney (Ed.), *Mechanisms of language acquisition* (pp. 249–308). Hillsdale, NJ: Lawrence Erlbaum Associates.

Markman, E. M. (1989). *Categorization and naming in children.* Cambridge, MA: MIT Press.

Markman, E. M., & Hutchinson, J. E. (1984). Children's sensitivity to constraints on word meaning: Taxonomic vs. thematic relations. *Cognitive Psychology, 16,* 1–27.

McShane, J., & Whittaker, S. (1988). The encoding of tense and aspect by three- to five-year-old children. *Journal of Experimental Child Psychology, 45,* 52–70.

Merriman, W. E. (1986). Some reasons for the occurrence and eventual correction of children's naming errors. *Child Development, 57,* 942–952.

Merriman, W. E., & Bowman, L. (1989). The mutual exclusivity bias in children's word learning. *Monographs of the Society for Research in Child Development, 54* (3–4, Serial No. 220).

Miller, G. A. (1972). English verbs of motion: A case study in semantics and lexical memory. In A. W. Melton & E. Martin (Eds.), *Coding processes in human memory* (pp. 335–372). Washington, DC: Winston.

Miller, G. A., & Johnson-Laird, P. N. (1976). *Language and perception.* Cambridge, MA: Harvard.

Naigles, L. (1990). Children use syntax to learn verb meanings. *Journal of Child Language, 17,* 357–374.

Nelson, K. (1973). Structure and strategy in learning to talk. *Monographs of the Society for Research in Child Development, 38* (1–2, Serial No. 149).

Nelson, K. (1988). Constraints on word learning? *Cognitive Development, 3,* 221–246.

Pinker, S. (1984). *Language learnability and language development.* Cambridge, MA: Harvard University Press.

Pinker, S. (1989). *Learnability and cognition.* Cambridge, MA: Harvard University Press.

Robertson, S., & Suci, G. J. (1980). Event perception by children in the early stages of language production. *Child Development, 51,* 89–96.

Rosch, E. (1978). Principles of categorization. In E. Rosch (Ed.), *Cognition and categorization* (pp. 1–28). Hillsdale, NJ: Lawrence Erlbaum Associates.

Schwartz, R. G., & Terrell, B. Y. (1983). The role of input frequency in lexical acquisition. *Journal of Child Language, 10,* 57–64.

Shatz, M. (1988). Bootstrapping operations in child language. In K. E. Nelson (Ed.), *Children's language* (Vol. 6, pp. 1–22). Hillsdale, NJ: Lawrence Erlbaum Associates.

Smith, E. E., & Medin, D. (1981). *Categories and concepts.* Cambridge, MA: Harvard University Press.

Talmy, L. (1985). Lexicalization patterns: Semantic structure in lexical forms. In T. Shopen (Ed.), *Language typology and syntactic description* (pp. 75–141). Cambridge, England: Cambridge University Press.

Taylor, M., & Gelman, S. A. (1988). Adjectives and nouns: Children's strategies for learning new words. *Child Development, 59,* 411–419.

Thelen, E. (1989). Self-organization in developmental processes: Can systems approaches work? In M. Gunnar & E. Thelen (Eds.), *Systems in development: The Minnesota Symposium in Child Psychology* (Vol. 22, pp. 77–117). Hillsdale, NJ: Lawrence Erlbaum Associates.

Thelen, E., & Ulrich, B. D. (1991). Hidden skills. *Monographs of the Society for Research in Child Development, 56* (1, Serial No. 223).

Tomasello, M. (1992). *First verbs.* Cambridge, England: Cambridge University Press.

Tomasello, M., & Farrar, M. J. (1986). Joint attention and early language. *Child Development, 57,* 1454–1463.

Tomasello, M., & Kruger, A. C. (1992). Joint attention on actions: Acquiring verbs in ostensive and non-ostensive contexts. *Journal of Child Language, 19,* 311–333.

van Geert, P. (1991). A dynamic systems model of cognitive and language growth. *Psychological Review, 98,* 3–53.

Ward, T. B. (1990). Further comments on the attribute availability hypothesis of children's category learning. *Child Development, 61,* 611–613.

Ward, T. B., & Scott, J. (1987). Analytic and holistic modes of learning family-resemblance concepts. *Memory and Cognition, 15,* 42–54.

Ward, T. B., Vela, E., & Hass, S. D. (1990). Children and adults learn family resemblance categories analytically. *Child Development, 61,* 593–605.

Waxman, S. R., & Gelman, R. (1986). Preschoolers' use of superordinate relations in classification and language. *Cognitive Development, 1,* 139–156.

PART THREE

THE ROLE OF ARGUMENT STRUCTURE

Verbs of a Feather Flock Together: Semantic Information in the Structure of Maternal Speech

Anne Lederer
Henry Gleitman
Lila Gleitman
University of Pennsylvania

Linguistic theorizing about language acquisition has primarily focused on phonetic and syntactic issues. A much ignored stepchild of the research enterprise has been the topic of word meaning: How do children aged 5 or 6 years come to know 15,000 or so words such that they can utter and understand them? The major reason for this benign neglect among linguists is that word learning has traditionally been seen as a problem with no interesting internal structure, solved by the particularistic business of lining up each word length formative with its extralinguistic contexts. For instance, the sound "aard-vark" occurs most regularly in the presence of aardvarks, the sound "receive" in the presence of receiving, and so on, and so the child can associate each sound with its meaning—a putatively simple and transparent mapping procedure.

However, challenges to the sufficiency of this approach go back at least to Plato and were compellingly explicated by Quine (1960): Any real-world observation in principle can support a bewildering variety of descriptions. An observed rabbit is also an observed animal, furriness, temporal rabbit stage, and collection of undetached rabbit parts. A substantive psychological literature responding to this challenge has now appeared, concerning constraints on the child's representational (perceptual and conceptual) biases (Carey, 1978; Hall & Waxman, 1993; Keil, 1989; Landau, in press; Landau, Smith, & Jones, 1988; Markman, in press; Soja, Carey, & Spelke, 1991; and many other sources).

More relevant to the work we present here, constraints on the interpretation of a new word also derive from the child's emerging understanding of language design. To put this as baldly as possible, things tend to surface as nouns, properties as adjectives, and actions as verbs. Thus a child who hears a new word can be guided in its mapping by noticing the telltale markings of its lexical class (e.g., whether she hears "a gorp," "gorpish," or "gorping"; Brown, 1957; Grimshaw, 1981; Pinker, 1984). This view has been extended by showing that there are cues to word meanings within as well as across lexical classes. Particularly, potential cues to the meaning of a new verb reside in the subcategorization frames in which it occurs in caretaker speech (Fisher, Gleitman, & Gleitman, 1991; Fisher, Hall, Rakowitz, & Gleitman, 1994; Gleitman, 1990; Landau & Gleitman, 1985).

The present article contributes to this position by analyzing maternal verb use to young children. We begin with a brief sketch of how verb syntactic structure appears to covary with verb semantic similarity and discuss how this covariance may facilitate learning. We then present an analysis of form/meaning relations in the speech of mothers talking to their infants. This analysis shows that frame-range information that distinguishes among the mothers' verb meanings is available in the children's input at the time in life when they are just beginning to learn their first verbs.

SYNTACTIC CORRELATES OF VERB MEANINGS

Sentences are the surface expressions of underlying predicate–argument structure, with the verb expressing the specific predicate and the nominals expressing the arguments. The mapping from underlying to surface structure, though complex, generally preserves this relationship (as codified in the *projection principle*; Chomsky, 1981). For example, a unary relation such as *fall* is expressed with an intransitive (one-argument) sentence, and a binary relation such as *push* is expressed with a transitive (two-argument) sentence. More generally, verbs that describe motion caused by voluntary adjustments of the organism's musculature typically occur with null complements:

(1) John giggled/climbed/fell/sneezed.

If the motion is necessarily caused by an external agent, there usually will be an additional NP to represent that cause, as in:

(2) Mary pushed/hit/rotated/lifted John.

Verbs can also encode the path over which or the location or state in which the affected entity ends up, as in:

(3) John put the ball on the table/poured juice into the glass/sent the tigers into a frenzy.

In English, these properties are typically represented by a prepositional phrase that describes this path (Gruber, 1967; Jackendoff, 1978; Landau, in press; Talmy, 1985). Thus, not only the number but also the position and case marking of NPs is related to the sense of the verb. As another example of the relation between surface form and predicate–argument structure, verbs that describe aspects of perception and cognition characteristically accept clausal complements. Compare, for example:

(4) John explains/thinks that Frank caught a wolverine.

(5) John *sleeps/*puts that Frank caught a wolverine.[1]

The difference in acceptability between Examples 4 and 5 makes sense because the verbs of Example 4 express a relation between an actor (John) and an event (Frank catching wolverine) and clauses are the linguistic expressions of whole events (Vendler, 1972).

These samples do not even scratch the surface of verb lexical organization, of course. The regards in which the complementation privileges of verbs are semantically conditioned have been a traditional focus of investigation by linguists (e.g., Jespersen, 1927), and remain so (Dowty, 1979; Fillmore, 1968; Hoekstra, 1992; Jackendoff, 1990; Levin, 1993; Pinker, 1989; Talmy, 1975; among scores of important sources). Our question here concerns the ways that these form–meaning correspondences might be exploited by a language acquisition procedure.

CLAUSE STRUCTURE AND LEARNING

If the clause structures are projections from the semantics of verbs, then a child who has extracted a verb meaning from observing the contexts of its use can predict its structural privileges. This idea was developed and eloquently supported in the work of Grimshaw (1981) and that of Pinker and his collaborators (Gropen, Pinker, Hollander, & Goldberg, 1991; Pinker, 1984).

We concentrate here on a converse claim: The child who understands the semantic implications of syntactic environments can recover aspects of the meanings of unknown verbs (Bloom, in press; Landau & Gleitman, 1985; Naigles, 1990; Naigles, Gleitman, & Gleitman, 1993; Waxman, in press). For example, if one hears *John is gorping*, it is unlikely that *gorp* means 'hit' and more likely that it means 'sneeze.'

---

[1]"*" represents sentences judged to be ill formed or unacceptable in everyday speech.

The chief argument for supposing that learners exploit this information source has to do with the difficulty of identifying a verb's meaning from observation of its extralinguistic concomitants. A significant proportion of verb utterances, even to babies, are not about the here and now (Beckwith, Tinker, & Bloom, 1989). Even if the context in which a novel verb occurs is pertinent, more than one thing is usually happening such that there is no unique interpretive choice. For example, John may sneeze while he hits Bill. The distinction between the two verbs can in the long run be extracted by cross-situational observation (see Pinker, 1984), but attention to the structure is a handy alternate route and has promise for explaining how children so often derive the sense correctly from a single scene–sentence exposure. Moreover, attention to the syntactic structure and the placement of nominals is especially important for disentangling the many paired verbs that just about always occur under the same real-world circumstances (e.g., *give/receive, chase/flee*; Fisher et al., 1994). Finally, syntactic deduction appears to be a necessary component in identifying such verbs as *want* and *believe*, whose mental senses are evidently impossible to cull from observing scenes in the world, but whose syntactic properties (clausal complements) are especially revealing (for experimental evidence see Gillette, 1992).

Examination of these issues has led us to a structure-sensitive approach to verb learning, one that works in tandem with the meaning-to-form deductions as described by Grimshaw and Pinker. In our view, learners do not acquire verb meaning by pairing the new word, as an isolated formative, with its real-world contingencies. Rather, they perform a sentence-to-world pairing. The structure of the sentence narrows the interpretive options left open by scene inspection by exposing the argument-taking properties of the novel verb. This allows the learner to decide whether to focus on the hitting or the sneezing aspect of the scene in view, to zoom in on only certain aspects of the extralinguistic context. This focusing role of the syntax accomplished, the precise identification of the verb is derived by inspection of its environmental contingencies.

An extension of this position attempts to respond to the fact that the sentence-to-world pairing procedure still seems too weak, even when amplified by cross-situational observation. This is because too many verbs share a surface environment and are used in situations that can easily be misleading. For example, the most frequent environment in maternal speech for both *want* and *eat* is a simple transitive: "Did you eat the cookie?" "Do you want a cookie?" Observers are biased to identify a novel verb as related in meaning to *eat* if shown a relevant scene and informed of this structure (Gillette, 1992). Even if shown further scenes in which *eat* cannot be the correct construal (e.g., a scene in which the mother offers a drum to the child), subjects guess another physical action term (e.g., *take* or *get*) and are mulishly resistant to conjecturing a mental term such as *want*. However, if they hear a disambiguating syntactic structure (and even if the content words in this structure have been converted to nonsense, e.g., "Did vany GORP to blitso the ribenflak?"), they guess a mental verb. The suggestion is that although single sentence–scene observations are often uninformative, a small and manageable set of sentence–scene observations allows convergence on the correct interpretation.

It is this suggested procedure whose data basis is examined in the analysis now presented. We ask whether the set of syntactic environments offered by mothers to the learning child inevitably places the learner in the correct semantic neighborhood—whether verbs whose range of syntactic privileges is similar share components of their interpretations. If this is not so in the child's real learning environment, it follows that syntactic range can play no part in the learning procedure. But if it *is* so, then the approach gains plausibility.

AN ANALYSIS OF MATERNAL SYNTACTIC USAGE

This analysis describes the verb use of native English-speaking mothers talking to their young children.

Subjects

The subjects were 8 middle-class English-speaking mothers. Their children ranged in age from 12 months, 5 days to 25 months, 3 days (mean = 20 months, 9 days). The mean length of the children's utterances (MLU) ranged from 1.2 to 1.6 (mean = 1.5). Their vocabulary consisted predominantly of simple nouns and social words (e.g., *bye-bye*), with few or no verbs, but they were just at the point where verb learning begins in earnest.

The Corpus

Maternal speech was videotaped during hour-long sessions in a laboratory playroom. The mothers were instructed to play with their children, using the toys that were scattered around the room. An experimenter who minimally interacted with the mother and child was also present.

Materials, Coding, and Preliminary Analysis

The videotapes were transcribed, and all transcribed utterances containing a verb were extracted from each mother's speech sample (copulas and auxiliaries were excluded). The frequency of each verb in each mother's speech was calculated. We retained for further analysis all verbs that appeared (across mothers) at least 32 times and had been uttered by at least half of the mothers. This yielded an average of four uses of each verb by each mother. A total of 24 verbs satisfied these criteria, yielding a total of 2,183 utterances for the analysis. The 24 verbs are listed, in descending order of frequency, in Table 10.1.

Syntactic Analysis

The verbs were analyzed according to the structures in which they appeared in the maternal speech, as follows.

Number and Type of Complement. The subcategorization frames were extracted in an orthodox fashion. For example, the sentences

1. The elephant is sleeping.
2. Bonnie saw the dog.

TABLE 10.1
Verbs Included in Analysis of Maternal Usage

Verb	Frequency Across Mothers	Number of Mothers Who Used Verb
go	179	8
see	171	8
come	166	8
say	157	8
do	145	8
put	142	8
get	137	8
look	136	8
want	118	8
have	110	8
know	94	8
like	78	8
think	67	8
take	65	8
find	53	6
play	49	7
push	49	5
show	45	7
sit	41	6
catch	39	4
call	37	7
make	36	6
eat	36	7
pull	33	6

3. Johnnie put the book on the table.
4. I know you like ice cream.
5. Do you want to pick up the blocks?
6. Look how I do it!

were coded as

1. V
2. V NP
3. V NP PP
4. V S_t
5. V S_u
6. V S_{fr}[2]

Intonation. We used the maternal intonation in certain cases to decide whether the utterance was a question or imperative. This was done because verbs vary as to whether they license imperatives (compare, e.g., "Accuse him of treason!" and *"Suspect him of treason!"). Although this distinction is not one of subcategorization as usually conceived, it is a distinction of syntactic environment that is informative of the semantics of activity versus state. Intonational features were also used to distinguish quotation contexts such as, "So she goes/says, 'Don't touch that!' "[3]

Progressive Versus Simple Past/Present. Only some verbs are comfortable in the progressive form as a consequence of the active/stative distinction in their semantics (compare "I am thinking of you" and *"I am believing in you").

Matrices of Verb Use

A verb by frame matrix for each mother was constructed. Across all mothers, the 24 verbs appeared in 71 structural environments, as these were defined in the preceding section. A verb was said to occur in a particular environment in the usage of a mother if it appeared in that environment at least twice.

---

[2] S_t = tensed sentence complement, S_u = untensed sentence complement, S_{fr} = sentence complement introduced by a free relative.

[3] This last decision is admittedly problematical. We have no hard evidence that the direct quotation intonation differs from that of tensed sentence complements when these are introduced without a complementizer (e.g., "He thinks John is coming"), for we performed no physical analysis of the stimuli. Skeptical readers should simply excise this variable from their interpretations of the result tables with the consequence that the set of distinctions shown here to be cued by frame-overlap becomes somewhat smaller.

Differences in frequency of appearance in these environments were ignored: For the purpose of this analysis, the question is only whether each verb does or does not appear in each environment. The outcome, then, is a 71 × 24 matrix for each mother.

A sample portion of such a matrix is shown in Table 10.2. To read this table, notice that *know* and *get* are distinct in Environment 1 (appearance with null complements, i.e., bare intransitives), share Environment 2 (appearance with NP complements), and so forth. It is these overlaps and nonoverlaps that are the information sources for a hypothetical structure-sensitive verb learning procedure.

Collapsing the Matrices: Similarities Across Mothers

Before examining these matrices, we first assessed how similar the mothers were in their verb use. This is because the idea that structural privileges play a causal role in learning would be falsified if it turned out that different mothers used the verbs in different structural environments while the children all acquired the same meanings for them.

Using Hildebrand's *del* statistic (see later discussion for an explanation of Hildebrand's *del*), we assessed the strength of the relation in syntactic usage between all possible pairs of mothers in the sample of 8 mothers. There were 28 such pairs. The finding was that the similarity between each pair was significant ($p < .0001$): All mothers used about the same structural environments for each of the 28 verbs. This obtained similarity across mothers justifies pooling all the maternal data into a single matrix, henceforth called the *supermatrix*.

The Structural Environments of Maternal Verb Use

No 2 of the 24 verbs appeared in all and only the same structural environments in any of the 8 mothers' usage or in the supermatrix. This result is not very interesting as it stands, for it is likely that in a larger sample some

TABLE 10.2
Sample Matrix of Maternal Usage

	Verbs			
Frames	*know*	*get*	*put*	*come*
V NP PP		+	+	
V NP	+	+		
V	+			+
V S	+			

Note. A + indicates that the verbs appeared with the frame on that row.

verbs would completely overlap in their syntactic ranges. The question of interest is whether degree of frame overlap is predictive of semantic similarity over the verb set as a whole: Do verbs whose meanings are alike tend to occur in the same syntactic environments? Preliminary experimental evidence exists to support such a conclusion about the organization of the English verb lexicon (Fisher et al., 1991); moreover, closely related findings have been obtained in a replication for Hebrew (Geyer, Gleitman, & Gleitman, 1993). Our question is whether mothers come close to this same picture.

To find out required three steps. First, we performed an analysis to discover which of the 24 verbs overlap syntactically (i.e., share certain frames). Second, we performed an experiment and an analysis to discover which of these verbs are semantically similar. Third, we asked if the syntactic and semantic similarity spaces, so derived, are essentially the same: Is the semantic similarity space predictable from the syntactic similarity space? If so, then the potential usefulness of frame ranges for narrowing the hypothesis space for verb learning receives support.

Discovery of the Syntactic Clusters

To compute a syntactic similarity score for each verb pair, we used a measure of the number of structural environments on which the two verbs matched syntactically in the supermatrix. Such an analysis is by no means simple to carry out realistically, for matching on certain structural criteria may be more informative for a learning procedure than matching on others. For example, literally thousands of verbs accept the simple transitive environment of (2); thus, this environment does little to differentiate among verbs. In contrast, a very small subset of verbs appears with sentence complements, as in (4); thus, appearance in this latter structure can be very informative.

To mirror this difference in the information value of individual structures, we weighted the matches between verbs by the frequency of the structures themselves across verbs in the set of 24. That is, the similarity score for each pair of verbs was equal to the sum of the weighted structural matches; each match was weighted by the frequency with which the frame occurs in the set of verbs as a whole. Using this weighted measure, we constructed a syntactic similarity matrix for the 24 verbs.

This new matrix was subjected to an overlapping cluster analysis to extract regularities in the syntactic organization of the supermatrix. Cluster analysis refers to a class of methods for picking out natural "clumps" in similarity data (Gordon, 1981). The algorithm located overlapping clusters, in which each verb in the set could be a member of more than one cluster. This overlapping cluster analysis is the only realistic one for the kind of data we are considering, for verbs participate in several cross-cutting subcategorizations. Thus, for example, verbs like *think* and *explain* match in accepting certain sentence complement environments (e.g., John thinks/explains that

Claire is clever) that *give* does not accept (e.g., *John gives that Claire is clever). In a cross-cutting categorization, *give* and *explain* but not *think* share a three-NP environment (e.g., John gives/explains/*thinks a book to Joe). Thus the patterning is complex, and it is the complexity itself that is revealing: Because *think* and *explain* involve mental events, they share the sentence complement environment, but because *explain* and *give* involve transfer (in this case, transfer of a book), they share the ditransitive environment. Thus, *explain* describes mental transfer, that is, communication (Zwicky, 1971). The cluster analysis is designed to draw out these cross-cutting patterns. Its results with the supermatrix yield seven overlapping clusters, as shown in Table 10.3.

In essence, these clusters are the groups of syntactically congruent verbs that fall out of the syntactic overlap in the mothers' speech. The clusters provide a good representation of the syntactic similarity data, yielding an overall r^2 of .70. Notice in Table 10.3 that each cluster is well described by overlap on a single frame. For example, *come, go,* and *look* (cluster 1) all accept intransitive environments with a prepositional frame: John comes into the room, John looks at the table. Both *want* and *like* accept untensed sentence complements (cluster 3, e.g., I want him to go to the store; I'd like him to whistle).

Informally, there is a whiff of semantic substance to these patterns of verb use. Cluster 1 verbs seem to pertain to physical or perceptual motion with directional paths (Gruber, 1967; Jackendoff, 1983) and cluster 3 verbs

TABLE 10.3
Syntactic Clusters

Cluster	Frame Variable	Example Frame	Verbs	Cumulative r^2
1	V PP[a]	John goes to the store.	come, go, look	.26
2	V S$_r$[b], V S$_{fr}$[c]	John knows who he likes. John sees how to do it.	know, see	.39
3	V S$_u$[d]	John likes to go to the store.	like, want	.44
4	V NP PP[e]	John put the ball on the table.	call, get, pull, push, put, take	.58
5	V PA[f]	Sit up! Get on!	come, get, go, sit	.64
6	V S$_c$[g]	I know that you are happy.	know, think	.67
7	V DI[h]	I said, "Get off the couch!"	call, do, go, say	.70

[a]V PP = A verb taking a prepositional phrase.
[b]V S$_r$ = A verb taking a sentence complement introduced by a relative pronoun.
[c]V S$_{fr}$ = A verb taking a sentence complement introduced by a free relative (e.g., *how, if*).
[d]V S$_u$ = A verb taking an untensed sentence complement.
[e]V NP PP = A verb taking a noun phrase and a prepositional phrase.
[f]V PA = A verb taking a particle (e.g., *on, up*).
[g]V S$_c$ = A verb taking a sentence complement introduced by a complementizer (e.g., *that*).
[h]V DI = A verb taking a whole sentence that is quoted to its right.

pertain to states of desire (Vendler, 1972). But we do not really want to make claims about the semantic correlates of these syntactic patterns based on such informal intuitions. Rather, we develop an experimental approach to this question in the next section.

Here, it is important to note only that the patterns of maternal syntactic usage, even in the space of a one-hour play period, yield a number of rather refined groupings. This opens the door for hypothetical learners disposed by nature to exploit these patterns as a basis for semantic inferences. Similarly, they provide the exemplars for hypothetical learners who, having made semantic inferences from extralinguistic observation, are disposed to project the structures onto semantically similar verbs that they may subsequently encounter (Bowerman, 1982).

Experimental Discovery of the Semantic Space

We consider the semantic space for the same set of verbs. The semantic space of interest is the one that characterizes the adult lexicon. This is the target toward which the learners are aiming. The first question, then, is how the 24 verbs under consideration are semantically related to one another as judged by adult speakers. Once we have determined the semantic groupings, we ask how these are related to the syntactic groupings derived in the analysis just presented.

Method. Subjects were presented with all possible triads of the set of 24 verbs without syntactic context and were asked to choose the semantic outlier in each triad. The final measure of the semantic relatedness of any two verbs was the percentage of times they stick together (i.e., are not chosen as outliers) in the triad judgment in the context of all third verbs with which they are presented. The idea is that if no third verb (in the set) is semantically closer to either of these verbs than the two are to each other, then the two must be very close in their meaning. This method was previously used by Fisher et al. (1991) and Geyer et al. (1993) to study form–meaning linkages in the adult lexicon.

Subjects. The subjects were 28 native English speakers, students at the University of Pennsylvania.

Stimuli. The stimuli were all possible triads of the 24 verbs in Table 10.1.

Procedure. Subjects was shown three verbs on a CRT screen. They were asked to choose the one verb of these three that was "the least similar in meaning" to the other two. They began with 10 practice trials consisting of verbs not in the experimental set. Because it would border on torture to ask a single subject to respond to all of the 2,024 possible sets of the 24 verbs taken three at a time, we broke down the set of triads into smaller groups. Each subject was presented with 150 triads, selected randomly from the complete set of 2,024. Thus, it takes 14 people to make a "composite subject." Two such composite subjects (28 individual subjects) were run.

Scoring. The subjects gave judgments of the degree of similarity of each verb pair in the context of all other (22) verbs in the set. We computed an index of similarity of the verbs by counting the number of times that any pair of verbs stuck together in the contexts of other verbs (following Fisher et al., 1991). Because there were 24 verbs, each pair appeared in the context of 22 other verbs. Therefore the similarity score for any given pair could range from 0 to 22.

Reliability. We tested to be sure that there was a high level of reliability between the two composite subjects, obtaining a Spearman's rho of .78. This level of concordance is significant at the .001 level as calculated by Hubert's conservative estimate and is similar to the level of concordance achieved by prior studies using this method. This result justified pooling the responses of the two groups.

Extracting the Semantic Organization of the Verb Set. We subjected the semantic similarity matrix obtained to the same overlapping cluster analysis used to construct the syntactic similarity matrix. Just as in the syntactic analysis, using a cutoff of r^2 of .70 we obtained seven semantic clusters. These are shown in Table 10.4. These clusters represent the structure implicit in our subjects' judgment of the meaning overlap of the verbs in our set. In Table 10.4, we have (rather clumsily) provided these clusters with semantic labels, but we should emphasize that these labels are rather arbitrary and are presented in the table only for their gross value as pointers to (whatever) may be the real semantic identifiers of these groups. It should not be surprising to find that this semantic labeling is rough. After all, the semantic organization of verbs across the mental lexicon is unlikely to be expressible with a small set of (other) words or phrases of English. In fact, that the method of triads does not force us to provide a label for these semantic generalizations is one of its major strengths. In the usual methods of linguists in this regard, the logically distinct problems of discovering a semantic correlate of a syntactic property and labeling that semantic correlate are conflated. In contrast, the semantic groupings we obtained derived from the subjects' own judgments as they fell out of the cluster analysis shown in Table 10.4, and the syntactic groupings fell out of an independent cluster analysis of maternal usage (see Table 10.3).

TABLE 10.4
Semantic Clusters

Cluster	Semantic Label	Verbs	Cumulative r^2
1	Cognition/Perception	*find, have, know, like, look, see, think, want*	.10
2	Active	*call, catch, come, do, eat, find, get, go, make, play, pull, push, put, show, sit, take*	.45
3	Discovery/Communication	*call, find, look, say, see, show*	.53
4	Mental	*do, get, know, look, make, say, see, show, think*	.56
5	Transfer	*catch, find, get, pull, push, put, take*	.64
6	Cognition	*know, like, think, want*	.68
7	Possession	*get, have, take, want*	.70

Two properties of the clusters in Table 10.4 should be noted particularly. The first is that many verbs whose overall meanings differ exceedingly appear in each cluster. All the same, the clusters represent some shared aspect of construal that subjects (implicitly) perceived and that contributed to the judgmental patterns. Although *push* and *take* are quite different, they have a likeness that we have labeled *active transfer* (cluster 5). Second, the overwhelming majority of verbs appear in more than one cluster. For instance, *want* shows up both as a verb of cognition (cluster 6) and as a verb of possession (cluster 7). In some ways, then, the outcomes of this analysis appear to have some fidelity to the relations among the verb meanings, and the clusters appear to represent components of these overall meanings rather well.

Analysis for Semantic/Syntactic Relations

At this point, we have extracted two similarity spaces. The first is a syntactic space derived from overlap in the frame-range privileges for verbs exhibited in maternal speech (Table 10.3). The second is a semantic space derived from adult choices of semantic outliers in the triad task (Table 10.4). We next wanted to examine how these two spaces overlap. That is, we wanted to know whether the syntactic groupings of the verbs are predictive of the semantic groupings of the verbs.

Comparing the Two Matrices. To accomplish this comparison, we set up a new matrix, shown as Table 10.5. In Table 10.5, the column headings are the seven syntactic clusters obtained from the syntactic analysis (see

TABLE 10.5

Matrix of the Relation Between Syntax and Semantics in Maternal Usage

Semantic Clusters with Semantic Labels	Syntactic Clusters with Frames						
	Cluster 1: V PP (3)[a]	Cluster 2: V S_r (2)	Cluster 3: V S_u (2)	Cluster 4: V NP PP (6)	Cluster 5: V PA (4)	Cluster 6: V S_c (2)	Cluster 7: V DI (4)
Cluster 1: Cognition/Perception	1[b]	2	2	0	0	2	0
Cluster 2: Active	2	0	0	6	4	0	3
Cluster 3: Discovery/Communication	1	1	0	1	0	0	2
Cluster 4: Mental	0	2	0	1	0	0	2
Cluster 5: Transfer	0	0	0	5	1	0	0
Cluster 6: Cognition	0	1	2	1	0	2	0
Cluster 7: Possession	0	0	1	2	1	0	0

[a]Numbers in parentheses indicate total number of verbs in each syntactic cluster.
[b]Numbers in each cell indicate the number of verbs in the syntactic cluster in the column that appeared in the semantic cluster intersecting at that row. In other words, each cell indicates the overlap in membership of the verbs in each syntactic and semantic cluster.

Table 10.3). The row headings are the seven semantic clusters obtained from the semantic analysis (see Table 10.4). Each cell indicates the number of verbs common to the semantic cluster and the syntactic cluster that intersect at the cell. For example, the verbs in syntactic cluster 1 (V PP) are *come, go,* and *look.* The verbs in semantic cluster 1 (Cognition/Perception) are *find, have, know, like, look, see, think,* and *want.* Because *look* is the only verb common to both clusters, the entry in this cell (row 1 and column 1) is 1. As another example, the verbs in syntactic cluster 4 (V NP PP) are *call, get, pull, push, put,* and *take.* The verbs in semantic cluster 2 (Active) are *call, catch, come, do, eat, find, get, go, make, play, pull, push, put, show, sit,* and *take.* Because all six verbs in syntactic cluster 4 appear in semantic cluster 2, the entry in the appropriate cell (row 4 and column 2) is 6. In sum, each cell in the matrix consists of the number of verbs that appear in both the semantic cluster and the syntactic cluster that make up that group.

If there were no relation between the syntactic and semantic clusters, then the numbers in each cell of Table 10.5 would be distributed randomly. Inspection suggests that the distribution is nonrandom, for some cells contain large numbers and others are empty. The question was how to determine whether this pattern could be obtained by chance.

The usual statistic for assessing the relationship between two categorical variables is chi square. However, as Table 10.5 shows, there are many zero cells in the matrix, and many verbs that appeared in one category also appeared in another. As a result, using the chi square was ruled out. We therefore turned to another test, Hildebrand's *del* statistic, which was designed to handle data of just this sort (Hildebrand, Laing, & Rosenthal, 1977; Hildebrand, 1986). The *del* assesses the strength of the relation between two categorical variables by comparing the number of errors generated by the actual data to the number of errors generated by a randomized replication of the data. However, its application requires some principle that allows us to predict an expected set of cell frequencies that can then be compared to the number that was actually obtained.[4]

Predicting the Relation Between the Categories.   To develop a principle on the basis of which we could predict the overlap between the syntactic and semantic categories, we made two assumptions. First, following Jackendoff (1983) and Pinker (1984), we assumed that the child believes verb construals are drawn from some large but limited set of overarching conceptual categories: physical motions, including their paths and goals;

---

[4]In assessing the overlap in the syntactic usage among the mothers, we had run into similar problems with chi square. The number of zero and small cells was just too great to warrant that test. Therefore, as described earlier, we used the *del* also to assess the similarity in syntactic usage among the mothers in the study.

mental acts and states; and so on. For the 24 maternal verbs, these categories are represented by the clusters of Table 10.4—the semantic space extracted from adult judgments. Second, based on a body of findings from linguists and developmental psychologists, we assumed that the argument-taking properties of verbs are reflected systematically in the surface structures that they accept and that these patterns are—correcting for architectural distinctions—much the same across languages of the world (Chomsky, 1981; Grimshaw, 1981; Jackendoff, 1978). These assumptions granted, a learning procedure that derives aspects of a new verb's meaning from inspection of its syntactic correlates can operate on the following principle:

> If a verb belongs to syntactic group X and assigns some semantic property p to this syntactic group, all verbs subsequently observed to fall into syntactic group X will be assigned property p. Verbs of a feather flock together.

Notice that this hypothetical learning principle is attentive to positive information only. It draws inferences about semantics only from structures in which a new verb is observed to occur. No inferences are based on the absence of some structure in the database for a new verb. After all, further structures may be observed at some later time; their current absence may be of little significance.

Applying this principle to predict from syntax to semantics without error, it would have to be the case that every time a member of a syntactic cluster is a member of a semantic cluster, all other members of that same syntactic cluster are also members of that same semantic cluster. We can clarify this generalization by inspection of cluster 6 in Table 10.5, in which just this relationship obtains. *Know* and *think* are the verbs that comprise syntactic cluster 6, and for every semantic cluster of which *know* is a member, *think* is also a member.

If this type of relation between the syntactic and semantic clusters held across the board, then we could predict from syntax to the semantic classification of Table 10.4 without error. Inspection of Table 10.5 shows that this perfect relation does not hold, except for syntactic cluster 6. Thus, it is clear that in trying to predict from syntax to the semantic groups, our hypothetical learner would make some errors. However, it is also clear from inspection of the matrix that the proportion of errors would be small.

The learning principle provides the prediction rule that allows us to compare the number of errors generated given the actual cell frequencies in the matrix to the number of errors generated given the expected cell frequencies. The *del* is the percent error reduction from the random replication to the actual obtained data.

Using this statistic, we determined whether the number of errors the child will make (given the obtained syntactic and semantic spaces of Tables 10.3 and 10.4) is significantly smaller than the number of errors he or she would make if only a chance relation existed between the two spaces. That is, if the relation between the two spaces is not at chance, we can assess how much power the structural facts about the verbs in our corpus give the child for predicting the semantic organization of these verbs.

We found that the syntactic formats have considerable predictive power. According to the *del* statistic, children would make 49% fewer errors than expected by chance in organizing the verb set semantically if they had knowledge of the syntactic organization of the verb set. This finding is significant at the .0001 level. The magnitude and reliability of this obtained relationship is quite remarkable considering the indirectness of the triad procedure we have used to extract the semantic organization of the 24 verbs.

Summary of the Findings

Our results show that caregivers provide rich syntactic information about common verbs for their very young children. Each verb had a distinctive distribution of subcategorization frames for each mother. The distribution was highly similar for all mothers, even in these small (one-hour long) corpora. Our question was how well the distributional structure of the corpora mapped onto the target semantic space, as assessed independently from the triad procedure. The answer was that overlap in frame range was a powerful predictor of the semantic organization of the maternal verb set. Thus, the database provided to children embodies the form–meaning correlations that are required for the syntactically sensitive verb learning procedure first suggested by Landau and Gleitman (1985).

DISCUSSION AND CONCLUSIONS

The form–meaning linkages in maternal—and all—speech appear to serve language learning in more than one way. The first, suggested in a seminal discussion from Grimshaw (1981), is to reduce two learning tasks to one: To the extent that a verb's meaning can be acquired from observing its contexts of use, aspects of its structural privileges follow, namely those that are consequences of the argument structure implied by the verb semantics. This position (elaborated significantly by Pinker, 1984) assumes the universality of these mappings and assigns them as a feature of the innate apparatus that children bring into the language learning task.[5] The evidence supporting such a view is strong. Linguists' investigations of the languages of the world over the past several decades demonstrate that, correcting for the architecture of specific languages, the same mappings characterize lexical structure in diverse languages. Moreover, Bowerman's (1982) analyses of child errors of subcategorization are best understood as corrections for local quirks in these mappings in the target language. Additionally, the study of manual communication systems spontaneously developed by deaf children of hearing parents (Feldman, Goldin-Meadow, & Gleitman, 1978; Goldin-Meadow & Feldman, 1977) shows that, without a model, children can project these same mappings (e.g., one noun phrase for sentences with *sleep*, two for sentences with *hit*, and three for sentences with *give*). The clause structure, in the relevant regards, can be bootstrapped from knowledge of the verb semantics.

We have argued here and elsewhere that built-in knowledge of the form–meaning linkages can also be used in the reverse direction: A verb's appearance in some particular structure constrains the logic it can be expressing. As we remarked in the introduction to this chapter, such constraints on the search space for verb meaning are particularly useful where observation provides little evidence. It is hard to parse scenes to come up with interpretations like "want" and "believe," but clausal complements can suggest that the speaker had mental acts and states in mind. More generally, the argument structure of a new verb can be bootstrapped from its linguistic context, putting the learner in a narrow neighborhood concerning its precise meaning. Given such constraints from structure on the semantic search space, learning the verb from its contexts of use becomes feasible. The present analysis provided one demonstration required by such a claim: The maternal corpus embodies the form–meaning linkages quite regularly.

This is not the place to review the form-to-meaning feature of verb learning in detail. However, a few words are in order about the nature of the hypothesis (see Fisher et al., 1994, for a full discussion). It goes without saying that one cannot learn the meaning of a verb (or any word) "from" its syntactic contexts. The subcategorization frames provide only information relevant to the argument structure, and that information is shared across many verbs. For example, *roll, bounce, slide*, and many other verbs are verbs of motion that can express a path as well as the agent causing the motion. These similarities in their meanings lead to identity in their argument structures and thus frame ranges (e.g., John rolls/bounces the ball down the hill; The ball rolls/bounces down the hill). But these verbs are not synony-

---

[5]It is presumed by most investigators that not all complementation is semantically conditioned, that there are some semantically arbitrary facts about subcategorization in natural languages at every point in their history. Because this is likely so, the deductions from form to meaning and from meaning to form can succeed only probabilistically. The necessarily errorful nature of these deductions is best revealed in the work of Bowerman (1982) on child errors in subcategorization, such as, "He falled me down."

mous, for they differ in the type of motion described. Acquiring these distinctions of manner requires observation of the verbs' distinctive contexts of use. At best, then, the frame range for these verbs can reveal that these are motion/path verbs of some kind. Our position is that this partial information is a requirement for inspecting the extralinguistic world relevantly. For instance, thoughts, desires, purposes, and so forth are aspects of the real world that may be present during the utterance of *bounce*. As we have shown elsewhere, this complexity in the environment renders both adult and child subjects helpless to identify the meaning of a novel verb from scene information alone. However, they correctly conjecture the right meaning when they receive scenes paired with structures. Successful identification of a new verb requires a sentence-to-world pairing rather than a word-to-world pairing.

Our position is not that there are verb classes associated with different ranges of subcategorization frames as a consequence of their semantics. Rather, verbs have meanings, and sentence frames have semantic implications. Whether a verb appears in a particular frame is a matter of the compatibility of its meaning with the argument structure implied by the frame. Thus, given the meaning of *dance* it is unlikely to occur in a transitive structure, but this verb in this structure is perhaps not ungrammatical or even uninterpretable as the verb class position would have it. After all, one can say "Gepetto danced Pinocchio." What evidently happens here is that the sentence takes on the interpretation implied by the verb sense and the frame implication taken together. That is, if *dance* occurs in a transitive structure, then the motion (though ordinarily voluntary) was caused by an external agent. This is plausible when the dancer lacks volition, as a puppet.

This position implies that any verb can occur in any structure. In essence, the child need not learn the subcategorization facts about any verb, for there are no such facts, only relative likelihoods that verbs with certain meanings will appear in certain structures. Hearing "John gorps that Mary is hungry" raises the likelihood that *gorp* means "think" and lowers the likelihood that it means "eat." It is such compatibility relations that yield the usage picture laid out in Table 10.5 and help the child decide which verb has which meaning.

REFERENCES

Beckwith, R., Tinker, E., & Bloom, L. (1989, October). *The acquisition of non-basic sentences.* Paper presented at the Boston University Conference on Language Development, Boston, MA.

Bloom, P. (in press). Possible names: The role of syntax-semantics mappings in the acquisition of nominals. *Lingua.*

Bowerman, M. (1982). Reorganizational processes in lexical and syntactic development. In E. Wanner & L. R. Gleitman (Eds.), *Language acquisition: The state of the art.* New York: Cambridge University Press.

Brown, R. (1957). Linguistic determinism and the part of speech. *Journal of Abnormal and Social Psychology, 55*, 1–5.

Carey, S. (1978). The child as word learner. In M. Halle, J. Bresnan, & A. Miller (Eds.), *Linguistic theory and psychological reality* (pp. 264–293). Cambridge, MA: MIT Press.

Chomsky, N. (1981). *Lectures on government and binding.* Dordrecht: Foris.

Dowty, D. R. (1979). *Word meaning and Montague grammar.* Dordrecht: Reidel.

Feldman, H., Goldin-Meadow, S., & Gleitman, L. R. (1978). Beyond Herodotus: The creation of language by linguistically deprived deaf children. In A. Lock (Ed.), *Action, symbol, and gesture: The emergence of language* (pp. 253–274). New York: Academic Press.

Fillmore, C. J. (1968). The case for case. In E. Bach & R. T. Harms (Eds.), *Universals in linguistic theory* (pp. 1–88). New York: Holt, Rinehart & Winston.

Fisher, C., Gleitman, L. R., & Gleitman, H. (1991). On the semantic content of subcategorization frames. *Cognitive Psychology, 23*, 331–392.

Fisher, C., Hall, D. G., Rakowitz, S., & Gleitman, L. R. (1994). When it is better to receive than to give: Structural and conceptual cues to verb meaning. *Lingua, 92*, 333–375.

Geyer, H., Gleitman, H., & Gleitman, L. R. (1993). *Subcategorization as a predictor of verb meaning: Evidence from modern Hebrew.* Unpublished manuscript, University of Pennsylvania, Philadelphia.

Gillette, J. (1992). *The acquisition of mental verbs.* Unpublished manuscript, University of Pennsylvania, Philadelphia.

Gleitman, L. R. (1990). The structural sources of word meaning. *Language Acquisition, 1*, 3–55.

Goldin-Meadow, S., & Feldman, H. (1977). The development of language-like communication without a language model. *Science, 197*, 401–403.

Gordon, A. D. (1981). *Classification.* London: Chapman & Hall.

Grimshaw, J. (1981). Form, function, and the language acquisition device. In C. L. Baker & J. J. McCarthy (Eds.), *The logical problem of language acquisition.* Cambridge, MA: MIT Press.

Gropen, J., Pinker, S., Hollander, M., & Goldberg, R. (1991). Affectedness and direct objects: The role of lexical semantics in the acquisition of verb argument structure. *Cognition, 41*, 153–195.

Gruber, J. S. (1967). Look and see. *Language, 43*, 937–947.

Hall, D. G., & Waxman, S. R. (in press). How 2- and 4-year-old children interpret adjectives and count nouns. *Child Development.*

Hildebrand, D. K. (1986). *Statistical thinking for behavioral scientists.* Boston: Duxbury Press.

Hildebrand, D. K., Laing, J. D., & Rosenthal, H. (1977). *Prediction analysis of cross classifications.* New York: Wiley.

Hoekstra, T. (1992). Aspect and theta theory. In I. M. Roca (Ed.), *Thematic structure: Its role in grammar.* Berlin: de Gruyter.

Jackendoff, R. S. (1978). Grammar as evidence for conceptual structure. In M. Halle, J. Bresnan, & G. Miller (Eds.), *Linguistic theory and psychological reality.* Cambridge, MA: MIT Press.

Jackendoff, R. S. (1983). *Semantics and cognition.* Cambridge, MA: MIT Press.

Jackendoff, R. S. (1990). *Semantic structures.* Cambridge, MA: MIT Press.

Jespersen, O. (1927). *A modern English grammar on historical principles.* Heidelberg: Carl Winters.

Keil, F. C. (1989). *Concepts, kinds, and cognitive development.* Cambridge, MA: MIT Press.

Landau, B. (in press). Where's what and what's where: The language of objects in space. *Lingua.*

Landau, B., & Gleitman, L. R. (1985). *Language and experience: Evidence from the blind child.* Cambridge, MA: Harvard University Press.

Landau, B., Smith, L., & Jones, S. (1988). The importance of shape in early lexical learning. *Cognitive Development, 3*, 299–321.

Levin, B. (1993). *English verb classes and alternations: A preliminary investigation.* Chicago, IL: University of Chicago Press.

Markman, E. M. (in press). Constraints on word meaning in early language acquisition. *Lingua.*

Naigles, L. (1990). Children use syntax to learn verb meanings. *Journal of Child Language, 15,* 257–272.

Naigles, L. G., Gleitman, H., & Gleitman, L. R. (1993). Children acquire word meaning components from syntactic evidence. In E. Dromi (Ed.), *Language and cognition: A developmental perspective* (pp. 87–102). Norwood, NJ: Ablex.

Pinker, S. (1984). *Language learnability and language development.* Cambridge, MA: Harvard University Press.

Pinker, S. (1989). *Learnability and cognition: The acquisition of argument structure.* Cambridge, MA: MIT Press.

Quine, W. V. O. (1960). *Word and object.* Cambridge, MA: MIT Press.

Soja, N., Carey, S., & Spelke, E. (1991). Ontological categories guide young children's inductions of word meaning: Object terms and substance terms. *Cognition, 38,* 179–211.

Talmy, L. (1975). Semantics and syntax of motion. In J. Kimball (Ed.), *Syntax and semantics* (Vol. 4, pp. 181–238). New York: Academic Press.

Talmy, L. (1985). Lexicalization patterns: Semantic structure in lexical forms. In T. Shopen (Ed.), *Language typology and syntactic description: Vol. 3. Grammatical categories and the lexicon* (pp. 57–149). Cambridge, England: Cambridge University Press.

Vendler, Z. (1972). *Res cogitans.* Ithaca, NY: Cornell University Press.

Waxman, S. (in press). The development of an appreciation of specific linkages between linguistic and conceptual organization. *Lingua.*

Zwicky, A. (1971). In a manner of speaking. *Linguistic Inquiry, 2,* 223–233.

CHAPTER ELEVEN

Syntactic Bootstrapping from Start to Finish with Special Reference to Down Syndrome

Letitia G. Naigles
Yale University

Anne Fowler
Bryn Mawr College and Haskins Laboratories

Atessa Helm
Yale University

Discussions of the close relation between verbs and syntactic structures are not new to either linguistics or psychology. Linguists from very different traditions (e.g., Chafe, 1970; Chomsky, 1965; Fillmore, 1968) have relied on distinctions between verbs to illustrate and in some cases to motivate critical syntactic distinctions (for more recent work, see Grimshaw, 1990; Wierzbicka, 1988). Likewise, in psychology, models of language processing have exploited verb differences to demonstrate and explain differences in the retention and processing of syntax (e.g., Fodor, Garrett, & Bever, 1968; Wanner, 1974; more recently, Carlson & Tanenhaus, 1988; Shapiro, Zurif, & Grimshaw, 1987). Finally, in the field of language acquisition, the verb–syntax correspondence has been implicated in the acquisition of syntax (Bloom, 1970, 1981; Pinker, 1984, 1989; Tomasello, 1992). With few exceptions, this research involving verb–syntax relations has been uni-directional, focusing on what verbs and verb meanings reveal about syntax and syntactic acquisition (but see Bowerman, 1974, 1982; Jackendoff, 1983, 1990). Our work joins a recent reversal of this direction of focus (e.g., Gleitman, 1990; Gleitman & Gleitman, 1992); we study what syntax reveals about the acquisition and development of the verb lexicon.

SYNTAX PROVIDES TWO WINDOWS ON VERB
ACQUISITION

Our guiding principle in this chapter is that, by virtue of the correspondences between syntax and verb meaning, syntax and tasks requiring sensitivity to syntax can be exploited to tap into the process and products of verb acquisition. At the beginning of verb learning, a major concern is characterizing how the child maps the correct referent onto a new verb. We provide evidence that the syntactic frame in which the verb is presented can be exploited by the learner to aid in selecting among the plethora of meanings allowed by observation alone. As verb acquisition progresses, the concern becomes how we finally achieve fully elaborated and stable verb meanings. We argue here that how children resolve novel combinations of familiar verbs and syntactic frames provides insights into the stability and formation of their verb representations. Finally, to add to our growing body of evidence on normally developing children, in this chapter we present converging evidence from a special population also faced with sorting out verbs and their syntactic frames. We suggest that schoolchildren and adolescents with Down syndrome, in their interpretation of novel pairings of verbs and frames, are guided by many of the same principles apparent in the interpretations of preschoolers at a similar syntactic level.

How Verb Acquisition Begins

At the beginning of verb learning, the child's task is to select the right action, process, or state (i.e., the meaning) from those supported by the context and to attach it to the designated lexical item. That is, to learn what *skid* means, the child must map skidding actions present in the visual-spatial context onto the word *skid*. This mapping task is not as straightforward as it may seem, though. As discussed in detail by Quine (1960; see also Wittgenstein, 1953), Landau and Gleitman (1985), Gleitman (1990), and Naigles, Gleitman, and Gleitman (1992), among others, there is a multitude of possible meanings available in the real-world scene that can be attached to a new verb. For example, a child hearing "skidding" and observing his mother pushing a truck such that it moves across the floor in a skidding manner cannot know whether "skid" refers to the mother's pushing (the causal action), or the truck's skidding (the manner of action), or traversing the floor (the path of the action). In these circumstances, one might expect children to be cautious or error-prone in using new verbs; however, the evidence to date (Carey, 1978, 1982; Tomasello, 1992) indicates that few mistakes are made.

Researchers have therefore suggested that children are not completely openminded in their acquisition of verbs. They have proposed that children approach the verb-learning task with specific biases in mind. For example,

Gentner (1978), Gropen, Pinker, Hollander, and Goldberg (1991), and Golinkoff, Hirsh-Pasek, Mervis, Frawley, and Parillo (this volume) all provided evidence that 3- and 4-year-old children find the manner of a novel action more salient for the referent of a novel just-presented verb than the instrument or endstate of the action (see also Behrend, 1990, and Fisher, Hall, Rakowitz, & Gleitman, 1994). Such semantic biases provide a basis from which young verb learners select some elements of verb meaning from among the possibilities.

However, semantic biases are not sufficient to account for the beginnings of verb acquisition because not all verbs in a language are consonant with the biases. For example, if children have a bias to assume that a novel verb refers to the manner of an action in the real-world scene, how will they learn all the verbs that do not encode manner or encode manner plus other components? What if the articulated verb in the *pushing/skidding/traversing* scene were "push" or "cross" instead of "skid"? Operating with a manner bias alone would lead a verb learner to make numerous errors. This becomes even more of an issue from a cross-linguistic perspective. Although in English the manner of motion or action is usually encoded in the verb, in Spanish, French, and other Romance languages the verb encodes the path of the motion (Choi & Bowerman, 1991; Talmy, 1985). Hence, the English sentence

(1) He is running down the stairs.

translates into French as

(2) Il descend l'escalier courant.

Literally, *He is-going-down the stairs runningly*. Therefore, a manner bias may be detrimental to a young Romance verb learner; children at least seem to have to learn their language-specific biases in verb encoding (Choi & Bowerman, 1991; Gentner, 1982; Naigles, 1991; Naigles, Eisenberg, & Kako, 1992).

In sum, children need more than the real-world scene and their semantic biases to begin to learn many novel verbs. In several recent papers, Gleitman (1990; Gleitman & Gleitman, 1992; Landau & Gleitman, 1985) proposed the *syntactic bootstrapping* process: Children use the syntactic frames in which verbs are placed to help determine the meaning of novel verbs. Recall our *push/skid/traverse* scene. If the verb is placed in an intransitive syntactic frame (e.g., "The truck is X-ing"), then the intended action is probably *skidding*, given the manner bias in English. If, however, the verb is placed in a transitive frame (e.g., "Mom is X-ing the truck"), then *skidding* becomes a less-favored option, and *pushing* becomes more plausible as the intended referent. The syntactic frames are informative precisely because they have certain semantic implications: Transitive frames canonically signal causative meanings (such as *push*), whereas intransitive frames implicate noncausative meanings (Bowerman, 1982; Fisher, Gleitman, & Gleitman, 1991; Jackendoff, 1983; Levin, 1985; Pinker, 1989). Thus, the syntactic bootstrapping hypothesis predicts that these correlations between syntax and verb meaning will be exploited early in the process of learning new verbs.

Empirical support for syntactic bootstrapping derives from several recent studies conducted by ourselves and our colleagues (Fisher et al., 1994; Naigles, 1990; Naigles & Kako, 1993), in which young children were taught novel verbs that were paired with videotaped scenes depicting multiple or ambiguous actions. In one such study (Naigles, 1990), the videos showed two characters (a duck and a rabbit) performing two simultaneous actions: The duck was forcing the rabbit to bend over (i.e., a causal action), and the duck and the rabbit were each moving their left arms in unison (i.e., a noncausal, synchronous action). Coincident with this scene, a novel verb was presented in either a transitive frame (e.g., "Look! The duck is gorping the bunny!") or an intransitive frame (e.g., "Look! The duck and the bunny are gorping!"). After several such presentations, the actions were separated, and the causal action was shown on one screen while the synchronous action was shown on the other screen. At this juncture the children were encouraged to "find gorping," and their looking patterns were recorded and analyzed using the preferential-looking paradigm developed by Hirsh-Pasek and Golinkoff (1991; Golinkoff, Hirsh-Pasek, Cauley, & Gordon, 1987). The results showed that young 2-year-olds ($M = 25$ months) modified their looking preferences based on the syntactic frame of presentation: When *gorp* had been presented in the transitive frame they looked longer at the causative action, but when *gorp* had been presented in the intransitive frame they watched the synchronous action.

This finding was replicated and extended by Naigles and Kako (1993) with the substitution of contact actions for causative actions and with the addition of a third audio condition in which the novel verb was presented with no syntactic frame (e.g., "Look! Gorping!"). The initial multiple-action scene depicted the duck and frog characters performing a synchronous action while the duck contacted the frog's head with a vertical sweeping motion. The two actions were again separated for the test trials, with the synchronous action shown on one screen and the contact action shown simultaneously on the other. There were three audio conditions for the novel verb: transitive, intransitive, and frameless. The looking preferences indicated that when the novel verb was presented in isolation or in an intransitive frame, the children chose the synchronous action as the referent of the novel verb. In contrast, in the transitive audio condition, a clear effect of syntax was obtained: The children looked significantly longer at the contact action. Thus, both studies demonstrate that young 2-year-old verb learners can exploit the syntactic frame around a novel verb to narrow or constrain the referents of that novel verb. Hence, syntax appears to be an important and exploited source of information during early verb learning.

When Verb Acquisition Ends and How We Can Tell

Even with the addition of semantic biases and syntactic frames, the full complexity of most verb meanings cannot be captured in a single coincident presentation of verb and scene. Consider the causative verbs taught to 2-year-olds in the preferential-looking paradigm. After watching a duck making a rabbit bend over paired with the verb *gorp* in a transitive frame, the children deduced that *gorp* referred to the causing-to-bend-over action rather than the synchronous arm bends. Did the children think that *gorp* can also refer to noncausal bending-over actions? In English, verbs can be more or less flexible in their encodings of semantic components such as cause.[1] For example, *go* is quite restricted with respect to cause of motion: One can only go on one's own, noncausally. If one is causing another to go, then either the periphrastic construction must be used (e.g., "He made the truck go up the hill"), keeping the causal element external to the main verb (and thus implying indirect rather than direct causation, see Fodor, 1970), or an entirely different verb must be used (e.g., *take, push*). *Bring* and *take* are restrictive in the opposite fashion, as these verbs must include causal components (e.g., one can only bring by causing something to change its location). Finally, there is a set of verbs in English, including *move, sink, drop*, and *break*, which allow either a causal or a noncausal interpretation (e.g., The pirate sank the ship, The ship sank). Thus, verbs differ as to the components they encode and on the flexibility or rigidity of each componential distinction.

It therefore seems reasonable to assume that after a single presentation of, for example, "sink" or "go," children have not learned everything about the set of components of meaning that the verb encodes. They cannot know, for example, that *sink* can participate in either a causal or a noncausal interpretation until they hear the verb referring to both causal and noncausal events. They cannot immediately conclude that *go* allows only a noncausal interpretation, having heard it only in reference to a noncausal event, because *go* could be a verb in the *sink* class. Likewise, they cannot conclude that *take* allows only a causal interpretation after hearing it used to refer to a

---

[1]Of course, this is not solely an issue for verb components that correlate with surface syntax (e.g., cause). For example, with regards to the manner component of verbs, *walk* is quite rigid as to its manner of motion (i.e., only walking will do), but *go* is quite flexible: One can go by skipping, stomping, sashaying, sidling, swimming, or skateboarding. Because our focus in this paper is on those aspects of verb meaning that are related to syntax, though, we do not further address these other components (see Fisher, Gleitman, & Gleitman, 1991, for further discussion).

causal event because a noncausal reference may be imminent. Eventually, however, English learners must arrive at each of these conclusions. The major question here, of course, is how children make these determinations, especially as they are unlikely to receive explicit negative instruction. In the section following, we discuss three hypotheses, namely, *conservatism* (Baker, 1979), *maturation* (Pinker, 1989), and *lexical knowledge* (Naigles, Fowler, & Helm, 1992). The purpose of the study following the discussion is to begin to distinguish among them.

Prior to addressing this question, another one must be answered: How can we determine when children have made these conclusions and so have arrived at the adult meaning of a verb? The most obvious route involves checking their spontaneous productions to see when they arrive at consistently correct usage (e.g., Brown, 1973); however, this route fails because incorrect verb usage is uncommon at any age. Children do not seem to need many presentations of a new verb in order to use it in production, and they appear to use it correctly from the start (Gropen et al., 1991; Maratsos, Gudeman, Gerard-Ngo, & DeHart, 1987). The major exceptions to this overwhelmingly correct verb usage are the spontaneous errors documented and analyzed by Bowerman (1974, 1977, 1982). These errors primarily involved using a familiar verb in an incorrect syntactic frame, such as

(3) Don't fall that on me.

(uttered to protest the impending dropping of something by a sibling). Because *fall* is an intransitive, noncausative verb, this use of it in a transitive frame indicating a causative meaning was both creative and incorrect. Evidently, the child had made an *overgeneralization*, extending the transitive–causative correlation to a verb that does not allow it. Interestingly, these errors did not occur until after at least three months of frequent and correct usage of the verb subsequently overgeneralized. This indicates that although the children had been using these verbs correctly, they had not yet arrived at a complete understanding of them, or they would not have made the errors. Correct usage, therefore, does not always imply complete knowledge. In fact, the children's knowledge may be incomplete on two levels: Not only do they violate semantic constraints (in that noncausative verbs are used to describe causal events), they also violate syntactic constraints (i.e., transitive frames are used with usually intransitive verbs).

One need not wait for these overgeneralizations to occur spontaneously in order to gauge the status of children's verb meanings. A related method involves examining how readily they accept sentences containing such overgeneralized verbs (e.g., "the tiger goes the lion"). If children are still learning about a verb, then its appearance in an incorrect frame may not be recognized as incorrect, and the verb may even be reinterpreted in accordance with this (novel) presentation. Thus, transitive *go* may be interpreted as causative and nonrestrictive. By contrast, if the verb has been fully acquired, then the information encapsulated in the incorrect form will be rejected, and the utterance will have to be repaired, perhaps rephrasing it as "the tiger goes TO the lion." Clark and Garnica (1974) made a similar proposal in their study of the acquisition of the deictic specifications of *come* and *go* (i.e., *come* here versus *go* there). They found a surprisingly late differentiation of the two verbs in comprehension (only by 9 years), even though in spontaneous production children generally use the verbs correctly by the age of 3 or 4 (see also Gentner, 1978). They suggested that the point of full acquisition may best be revealed by testing children with inappropriate descriptions or forms, that is, ones that selectively do not match the adult representation.

A straightforward grammaticality judgment task may seem to be the easiest way to implement this suggestion; however, one would then be restricted to studying children no younger than 5 years of age. For example, Hochberg (1986) found that only two-fifths of the 3- and 4-year-olds in her original sample performed consistently enough when asked to make such judgments to be included in the final pool. Because Bowerman's (1974, 1977) data suggest that the work of establishing verb restrictions is going on in the preschool years, a task that is accessible to this age group is preferable. In the studies described in the following sections, we used a sentence enactment task that elicits systematic effects in adults and can be performed consistently by subjects as young as 2½ years of age (Bever, 1970).

An additional advantage of the enactment task is that it reveals how subjects interpret the different types of sentences. That is, the enactments may reveal whether the subjects considered the novel (ungrammatical) frames as information still relevant to the verb's meaning. For example, for the ungrammatical sentence "*the tiger goes the lion," would subjects enact the tiger going TO the lion, thus showing they know that *go* must be noncausal? Or would they enact the tiger causing the lion to go by pushing it, thereby suggesting that *go* in that frame must be causal? In their enactments, the subjects can either follow the restrictions of the verb and repair the sentence (*Verb Compliance*) or follow the restrictions of the frame and adjust the meaning of the verb (*Frame Compliance*).

The Data Thus Far

In two studies, we asked children and adults to enact both grammatical and ungrammatical sentences, using a "Noah's Ark" and toy wooden animals as props (Naigles, Fowler, & Helm, 1992; Naigles, Gleitman, & Gleitman, 1993). The ungrammatical sentences were constructed by placing transitive verbs (*bring, take, push, put*) in intransitive frames (e.g., NV: "*The zebra brings,"

NVPN: "*The lion puts in the ark") and intransitive verbs (*come, go, fall, stay*) in transitive frames (e.g., NVN: "*The elephant comes the giraffe," NVNPN: "*The camel stays the penguin next to the ramp"). These sentences were presented to 120 children between the ages of 2½ and 12 years and 20 undergraduates at the University of Pennsylvania.

The results (see Fig. 11.1) demonstrate that younger subjects, especially the 2-year-olds, were more Frame Compliant. They enacted the ungrammatical sentences in accordance with the demands of the frame, changing the meaning of the verb (i.e., they were doing syntactic bootstrapping). Older subjects, especially the adults, tended to be more Verb Compliant, following the restrictions of the verb and repair the sentence. Thus, as we conjectured, the 2-year-olds allowed the novel frames to influence their enactments of these familiar verbs, whereas the adults tended to reject the novel frames and enact the verbs according to their known restrictions. The children at the intermediate ages were en route from the 2-year-old state to the adult state.

Interestingly, the shift from Frame Compliance toward Verb Compliance was not an across-the-board phenomenon, nor did it happen all at once.

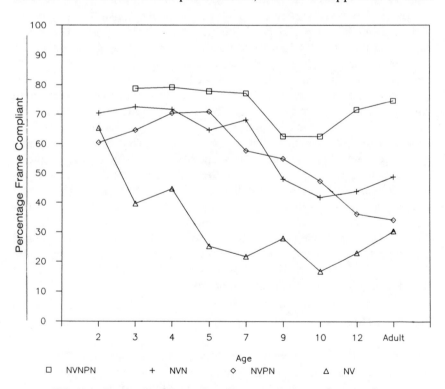

FIG. 11.1. Percentage of Frame Compliant enactments as a function of age group and syntactic frame. For normal-IQ subjects. From Naigles, Fowler, and Helm (1992). Adapted by permission.

Rather, the shift with age toward Verb Compliance varied as a function of syntactic frame (see Fig. 11.1). That is, the NV frame elicited both Verb Compliant and Frame Compliant responses from the 3- and 4-year-olds but elicited adult levels of Verb Compliant enactments from subjects aged 5 years and older. For this frame, the shift begins during the preschool years and is complete by age 5. By contrast, the NVPN frame showed a much more gradual shift toward Verb Compliance, reaching adult levels only by age 12. The NVN frame elicited adult levels of Verb Compliance between the ages of 9 and 10, whereas the NVNPN frame elicited mostly Frame Compliant enactments from subjects of all ages.

The shift toward Verb Compliance also differed as a function of individual verb. For both the NVN and NVNPN frames, the verbs *come* and *go* elicited Verb Compliance earlier and to a greater extent than did *fall* or *stay*. Similarly, *push* elicited Verb Compliance earlier than the other three transitive verbs in the NV frame, and *take* elicited Verb Compliance much later than the other three verbs in the NVPN frame. Our conjectures as to the bases of these frame and verb effects are discussed in detail in Naigles, Fowler, and Helm (1992) and Naigles et al. (1993). Two points are important here: The systematic effects of frame and verb suggest that the shift is not triggered by a general developmental change in how our subjects approached the task, and the fact that the shift follows a different course for different verbs suggests that verb knowledge itself is exerting an important effect.

How Verb Meanings Become Fully Established

Having suggested one method for determining when verb meanings become complete, we can return to the question asked previously. Given that one example of a verb in conjunction with its linguistic and extralinguistic contexts is not sufficient to reveal the entire meaning of that verb, how is this complete meaning finally established? This question has already been studied extensively from the opposite angle: Instead of posing the problem as one of how syntax aids in the acquisition of semantics, the issue has involved the influence of specific verbs on syntax and has been couched as the acquisition of argument structure. Baker (1979) was among the first to lay out the problem that the verbs that are allowed in particular syntactic frames appear to be arbitrarily selected; for example, why can something be dropped but not fallen? How might this difference be learned? Baker's solution involved rejecting the very notion of general form–meaning relations or rules. He suggested that the frames that a verb takes are learned by attending only to attested examples and resisting the formation of generalizations. If no generalizations are formed in early childhood, then none need be unlearned later on. Thus, children are expected to be conservative in allowing verbs to appear in unattested frames.

Baker seems to have been unaware, though, of the spontaneous over-generalizations observed by Bowerman and others (for a summary, see Pinker, 1989). These errors indicate that productive generalizations with argument structure are made during development (see also Gropen et al., 1991; Gropen, Pinker, Hollander, Goldberg, & Wilson, 1989), and so one is forced to consider how children recover from such errors to form stable (i.e., adultlike) argument structures). The just-described findings of Frame Compliance in younger children are reminiscent in many ways of these spontaneous overgeneralizations; they are in fact mirror images. Thus, the process of recovery from the overgeneralizations—of learning that these are errors and of forming argument structures—may be considered the same as the process of shifting from Frame Compliance to Verb Compliance. The question we are addressing, then, is how children determine that the rules or relations do not apply indiscriminately.

The most recent theory concerning the retreat from overgeneralizations, put forth by Pinker (1989; see also Bowerman, 1983), relies partly on the child's increasing lexical knowledge to constrain each verb's argument structure. In brief, Pinker holds that verbs become organized into semantic sub-classes (*narrow range subclasses*) as their representations are refined and elaborated during acquisition. The semantics of the subclasses predict whether the verbs allow such syntactic–semantic alternations as the causative, which can alternate between transitive and intransitive frames or causative and noncausative meanings. For example, motion verbs that encode manner (e.g., *roll* and *bounce*) allow both causative and noncausative in-terpretations, whereas motion verbs that encode path (e.g., *take* and *bring, come* and *go*) allow either a causal interpretation (for the first two) or a noncausal one (for the latter two), but not both. The crucial point is that when the representation of a verb matches that of another verb that is known to alternate, the former verb is licensed to alternate as well. Pinker (1989) spent three chapters discussing the grammatically relevant ways in which this matching is to be specified. Thus, as the representations of verbs are accrued during acquisition, they fall naturally into either licensing or non-licensing narrow range subclasses. When verbs such as *come* and *go* fall into their nonlicensing subclass, they are no longer overgeneralized because broader lexical rules such as the transitive–causative correlation only apply to the licensing subclasses. (This is a very brief synopsis; see Pinker, 1989, and Naigles, 1991, for details.)

According to Pinker, the shift from Frame Compliance to Verb Compliance may occur because the verb representations are elaborated to the extent that they have formed grammatically relevant narrow range subclasses. Verbs such as *come* and *go* no longer allow the causative interpretation (i.e., become Verb Compliant) because they do not fit the semantic specifications of subclasses that "causativize" (i.e., they do not encode manner of motion).

Notice that this account predicts that *fall* and *stay* will also eventually fall into nonlicensing subclasses (i.e., *fall* will be in the same subclass as *come* and *go* because the verbs only differ on the specified path of motion, which Pinker claimed is not grammatically relevant. These verbs will thus eventually disallow the causative interpretation. Our subjects, however, continued to allow *fall* and *stay* to be causativized well past the shifts for *come* and *go*. In fact, even our adults were predominantly Frame Compliant (68%) for "the lion falls the chicken" and "the penguin stays the bird." Within Pinker's narrow range subclasses, all verbs are supposed to behave similarly with regard to argument structure, yet our data show that at least one of the verbs in the *come* subclass exhibits quite a different degree of flexibility.

A second feature of Pinker's account concerns the mechanism involved in the achievement of stable argument structures. Because assignment to an alternating subclass depends upon positive evidence to that effect (e.g., that children hear "sink" being used in both transitive and intransitive frames), it should in principle always remain possible that the next utterance the child hears will contain a critically relevant datum. However, Pinker argued—and our data confirm—that children eventually become more definitive about the status of nonalternating verbs such as *go* and *bring*. Having not heard these verbs in the alternate syntax, they somehow come to expect that they will not. Pinker's explanation for this "closing off" of the argument structure is maturational in nature: At the time of puberty, those subclasses of verbs for which there has been no evidence of alternation become fixed as nonalternating subclasses, and the adult state is achieved. Beyond this point, no new information about these verbs is accepted. Our results are not entirely inconsistent with this hypothesis: The 12-year-olds in the study by Naigles, Fowler, and Helm (1992) were indeed indistinguishable from adults in this regard, and there was considerable growth until this point.

On the other hand, we have reason to be skeptical about this maturational account as telling the whole story. For example, why is it that the tendency to reject novel syntactic information begins as early as age 3, is complete for the NV frame by age 5, and varies as a function of syntactic frame and individual verb? Such findings are clearly not supportive of a strict maturational account, as they indicate that some verbs and frames achieve stability well before puberty. In fact, because of the verb-by-verb nature of the shift toward Verb Compliance, we put forth a hypothesis, which we dubbed *lexical knowledge*, which focuses even more specifically on the role of individual verb knowledge in the construction of verb representations (Naigles et al., 1993). In particular, we suggested that the observed developmental shift may be displaying the gradual accrual of verb knowledge over time, so that Verb Compliant behavior is a function of verb-specific experience. Thus, our proposal was that the actual closing off of verbs and their argument structures is governed by the accrual of lexical knowledge.

Our purpose in the study presented next was twofold. First, to further refine the concept of lexical knowledge, we consider a new population whose syntactic and lexical skills are divergent. Second, we consider a maturational account in a somewhat different light: Regardless of when verbs and argument structures *begin* to achieve stability, is puberty the point at which the verb acquisition process necessarily *ends*?

THE END OF VERB ACQUISITION IN SUBJECTS WITH DOWN SYNDROME

To address the issues presented previously, we turned to a different population of verb learners, namely, schoolchildren and adolescents with Down syndrome (DS). Our subjects were individuals whose language learning was often far from complete but who either had attained puberty or were prepubescent. How flexible would they be in interpreting familiar verbs in novel syntactic frames? This is not the first time researchers have turned to individuals with DS to investigate critical-period questions. Indeed, the evident lack of growth in sentence structure among individuals with DS beyond puberty (Lenneberg, Nichols, & Rosenberger, 1964) was cited as one of the key pieces of evidence in the most comprehensive and influential critical-period hypothesis ever put forth (Lenneberg, 1967). What is particularly exciting in the study presented here is that we have the opportunity to investigate not what these individuals have acquired but how they respond to new input.

When we ask whether students with DS respond in accordance with chronological age (CA) or language level, a particularly intriguing question concerns how their language state is defined. It is a well documented fact about individuals with DS that their language skills split in an interesting fashion—generally portrayed as distinguishing between lexical and syntactic knowledge or vocabulary and grammar (for reviews, see Fowler, 1988; Miller, 1988). Specifically, receptive vocabulary growth, although well behind CA, proceeds well in advance of syntactic knowledge (e.g., MLU, auxiliary use). For example, in a study of adolescents with DS, Fowler (1990) reported that children with vocabulary ages of 6 years had "syntactic ages" closer to 3 years (see also Evans, 1977; Hartley, 1982). This dichotomy creates considerable interest for our inquiry into verb acquisition, an area that clearly straddles the boundary between lexical and syntactic development. Do schoolchildren with DS respond to novel sentences in accordance with general lexical knowledge as assessed by their vocabulary or mental age, or more in accordance with their level of syntactic development? Given the oft-cited discrepancy between vocabulary and syntactic development, it should in principle be possible that students acquire vocabulary well in advance of their syntactic development, yielding verb compliance out of keeping with that found among peers defined on a syntactic basis.

Thus, our goal in the study was to determine those factors that bear on verb interpretation in individuals for whom the usual course of maturational, lexical, and syntactic development has become dissociated (see also Gopnik, 1992). To this end, we gave the Noah's Ark task to both pre- and postpubescent schoolchildren with DS and assessed syntactic and lexical skill independently via standardized measures. Our design allowed us to explore two different hypotheses. First, if Pinker and Lenneberg were correct regarding maturational factors, then adolescents with DS will be no more Verb Compliant than their prepubescent counterparts. On the other hand, if our lexical knowledge hypothesis is correct, then adolescents with DS who have accrued more linguistic knowledge will be more Verb Compliant than prepubescents with DS. Second, if the subjects with DS are as Verb or Frame Compliant as their normal-IQ mental-agemates, then we can assume that the Noah's Ark task (and perhaps verb acquisition more generally (is primarily tapping into lexical knowledge. If they perform more in keeping with their syntactic agemates, then we have additional evidence that the acquisition of verbs has a strong syntactic component.

Method

Subjects.   The subjects were 24 middle-class children with Down syndrome from elementary and secondary schools in Connecticut and Pennsylvania; all were enrolled in outstanding programs for children with special needs, and all were native speakers of English. Twelve of the children were gradeschoolers between the ages of 9;0 and 11;8 (MA = 10.12 years), and 12 were adolescents between the ages of 12;0 and 17;11 (MA = 14.90 years). All but one of the subjects had full trisomy 21; the youngest child had a mosaic form of trisomy 21. The mental ages of the grade school children ranged from 4;2 to 7;8, with a mean of 5;4. These were derived from recent school-administered omnibus IQ tests, including the Stanford-Binet and the WISC-R. A *language age* measure for these children was based on mean length of utterance (MLU), calculated on the basis of their spontaneous comments during the experimental sessions. Their MLUs ranged from 1.0 to 3.21, with a mean of 2.08, making their mean language age around 2;3 (Miller, 1980) and confirming prior studies finding MLU to lag well behind mental age (Fowler, 1990; Miller, 1987). Mental ages for the adolescents were estimated on the basis of the PPVT-R test (Dunn & Dunn, 1981), which correlates highly with the Stanford-Binet and WISC-R. The resulting mental ages ranged from 4;6 to 10;8, with a mean of 6;6. Language age in these subjects was based on the Test of Auditory Comprehension of Language-Revised (TACL-R; Carrow-Woolfolk, 1985); subjects' performance placed them at the 5;7 age-equivalent level on both the grammatical markers and elaborated sentences subsections (range 3;5 to 9;9). It seems from these scores that the adolescents did not show the typical split between language age and mental age. We suspect that this is entirely an artifact of the language measure used. The TACL-R assesses comprehension rather than production, and a high level of performance can be obtained with well-developed lexical skills. In short, it captures some of the same skills as the PPVT-R; a production measure would presumably be much lower (Miller, 1987).

To be included in this study, all subjects had to meet our criterion of enacting the grammatical control sentences correctly at least 75% of the time; six additional children with DS were tested but failed to reach this criterion.

Stimuli and Design. The stimuli and design were exactly the same as those reported in Naigles et al. (1993); the reader is directed to that paper for details. Briefly, 40 experimental sentences were designed by fitting each of 10 motion verbs into four sentence frames (NVNPN, NVN, NVPN, NV). Four of the verbs were transitive (*bring, take, push, put*), four were intransitive (*come, go, fall, stay*), and two (*move, drop*) could legitimately appear in both transitive and intransitive frames. Of the 40 sentences, 16 were ungrammatical and 24 were grammatical.

Procedure. The subjects were tested individually in a room provided by the school. Each subject was asked to name the characters and practice was provided in the case of any confusion. In general, however, subjects did know the names. When working with the normal-IQ children in Naigles, Fowler, and Helm (1992) and Naigles et al. (1993), all animals were placed within easy access of the children, and the children then chose the animals needed to enact each sentence in turn. However, pilot testing revealed that the selection of animals distracted the children with DS; they often forgot the test sentence in the process. These children were therefore only given access to the named characters plus deliberate foils. For the adolescents, three or four characters were set up by the experimenter within easy reach of the subjects, who were then directed to choose the one(s) they needed to enact each sentence. For the grade schoolers, the named characters were placed on the stage, and the children were told to use these to enact each sentence. For 6 of the gradeschoolers, an extra animal (usually a bird) was placed right next to the stage for each sentence in which a direct object was missing (e.g., "the tiger takes," "the elephant pushes toward the ark"); no particular instructions were given about this extra animal. For both groups, after each enactment, the animals were removed from the stage.

Verbal memory limitations of the subjects with DS also led us to modify presentation of the test sentences. The normal-IQ children generally needed to hear just one presentation to produce an enactment; however, the subjects with DS required multiple repetitions, lengthening considerably the necessary time to administer the test. Whereas the entire procedure was administered in one session for the normal-IQ children over age 5, 2 of the grade-school children with DS needed two sessions and one needed three sessions to complete the entire task. For both groups, feedback was always positive, regardless of accuracy. The subjects' responses were recorded on videotape for later coding.

Coding. The coding scheme employed is fully described in Naigles (1988), Naigles, Fowler, and Helm (1992), and Naigles et al. (1993). Each enactment of a sentence was first described using a detailed inventory of action descriptions, such as "tiger pushes lion over to ark." The major focus of these descriptions was whether the verb was enacted as a causal or a noncausal action; in this example the action was causal. If the stimulus sentence was grammatical, the description was then coded for *correctness*; if the stimulus sentence was ungrammatical, it was coded for *compliance*. For example, the ungrammatical transitive sentences (e.g., "*the tiger goes the lion") were coded as Frame Compliant if the enactment was causal (e.g., the tiger makes the lion go) and Verb Compliant if the enactment was noncausal (e.g., the tiger and lion go separately). The ungrammatical intransitive sentences (e.g., "*the tiger brings to Noah") were coded as Frame Compliant if the enactment was noncausal (e.g., the tiger moves alone to Noah) and Verb Compliant if the enactment was causal (e.g., the tiger brings the bird to Noah).

An enactment was coded as *other* if it did not fit into either of the two preceding categories. For example, the child employed wrong movements (e.g., a vertical motion for *come* or no motion at all) or reversed the thematic roles of the sentence, such as making the bird knock the lion over in response to "*the lion falls the bird." Although the latter enactment is causal and so partially fits the Frame Compliant criteria for the ungrammatical transitives, the subject of this sentence is cast as the experiencer of the action rather than its agent, thus partially fitting the Verb Compliant criteria. Finally, occasional enactments suggested that the child misheard some part of the sentence, as when the lion was made to move behind the bird in a sentence containing *fall* (i.e., "fall" may have been confused with *follow*).[2]

---

[2]After coding the enactments according to the specifications just detailed, we made a small number of modifications to take into account the children's enactments of the grammatical sentences. The grammatical and ungrammatical sentences were paired according to their causal and noncausal counterparts for each frame. Thus, ungrammatical *come, go, stay,* and *fall* were paired with grammatical *bring, take, put,* and *drop,* respectively (e.g., "*the elephant comes the giraffe" was compared with "the tiger brings the bird"). Likewise, ungrammatical *bring, take, push,* and *put* were paired with grammatical *come, go, move,* and *stay,* respectively (e.g., "*the lion puts" was compared with "the kangaroo stays"). The pairs of sentences were then compared, with the grammatical enactment providing the basis for our interpretation of the ungrammatical enactment. For example, if a child's enactment of "the tiger brings the bird" (a grammatical sentence) involved the tiger and bird moving side by side in two hands without

The enactments for all the sentences were initially described and then coded by the experimenters. The entire set of enactments was described and coded a second time by LGN; agreement among coders averaged 85%, and disagreements were resolved by discussion. This is the same level of reliability as was obtained when coding the normal-IQ toddlers and preschoolers (Naigles et al., 1993) and gradeschoolers (Naigles, Fowler, & Helm, 1992).

Results and Discussion

Each subject enacted at least 75% of the grammatical sentences correctly, and the mean percentage correct for both the gradeschoolers and adolescents was 88%. Consistent with our expectations and with the performance of their normal-IQ peers, the children with DS readily understood the task and were quite accurate when the verbs occurred in familiar structures. The children also enacted the ungrammatical sentences in an interpretable fashion: Responses coded as other (neither Frame Compliant nor Verb Compliant) were relatively uncommon, constituting 10.8% of the responses for both age groups. This level of other responses is higher than that of the normal-IQ gradeschoolers but the same as that of the normal-IQ preschoolers (see Naigles et al., 1993). Because these other responses did not differ as a function of frame type or subject age and did not appear to follow any discernible pattern, they were omitted from the statistical analyses that follow. All tabular presentations and analyses are based on the 89.2% of responses that were coded as either Frame Compliant or Verb Compliant.

Two questions were addressed by the analyses below. First, how Frame Compliant were the subjects with DS? Did they tend to follow the frame and change the verb, as the normal-IQ preschoolers did, or did they follow the verb and repair the frame, as the gradeschoolers and adults from the normal-IQ population had? Second, was there a shift with age among the

---

touching (coded as incorrect because it was noncausal), and if the same child's enactment of "the elephant comes the giraffe" involved the same noncausal action (initially coded as Verb Compliant because it was noncausal), then the latter enactment was recoded as Frame Compliant because of its close similarity to the enactment of the grammatical sentence. Likewise, if a child's enactment of "the kangaroo stays" involved simply putting the kangaroo on the stage, motionless, and if the same child's enactment of "*the lion puts" involved putting the lion motionless on the stage and also putting the bird motionless on the stage (initially coded as Frame Compliant because it was noncausal), then this latter enactment was recoded as Verb Compliant because of its dissimilarity to the enactment of the grammatical sentence (i.e., a second animal was introduced for the ungrammatical sentence but not the grammatical one). Only pairs of sentences within the same frame were compared; thus, if the child who enacted *come* and *bring* in the NVN frame as described previously also enacted *come* noncausally in the NVNPN frame but did not enact *bring* noncausally in the NVNPN frame, then the Verb Compliant coding of *come* in the NVNPN frame was maintained. A total of 23 enactments (out of 384: 6%) were changed in this fashion; 5 were changed from Frame Compliant to Verb Compliant, and 18 were changed from Verb Compliant to Frame Compliant.

subjects with DS, away from Frame Compliance and toward Verb Compliance? If so, was it uniform or does it vary as a function of frame and verb? A final analysis assessed whether implicit and explicit recognition of ungrammaticality were precipitating factors in the shift towards Verb Compliance and, by extension, toward stable argument structures.

How Frame Compliant Are Subjects With DS? Table 11.1 shows the percentage of Frame Compliant enactments for each DS age group. Both age groups were quite Frame Compliant: The gradeschool children performed Frame Compliantly almost 75% of the time and the adolescents almost 67% of the time. This finding, together with the small percentage of other responses reported previously, indicates that the children with DS systematically exploited the aforementioned correlations between verb meaning and surface syntax (i.e., transitive–causative) and so made systematic predictions about verb meaning based on syntax. With the obvious caveat that these verbs were familiar rather than novel, it seems clear that children with DS can bootstrap syntactically.

The subjects with DS seemed even more Frame Compliant than many of the normal-IQ subjects studied by Naigles, Fowler, and Helm (1992) and Naigles et al. (1993). In the ANOVAs (Group × Frame) that follow, the percentage of Frame Compliance demonstrated by subjects with DS was compared with that generated by their chronological agemates (CA-mates), their mental agemates (MA-mates), and the normal-IQ 2- and 3-year-olds who were closest to their syntactic agemates. Across all four frames, the gradeschoolers with DS performed significantly more Frame Compliantly than the normal-IQ 10-year-olds ($F(1, 23) = 19.54$, $p < .001$) and the normal-IQ 5-year-olds ($F(1, 22) = 6.34$, $p < .02$). There was a nonsignificant trend toward greater Frame Compliance in the DS gradeschoolers than the normal-IQ 3-year-olds ($F(1, 30) = 2.81$, $p = .10$), and there was no difference between the DS gradeschoolers and the normal-IQ 2-year-olds for the NVN and NVPN frames ($F(1, 30) < 1$, ns) or for the NV frame ($F(1, 29) < 1$, ns). Thus, the gradeschool children with DS were more Frame Compliant than either their CA- or MA-mates; the normal-IQ group they most resembled was the 2-year-old group.

As with the younger group, the adolescents with DS performed significantly more Frame Compliantly across all four frames than did the normal-IQ 12-year-olds ($F(1, 22) = 6.40$, $p < .02$) or the normal-IQ 9-year-olds ($F(1, 22) = 4.996$, $p < .05$). They performed like the normal-IQ 7-year-olds for all frames except NV; they were somewhat more Frame Compliant for this frame ($F(1, 22) = 3.25$, $p < .09$). Their performance was not different from that of the normal-IQ 3-year-olds on any frame ($F(1, 30) < 1$, ns), nor was it different from that of the normal-IQ 2-year-olds on frames NVN and NVPN ($F(1, 30) < 1$, ns). They were, however, significantly less Frame Compliant

TABLE 11.1
Mean Percentage Frame Compliant Enactments

Down Syndrome Subjects

	Age	
	Grade School	Adolescent
Across Frames	73.38	62.50
Frame 1: NVNPN	78.47	63.19
Frame 2: NVN	71.97	67.36
Frame 3: NVPN	68.06	75.69
Frame 4: NV	75.00	43.75
Chronological Age	10.12 years	14.90 years
Mental Age	5.33	6.65
Syntactic Age	2.29 (MLU)	5.66 (TACL-R)

Normal IQ Subjects

	Age								
	2	3	4	5	7	9	10	12	Adult
Across Frames	64.96	63.26	66.46	59.55	56.08	48.27	42.02	43.58	47.60
Frame 1: NVNPN		78.75	79.20	77.78	77.08	62.50	62.50	71.53	75.85
Frame 2: NVN	69.10	70.45	71.65	64.58	68.06	47.92	41.67	43.75	50.00
Frame 3: NVPN	60.40	63.85	70.45	70.83	57.64	54.86	47.22	36.11	34.15
Frame 4: NV	65.37	40.00	44.55	25.00	21.53	27.78	16.67	22.92	30.40

than the 2-year-olds for the NV frame ($F(1, 29) = 3.74$, $p < .06$). In sum, the adolescents with DS were much more Frame Compliant than their CA-mates and somewhat more Frame Compliant than their MA-mates (i.e., for the NV frame). These subjects most resembled the preschool-aged normal-IQ group.

These analyses suggest that there is an age effect within the DS population; that is, the adolescents with DS were less Frame Compliant than the gradeschoolers with DS and so may be beginning to shift toward Verb Compliance. An ANOVA was performed (Age × Frame) comparing the two DS groups, and although it yielded no main effect of age ($F(1, 22) = 2.26$, $p > .10$), the interaction of age and frame approached significance ($F(3, 66) = 2.25$, $p < .09$). Post hoc Tukey tests revealed that the adolescents were significantly less Frame Compliant than the gradeschoolers for the NV frame only ($p < .01$). Thus, whereas the gradeschool children with DS performed at approximately the same level of Frame Compliance with all four frames, the adolescents with DS performed less Frame Compliantly with the NV frame than with the other three frames ($F(3, 33) = 3.08$, $p < .05$). This effect is shown graphically in Fig. 11.2. Thus, it appears that the adolescents with DS had begun to shift toward Verb Compliance with the NV frame.[3]

Our final analysis of Frame and Verb Compliance investigated possible verb effects across age groups. Table 11.2 shows the percentage of Frame Compliant enactments elicited for each verb in its two frames. Our first comparison was motivated by a result from Naigles et al. (1993), who found that normal-IQ gradeschool subjects enacted sentences with *come* and *go* less Frame Compliantly than sentences with *fall* and *stay*, with *come* and *fall* the most and least Frame Compliant, respectively. Although the number of DS subjects was much smaller (24 DS subjects versus 60 normal-IQ subjects in Naigles et al., 1993), these subjects followed a similar pattern: Across both

---

[3]At this point, a methodological issue must be addressed. Recall from the procedure section that all the adolescents with DS were presented with extra animals for each sentence enactment, whereas only half of the DS gradeschoolers had access to extra animals. That is, upon hearing "the tiger brings," an adolescent always had access not only to the tiger but also to at least one other animal, which he or she could exploit as the patient of the tiger's bringing. Half of the gradeschoolers with DS, on the other hand, were only presented with the tiger; perhaps they did not pick up another animal (and so perform Verb Compliantly) because they believed they were restricted to the animals accessible. Might this procedural difference be the reason that the gradeschoolers with DS performed more Frame Compliantly with the NV frame? There are two reasons why this explanation cannot entirely account for the age difference. First, the gradeschoolers who were not presented with an extra animal sometimes performed Verb Compliantly with the NV sentences; they were Verb Compliant 16.7% of the time and exploited other props such as the ark and the ramp as the patients of the action. Second, the gradeschoolers who received the extra animal did not always make use of it. In fact, they performed Verb Compliantly only 33.3% of the time, which is much less than the 57% Verb Compliance of the adolescents. In sum, although the addition of an extra animal probably helped the subjects with DS to perform Verb Compliantly once they realized a sentence warranted it, it is unlikely that the presence of the extra animal instigated the Verb Compliant enactments.

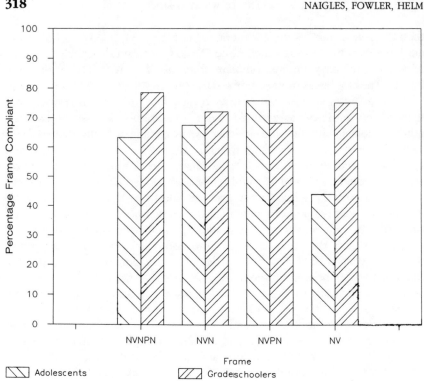

FIG. 11.2. Percentage of Frame Compliant enactments as a function of frame for the subjects with Down syndrome.

frames, *come* elicited Frame Compliant enactments around 50% of the time, whereas *fall* elicited Frame Compliant enactments around 80% of the time (by items, $t(2) = 9.5$, $p < .05$), with *go* and *stay* falling in between. For these data, then, the verb effects gain in generality. Naigles et al. (1993) also found that for the NVPN frame, *take* elicited the most Frame Compliance; however, with the DS subjects, *put* elicited significantly more Frame Compliance than

TABLE 11.2
Percentage Frame Compliance by Verb and Frame

	Come	Go	Fall	Stay
NVNPN	0.52	0.73	0.87	0.67
NVN	0.53	0.62	0.85	0.70

	Bring	Take	Push	Put
NVPN	0.67	0.58	0.58	0.96
NV	0.71	0.48	0.50	0.71

the other three verbs (by subjects, Cochran's $Q(2)$ > 7.0, p < .05 for each verb). Within the NV frame, Naigles et al. found that *push* elicited the *least* Frame Compliance; *take* had that distinction with the DS subjects, although *push* came very close (*take* differs significantly only from *put* [Cochran's $Q(2)$ = 6.0, p < .05]). Thus, some but not all of the verb effects from Naigles et al. (1993) were revealed by the subjects with DS. What is more interesting is that verb effects were again present. Together with the significant frame effect, the verb effects indicate that the children's Frame Compliance has a linguistic aspect to it; it is not simply a function of slavishly obeying the experimenter.

To summarize, the gradeschool children with DS enacted the ungrammatical sentences predominantly Frame Compliantly. Despite their chronological age of 10 and their mental age (calculated mostly from vocabulary tests) of 5, their enactments of these sentences were most akin to those of normal-IQ 2-year-olds. They accepted the novel frames for the familiar verbs and reinterpreted the verbs' meanings almost 75% of the time. By contrast, the adolescents with DS appear to have begun to shift away from Frame Compliance and toward Verb Compliance with at least one of the four frames. They were more Frame Compliant than their CA-mates and slightly more Frame Compliant than their MA-mates. Like the preschoolers they most closely resemble, they seem to have begun to reject novel frames for some transitive verbs and seem to be beginning to build an argument structure for these verbs.

What Precipitates the Shift? A Measure of Grammaticality. An additional advantage inherent in studying children with DS is that because of their extremely slow but normal development, milestones that pass swiftly in normal-IQ children can be studied in greater detail in children with DS. For example, in the normal-IQ population, 2-year-olds are Frame Compliant with all frames, whereas 3-year-olds are significantly less Frame Compliant with the NV frame—the beginning of the shift is swift. Within the DS population, though, the commencement of the shift is drawn out over a number of years. The issue at hand involves the precipitation of the developmental shift toward Verb Compliance. The most straightforward hypothesis concerning the start of the shift toward Verb Compliance (and by extension toward stable verb meanings and argument structures) involves the attribution of ungrammaticality to the novel sentences. That is, perhaps the realization that a sentence is ungrammatical is what precipitates the formation of stable argument structures for specific verbs. Alternatively, though, such a realization may be a result of the stable structures, not an instigating factor. Our data speak to this.

None of the Noah's Ark studies specifically tested for grammaticality judgments; however, the subjects sometimes commented on the sentences, and many of the comments were quite revealing of difficulty with the sentences (e.g., "I don't know what *come* means" from a 4-year-old and "The tiger brings what to Noah?" from an adult). The comments, then, can be regarded as fairly explicit indications of whether the subjects viewed the sentences as grammatical or not. However, not every subject chose to comment on every sentence; in fact, some hardly spoke at all. Therefore, the more pervasive measure of latency to enact the sentences was used as an implicit measure of grammaticality. That is, if the sentence is regarded as ungrammatical, it may take longer to begin the enactment.

The spontaneous comments of all of the adults, 4-, 3-, and 2-year-olds who participated in the Naigles et al. (1993) study, as well as comments from the subjects with DS in the study described here were transcribed and categorized as relevant or irrelevant to grammaticality. Comments considered to be relevant to grammaticality were those that indicated some kind of uncertainty on the part of the subject: requests for repetition (e.g., "What?" "Say that again?"), requests for information (e.g., "Where?" "Brings what?"), comments on the characters (e.g., "Noah?" "Where's the ramp?"), declarative repetitions (e.g., "The elephant comes the giraffe"), interrogative repetitions (e.g., "Comes the giraffe?"), and explicit statements of confusion (e.g., "I don't know what that means," "Help"). Comments considered irrelevant to grammaticality included noises made while enacting the sentences (e.g., "vroom") and questions and declaratives off the subject (e.g., "what's your name?" "I like the tiger"). The latency to enact the sentences was also recorded for all the adults, 15 randomly selected 3- and 4-year-olds, 7 randomly selected 2-year-olds, and all the subjects with DS. Latency was recorded in seconds with a handheld stopwatch, starting at the end of the experimenter's first articulation of the test sentence and ending at the beginning of the subject's first attempt at enacting the sentence.

The results are presented in Tables 11.3 and 11.4. Consistent with our hypothesis, the normal-IQ adults and preschoolers took longer to enact the ungrammatical sentences than the grammatical sentences (by items, $t(32) = 62.14$, $p < .001$ and $t(32) = 30.05$, $p < .001$, respectively). Both groups also produced more comments about the ungrammatical sentences than about the grammatical sentences (by items, $t(6) = 7.6$, $p < .05$; $t(6) = 6.94$, $p < .05$; and $t(6) = 34.08$, $p < .005$; for the adults, 4-year-olds, and 3-year-olds, respectively). In contrast, the normal-IQ 2-year-olds did not distinguish the two types of sentence either in their comments or in their latency of enactment. It seems then, among normal-IQ individuals, that the only age group to perform predominantly Frame Compliantly with all frames was the same age group that demonstrated neither implicit nor explicit recognition of the ungrammaticality of the sentences. The next oldest group, the 3-year-olds, had both begun to shift toward Verb Compliance with one frame (NV) and demonstrated both implicit and explicit recognition of the ungrammaticality

TABLE 11.3
Latency to Enact Sentences

Age Group	Grammatical	Ungrammatical
Adult	4.573	7.473**
Preschool	8.949	12.514**
Two	8.322	7.676
DS-gradeschool	6.144	7.419*
DS-adolescent	8.889	10.276*

*$p < .05$. **$p < .01$.

of the sentences. Here, then, is a case in which the subjects with DS, with their slower development, may shed light on the type of recognition that is more indicative of the beginnings of the formation of argument structure.

The mean latencies of enactment and percentage of comments produced by the DS subjects are also presented in Tables 11.3 and 11.4. As Table 11.3 shows, both the gradeschool and adolescent subjects with DS took longer to enact the ungrammatical sentences than the grammatical ones (by items, $t(32) = 6.55$, $p < .02$ and $t(32) = 3.84$, $p < .06$, for the gradeschoolers and adolescents, respectively). Thus, both age groups demonstrated implicit recognition of the ungrammaticalities. Although both age groups also produced a higher percentage of comments on the ungrammatical sentences than on the grammatical ones (see Table 11.4), this was not significant for either age group. That is, neither age group with DS exhibited explicit recognition of the grammatical/ungrammatical distinction. It appears, on this initial analysis, that neither of these measures distinguishes the gradeschool children with DS from the adolescents with DS.

Interestingly, the subjects with DS were much more talkative overall than either the normal-IQ adults or the preschoolers; the normal-IQ subjects tended to enact the sentences in silence, with just a few comments interspersed. The children with DS, on the other hand, tended to repeat almost every test sentence, sometimes asked for repetitions of every sentence, and

TABLE 11.4
Percentage of Sentences With Comments

Age Group	Grammatical	Ungrammatical
Adult	2.7	10.6*
Four	22.9	36.9*
Three	13.1	25.9**
Two	7.5	8.6 ns
DS-gradeschool	21.5	26.6 ns
DS-adolescent	45.5	52.6 ns

*$p < .05$. **$p < .01$.

very often queried the experimenter about the animals. Thus, perhaps only the outright statements of confusion are truly indicative of grammatical uncertainty in this population. If only these statements are considered, we see a split between the adolescents and gradeschool children: Of the 12 statements of confusion expressed by the adolescents, 10 co-occurred with ungrammatical sentences. Only one statement of confusion was produced by any gradeschooler; the fact that this also co-occurred with an ungrammatical sentence is difficult to assess, given the small numbers.[4] Thus, although the gradeschoolers with DS talked about half as much as the adolescents, they produced disproportionately fewer statements of confusion in response to the ungrammatical sentences. This suggests that the gradeschoolers' explicit recognition of the ungrammaticality of these verbs in unattested frames is less well developed than that of the adolescents.

General Discussion

In the experiment presented, we explored the extent to which maturational, lexical, or syntactic factors affected how schoolchildren and adolescents with Down syndrome interpreted familiar verbs in novel syntactic frames. Prior work with normal-IQ individuals (Naigles, Fowler, & Helm, 1992; Naigles et al., 1993) suggested that when children are very young, the argument structure for any given verb is sufficiently flexible that it can accommodate to a novel syntactic frame; the frame therefore tends to determine the interpretation. By adulthood, the argument structure of the verb has apparently stabilized enough to override most contradictory information provided by the syntactic frame. In short, in the normal-IQ case, we know that performance shifts from predominantly Frame Compliant to more Verb Compliant as children grow simultaneously older, smarter, and linguistically more sophisticated. But which of these three factors bears on their construal of the task and the verbs placed before them? We suggest that by studying schoolchildren and adolescents with DS—individuals for whom maturational, cognitive, and linguistic development are not as tightly linked as in the normal case—we may identify the important catalyst(s) for change.

Before discussing our results, we stress that basic knowledge of all 10 verbs and four frames was well within the competence of all children who participated in the study; children who failed to meet these criteria were excluded from the study. Thus, Frame and/or Verb Compliance cannot be

---

[4]Outright statements of confusion were also more evident in response to ungrammatical sentences than to grammatical ones for the normal-IQ adults, 4-year-olds, and 3-year-olds (1, 7, and 6 statements with grammatical sentences; 5, 14, and 12 statements with ungrammatical sentences; for the adults, 4-year-olds, and 3-year-olds, respectively). The 2-year-olds, by contrast, produced only two statements of confusion, one co-occurring with a grammatical sentence and one with an ungrammatical sentence.

attributed to a lack of any familiarity with the verbs nor to an insensitivity to the frame presented. Our major findings were that the gradeschoolers with DS performed Frame Compliantly with every syntactic frame and that the adolescents with DS had begun to shift toward Verb Compliance with the NV frame. Within this population, then, we observed both an age effect and a frame effect. In the following section, we discuss what these effects reveal about language in the DS population and what they reveal about the acquisition of verbs and argument structure more generally.

Language in the DS Population. The results from the Noah's Ark task indicate that schoolchildren with DS perform much like normal-IQ 2-year-olds with regard to their degree of Frame Compliance. This is consistent with their language age and well behind expectations based on general cognitive growth. The adolescents with DS also performed well behind mental age; their degree of Frame Compliance was closest to that of the normal-IQ preschoolers. Insofar as our Noah's Ark task is construed to be syntactic in nature, these results corroborate evidence using other methodologies and looking at other aspects of syntax (e.g., Fowler, 1990). That is, the syntactic knowledge of individuals with DS is disproportionately delayed relative to their mental age.

Our second finding, that the adolescents with DS appear to have begun to shift toward Verb Compliance with the NV frame, suggests that language acquisition continues during the gradeschool years and perhaps into adolescence. As in other studies, what appears to be a plateau is followed by an upswing in language growth at a surprisingly late point in development. Although these results are suggestive, they may ultimately challenge the prevailing view of a shutdown of language acquisition in adolescence (see also Fowler, 1988; Meyers, 1988; Miller, 1988). The significance of this finding for the role of maturation specifically in the acquisition of verbs and their argument structures is discussed in more detail in the sections following.

The Acquisition of Verbs and Argument Structure. The adolescents with DS were considerably more Frame Compliant than most of the normal-IQ comparison groups. Nonetheless, they were identical to the comparison groups with respect to the developmental sequence. That is, the first frame to elicit substantial amounts of Verb Compliance in both normal-IQ and DS individuals was the NV frame. This finding reinforces the contention of Naigles, Fowler, and Helm (1992) that the pattern of frames shifting toward Verb Compliance, at least for the four frames tested, is a principled one based more on differential linguistic complexity than on particular strategies for handling unattested sentences. Children with DS are often relatively adept at using nonlinguistic or pragmatic strategies to handle difficult linguistic (especially syntactic) tasks (Beeghley, Weiss-Perry, & Cicchetti, 1990;

Price-Williams & Sabsay, 1979); however, if those factors alone had led to the shift in the responses to our "Noah's Ark" task, we would not have obtained the significant frame effect from the adolescent group. It seems clear that this task is tapping developing lexical and syntactic knowledge in both normal-IQ and DS subjects.

The subjects with DS also bear on our conceptualization of verb acquisition by highlighting the problematic nature of the lexicon/syntax split. Recall that the DS subjects' performance most closely resembled that of their syntactic age-mates, thus suggesting that the task was tapping syntactic knowledge. On the other hand, even within this generally Frame Compliant group, some verbs—usually the same ones as had been observed in the normal-IQ groups—were enacted Verb Compliantly both earlier and more consistently than others. This finding implicates a significant lexical component in the task. We believe that these findings are not contradictory; rather, they are the inevitable result of dealing with verbs. Verbs, by their very nature, incorporate general conceptual knowledge (e.g., certain verbs encode movement), language-specific semantic knowledge (e.g., certain verbs encode the manner of movement), and specific syntactic knowledge (e.g., certain verbs involve particular argument structures). In sum, verbs are difficult to categorize as lexical or syntactic *because* they have multiple components.

The Noah's Ark task, which involves (depending on one's perspective) verbs in ungrammatical sentence frames or sentences containing the wrong verbs, investigates several of these components simultaneously. In fact, we suggest that, for the youngest normal-IQ group and the schoolchildren with DS, the task is predominantly syntactic. These subject groups, like 2-year-olds encountering novel verbs in a preferential-looking paradigm (Naigles, 1990; Naigles & Kako, 1993), relied wholly on the syntactic frame to interpret verb meaning. In contrast, for older normal-IQ children and for adolescents with DS, the task was lexical. These groups disallowed ungrammatical argument structures on a verb-by-verb basis. The questions produced by the subjects supported this lexical focus, singling out the verb as the source of concern in their enactments (e.g., "I don't know what *comes* means" and "Brings? Brings what?"). Thus, whether the task is viewed as predominantly syntactic or predominantly lexical may well depend on the level of linguistic knowledge of the individual subject.

Finally, the data suggest that the shift toward Verb Compliance does not seem to be maturationally bound, either at the beginning or at the end of development. Previous work has demonstrated that the shifts toward Verb Compliance begin anywhere between the ages of 2 and 7 in the normal-IQ population (Naigles, Fowler, & Helm, 1992; Naigles et al., 1993; see also Fig. 11.1). The study presented here expands this range, showing that subjects with DS begin to shift toward Verb Compliance at or beyond the onset of puberty. It therefore does not seem to be the case that, whatever the degree of Frame Compliance achieved by children before puberty, no further development can occur in adolescence. Rather, there is evidence of modest but significant syntactic and lexical growth during the teenage years. This continued growth, combined with the findings from the normal-IQ population, suggests that what one knows about the language itself may play a much larger role than maturational factors in reducing flexibility.

This is not to say that maturation plays no role in language acquisition. In fact, research on both first and second language acquisition (Curtiss, 1979; Gleitman, 1981; Johnson & Newport, 1989; Newport, 1990) has provided important evidence that the ability to learn particular aspects of a language declines over age. Interestingly, much of this evidence for maturational constraints has involved linguistic structures rather distinct from verb argument structure, including auxiliary verbs, inflections, classifiers, determiners, and pronouns. Our data suggest only that it is unlikely that verb argument structures become rigid at some maturationally determined date. Thus, verb argument structures, at the very nexus of syntax and semantics, may not be nearly as dependent on maturational factors as the closed-class items.

So how are verbs and their argument structures acquired? At the beginning of verb learning, general rules that link verb meaning and syntax are exploited, allowing syntax to constrain the meanings of novel verbs. This general rule usage, known as syntactic bootstrapping, remains in effect for novel verb learning in adulthood; however, new syntactic information no longer affects the construals of familiar verbs in an indiscriminate fashion. Rather, for both normal-IQ subjects and those with DS, prohibition of novel syntax takes hold frame by frame and verb by verb. In accord with our lexical knowledge hypothesis, we proposed that specific lexical and syntactic information concerning each individual verb must be accrued in order to establish stable verb representations. This accrual may be aided by principles such as *uniqueness* (e.g., Clark, 1987; Wexler & Culicover, 1980) and by attention to the frequency and diversity of verb presentations in the input. For example, the principle of uniqueness can account for the shift toward Verb Compliance for transitive *come* and *go*, in that the attested transitive and causative verbs *bring* and *take* preempt the other, virtually synonymous entries. Likewise, the attested intransitive verbs *come* and *go* may preempt intransitive *bring* and *take*. To explain the sequence of these preemptions in development, we appealed to demonstrated differences in the use of these verbs to young children, in that *come* and *go* are used much more frequently than *bring* and *take*. We conjectured that verbs that are more commonly encountered allow the child to activate preemption much earlier.

In the case of children with DS, it may be the very lack of accrual of information about verbs and their cues that slows them down. For example, it appears that both phonological memory and phonological codes for individual words are often deficient compared to other children matched on receptive vocabulary age (Fowler, Doherty, & Boynton, 1992). These factors were found to slow further lexical development in other populations (Gathercole & Baddeley, 1989). This poorly detailed database, compounded by the demonstrably impoverished syntax of children with DS, may certainly hamper the successful exploitation of the principle of uniqueness as well as of the information in the input.

CONCLUSIONS

In this chapter we discussed the complex intertwining of syntax and semantics in the development of verb meanings. Our aim was to show how reversing the usual approach and focusing on how syntactic knowledge and syntactic tasks shed light on verb meaning can be revealing with respect to the acquisition of verbs. Prior research has shown that familiar syntactic frames can be used by very young children as information about the meaning of a novel verb (i.e., syntactic bootstrapping). Furthermore, children's interpretations of familiar verbs in novel syntactic frames in the Noah's Ark task can reveal how their verb meanings and argument structures are finally established. We presented a new study employing the same task with a new population, namely, children with DS and obtained the same interdependence of verb syntax and verb semantics. On the one hand, children with DS perform most like their normal-IQ syntactic peers, not like chronological or vocabulary peers, yet their eventual shift toward Verb Compliance seems to be dependent on features of individual verbs. Determining the meaning of a verb is partly dependent on the syntactic frames in which it appears, and establishing those syntactic frames in which it can appear is partly a function of the meaning thus far constructed. We therefore suggest that where the child is in the process of verb learning—that is, whether syntax is allowed to be informative about verb meanings—is dependent not on intelligence or maturational status but on the child's level of linguistic sophistication.

ACKNOWLEDGMENTS

We thank the teachers, parents, and children of the Julian Curtiss and Jennings schools in Greenwich and Fairfield, CT, and St. Katherine's Day School, Lower Merion High, and Bala Cynwyd Junior High in Merion, PA, for their cheerful cooperation. We also thank Brian Doherty and Laura Boynton for their assistance in running subjects and Anna Hradnansky and Edward Kako for their help with data coding. We are grateful to William Merriman and

Michael Tomasello for their comments on an earlier version of this chapter. The research was supported by NIH FIRST Award HD26595 to L. Naigles and a National Down Syndrome Society Scholar Award to A. Fowler. Portions of the data were previously reported at the 1991 Biennial Meeting of the Society for Research in Child Development, Seattle, WA.

REFERENCES

Baker, C. L. (1979). Syntactic theory and the projection problem. *Linguistic Inquiry, 10*, 533–581.

Beeghly, M., Weiss-Perry, B., & Cicchetti, D. (1990). Beyond sensorimotor functioning: Early communicative and play development of children with Down syndrome. In D. Cicchetti & M. Beeghly (Eds.), *Children with Down syndrome: A developmental perspective* (pp. 329–368). New York: Cambridge University Press.

Behrend, D. (1990). The development of verb concepts: Children's use of verbs to label familiar and novel events. *Child Development, 61*, 681–696.

Bever, T. (1970). The cognitive basis for linguistic structures. In J. Hayes (Ed.), *Cognition and the development of language* (pp. 279–362). New York: Wiley.

Bloom, L. (1970). *Language development: Form and function in emerging grammars.* Cambridge, MA: MIT Press.

Bloom, L. (1981). The importance of language for language development: Linguistic determinism in the 1980s. *Annals of the New York Academy of Sciences, 379*, 160–171.

Bowerman, M. (1974). Learning the structure of causative verbs: A study in the relationship of cognitive, semantic and syntactic development. *Proceedings on Research in Child Language Development, 8*, 142–178.

Bowerman, M. (1977). The acquisition of rules governing "possible lexical items": Evidence from spontaneous speech errors. *PRCLD, 13*, 148–156.

Bowerman, M. (1982). Starting to talk worse: Clues to language acquisition from children's late speech errors. In S. Strauss (Ed.), *U-shaped behavioral growth.* New York: Academic Press.

Bowerman, M. (1983). Evaluating competing linguistic models with language acquisition data: Implications of developmental errors. *Quaderni de Semantica, 3*, 5–66.

Brown, R. (1973). *A first language.* Cambridge, MA: Harvard University Press.

Carey, S. (1978). The child as word learner. In M. Halle, J. Bresnan, & G. Miller (Eds.), *Linguistic theory and psychological reality* (pp. 264–293). Cambridge, MA: MIT Press.

Carey, S. (1982). Semantic development: The state of the art. In E. Wanner & L. R. Gleitman (Eds.), *Language acquisition: The state of the art* (pp. 347–389). Cambridge, England: Cambridge University Press.

Carlson, G., & Tannenhaus, M. (1988). Thematic roles and language comprehension. In W. Wilkins (Ed.), *Syntax and semantics: Thematic relations* (pp. 263–288). San Diego, CA: Academic Press.

Carrow-Woolfolk, E. (1985). *Test for auditory comprehension of language—Revised.* Allen, TX: DLM.

Chafe, W. (1970). *Meaning and the structure of language.* Chicago: University of Chicago Press.

Choi, S., & Bowerman, M. (1991). Learning to express motion events in English and Korean: The influence of language-specific lexicalization patterns. *Cognition, 41*, 83–122.

Chomsky, N. (1965). *Aspects of a theory of syntax.* Cambridge, MA: MIT Press.

Clark, E. (1987). The principle of contrast. In B. MacWhinney (Ed.), *Mechanisms of language acquisition* (pp. 3–20). Hillsdale, NJ: Lawrence Erlbaum Associates.

328   NAIGLES, FOWLER, HELM

Clark, E. V., & Garnica, O. (1974). Is he coming or going? On the acquisition of deictic verbs. *Journal of Verbal Learning and Verbal Behavior, 13*, 559–572.

Curtiss, S. (1979). *Genie: A psycholinguistic study of a modern day "wild child."* New York: Academic Press.

Dunn, L., & Dunn, L. (1981). *Peabody Picture Vocabulary Test—Revised.* Circle Pines, MN: American Guidance Service.

Evans, D. (1977). The development of language ability in mongols: A correlational study. *Journal of Mental Deficiency Research, 21*, 103–117.

Fillmore, C. (1968). The case for case. In E. Bach & R. Harms (Eds.), *Universals in Linguistic Theory* (pp. 1–91). New York: Holt, Rinehart & Winston.

Fisher, C., Gleitman, H., & Gleitman, L. R. (1991). On the semantic content of subcategorization frames. *Cognitive Psychology, 23*, 331–392.

Fisher, C., Hall, D. G., Rakowitz, S., & Gleitman, L. R. (1994). When it is better to receive than to give: Syntactic and conceptual constraints on vocabulary growth. *Lingua, 92*, 333–375.

Fodor, J. A. (1970). Three reasons for not deriving "kill" from "cause to die." *Linguistic Inquiry, 1*, 429–438.

Fodor, J., Garrett, M., & Bever, T. (1968). Some syntactic determinants of sentential complexity. II: Verb structure. *Perception and Psychophysics, 3*, 453–461.

Fowler, A. (1988). Determinants of language growth in children with Down syndrome: A longitudinal investigation. In L. Nadel (Ed.), *The psychobiology of Down syndrome* (pp. 217–245). Cambridge, MA: MIT Press.

Fowler, A. (1990). Language abilities in children with Down syndrome: Evidence for a specific syntactic delay. In D. Cicchetti & M. Beeghly (Eds.), *Children with Down syndrome: A developmental perspective* (pp. 302–328). New York: Cambridge University Press.

Fowler, A., Doherty, B., & Boynton, L. (1994). *Phonological bases of reading and language problems in young adults with Down syndrome.* Unpublished manuscript, Bryn Mawr College, Bryn Mawr, PA.

Gathercole, S., & Baddeley, A. (1989). Evaluation of the role of phonological STM in the development of vocabulary in children: A longitudinal study. *Journal of Memory and Language, 28*, 200–213.

Gentner, D. (1978). On relational meaning: The acquisition of verb meaning. *Child Development, 49*, 988–998.

Gleitman, L. R. (1981). Maturational determinants of language growth. *Cognition, 10*, 103–114.

Gleitman, L. R. (1990). The structural sources of verb meaning. *Language Acquisition, 1*, 3–55.

Gleitman, L. R., & Gleitman, H. (1992). A picture is worth a thousand words, but that's the problem: The role of syntax in vocabulary acquisition. *Current Directions in Psychological Science, 1*, 31–35.

Golinkoff, R., Hirsh-Pasek, K., Cauley, K., & Gordon, L. (1987). The eyes have it: Lexical and syntactic comprehension in a new paradigm. *Journal of Child Language, 14*, 23–45.

Gopnik, M. (1992). A model module? *Cognitive Neuropsychology, 9*, 253–258.

Grimshaw, J. (1990). Argument structure. *Linguistics Inquiry Monograph* (Serial No. 18). Cambridge, MA: MIT Press.

Gropen, J., Pinker, S., Hollander, M., & Goldberg, R. (1991). Syntax and semantics in the acquisition of locative verbs. *Journal of Child Language, 18*, 115–151.

Gropen, J., Pinker, S., Hollander, M., Goldberg, R., & Wilson, R. (1989). The learnability and acquisition of the dative alternation in English. *Language, 65*, 203–257.

Hartley, X. Y. (1982). Receptive language processing of Down's syndrome children. *Journal of Mental Deficiency Research, 26*, 263–269.

Hirsh-Pasek, K., & Golinkoff, R. (1991). Language comprehension: A new look at some old themes. In N. Krasnegor, D. Rumbaugh, M. Studdert-Kennedy, & R. Schiefelbusch (Eds.), *Biological and behavioral aspects of language acquisition* (pp. 301–320). Hillsdale, NJ: Lawrence Erlbaum Associates.

Hochberg, J. (1986). Children's judgments of transitivity errors. *Journal of Child Language, 13,* 317–334.

Jackendoff, R. (1983). *Semantics and cognition.* Cambridge, MA: MIT Press.

Jackendoff, R. (1990). *Semantic structures.* Cambridge, MA: MIT Press.

Johnson, J., & Newport, E. (1989). Critical period effects in second language learning: The influence of maturational state on the acquisition of English as a second language. *Cognitive Psychology, 21,* 60–99.

Landau, B., & Gleitman, L. R. (1985). *Language and experience.* Cambridge, MA: Harvard University Press.

Lenneberg, E. H. (1967). *Biological foundations of language.* New York: Wiley.

Lenneberg, E. H., Nichols, I., & Rosenberger, E. (1964). Primitive states of language development in mongolism. *Research Publications, Association for Research in Nervous and Mental Disease, 42,* 119–147.

Levin, B. (1985). Lexical semantics in review: An introduction. In B. Levin (Ed.), *Lexical semantics in review.* Lexicon Project Working Papers, Center for Cognitive Science, MIT. Cambridge, MA.

Maratsos, M., Gudeman, R., Gerard-Ngo, P., & DeHart, G. (1987). A study in novel word learning: The productivity of the causative. In B. MacWhinney (Ed.), *Mechanisms of language acquisition* (pp. 89–113). Hillsdale, NJ: Lawrence Erlbaum Associates.

Meyers, L. (1988). Using computers to teach children with Down syndrome spoken and written language skills. In L. Nadel (Ed.), *The psychobiology of Down syndrome* (pp. 247–265). Cambridge, MA: MIT Press.

Miller, J. (1980). *Assessing language production in children: Experimental procedures.* Baltimore: University Park Press.

Miller, J. (1987). Language and communication characteristics of children with Down syndrome. In S. Pueschel, C. Tingley, J. Rynders, A. Crocker, & C. Crutcher (Eds.), *New perspectives on Down syndrome* (pp. 233–262). Baltimore: Brookes.

Miller, J. (1988). The developmental asynchrony of language development in children with Down syndrome. In L. Nadel (Ed.), *The psychobiology of Down syndrome* (pp. 167–198). Cambridge, MA: MIT Press.

Naigles, L. (1988). *Syntactic bootstrapping as a procedure for verb learning.* Unpublished doctoral dissertation, University of Pennsylvania, Philadelphia.

Naigles, L. (1990). Children use syntax to learn verb meanings. *Journal of Child Language, 17,* 357–374.

Naigles, L. (1991). Review of *Learnability and Cognition. Language and Speech, 34,* 63–79.

Naigles, L., Eisenberg, A., & Kako, E. (1992, November). *The acquisition of a language-specific lexicon: Motion verbs in English and Spanish.* Paper presented at the annual meeting of the International Pragmatics Association, Antwerp, Belgium.

Naigles, L., Fowler, A., & Helm, A. (1992). Developmental shifts in the construction of verb meanings. *Cognitive Development, 7,* 403–428.

Naigles, L., Gleitman, L. R., & Gleitman, H. (1993). Children acquire word meaning components from syntactic evidence. In E. Dromi (Ed.), *Language and cognition: A developmental perspective* (pp. 104–140). Norwood, NJ: Ablex.

Naigles, L., & Kako, E. (1992). First contact in verb acquisition: Defining a role for syntax. *Child Development, 64,* 1665–1687.

Newport, E. (1990). Maturational constraints on language learning. *Cognitive Science, 14,* 11–28.

Pinker, S. (1984). *Language learnability and language development.* Cambridge, MA: Harvard University Press.

Pinker, S. (1989). *Learnability and cognition: The acquisition of argument structure.* Cambridge, MA: MIT Press.

Price-Williams, D., & Sabsay, S. (1979). Communicative competence among severely retarded persons. *Semiotica, 26,* 35–63.

Quine, W. V. O. (1960). *Word and object.* Cambridge, MA: Harvard University Press.

Shapiro, L., Zurif, E., & Grimshaw, J. (1987). Sentence processing and the mental representation of verbs. *Cognition, 17*, 10–28.

Talmy, L. (1985). Lexicalization patterns: Semantic structure in lexical forms. In T. Shopen (Ed.), *Language typology and syntactic description* (pp. 57–149). New York: Cambridge University Press.

Tomasello, M. (1992). *First verbs: A case study of early grammatical development.* Cambridge, England: Cambridge University Press.

Wanner, E. (1974). *On remembering, forgetting, and understanding sentences.* The Hague: Mouton.

Wexler, K., & Culicover, P. (1980). *Formal principles of language acquisition.* Cambridge, MA: MIT Press.

Wierzbicka, A. (1988). *The semantics of grammar.* Philadelphia: John Benjamins.

Wittgenstein, L. (1953). *Philosophical investigations.* New York: Macmillan.

CHAPTER TWELVE

Missing Arguments and the Acquisition of Predicate Meanings

Matthew Rispoli

Northern Arizona University

The objective of this chapter is to contribute to a realistic explanation of how the semantic representations of verbs are acquired. The narrower focus of this chapter is the question of information sources; that is, what sources of information are used by children to establish the semantic representation of a verb? In particular, it is proposed that children as young as 18 months old take note of the communicative intents of conversational partners and the pragmatic status of referents, overt and implied, and that children use this information when constructing the meaning of a predicate.

It has been argued that the acquisition of a verb's meaning cannot in principle proceed by matching a word like *give* to the nonverbal context in which it is used. In part, the problem lies in the multitude of elements in the environment that can constitute noise in the process. As Gleitman wrote, "The very richness of perception guarantees multiple interpretive possibilities at many levels of abstraction for single scenes; but the problem for word learning is to select from among these options the single interpretation that is to map onto a particular lexical item" (1990, p. 13). In response to this problem Gleitman proposed that children use syntactic bootstrapping to acquire a verb's meaning. As Gleitman explained, "The idea . . . is that children deduce the verb meanings in a procedure that is sensitive to their syntactic privileges of occurrence" (1990, p. 5). It is argued that if a child hears a sentence such as "x zub y," the child will know that this is a transitive sentence, with x equaling the actor and y equaling an undergoer. Knowing this, the child can acquire an important aspect of the semantic representation of this predicate through the syntax alone.

Syntactic bootstrapping is a procedure bounded in applicability. A lower boundary exists, below which syntactic bootstrapping cannot be used. This lower boundary exists because linking rules between the syntactic roles of *noun phrase* (NP) arguments and their semantic roles must be established before the syntactic roles can be interpreted. The knowledge that "x zub y" is parsed as "actor zub undergoer" is not given a priori but must be acquired by observation of the nonlinguistic context. Gleitman recognized this fact and pointed out that the child must "understand the semantic values of subcategorization frames" in order to bootstrap the meaning of a new verb syntactically (1990, p. 38). There is also an upper boundary to this procedure, a point beyond or above which syntax is no longer indicative or reflective of elements in the semantic representation. This occurs when the child encounters semantically indeterminate argument structures. I explore one such indeterminate structure in a later section. The two boundaries, upper and lower, are graphically presented in Table 12.1.

In this chapter I consider what happens at these boundaries. The exploration is crosslinguistic. I examine the acquisition of Japanese because the typology of Japanese may cause the period before the establishment of the lower boundary to be protracted, allowing a closer look at how linking rules may be established. I then return to English, in which the acquisition of optional undergoer verb lies at the upper boundary of the applicability of syntactic bootstrapping. However, before we embark on our crosslinguistic journey we must reconsider the basic psycholinguistic problem: How do children acquire the meanings of verbs? We must also review several weak points in the syntactic bootstrapping approach to the problem, in particular the need for an independently motivated semantic theory.

In Gleitman's (1990) exposition of syntactic bootstrapping, continual reference is made to the construct *verb*, but the term is used in a variety of ways. For example, when Gleitman asked, "How does the learner decide which particular phonological object corresponds to which particular verb concept?" (1990, p. 4), "verb" referred to something at the conceptual level. On the other hand, when Gleitman wrote, "The idea here is that children deduce the verb meanings . . ." (1990, p. 5), "verb" referred to something in the semantic component of grammar. Finally, when Gleitman discussed the problems of idiomatic verb uses such as the use of *saw* in "John saw his brother out of the room" (1990, pp. 31, 49), "verb" referred to a lexical item as a phonological string, without regard to meaning. This ambiguity in the use of the term verb clouds matters. Thus, some definitions are in order. In this chapter, verb is a morphological and syntactic designation, not a semantic one. Following Kempson (1977, pp. 88–101) I use the term *predicate* as a semantic term. The terminology is borrowed from predicate cal-

TABLE 12.1
The Bounded Nature of Syntactic Bootstrapping

	Prior to Establishment of Linking Rules	Syntactic Bootstrapping Can Apply	Interpretation of Syntactically Indeterminate Structures
Examples	Actor = Nominative case		Intransitive eat, shave, win, swallow.
Explanation	The child must establish reliable links between semantic roles and case before syntactic bootstrapping can take place.	After linkages are established the child can use case to deduce something about the meaning of a new predicate	Some argument structure alternations are ambiguous as to the predicate types they encode. The child must use semantic and discourse–pragmatic information to establish the meanings of these predicates.

culus. Let us represent the internal structure of a proposition as F_a, in which F is a property, or in semantic terms, a predicate, which is predicated of some individual a, in semantic terms, an *argument*. Therefore, when we say that children learn the meanings of verbs, we are being imprecise. More precisely, children learn the meanings of predicates.

Does this change in terminology alter our understanding of the acquisition problem? Yes. The following commonplace example serves as a demonstration. Suppose we ask the question, how does the child acquire the meaning of the verb *took*? In example (1a) following, *took* is a verb that subcategorizes for an NP, *a spoon*, and a locative prepositional phrase, *from the drawer*. At the semantic level, *took from* is a predicate predicated of three arguments: I, spoon, and drawer. Note that we are considering *took from*, not just took, as the predicate here. This is because *took from* takes an location argument: the place from which something was taken. In (1b), we have a very different predicate, despite the fact that we have the same verb, *took*. It is arguable as to whether the predicate in (1b) has one argument, I, or two, both I and bath. This is not the crucial point here. What is important is the fact that the predicate in (1b) cannot take a third location argument. That is, baths are not taken from a location, and this is why Example 1c is nonsensical.

(1a) I took a spoon from the drawer.

(1b) I took a bath.

(1c) *I took a bath from the bathroom / from the bathtub.

Consider what happens to the meaning of sentences (1a) and (1b) when they are modified by the temporal expression *for an hour*, as in Examples

2a and 2b. In Example 2a, *for an hour* refers to the length of time for which I had possession of the spoon. In contrast, in Example 2b, *for an hour* refers to the length of time for which I bathed. The predicate in (2a) tells us something about the location of its arguments relative to one another. The predicate in Example 2b tells us nothing about the location of the arguments relative to one another. For the same reasons, Example 3a makes sense but Example 3b makes no sense whatsoever.

(2a) I took a spoon from the drawer for an hour.

(2b) I took a bath for an hour.

(3a) I took a spoon from the drawer for an hour but put it back.

(3b) *I took a bath for an hour but put it back.

How does the child learn the meaning of the verb *took* when it appears to mean so many different things? The answer is that the child does not learn the meaning of a verb per se. Children learn that the verb *took* is used in the expression of a number of different predicates and do not attempt to select "the single interpretation that is to map onto a particular lexical item" (Gleitman, 1990, p. 13).

By adopting the position that children acquire the meanings of predicates rather than verbs, we move our focus away from syntactic privileges of occurrence, because syntactic privileges are aspects of lexical items. Rather, I argue that children use morphological and discourse-pragmatic information to interpret missing arguments and in so doing, construct the meanings of predicates. Such a claim, however, needs a theory of how morphological and pragmatic information can implicate aspects of a predicate's meaning. Therefore, before proceeding to data, we need to dwell on some theoretical underpinnings.

THEORETICAL FRAMEWORK

If the psycholinguist's question is how children build semantic representations, then the psycholinguist must have some working theory of semantic representations that does not confuse semantic representation with syntactic representation (or for that matter, the nonlinguistic, conceptual representation). In this chapter, the grammatical framework known as *role and reference grammar* (RRG) is used. RRG was chosen because of its detailed theory about the interface between semantic representations, case systems, and grammatical relations, as well as its crosslinguistic orientation. For these reasons, RRG is well suited for exploring the upper and lower boundaries of syntactic bootstrapping. This synopsis of pertinent aspects of role and reference grammar serves as an introduction to the larger theoretical framework (Foley & Van Valin, 1984; Van Valin, 1990, in press).

A predicate in RRG has a skeletal semantic representation called a logical structure. The classification recognizes four types of predicate, classified according to their inherent temporal contours and causal relationships: states, achievements, accomplishments, and activities, displayed diagrammatically in Table 12.2. There are two basic operators for logical structures, BECOME and CAUSE. BECOME is a symbol for the fact that achievements entail a culmination point that divides two phases of an action, pre- and post-culmination phases (Lys & Mommer, 1986). Activities and states do not entail a culmination point and therefore do not have the BECOME operator in their logical structures. Accomplishments are decomposable into two component predicates, the second of which is either an achievement or activity. The two predicates are connected symbolically by the CAUSE operator.

These logical structures provide information for the first step in determining *thematic roles* for a given predicate. Thematic roles are a feature of many linguistic frameworks, largely because of the relation between these roles and verb-argument structure (Fillmore, 1968; Foley & Van Valin, 1984; Grimshaw, 1990; Gruber, 1976; Jackendoff, 1972; Van Valin, 1990). If we begin with the notion that predicates take arguments, we can imagine that there are no general classes of arguments. That is, every time we have a new predicate, it is associated with arguments that are essentially unique to that predicate only. However, empirical evidence suggests that this is not the case. The evidence is morphosyntactic. Syntax and morphology treat arguments not as individual and unique but as differentiated classes. RRG recognizes a series of approximately six thematic roles: agent, effector, ex-

TABLE 12.2
Predicate Class and Logical Structure in RRG

Predicate Class	Logical Structure
State	predicate' (x) or (x, y)
The clock is broken.	broken' (clock)
John is a lawyer.	be' (John, [lawyer'])
Achievement	BECOME predicate' (x) or (x, y)
The clock broke.	BECOME broken' (clock)
John became a lawyer.	BECOME be' (John, [lawyer'])
Activity	do (x) [predicate' (x) or (x, y)]
The children cried.	do (children) [cry' (children)]
Larry ate fish.	do (Larry) [eat' (Larry, fish)]
Accomplishment	@ CAUSE %
	(where @ is an activity, and % is an activity or accomplishment).
The child broke the clock.	[do (child)] CAUSE [BECOME broken' (clock)]

periencer, locative, theme, and patient. Roughly speaking, (a) agents are intentional, animate effectors, (b) effectors are energetic entities, (c) experiencers are entities capable of psychological experience, (d) locative is a place (further broken down into source and goal), (e) themes are objects or entities that move, change location, or change orientation, and (f) patients are objects or entities that change state or endure a state.

An important feature of the RRG framework is that thematic roles are not ad hoc features of a predicate. Rather, strict relations exist between logical structures and thematic roles. Understanding these relations is essential for understanding how an RRG-based approach can explain the acquisition of predicates. The relations are basically as follows: (a) Effectors are energetic entities and must be associated with activities (e.g., the wheel is rotating, the flag is waving); (b) Agents are animate effectors acting intentionally (e.g., The man is waving goodbye); (c) States cannot have effectors associated with them because states are not dynamic; and (d) Patients are arguments only of states, but states can be embedded in achievements and accomplishments. It is assumed that these relations between predicate type and thematic role exist a priori; that is, they are part of *universal grammar* (UG), as defined by RRG.

RRG does not posit the grammatical relations subject and object as part of UG. Rather, RRG recognizes that human beings (including children) can construct a level of semantic role broader than thematic roles. This broader level is the level of *macrorole*. There are two macroroles allowed in a sentence: *actor* and *undergoer*. This broad level of macrorole was hypothesized to account for the tendency of case systems to group the more specific thematic roles into a more general dualistic system (e.g., the English nominative–accusative case system, the Mayan ergative-absolutive case system, and the Georgian active–stative case system). In RRG, a verb that takes both macroroles in a sentence is a transitive verb, whereas a verb that takes only one macrorole (and this could be either an actor or an undergoer) is an intransitive verb. In RRG, the terms transitive and intransitive refer to a verb's valence—the number of macroroles with which a verb may appear (see Foley & Van Valin, 1984; Rispoli, 1991a, 1991b; Van Valin, 1990).

It is a consequence of RRG's semantic theory that the child may use multiple linguistic and nonlinguistic sources of information to establish a predicate's logical structure. Let us take a concrete problem of predicate differentiation common in child language. Consider two different predicates, the state "hurt" and the accomplishment "hurt," examples of which are given in Examples 4a and 4b, respectively.

(4a) My arm hurts me.

(4b) You hurt me.

On the basis of empirically derived, linguistic facts, we establish that these are two different predicates. The first observation we make is that the two different predicates do not allow the same class of adverbial modifiers. The predicate in (5a) cannot be modified by either of the adverbs *accidentally* or *intentionally*, but the predicate Example 5b can.

(5a) My arm hurts *accidentally / *intentionally.

(5b) You hurt me accidentally / intentionally.

These adverbs refer to manner of causation, and only predicates that contain the CAUSE operator can be modified by these adverbs. Therefore, the Example 5a predicate does not contain the CAUSE operator in its logical structure, whereas the Example 5b predicate does.

Another indication that these are two different predicates is that they behave differently when modified by the same aspect. To see this we have to compare the meaning of the Example 6a and 6b predicates in both the progressive and nonprogressive aspect forms. For the Example 6a predicate there is a rough synonymy between the nonprogressive and the progressive aspects. There is no such synonymy between the nonprogressive and progressive aspect forms of the Example 6b predicate. Without going into excessive detail on why this is so (see Dowty, 1979, pp. 71–78), it suffices to note that the (6a) predicate can be used to refer to "now" in either aspect form, whereas the Example 6b predicate can be used to refer to "now" only in the progressive. The nonprogressive form of the Example 6b predicate must mean "not now."

(6a) My arm hurts me = my arm is hurting me.

(6b) You hurt me ≠ You are hurting me.

The last observation I make is that the Example 7a predicate cannot take an imperative, whereas the Example 7b predicate can. In most semantic decompositional theories (Dowty, 1979; Foley & Van Valin, 1984; Grimshaw, 1990; Jackendoff, 1972; Van Valin, 1990), this occurs because the predicate in (7a) does not contain a CAUSE operator in its logical structure. Note that the symbol ?! stands for a pragmatic anomaly.

(7a) ?! Don't my arm dare hurt me!

(7b) Don't you dare hurt me!

To summarize, the predicate in Examples 4a–7a, a state predicate, does not have a CAUSE operator in its logical structure. Therefore, it cannot have an agent thematic role and is not temporally dynamic. The empirical results are that it cannot be modified by adverbs that refer to manner of causation (e.g., accidently, intentionally), its nonprogressive form has rough synonymy with its progressive form, and it cannot take an imperative.

How does a child come to differentiate these predicates? Let us consider how syntactic bootstrapping answers this question. The first problem the syntactic bootstrapping procedure must face is that these two predicates use the same verb. Second, the predicates can both appear in the transitive frame, and the tendency of the syntactic bootstrapping process is to equate the meanings of *hurt* in Examples 4a and 4b on the basis of the syntactic form alone. This may lead to serious difficulty: The meanings of these predicates are radically different, and the child must at some point come to differentiate them.

The point is not that syntactic bootstrapping is uninformative or impossible. The point is that syntactic bootstrapping is clearly limited because it contains a theoretical lacunae, that children must come to recognize differences in meaning between predicates, regardless of whether the same verb is used in these predicates. Let us consider an alternative to how the child differentiates between predicates such as the two predicates for which we use the verb *hurt*. First, let us assume that the child has some notion of the speech act "imperative" or "request," in which the addressee is a potential agent. The relation between imperatives and agency is not dependent on overt NP arguments because imperatives often lack overt agent NPs. Rather, the relation is given directly by the interface between pragmatics and semantics assumed in RRG's theory of UG. Also given in RRG's theory of UG is the incompatibility of states with agents and effectors. UG tells the child that if the predicate can be used in a imperative, the predicate cannot be a state. However, the child also accumulates evidence over time that state predicates in English fit in the aspectual schema of (6a) (*see, hear,* and *be sick* are very common state predicates). When the child realizes that *hurt* in used with agents and also fits into the state predicate aspectual schema of English, the child is forced to make two separate logical structures that the single verb *hurt* is used to express. Gradually, the child's hypothesis that *hurt* is used in both state and accomplishment predicates is confirmed by additional evidence from adverbials, as in Example 5. Thus, the child has to make use of semantic information (i.e., aspect), morphological evidence (i.e., the suffix for the progressive), and pragmatic evidence (i.e., speech act information). This solution does not depend on overt NP arguments because imperatives do not need overt actor arguments. The process outlined here is one of accumulation of evidence in order to set or construct logical structures. This may be a long process, and its strength is probably not speed. However, it can lead to predicate differentiation, whereas syntactic bootstrapping cannot.

There is yet another alternative. If the child realizes that some situations are the result of natural causation and others are the result of intentional causation, the child could differentiate the state *hurt* and the accomplishment *hurt* on this basis. This alternative is not pursued here because it is entirely unclear what a 2-year-old child understands about intentional and natural causation.

RRG's semantic theory details an important relation among aspect, thematic roles, and speech acts that provides a solution to the problem of predicate differentiation as outlined for the English verb *hurt*. As discussed in the following section on the acquisition of Japanese, this relation may be crucial to understanding what happens at the lower boundary of syntactic bootstrapping where the initial links between syntax and semantics are made—Gleitman called this "the largest problem of all" (1990, p. 50). RRG's semantic theory can also help us explore the upper boundary of syntactic bootstrapping, where syntax is not indicative of important differences among logical structures. Consider those transitive verbs in English that can optionally appear without their undergoers. The intransitive alternates disguise a variety of predicate types, as can be seen in Examples 8a through 10b with *kick, swallow, read, eat, dress,* and *shave.*

(8a) The boy kicked the ball / swallowed the cookie.

(8b) The boy kicked / swallowed.

(9a) Tom read the book / ate the pizza.

(9b) Tom read / ate.

(10a) William shaved / dressed Tom.

(10b) William shaved / dressed.

We can discern at least three types of alternations in these sentences. The paired sentences of Examples 11a–11c capture these differing interpretations in everyday language.

(11a) The boy kicked = The boy's body moved (without contacting an object).

(11b) Tom read = Tom read something or other.

(11c) William shaved = William shaved himself.

For the *kick* type predicates, the omitted undergoer truly reflects the absence of an argument from the logical structure. For *read* type predicates the intransitive form signals a lack of commitment to the specificity of the erstwhile undergoer. When you read or eat, you must read or eat something. For the *shave* type predicates, the omitted undergoer is interpreted as being coreferent with the actor. The syntactic operation involved, the loss of the overt argument, cannot in principle inform a child of the semantic representation of the predicate involved. However, the actual interpretation of the missing argument affects the logical structure of the predicate. In Examples 12a–12c, the *kick* and *read* type predicates are *atelic* (a characteristic of activities), whereas the *shave* type predicate is *telic* (a characteristic of accomplishments). Note that telic predicates can be modified by any time-delimiting adverb such as *in fifteen minutes*, whereas atelic predicates cannot be so modified. Also note that only the telic predicate in Example 7, *shave*, is to be paraphrased as "it took fifteen minutes to finish shaving" (Dowty, 1979).

(12a) ?! The boy swallowed in fifteen minutes.
(≠ it took fifteen minutes to finish swallowing)

(12b) ?! Tom read / in fifteen minutes.
(≠ it took fifteen minutes to finish reading)

(12c) William shaved / in fifteen minutes.
(= it took fifteen minutes to finish shaving)

What is perhaps most intriguing about this tale, a piece of the story brought out rather well by the RRG framework, is that concomitant with these differences in logical structure are differences in the discourse-pragmatic privileges of these predicates. In the intransitive form, the *shave* type predicate's overtly missing argument is interpreted as a specific entity—in fact, as coreferential with the actor. Specificity can be seen as a discourse-pragmatic property. A referent is specific if a speaker believes that he or she knows the actual identity of the referent (Enç, 1991; Kuno, 1973). The absurdity of the nonspecific reading for a *shave* type predicate is reflected in the unacceptability of Example 13. In contrast, with *read* type predicates the identity of the referent of the missing undergoer can be nonspecific, literally unknown to the speaker. As a result, Example 14 makes sense.

(13) ?! When I peeked into John's room he was dressing; now I wonder whom he was dressing.

(14) I saw John eating, but I don't know what he was eating.

Fillmore (1986) termed this missing undergoer of *read* type predicates the *indefinite null complement* (INC). In Example 15, the topic of the question–response pair is *my sandwich*. The omitted undergoer is extremely odd with *eat* in the response.

(15) A: What happened to my sandwich?
B: ?! The dog ate.

As Fillmore points out, the INC "is markedly indefinite . . . it is obligatorily disjoint in reference with anything saliently present in the pragmatic context" (1986, p. 97).

At this upper boundary of syntactic bootstrapping, a connection exists between the interpretation of a missing argument, the logical structure, and the discourse-pragmatic status of the missing argument. If the missing argument is interpreted as reflexive, the logical structure is telic and the discourse-pragmatic status of the missing argument is specific. If the missing argument is truly missing or generic, the logical structure is atelic and the discourse-pragmatic status is nonspecific. What this particular framework reveals is that at the upper and lower boundaries of syntactic bootstrapping, there are connections between semantics and pragmatics that go beyond the syntax. The connection is that discourse-pragmatic status implies certain features of logical structure (i.e., the semantic representation of a predicate) independent of syntax. Let us then begin our crosslinguistic inquiry with Japanese and the establishment of links between syntax (more exactly, case) and the semantic representation of predicates.

THE ACQUISITION OF JAPANESE

Japanese is a nominative–accusative language. Case is marked by postpositions: *ga* for nominative and *o* for accusative, as can be seen in Example 16. The transitive accomplishment *ire-ta* [put in] takes both an actor (*kodomo* [child]) and an undergoer (*kugi* [nail]), whereas the intransitive achievement takes a single macrorole (*kugi* [nail]). The word order in example sentences presented here is actor-undergoer-verb, but this is only to simplify the exposition. Unlike English, word order is actually irrelevant to case assignment in Japanese and so is not relevant to the establishment of linking rules between an argument's semantic role and its syntactic case.

(16a) kodomo ga   kugi o   ire-ta
      child   NOM nail ACC put in—PAST
      Boy put nail in.

(16b) kugi ga   hait-ta
      nail NOM go in—PAST
      Nail went in.

In addition, Japanese has grammatically unrestricted zero anaphora. Any and all of the core arguments of a predicate can be omitted in a grammatical sentence, as in Example 17 (Hinds, 1982; Okamoto, 1985).

(17) kugi o   ire-ta
    nail ACC put in—PAST
    Put in nail.

Furthermore, in the familiar register of Japanese the postpositions *ga* [nominative] and *o* [accusative] are often omitted, as in Example 18 (Shibamoto, 1985; Tsutsui, 1983).

(18) kugi ire-ta
      nail put in—PAST

A sentence like Example 18 is syntactically indeterminate. Because there is no syntactic indication of the case of *kugi* in (18), it is entirely unclear as to whether *ire-ta* is a transitive or an intransitive verb. For that matter, Example 16b is also indeterminate because all the syntax tells us is that *kugi* is nominative. Based on syntax alone, we have no idea if an undergoer was omitted from Example 16b. If a child had to classify a verb as transitive or intransitive based on syntax alone, the only truly informative sentences would be those with an undergoer overtly marked by the accusative postposition *o*, such as Examples 16a and 17.

Syntactic indeterminacy would not be a problem if Japanese children were often exposed to syntactically determinate input sentences. Unfortunately, caregiver speech to young Japanese children is in the familial register, which means zero anaphora and the omission of postpositions is the norm. A sample of 450 action sentences from 9 Japanese caregivers to their children was examined by Rispoli (1991a) to determine the percentage of sentences that were syntactically determinate. Here, I focus on the transitive sentences, summarized in Table 12.3. Of the original 450 sentences examined by Rispoli (1991a), 226 were transitive. Of these 226 transitive sentences, only 19 had the postposition *o* [accusative]. That is, only 9% of the caregiver transitive sentences were syntactically determinate. Most telling is the fact that only 1% of the transitive sentences had a full complement of two overt, syntactically distinguished macroroles. The implication here is that, if Japanese

TABLE 12.3
Frequency of Overt Macrorole NPs and Case Postpositions in Japanese
Caregiver's Transitive Sentences

Sentence Type	Frequency	Percentage of Total
V	73	32
NP V	103	46
NP *o* V	15	7
NP *ga* V	8	4
NP *ga* V (passive)	2	1
NP NP V	18	8
NP *ga* NP	3	1
NP NP *o* V	2	1
NP *ga* NP *o* V	2	1

children relied only on syntactic information for the classification of verbs into the transitive class, they would have to wait for a set of very rare input sentences to accomplish this classification. This may seem unlikely but not impossible. Perhaps Japanese children are especially gifted at discovering needles in haystacks.

Moreover, the rare but informative sentences crucially involve the post-positions *ga* and *o*, and Japanese children must have acquired the linkage between case and semantic roles before they can use these sentences. Here we confront empirical disconfirmation. The evidence shows clearly that Japanese children have difficulty learning the case system of Japanese. Errors in the use of *o* and *ga* have been observed among children between the ages of 2 and 4 years old (Clancy, 1985; Rispoli, 1987; Yokoyama & Schaefer, 1986). Example 19 is an example of this error, taken from Clancy (1985).

(19) *omizu ga   ire-ta   no ni.
     water   NOM put in—PAST although
     "Although (she) put in water" (Clancy, 1985, p. 389).

Furthermore, experimental results on the comprehension of these case post-positions by older children have shown that as late as 5 years of age, case marking is still not controlled (Hakuta, 1982; Hayashibe, 1975). Hayashibe studied children between the ages of 3;0 and 5;11 and tested whether children used word order, postpositions, or plausibility (i.e., animacy) as cues to interpretation of simple, active transitive sentences. Among the findings was the strong effect, obtained from the earliest age, that plausibility in interpretation, based on animacy, overrode case particles *o* and *ga*. Given the evidence, we must conclude that for 2-year-olds, plausibility and not case marking determines comprehension. It is highly doubtful that 2-year-old Japanese children find sentences with *o* and *ga* informative for syntactic bootstrapping.

Japanese children receive extremely little by way of useful, syntactically determinate input sentences, and they do not acquire linkages between case and semantic roles until rather late, perhaps as late as 5 years of age. Does this mean that Japanese children fail to acquire the meanings of important predicates such as *it-ta* [went], *ku-ru* [come], *suwat-te i-ru* [is sitting], and *ire-ta* [put in]? Absolutely not. There are many aspects of the grammar of a Japanese 2-year-old that indicate sophisticated semantic representations are being constructed before the acquisition of the case system. First, although Japanese children make errors with case postpositions, their use of action verbs is appropriate to the valence description of the verbs (i.e., the number of macroroles a verb takes). Two-year-olds use intransitive verbs with only one macrorole (Clancy, 1985; Rispoli, 1987, 1989; Yokoyama & Schaefer, 1986). Second, they use imperative, request, desiderative, and benefactive morphemes and constructions with the appropriate verbs, indicating that they are aware which predicates can have an agent argument. The competent production of morphemes entailing agency progresses far more rapidly than the sporadic and error-prone production of case postpositions *o* and *ga.* Early morphemes include -*te* [request], -*tai* [desiderative], -(*y*)*o* [hortatory], and -*cha dame* [prohibitional] (Clancy, 1985; Okubo, 1967; Rispoli, 1987). Third, 2-year-olds appear to acquire a significant aspectual schema (Rispoli, 1990). There are two sides to this aspectual schema. One side is that the -*te i-ru* (continuative) aspect of achievement predicates entails the -*ta* (completive) aspect, as in Example 20a, where the verb *hair-* [enter] is an achievement predicate. The counter side of this schema is that this relation does not hold for activity predicates, as in Example 20b, where the verb *asob-* [play] is an activity predicate.

(20a) x hait-te iru *entails* x hait-ta
       x is entered *entails* x has completed entering

(20b) x ason-de iru *does not entail* ason-da
       x is playing *does not entail* has completed playing

As 2-year-old Japanese children acquire the aspectual schemata, they begin to have dialogues such as that in Example 21. In this example, a 22-month-old child is attempting to insert a doll's thumb into its mouth, but the thumb keeps popping out. The child's father asks if the child has been successful by asking a question with the completive form *haitta* [did it enter?]. The 22-month-old answers negatively by using the negative continuative in accordance with the aspectual schema in Example 20a, saying simply, *haittenai* [it is not entered]. (The example is taken from Rispoli, 1990. Note the missing subject NP.)

(21) Father: hait-ta?
              enter-COMPLETIVE?
              Did (it) enter?
     Child: hait-te i-nai.
              enter-PRESENT CONTINUATIVE-NEGATIVE
              (It) isn't entered.

This is an important milestone in the acquisition of the inflectional aspect system of Japanese and is on a parallel with an English-speaking child acquiring the aspectual schemata involving the progressive and nonprogressive aspect forms exemplified in Examples 6a and 6b. This development suggests that Japanese 2-year-olds are acquiring the logical structures of predicates.

Finally, in the sentences of Japanese children observed by Rispoli (1987), the animacy of theme and patient referents was highly correlated with the syntactic distinction of transitivity among action verbs, with transitive verbs having almost exclusively inanimate theme and patient referents. This is what one would expect if children were paying attention to the nonlinguistic context and tracking the animacy of participants in a referenced action. Taken together, these four characteristics of a Japanese 2-year-old's grammar suggest that the children are subcategorizing verbs. Children recognize that a particular verb is used for particular types of predicates and not for others. It appears that Japanese children acquire semantic representations without the aid of the case system. This is tantamount to saying that Japanese children acquire the meanings of predicates without the aid of syntactic information.

Let us summarize the main points of this review of the acquisition of Japanese. According to our best estimates, only 9% of the action transitive sentences caregivers speak to their children are syntactically determinate, and only 1% are fully determinate with overt, case-marked actors and undergoers. This casts doubt on the idea that Japanese children need case-marked NPs to begin to acquire the meanings of predicates. In fact, Japanese children do not acquire the case system until rather late, perhaps as late as 5 years old. However, there is substantial evidence that 2-year-old Japanese children are well into the acquisition of predicates before they have acquired the case system and therefore are not using syntax as the primary means of acquiring the semantic representations of these predicates.

Because of the typological characteristics of Japanese, children acquire predicates before they acquire case. Perhaps the lower boundary of syntactic bootstrapping is, in effect, protracted in Japanese. One important property of early child Japanese is the acquisition of morphemes encoding imperative, request, desiderative, and so on. This suggests that Japanese children have at their disposal an avenue for determining agency that does not depend on syntactic bootstrapping but rather connects the predicate to the speech act and the bound morphology used to signal that speech act. Thus, at the lower boundary of syntactic bootstrapping, we find pragmatics and possibly inflectional morphology as information sources for the construction of the semantic representations of predicates.

ON THE ACQUISITION OF EAT

English word order is strict, and zero anaphora is highly restricted. Therefore, syntactic bootstrapping may be much more prevalent in English than it is in Japanese (for counter-evidence, see Olguin & Tomasello, in press). Nevertheless, English speaking children may also be sensitive to discourse-pragmatic information, but this sensitivity may be most important at the upper boundary of syntactic bootstrapping, where syntax cannot inform the child about important aspects of a predicate's semantic representation.

I noted in the introduction that the intransitive form of optional undergoer verbs disguise at least three different predicate types. Concomitant with these differences in predicate type are differences in the discourse-pragmatic status of the implicit undergoer. Recall that in the surface intransitive form, the status of the implicit undergoers of *shave* type predicates is specific. In contrast, with *read* type predicates the identity of the referent of the missing undergoer can be nonspecific. When the child encounters a verb that optionally appears with an omitted undergoer, the child must discover which semantic and pragmatic features constrain the interpretation of the implicit undergoer.

One piece of evidence that 2-year-old children are actually discovering these features comes from a study of the acquisition of the English verb *eat* (Rispoli, 1992). The subjects for this study were 40 children, 18 boys, and 22 girls, audiotaped at home for an hour every month from age 1;0 to 3;0. The transcribed utterances were grouped into episodes and turns: An episode boundary was defined as a 5-second or longer gap between utterances, and a turn was defined as an uninterrupted string of utterances by one speaker. The MLU for each monthly sample was calculated following procedures outlined by Brown (1973). A lexicon was compiled containing every word (type) on the audiotapes and the date of the word's first appearance in each child's lexicon. The verb *eat* was the focus of this study because according to the adult grammar, *eat* takes the indefinite null complement (INC) and all 40 children used this verb. No other INC-taking verb was used as early and with such frequency.

The children's sentences were coded for the presence of an overt undergoer. Food items and meal names were assumed to be undergoers, as in Example 22a. Inanimate pronouns and quantifiers found in postverb position were also automatically coded as undergoers, as in Example 22b.

(22a) We're eating supper.
(22b) Eat it / all of it.

Two contrasting discourse contexts were defined, a context in which a potential undergoer for the verb *eat* was readily available in the discourse context (*undergoer accessible* context) and another that was open to undergoer omission (*open* context). The contrast in discourse context was applied only to response sentences, that is, children's sentences that responded to another speaker's immediately prior utterance within a single episode. Sentences that either initiated an episode or continued a child's turn were not coded for discourse context. The undergoer accessible context was defined by characteristics of what was said in the preceding discourse.

Contexts were considered undergoer accessible if, in the preceding discourse, either the interlocutor or the child produced an utterance containing either the verb *eat* with an overt undergoer NP or a food item or meal name NP. At least one of the two criteria for the undergoer accessible context had to be found within a delimited stretch of discourse preceding a child's response sentence. Preceding discourse was divided into two sections, the immediately prior interlocutor turn (*prior turn*) and an extended segment of discourse (*extended segment*). Examples 23 and 24 were classified as undergoer accessible contexts because at least one of the criteria was found in the prior turn, *something to eat* in Example 23, and *a whole lot of bacon* in example (24). *Something to eat* is an example of the verb *eat* with an overt undergoer; *a whole lot of bacon* is an example of a food item NP. In the examples, P = parent, C = child.

(23) (Child 2;6, MLU = 2.76)
   P: Oh I want something to eat.
   C: Eat that!

(24) (Child 2;7, MLU = 2.71)
   P: We got whole lot of bacon.
   C: Can I eat it?

If neither of the two criteria were found in the prior turn, the search for the criteria proceeded into the extended segment of preceding discourse. The extended segment ended with the prior turn and began at an initiation point. The initiation point was a lexical, inanimate NP. This initiation point was chosen for two reasons. First, the conventional undergoer of *eat* is a food item, always a lexical inanimate NP. Second, lexical NPs are discourse prominent; that is, they can be focal or contrastive, whereas unstressed anaphors cannot be focal or contrastive (Chafe, 1976; Lambrecht, 1987). If the most recently lexicalized inanimate NP in a conversation is a food item, it is reasonable to assume that the item has some discourse prominence. Example 25 was classified as undergoer accessible because the food item *candy cane* was the initiation point of the extended segment.

(25) (Child 2;11, MLU = 3.41)
   P: Does that look like a candy cane?   < extended segment
   C: Yeah.
   P: Yeah.
   C: Here.
   P: It does.   < prior turn
   C: Eat it.
   P: You can eat it,
        but it won't taste very good.

If the initiation point was formed by a lexical, inanimate NP that was not a food item or meal name, the context was coded as open, as in Example 26. If there was no full lexical, inanimate NP between the prior turn and the preceding episode boundary, then the context was classified as open by default.

(26) (Child 2;11, MLU = 3.53)
    C: Goldilock have that spoon.   < extended segment
    P: Goldilock.
    C: That's the mother's.
    P: Now what (—[1]).
    C: I don't know.
    P: You don't know?   < prior turn
    C: Her wanna eat.

Although MLU was calculated for every sample, *cumulative verb lexicon* (CVL) was used as a general measure of linguistic development for two reasons. First, CVL is cumulative with age, whereas MLU is not. Second, as children acquire more verbs, they move closer to the upper boundary of syntactic bootstrapping's applicability. Five CVL levels were used: (a) CVL less than or equal to 75 verb types, (b) CVL less than or equal to 150 verb types, (c) CVL less than or equal to 225 verb types, (d) CVL less than or equal to 300 verb types, and (e) CVL greater than 300 verb types.

A total of 1,276 sentences with the verb *eat* were analyzed. Table 12.4 presents the five CVL levels, the mean age at each CVL level, the mean MLU at each CVL level, and the number of *eat* sentences produced by the children at each level. Table 12.4 also presents the rate of undergoer omission at each CVL level. These data were pooled across children. It is not surprising that, as CVL size increased, the percentage of sentences without overt undergoers decreased. CVL is correlated with MLU, so that as the children were able to say more in an utterance, the rate of undergoer omission decreased. This general decrease in undergoer omission serves as a base rate in undergoer omission over time.

Table 12.5 presents the frequency and rate of undergoer omission for response sentences, further divided into undergoer accessible and open contexts. These frequencies are from pooled data. As a hedge against inflation of these frequencies by individual children, children who contributed over 20% of the response sentences at any single CVL level were dropped from the analysis. Only one child was dropped from the highest CVL level (CVL > 300). The undergoer omission rate was most similar across discourse conditions at the lowest CVL level (CVL ≤ 75): 66% in the undergoer accessible context and

---

[1]— = unintelligible segment of speech.

TABLE 12.4
Frequency of *Eat* Sentences Across Levels of Cumulative Verb Lexicon Size
(CVL)

CVL Levels	Mean Age	Mean MLU	Total Sentences	Rate of Undergoer Omission
≤ 75	1;10	1.60	180 (n = 34)	72%
75 < CVL ≤ 150	2;3	2.40	315 (n = 37)	36%
150 < CVL ≤ 225	2;6	3.05	327 (n = 35)	31%
225 < CVL ≤ 300	2;8	3.56	205 (n = 26)	22%
> 300	2;9	3.86	249 (n = 15)	20%

70% in the open context. At the next highest CVL level (CVL > 75 ≤ 150), there is a noticeably greater difference in the omission rate across contexts: 26% in the undergoer accessible context and 45% in the open context, a difference of 19%. By the fifth and highest CVL level (CVL > 300), the omission rate in the undergoer accessible context was 2%, whereas in the open context, the omission rate was 30%, a difference of 28%. Recall that the data from one child were removed from pooled data at the highest CVL level (CVL > 300). If this child's data were included, the difference in omission rate across discourse contexts would become even greater.

As one might expect, the children's sentences without undergoers in undergoer accessible contexts sounded strange. The dialogue in (27) provides an example. The parent's reply to the child's sentence refers back to an NP mentioned by the parent previously: *Some* refers back to the previously

TABLE 12.5
Frequency and Rate of Undergoer Omission in Conversational Responses

	Discourse Context			
	Undergoer Accessible		Open	
CVL Levels	+ U	− U	+ U	− U
≤ 75	12 (34%)	23 (66%)	16 (30%)	37 (70%)
75 < CVL ≤ 150	53 (74%)	19 (26%)	51 (55%)	42 (45%)
150 < CVL ≤ 225	61 (73%)	23 (27%)	33 (60%)	22 (40%)
225 < CVL ≤ 300	66 (90%)	7 (10%)	23 (62%)	14 (38%)
> 300	51 (98%)	1 (2%)	16 (70%)	7 (30%)

Note. + U = with overt undergoer, − U = missing overt undergoer.

mentioned popcorn. It appears that the parent considered popcorn to be part of the discourse topic even after the child used the verb *eat*. This supports the interpretation that the omission of the undergoer in these sentences was inappropriate.

(27) (Child 2;6, CVL 103, CVL Level 2, MLU 1.97)
     (P has just opened a bag of popcorn.)
     P: Popcorn.
     C: I eat.
     P: You gonna save some for your dad?

These data strongly suggest that 2-year-old American children are sensitive to a relation between undergoer omission and discourse context. This sensitivity manifests itself as early as CVL level 2 (75 < CVL ≤ 150), or an average age of 2;3 and average MLU of 2.4. At this CVL level the undergoer omission rate differed across discourse contexts by 19%: 26% in the undergoer accessible context and 45% in the open context. By CVL level 5 (CVL > 300), the difference in the undergoer omission rate had increased to 28%: 2% in the undergoer accessible context and 30% in the open context. These data show that 2-year-old children are sensitive to a connection between the intransitive form of the verb *eat* and its discourse context. At this time, we cannot say whether this sensitivity is general or verb specific. However, from a theoretical perspective, such sensitivity is a prerequisite to discovering the semantic and discourse-pragmatic features of an implicit undergoer. Note that in these data on the production of the verb *eat*, this sensitivity becomes increasingly more apparent as children become acquainted with more verbs, which is to be expected if we are looking at a process that occurs at the upper boundary of syntactic bootstrapping's applicability.

CONCLUSION

I began this chapter by noting that syntactic bootstrapping is bounded in applicability. A lower boundary exists, below which syntactic bootstrapping cannot be used. This lower boundary exists because linking rules between the syntactic roles of NP arguments and their semantic roles must be established before syntactic bootstrapping begins. There is also an upper boundary to this procedure, a point beyond or above which syntax is no longer indicative or reflective of elements in the semantic representation. I then looked at the acquisition of Japanese. Because of the typology of Japanese, with its ubiquitous zero anaphora and optional case marking, the lower boundary on syntactic bootstrapping may be protracted. There was substantial evidence that Japanese 2-year-olds do not control the case system of Japanese. There was also evidence indicating that at the same period in development, Japanese children have begun to build semantic representations of predicates. Returning to more familiar psycholinguistic territory, I then considered the acquisition of optional undergoer verbs in English. The acquisition of these verbs in their intransitive argument structures represents the upper boundary of syntactic bootstrapping's applicability because the same argument structure alternation disguises at least three different predicate types. The theoretical framework, based on RRG, revealed a relation between the interpretation of the omitted argument and the discourse-pragmatic properties of the intransitive form. A detailed look at the acquisition of the verb *eat* revealed evidence that children become sensitive to the relation between undergoer omission and discourse context sometime between the second and third birthdays. This is a prerequisite to their establishing the missing argument of intransitive *eat* as a nonspecific entity.

At either boundary of syntactic bootstrapping's applicability, we see children using discourse-pragmatic information. That is, discourse-pragmatics is another information source for the acquisition of a predicate's meaning. This is not to say that discourse-pragmatic information is used exclusively, but I should note that discourse-pragmatic information may be used concurrently with syntactic-bootstrapping. If children are using discourse-pragmatic information, they may be taking note of the communicative intents of the participants and the pragmatic status of referents, overt and implied. Furthermore, children may transfer this information to the semantic representation of predicates.

ACKNOWLEDGMENTS

The author acknowledges support from a National Research Service Award, T32 HD07181-08, which enabled me to conduct the research on Japanese children reported in this chapter. I also acknowledge the support of the National Institute of Child Health and Human Development (HD03144) to the Bureau of Child Research at the University of Kansas, enabling the research on American children reported here. I also thank Patricia Clancy for generous access to her Japanese data and Nancy Budwig, Patricia Clancy, Pamela Hadley, Betty Hart, Bill Merriman, Janna Oetting, Ceil Toupin, Dan Slobin, Michael Tomasello, and Robert Van Valin for thoughts, criticism, comments, and conversation.

REFERENCES

Brown, R. (1973). *A first language: The early stages.* Cambridge, MA: Harvard University Press.
Chafe, W. (1976). Giveness, contrastiveness, definiteness, subjects, topics, and point of view. In C. Li (Ed.), *Subject and topic* (pp. 25–55). New York: Academic Press.

Clancy, P. (1985). The Acquisition of Japanese. In D. Slobin (Ed.), *The crosslinguistic study of language acquisition* (pp. 373–524). Hillsdale, NJ: Lawrence Erlbaum Associates.

Dowty, D. (1979). *Word meaning and Montague Grammar.* Dordrecht: Reidel.

Enç, M. (1991). The semantics of specificity. *Linguistic Inquiry, 22,* 1–25.

Fillmore, C. (1968). The case for case. In E. Bach & R. Harms (Eds.), *Universals in linguistic theory.* New York: Holt, Rinehart & Winston.

Fillmore, C. (1986). Pragmatically controlled zero anaphora. *Berkeley Linguistics Society, 12,* 95–107.

Foley, W., & Van Valin, R. (1984). *Functional Syntax and Universal Grammar.* Cambridge, England: Cambridge University Press.

Gleitman, L. (1990). The structural sources of verb meanings. *Language Acquisition, 1,* 3–55.

Grimshaw, J. (1990). *Argument Structure.* Cambridge, MA: MIT Press.

Gruber, J. (1976). *Lexical structures in syntax and semantics.* Amsterdam: North Holland.

Hakuta, K. (1982). Interaction between particles and word order in the comprehension and production of simple sentences in Japanese children. *Developmental Psychology, 18,* 62–75.

Hayashibe, H. (1975). Word order and particles: A developmental study in Japanese. *Descriptive and Applied Linguistics, 8,* 1–18.

Hinds, J. (1982). *Ellipsis in Japanese.* Edmonton: Linguistic Research.

Jackendoff, R. (1972). *Semantic interpretation in generative grammar.* Cambridge, MA: MIT Press.

Kempson, R. (1977). *Semantic theory.* New York: Cambridge University Press.

Kuno, S. (1973). *The structure of the Japanese language.* Cambridge, MA: MIT Press.

Lambrecht, K. (1987). Sentence focus, information structure, and the thetic-categorical distinction. *Berkeley Linguistics Society, 13,* 366–382.

Lys, F., & Mommer, K. (1986). The problem of aspectual verb classification: A two-level approach. *Chicago Linguistics Society, 21,* 216–230.

Olguin, R., & Tomasello, M. (1993). Two-year-old children do not have a grammatical category of verb. *Cognitive Development, 8,* 245–272.

Okamoto, S. (1985). *Ellipsis in Japanese discourse.* Unpublished doctoral dissertation, University of California, Berkeley.

Okubo, A. (1967). *Yooji gengo no hattatsu.* Tokyo: Tokyodoo.

Rispoli, M. (1987). The acquisition of transitive and intransitive action verb categories in Japanese. *First Language, 7,* 183–200.

Rispoli, M. (1989). Encounters with Japanese verbs. *First Language, 9,* 57–80.

Rispoli, M. (1990). Lexical assignability and perspective switch: The acquisition of verb subcategorization for aspectual inflections. *Journal of Child Language, 17,* 375–392.

Rispoli, M. (1991a). The acquisition of verb subcategorization in a functionalist framework. *First Language, 11,* 41–63.

Rispoli, M. (1991b). The mosaic acquisition of grammatical relations. *Journal of Child Language, 18,* 517–551.

Rispoli, M. (1992). Discourse and the acquisition of *eat. Journal of Child Language, 19,* 581–595.

Shibamoto, J. (1985). *Japanese women's language.* Orlando: Academic Press.

Tsutsui, M. (1983). Ellipsis of *ga. Papers in Japanese Linguistics, 9,* 199–243.

Van Valin, R. (1990). Semantic parameters of split intransitivity. *Language, 66,* 221–260.

Van Valin, R. (in press). A synopsis of Role and Reference Grammar. In R. Van Valin (Ed.), *Advances in role and reference grammar.* Amsterdam: Benjamins.

Yokoyama, M., & Schaefer, R. (1986). Suspension of the case particle *o* in the acquisition of Japanese. *University of Kansas Working Papers in Language Development, 1,* 77–104.

CHAPTER THIRTEEN

Verb Argument Structure and the Problem of Avoiding an Overgeneral Grammar

Martin D. S. Braine
Patricia J. Brooks
New York University

An overgeneral grammar generates all the well-formed sentences of a language but also generates sentences that native speakers do not consider well-formed. That is, it is possible to have two grammars both of which generate the well-formed sentences, and which differ only in that one of them—the overgeneral grammar—also generates strings that are not grammatical to native speaker intuition. We face the following problem (Baker, 1979; Braine, 1971): Given that every sentence a child hears is consistent with both grammars, how does the child eventually settle on the correct grammar and not on the overgeneral grammar? The problem is particularly acute because the overgeneral grammar is usually intuitively simpler than the correct one. Moreover, young children are known to make errors consistent with overgeneral grammars.

The problem of how children avoid constructing overgeneral grammars has intrigued and perplexed many individuals interested in language acquisition since the 1970s. In the first part of this chapter we delineate the nature of the overgeneralization problem and relate it to children's acquisition of verb argument structure. Over the years, a number of partial solutions to the paradox have been proposed (see Bowerman, 1988, for a review). Some of the early theories failed because they were inconsistent with what is now known about children's overgeneralization errors and language acquisition in general. Other early theories failed to address the complexity of the problem as it pertains to children's acquisition of verb argument structures. In the second part of this chapter, we briefly review and critique this early work to provide a background for examining newer theories. Recently, two more promising solutions to the paradox have been proposed: The first is Steven Pinker's theory (fully developed in Pinker, 1989a) and the second is ours (stemming from ideas originally proposed in Braine, 1971, and most fully developed in this chapter). The remainder of this chapter examines these two theories in detail, with attention to the similarities and differences between them. Although the two theories have much in common, they differ considerably with respect to the nature of the mechanisms proposed to be available to children learning a language. In particular, the mechanisms proposed by Pinker require children to perform complicated distributional analyses of language input, which are not required of our model. In conclusion, we argue that our theory is the more parsimonious solution to the paradox, although the available data are not yet decisive.

THE NATURE OF THE PROBLEM

The simplest realistic example of the overgeneralization problem involves morphological exceptions. It is the one type for which a reasonably plausible solution exists, as we note later. As is well known, children often regularize exceptions; for example, they may say *goed* in place of *went*, *throwed* in place of *threw*, and *mouses* and *foots* in place of *mice* and *feet*. Now consider a grammar of English that differs from a standard grammar only because it contains the regularized forms as well as the exceptions; that is, it generates *goed, throwed, mouses*, and *foots* as well as *went, threw, mice*, and *feet*. Such a grammar is overgeneral—it generates the correct forms but also some incorrect ones; it is completely consistent with everything a child hears. Now, in the course of learning a correct exceptional form children often pass through a stage during which they sometimes use the correct form and sometimes use the regularized form. Their behavior in such a stage is consistent with the possibility that they have an overgeneral grammar. The question then arises: How could they learn that the regularized forms, like *goed* and *foots*, which are generated by the regular rules, are not in fact well-formed?

Other examples—the kind we shall concentrate on—involve verb argument structure. In addition to making errors involving morphological forms, children also make errors such as *he stayed it* for *he kept it, Shall I whisper you something* for *Shall I whisper something to you*, or *fill water into the glass* for *fill the glass with water*. These involve usage of an argument structure with a verb that is judged ungrammatical by adults. These kinds of errors demonstrate that children may spontaneously assign an argument structure to a verb even when they have not heard others use the verb in that particular argument structure. Errors of this sort commonly occur with argument structures associated with verb alternations such as the dative alternation (e.g., *she gave a book to me* alternates with *she gave me a book*), the causative/intransitive alternation (e.g., *he broke it* alternates with *it broke*), and the locative alternation (e.g., *he cleared dishes from the table* alternates with *he cleared the table*, and *he loaded wood onto the sled* alternates with *he loaded the sled with wood*). In each case, a number of verbs freely occur with both argument structures of the alternation; the problem facing the child involves determining exactly which verbs may occur in both argument structures and which verbs occur in only one.

Often the argument structures associated with an alternation express similar but not identical meanings. In particular, the two argument structures may be related in that one argument structure constitutes a syntactic reorganization of the arguments that occur with the other, in the case of the particular verbs that occur with both argument structures. Sometimes, one argument structure in an alternation may express additional arguments that do not occur in the other argument structure, as in the causative/intransitive alternation. In the case of each of the argument structures there is a canonical sentence schema[1] that associates the form of the argument structure with the interpretation consistently assigned to it. The ability of humans to incorporate newly invented verbs (e.g., *fax, email*) into their language easily and experimental subjects' ability to use novel verbs introduced in psychological experiments appropriately without prior exposure to usage (e.g., Braine, Brody, Fisch, Weisberger, & Blum, 1990; Gropen, Pinker, Hollander, Goldberg, & Wilson, 1989; Gropen, Pinker, Hollander, & Goldberg, 1991a, 1991b) attests for the psychological reality of these canonical sentence schemas. To illustrate the kinds of meaning changes that are characteristic of verb alternations and are captured by the canonical sentence schemas, we consider further the dative, causative/intransitive, and locative alternations in turn.

Although both argument structures of the dative alternation (i.e., "NP_x verb NP_y to NP_z" and "NP_x verb NP_z NP_y") may appear to be synonymous (e.g., compare the meaning of the prepositional object form *John gave a book to me* with the double object form *John gave me a book*), a closer examination reveals that the two argument structures are semantically distinct. First, as discussed by Green (1974) and Pinker (1989a), the prepositional object form of the dative conveys the meaning "X transfers Y to Z," whereas the double object form means "X causes Z to have Y"; thus, in the double object form the direct object noun phrase must correspond to a potential possessor of Y. This semantic difference accounts for the respective

---

[1]We use the term "canonical sentence schemas" to refer to cognitive structures functionally similar to those Pinker (1989) describes as "broad conflation classes." We prefer the term "canonical sentence schemas," originally introduced by Slobin and Bever (1982) and adopted by Braine, Brody, Fisch, Weisberger, and Blum (1990), because it seems more semantically transparent and intuitively understandable than "broad conflation classes."

grammaticality and ungrammaticality of sentences like *She carried the suitcase to the car* as compared to *She carried the car the suitcase*. Note, however, that although the canonical sentence schemas provide necessary conditions for well-formedness, they do not provide sufficient conditions for predicting which verbs occur with which argument structures. Hence, only a subset of verbs with meanings consistent with a canonical schema occur with its corresponding argument structure. To illustrate using the double object dative, the meaning of *donate* in *He donated the school some books* is entirely consistent with the canonical schema; that is, the school is understood to be the potential possessor of the books. However, for most speakers of English the sentence is ungrammatical—*He donated some books to the school* is preferred.

The notion of transfer associated with the dative alternation includes not only physical transfer but transfer of information as well. Thus, many verbs of communication alternate (e.g., *she told a story to the children* alternates with *she told the children a story*). There is also a more subtle distinction between the two forms of the dative alternation that has a pragmatic basis: In each argument structure, the direct object noun phrase tends to express old or given information, whereas the second noun phrase tends to provide new information (Erteschik-Shir, 1979).

The argument structures corresponding to the causative/intransitive alternation (i.e., "NP_x verb NP_y" and "NP_y verb") are more obviously semantically distinct than those of the dative alternation: Whereas the causative argument structure conveys the meaning "X directly causes Y to undergo a change of state or position," the intransitive variant simply means that "Y changes state or position." Thus, the two forms of the causative/intransitive alternation differ in terms of both the number of arguments expressed and the semantic role of the subject noun phrase.

Likewise, the argument structures associated with the locative alternation (i.e., "NP_x verb NP_y into/onto/out of/off of NP_z" and "NP_x verb NP_z {with/of NP_y}") differ somewhat in meaning (Gropen et al., 1991b; Levin & Rappaport Hovav, 1991; Pinker, 1989a): The "locatum-as-object" form, in which the direct object of the verb refers to the object undergoing movement to or from a reference object functioning as a location (e.g., *Jack splashed oil and vinegar onto the salad, Mary wiped dirt off the baby's face, Sara rinsed the soap from her hair*), conveys the meaning "X moves Y into/onto/out of/off of Z," whereas the location-as-object form, in which the direct object of the verb refers to the reference object (e.g., *Jack splashed the salad with oil and vinegar, Mary wiped the baby's face, Sara rinsed her hair*), conveys the meaning "X changes the state of Z as a consequence of the movement of Y into/onto/out of/off of Z." Thus, whereas the locatum-as-object form focuses attention on the movement of Y with respect to a reference object Z (i.e., a source or a goal), the location-as-object form emphasizes the resultant state of Z. As a result, the location-as-object form conveys the sense of Z as wholly affected by the movement of Y. Furthermore, as the examples attest, in the location-as-object form the object undergoing movement need not be explicitly stated; however, the existence of the locatum is implicitly a part of the meaning of the verb.

For each of the argument structure alternations discussed above, a number of researchers (e.g., Bowerman, 1978, 1982a, 1982b, 1983, 1987; Mazurkewich & White, 1984; Pinker, 1989a) have amassed considerable evidence suggesting that children often make errors by using verbs in argument structures judged ungrammatical by adults. To illustrate the kinds of errors children make, several examples taken from Melissa Bowerman's work are presented here, along with the age of the speaker.

Double object datives

3;1   I said her no.

3;6   Don't say me that or you'll make me cry.

3;9   I do what my horsie says me to do.

2;6   I want Daddy choose me what to have.

5+   Choose me the ones that I can have.

7;8   Shall I whisper you something?

3;4   Button me the rest.

Causatives

2;9   I come it closer so it won't fall.

3;4   She came it over there.

2;6   Mommy can you stay this open.

3;7   I want to stay this rubber band on.

4;5   Eva won't stay things where I want them to be.

3;0   Don't giggle me.

5;3   You cried her.

Locatives

3;0   Cause I'm gonna touch it on your pants.

3;11 Eva is just touching gently on the plant.

4;5   I'm gonna cover a screen over me.

4;11 I don't want it because I spilled it of orange juice (= spilled orange juice on it).

6;10 Feel your hand to that.

In the case of each of these alternations, one can envisage an overgeneral grammar of English according to which any verb that would make sense with both argument structures of a pair would alternate. Such grammars would be more regular than the real English grammar and would predict the children's errors just cited. The problem, then, is to explain how the overgeneral grammar is corrected, if it is acquired, or to provide an alternative account of development that explains the errors, the correct uses of the verbs, and why the errors disappear.

CORRECTION AS A POSSIBLE EXPLANATION

The problem posed by all these examples would be trivial if we could assume that children are always corrected for making mistakes—that is, if it were the case that some adult always tells children directly that people say *threw* and not *throwed, feet* and not *foots, report something to somebody* and never *report somebody something*, and *keep it there* and never *stay it there*. However, it is known that such corrections are rare, and certainly quite insufficient in number and consistency to provide a solution to the problems posed. There is some evidence that there are other kinds of cues, indirect ones, that give information about what is *not* a well-formed sentence (e.g., Demetras, Post, & Snow, 1986; Moerk, 1983). However, there is much doubt that such cues exist in sufficient quantity or that children make much use of them even when they are available (e.g., Braine, 1971; Brown & Hanlon, 1970; Morgan & Travis, 1989), and there is evidence that children can learn without such cues (see reviews by Bowerman, 1988, and Braine, 1988a; for experimental demonstrations of grammar acquisition without corrective feedback, see Braine, 1965, 1971, and Braine, Brody, Brooks, Sudhalter, Ross, Catalano, & Fisch, 1990).

THE HYPOTHESIS OF CONSERVATISM AND ITS FAILURE

This hypothesis attempted to account for the argument structure examples by proposing that children are effectively programmed so that they never acquire overgeneral rules initially and so do not have to learn to restrict them. In other words, children are conservative learners. Two potential ways of accomplishing this programming were proposed. Baker (1979) proposed a theory of lexical conservatism which posits that there are no general syntactic rules (i.e., transformations) that relate pairs of argument structures occurring with the same verbs (e.g., the double object and prepositional object forms of the dative alternation). Instead, systematic generalizations across lexical items are captured by lexical redundancy rules that state the form of the correspondence among argument structures. These lexical redundancy rules do not support generalization of an argument structure to a new lexical item or to an existing lexical item lacking that argument structure unless there is prior exposure to the usage of the verb in that argument structure. Thus, Baker suggested that an argument structure is added to a verb's lexical entry only when the child has heard the verb used in the argument structure. The theory explicitly denies the existence of cognitive structures functionally analogous to the canonical sentence schemas that would support usage of verbs in argument structures in the absence of positive evidence. As a consequence, Baker's theory predicts that children should not be prone to making overgeneralization errors.

Dell (1981) and Berwick (1985; Berwick & Weinberg, 1984) proposed a principle that has the same effect as Baker's theory: They suggest that children's usage of verbs in argument structures is constrained by the "subset principle." This principle is based on the assumption that all candidate (i.e., immature) grammars that children entertain are proper subsets of the correct adult grammar. The theory proposes that in order for a child to converge on the correct adult grammar in the absence of negative feedback, the child must begin by formulating the narrowest possible grammar that accommodates those sentences that the child has been exposed to. In the specific case of learning a verb argument structure (or a verb alternation), the child at first entertains the narrowest possible rule consistent with the verbs the child has heard used with the particular argument structure. Gradually, as the child hears more and more verbs occurring with an argument structure (or in both argument structures in the case of an alternation), the child's rule enlarges to accommodate the positive evidence until the child's rule is equivalent to that of adults. Because any candidate grammar that generates sentences judged ungrammatical by adults cannot, by definition, be a proper subset of the correct grammar and therefore violates the subset principle, this theory, like Baker's proposal, posits that children will not be prone to making overgeneralization errors.

Unfortunately, both theories hypothesizing strict conservativism on the part of the child do not fare well with the evidence of overgeneralization errors in children's spontaneous speech (e.g., Bowerman, 1974, 1982a, 1982b, 1983, 1987; Pinker, 1989a), as noted earlier, or with findings suggesting that children often judge as grammatical overgeneral forms adults consider ill-formed (Hochberg, 1986; Mazurkewich & White, 1984). Taken as a whole, this body of work indicates that Baker's proposal and the subset principle are both untenable as they stand.

A PARTIAL THEORY: PREEMPTION PLUS VARIATION IN LEARNING STRENGTH

One important kind of mechanism that has been proposed to help solve the overgeneralization problem is commonly called "preemption." Very roughly, preemption involves positing some sort of default assumption among children that linguistic forms and meanings are in one-to-one correspondence: Once one linguistic form for expressing a meaning has been learned, it preempts other forms that express the same meaning, unless the language input offers positive evidence for a second form. According to the simplest and most widely accepted form of preemption, once a child has rote-learned an irregular form the erroneous regularized form drops out of the child's repertoire—the rote-learned irregular form is said to preempt the form generated by rule (e.g., learning *broke* leads the child to stop saying *breaked*). This kind of preemption is entailed by several current theoretical proposals such as Clark's (1987, 1988) principle of contrast, the mutual exclusivity hypothesis (Markman, 1989; Merriman & Bowman, 1989), and the uniqueness principle (e.g., Pinker, 1984); it was posited earlier by Braine (1971), Baker (1979), and MacWhinney (1978).[2] Another closely related kind of preemption is also possible. In this, a secondary inflection (i.e., not the most common inflection) is shared by a subclass of items that have a common feature. Such subclasses represent secondary paradigms (e.g., declensions or conjugations). The common feature that marks the subclass may be either phonological (e.g., a particular final vowel) or semantic. Learning that the secondary inflection is associated with the feature preempts the use of the regular (most common) inflection for stems with the feature. All these kinds of preemption were proposed by MacWhinney (1978) and have been included in other models (e.g., Braine, 1988a; Pinker, 1984).

These kinds of preemption go far to solve the first class of example of the overgeneralization problem, those involving morphological exceptions. They do not completely solve it, however—an additional principle is needed. Taken alone, preemption predicts a sudden change in children from an incorrect regularized form to the correct irregular form: As soon as the child catches on to the correct form, the incorrect form will be instantly suppressed. But that does not happen. As we noted previously, there is often a period of apparently free variation between the correct irregular and the incorrect regularized form. This anomaly is easily explained if we add the principle that linguistic forms and patterns can vary in the strength with which they are known, and that strength is related to frequency variables such as past input frequency and density in the recent input (and to other things as well, no doubt). Then, as proposed in Braine (1971), a correct irregular form may pass through a period of instability (i.e., rises and falls in strength depending on the pattern of recent occurrences in the input) before it becomes solidly established in the permanent memory store. During this period, the child uses the correct form when he or she remembers it; otherwise, the incorrect rule-generated form is used.

---

[2]Although preemption is invoked as an explanatory principle in most current acquisition theories, all is not consensus: For example, Gathercole (1987, 1989) and Nelson (1988) expressed doubt about the validity of principles like contrast that imply uniqueness of forms, including the idea that regularized forms are preempted by conventional irregular ones (Gathercole, 1989, 695–696).

This theory (i.e., preemption, taken with variation in learning strength) solves the overgeneralization problem for morphological exceptions. However, it is not sufficient to solve the type of example that involves verb argument structure, including the examples cited earlier. For example, Bowerman (1988) cited occasional uses of *disappear* as a transitive verb meaning "make disappear." How do children confine *disappear* to intransitive status, given that there appears to be nothing that preempts the transitive use and given also that there are very many verbs like *break* that occur both transitively and intransitively? The usual kinds of preemption do not solve this problem.

TWO CONTENDING THEORIES

We now review two theories that attempt to do justice to more of the complexity of the phenomena. One theory, ours, stems from the original ideas of Braine (1971), developed further in Braine (1988a) and Braine, Brody, Fisch et al. (1990), and additionally elaborated here. The other is the theory of Pinker and his colleagues, maximally developed so far in Pinker (1989a; see also Gropen et al., 1989, and Gropen et al., 1991a, 1991b).

Pinker's Theory

Pinker (1989a) proposed a theory in which semantic constraints serve as conditions defining semantic classes of verbs that may or may not occur in particular argument structures. These semantic constraints come in two sizes, which Pinker called broad and narrow range rules; the constraints characterize the pattern of verb selectivity of each argument structure. Pinker's broad and narrow range rules define semantic classes of verbs called, respectively, broad and narrow conflation classes. The conflation classes are categories of verbs defined by semantic criteria that appear in particular argument structures. Pinker's broad conflation classes are functionally identical to the canonical sentence schemas described earlier.

Broad range rules denote changes in meaning that are associated with an argument structure alternation and dictate the assignment of grammatical functions (e.g., thematic roles) to the arguments occurring in each argument structure. The broad range rules impose a set of necessary conditions that must be satisfied if a sentence is to be judged well-formed. Consider a few examples involving the dative alternation. For the double object form of the dative (e.g., *John gave me a headache*), a broad range rule dictates that the first object must be construed as the potential possessor of the second object. If the first object fails to meet this criterion or the verb itself does not refer to a situation involving possession, then the sentence is ruled out. For the prepositional object form of the dative, the direct object must be something that can be transferred from one entity, state, or place to another; thus, although *John gave a necklace to me* is perfect, *John gave a headache to me* is odd because a headache is not something that can be transferred directly. Likewise, the broad range rule predicts the grammaticality of *John drove me to the shopping center*, which satisfies the condition of transfer, and the ungrammaticality of *John drove the shopping center me*, which fails to satisfy the condition of possession.

Unfortunately, the existence of broad range rules cannot wholly account for patterns of occurrence and nonoccurrence of verbs in particular argument structures. Many verbs exist that do not occur in particular argument structures, although the meanings of these verbs are entirely consistent with the associated broad range rules. For example, consider the following sentences judged ungrammatical by most speakers of English: *The charity distributed the homeless new clothing* and *The charity supplied the homeless new clothing*. In these sentences there is nothing inherent in the meaning of the verbs *distribute* or *supply* that blocks an interpretation in which the homeless are the potential possessors of the new clothing (compare *The charity gave the homeless new clothing*). Similarly, the broad range rule for the causative cannot block sentences like *The exterminator died many cockroaches* or *The exterminator disappeared many cockroaches* because the subject noun phrase may easily be interpreted as an agent directly causing a change of state in the patient. For the locative, *Joe filled the water into the glass* or *Joe robbed money from the bank* cannot be ruled out by a broad range rule dictating that the direct object noun phrase be construed as moving into/onto/off/out of a location. In Pinker's theory, although the broad range rules denote necessary conditions for the occurrence of a verb in a particular argument structure, the broad range rule is not a sufficient condition.

Thus, to obtain sufficient conditions that predict patterns of occurrence and nonoccurrence of particular verbs in particular argument structures, Pinker posited narrow range rules. Narrow range rules define semantic subclasses of verbs that have in common a narrower range of meaning than that associated with a broad conflation class (i.e., the class of verbs that satisfy the broad range rule for a particular alternation). Narrow range rules take into consideration subtle aspects of meaning such as whether or not the semantic representation of a verb specifies a manner of motion (e.g., *roll, float*) or motion in a specified direction (e.g., *enter, exit*); whether the verb involves motion, contact, or effect; whether communication is by means of a speech act (e.g., *ask, tell*), instrument (e.g., *telephone, email*), or manner of speaking (e.g., *shout, scream*); or whether cause of motion is continuous (e.g., *pull, push*) or instantaneous (e.g., *throw, toss*). In addition, verb alternations may be constrained by morphological criteria. For example, with the dative alternation, it is argued that members of some narrow conflation classes must be of Germanic rather than Latinate stock (or have Germanic rather than Latinate morphological shape) in order to alternate, whereas for other alternating subclasses, this morphological distinction is irrelevant. To illustrate this pattern, consider Pinker's three subclasses of verbs of communication: Members of the subclass of verbs denoting speech acts ("illocutionary communication") alternate if the verb is of Germanic stock (e.g., *Joe read the children a story* alternates with *Joe read a story to the children*); however, verbs in this subclass with Latinate roots do not alternate (e.g., *explain, recite*). Members of the subclass of verbs of communication via a lexically specified instrument alternate regardless of the morphological status of the verb (e.g., *Sara emailed me a message, Sara emailed a message to me*), and members of the subclass of verbs denoting manner of speaking do not alternate (e.g., *say, shout, scream*). In sum, Pinker's narrow range rules capture seemingly idiosyncratic aspects of meaning (and occasionally morphological form) which co-occur in small sets of verbs for which a particular argument structure is permissible or not permissible. The purpose of the narrow range rules is to indicate which verbs falling within the scope of the broad range rule alternate and which do not; this is done by specifying alternating and nonalternating narrow conflation classes.

Pinker proposed that children's overgeneralization errors are of two sorts. First, he suggested that a majority of children's errors are one-shot innovations that occur when the child occasionally uses a broad range rule to generate an argument structure for a verb. He argued that although all children are likely to make occasional overgeneralization errors, the actual proportion of errors as a fraction of the child's total usage of a particular argument structure is very low (i.e., far less than 1% of total usages; see Pinker, 1989a, p. 319). Thus, it appears that children are overwhelmingly biased toward using verbs in exactly the same argument structures that adults do.

However, not all errors are one-shot innovations, according to Pinker. He noted that data exist suggesting that children occasionally misanalyze the meaning of a verb and may systematically produce overgeneralization errors with such misanalyzed verbs over an extended period of time. Thus, he argued that a second sort of overgeneralization error exists, the product of the child's incomplete mastery of a verb's semantic representation. Evidence for such misanalyses is provided by Gropen et al. (1991b), who demonstrated that children tend to misinterpret locative change-of-state verbs (e.g., *fill, empty*) as verbs specifying a manner of motion (see also Gentner, 1978). When such misclassifications occur, children produce argument structure errors (e.g., *fill salt into the bear*) that reflect the child's current semantic representation of the verb (e.g., *fill* as "cause to become fuller by pouring"). Such errors cease to occur as the child learns the verb's real semantic structure as a consequence of exposure to the verb in discriminating contexts.

There are several points in Pinker's theory that we agree with. First, as noted earlier, the broad conflation class notion is equivalent to what we called a canonical sentence schema. Second, as discussed later, we largely agree with the explanation of children's errors—in particular with the idea that very many of them are performance errors that conform to the appropriate canonical sentence schema or broad conflation class (cf. Braine et al., 1990). The proposal that some errors reflect an imperfect semantic representation of a verb also seems reasonably well supported. The part of the theory that seems weak to us concerns the concept of narrow range rules and conflation classes. No experimental or observational data are presently available that indicate that narrow range rules play a role in the disappearance of overgeneralization errors (Ingham, 1992). An additional concern is that the process by which the child acquires the relevant semantic structure for a verb has not been worked out. Presumably, the child must rely on a sort of hypothesis-testing procedure by which semantic features are added to a verb's lexico-semantic structure if the semantic features are consistent with observations of how the verb is used across a variety of situations. Given the high degree of overlap in the situations in which both an alternating verb and a nonalternating verb are appropriate (e.g., *trip* and *stumble, drop* and *fall, tell* and *say, turn* and *revolve*), it is hard to imagine how the child would come up with the relevant semantic distinctions given a relatively impoverished database to work with (see Ingham, 1992, for further discussion and examples).

As noted by Bowerman (1988), most of the narrow semantic subclasses seem to be too small in their membership, and too inconsistent and riddled with exceptions, for it to be plausible that the child has learned that this, this, and this subclass alternate. In addition, the actual number of subclasses the child must acquire is huge. For the causative/intransitive alternation alone, Pinker posited that the child must recognize three subclasses of intransitive verbs that may causativize, five subclasses of intransitives that resist causativization, and three subclasses of transitive verbs that lack intransitive counterparts. For the other alternations the child is expected to construct an even larger number of subclasses. Although the subclasses posited appear at a glance to predict patterns of occurrence and nonoccurrence in argument structures for many verbs, there are numerous exceptions and qualifications. For instance, within the three subclasses of verbs that alternate between intransitive and causative sentence frames (i.e., "verbs of extrinsic change of state," "verbs for motions occurring in a particular manner," and "verbs of locomotion and verbs signifying an instrument of transportation"), there are many intransitive verbs that fail to causativize. The fact that they fail to alternate would presumably be unlearnable in the absence of negative evidence. Failure to causativize is evidenced by several verbs denoting extrinsic changes of physical state (e.g., *subside, wither, shrivel, fluctuate*) as well as manner of motion (e.g., *quiver, totter, ripple, revolve, waver, stumble, oscillate, vibrate*). Several verbs that belong to the nonalternating subclass "volitional or internally caused action" are apparently also members of the alternating subclass of verbs of locomotion (e.g., *walk, gallop,* and *jump,* as in *Jill walked her dog, Jill galloped her horse,* and *Jill jumped her horse*). Furthermore, there are numerous verbs denoting extrinsic changes of physical state that have causative sentence frames only, as well as numerous exceptions to each of the nonalternating subclasses posited by Pinker. Given the small number of verbs in each subclass, the existence of even a few exceptions and qualifications is enough to make the category induction problem facing the child infeasible.

Our Theory

Let us consider first why there are argument-structure errors like those illustrated earlier. Braine, Brody, Fisch, Weisberger, & Blum (1990) proposed that children acquire canonical sentence schemas from experience with the language they are exposed to. Although, like Pinker, they regarded such schemas as necessary rather than sufficient conditions for a verb to take a particular argument structure, they also proposed that canonical sentence schemas can sometimes assign an argument structure to a verb on-line. There are two main ways in which this may happen. First, early in learning a new verb, a child may know something about the action represented by the verb without having yet learned a specific argument structure for it. The child may then give the verb the argument structure of a canonical schema. The same kind of thing may happen for adults, too, we believe: New verbs (e.g., *email, fax*) or invented verbs used in tests (e.g., *tavicate,* meaning "to convey information telepathically") typically receive an argument structure by default from the canonical sentence schemas consistent with their understood meanings (thus we know, without actually hearing anyone use the verb *tavicate,* that both *I tavicated John the answers* and *I tavicated the answers to John* are possible). Second, later in learning, an incorrect argument structure that fits a canonical schema may still be assigned on-line under a discourse need to have a particular argument as subject.

Evidence that argument structures can be assigned to verbs in both these ways was reported in the study by Braine, Brody, Fisch, Weisberger, & Blum (1990), who investigated the acquisition of new causative and intransitive verbs. Novel action verbs were modeled: some as causative, some as intransitive, and some not marked for transitivity. Spontaneous usage was recorded along with responses to agent questions (e.g., "What is the [agent] doing?") and patient questions (e.g., "What is the [patient] doing?"). For comparison purposes, the same kinds of questions were asked for some familiar English verbs. In line with predictions, both children and adults were willing to use the novel verbs both transitively and intransitively (although they were slightly biased toward using the verb in the way they had heard it used). The discourse pressure of the agent and patient questions greatly affected the argument structure used—agent questions encouraged transitive usage, and patient questions encouraged intransitive usage. Although all subjects largely respected the transitivity of familiar verbs, there were a number of cases in which the 2- and 4-year-olds used familiar intransitive verbs (e.g., *fall* and *dance*) as causatives when asked what the agent was doing (e.g., *You're dancing him, I'm falling it*) and used familiar transitive verbs (e.g., *put, throw*) as intransitives when asked what the patient was doing (e.g., *It's putting in the jar, It throwed*). Such errors replicate the kinds of errors reported in the literature and confirm that a discourse need to have a particular argument as subject can be a potent stimulus to such errors. It was argued that the well-known errors observed by Bowerman (1974, 1982a), in which an intransitive verb is used causatively (e.g., *stay this open* [meaning, "keep this open"], *You ached me* [meaning, "you made me ache"], are similarly due to assignment of argument structures from canonical sentence schemas, especially under a need to have an agent as subject.

Note that, except in the circumstances discussed, the canonical sentence schemas are not productive rules, according to this conception. Speakers occasionally use them in generating sentences under the circumstances described, but they do not regularly do so. In the vast majority of circumstances that a verb is used, the argument structure employed is the one recorded in the lexical entry (or is one of those recorded in the lexical entry, if there are more than one). Thus, if a verb is only marked as intransitive, its causative use is inhibited; similarly, if it has been learned only as transitive, its intransitive use is inhibited. If a verb is freely used both ways, then both ways have been independently learned and are marked in the lexical entry. The argument structures listed in a verb's lexical entry are always consistent with canonical schemas, but some argument structures that would be consistent with canonical schemas may not be listed in a verb's entry. Thus, the transitive use of *fall* ("cause to fall") is consistent with the canonical schema agent–verb–patient described previously, but it is not sanctioned by the lexical entry for *fall*, which only marks it as intransitive. Similarly, *donate–somebody–something* and *give–somebody–something* are both consistent with a canonical schema, but only *give* has that argument structure listed in its lexical entry; hence, *donate somebody something* is not well-formed (although perfectly understandable). The circumstance in which a canonical schema is productive is the case, discussed earlier (*email, tavicate,* etc.), of novel or invented verbs that have no specific argument structure listed in their lexical entries but whose meaning is known well enough for the appropriate canonical schemas to be recognized.

There is a novel principle implicit in the content of the preceding paragraph, namely, that once a language learner has solidly learned an argument structure for a verb—that is, once that argument structure has been solidly recorded in the learner's lexical entry for the verb—he or she assumes (until the language they hear teaches them otherwise) that this is the verb's only argument structure. This principle amounts to a novel kind of preemption, that is, a kind of preemption that is additional to the kinds discussed earlier. It implies that once one argument structure is firmly learned for a verb, it tends to preempt other argument structures for that verb. We shall call this principle a "unique argument-structure preference." (The concept should probably be taken as including a unique subcategorization-frame preference,[3] but, with one exception, we do not discuss subcategorization frames that are not associated with argument structures.) According to this preference, once a transitivity status has been solidly learned for a verb (e.g., the intransitive use of *disappear*), this learning tends to block usage of another argument structure unless the other argument structure has been independently learned. Similarly, for a verb indicating transfer of information or object possession, once one of the argument structures, agent–verb–object–*to*–recipient or agent–verb–recipient–object, has been solidly learned, the other argument structure will tend not to be used unless and until it has been independently noted in the input.

The proposal, that once an argument structure has been solidly learned it is preferred over other possibilities, explains both why canonical sentence schemas are usually not productive and also the circumstance in which they are. The schemas are usually not productive because once an argument structure is solidly ensconced in a lexical entry it blocks other argument structures that are consistent with canonical schemas (except for occasional coinages, as discussed earlier). However, schemas are predicted to be productive at early stages of learning a verb when no argument structures have yet been solidly learned for it; then there is nothing to block the generative power of a schema. Thus the idea that canonical schemas represent necessary but not sufficient conditions for a verb to have a particular argument structure does not need to be stated as an independent theoretical principle. It is an automatic consequence of the unique argument-structure preference.[4]

---

[3]A subcategorization frame for a verb specifies the essential elements of the grammatical frames in which it can occur and its position with respect to those elements. For example, *donate* has the frame NP–NP (*to* NP)—the parentheses indicate optionality. In addition, an argument structure specifies the semantic roles of the elements that are arguments of the verb.

[4]It seems to us that something like a unique argument-structure preference is implicit in Pinker's theory, too, because in his theory, when a verb's lexical entry contains one argument structure, the default assumption is that only that argument structure is applicable. In his theory too, the preference can explain why broad conflation classes represent necessary but not sufficient conditions for a verb to accept a particular argument structure. The difference between the theories lies in the fact that narrow range rules override the preference in Pinker's theory.

The evidence that canonical schemas are productive at early stages of learning comes from experiments in which subjects are introduced to invented verbs for a relatively short period of time. Data from diaries and corpora do not show any particular proneness to argument structure errors for recently acquired verbs. Braine, Brody, Fisch, Weisberger, & Blum (1990) suggested that under normal conditions (outside experiments) children are hesitant to use freshly learned verbs when they are still uncertain how to use them; hence, they do not make many argument structure errors with them. In the experiments children may show resistance to using new verbs, but they are strongly encouraged and often pressed with questions; hence the experiments are likely to tap a stage of learning when the children know a meaning but have not yet firmly registered an argument structure.[5]

Note that the principle that a solidly learned argument structure tends to inhibit other argument structures, like the theory that morphological exceptions preempt rule-generated forms, presupposes a notion of learning strength; that is, it presupposes that linguistic properties can vary in the strength (or solidity) with which they are known. It is only when the strength or solidity of a verb's argument structure has reached a high enough level that the learner favors that argument structure and avoids argument structures for the verb that have not been independently noted. We take no stand on the precise quantitative relation between strength and usage—that will have to be determined by research. It could be that as the strength of one argument structure in a lexical entry increases, the probability that it will be chosen on an occasion of usage also increases and the probability of a nonrecorded argument structure being chosen decreases (becoming essentially zero when the strength of the learned argument structure has reached asymptote); or it could be that there is a threshold of strength such that only argument structures above the threshold are considered correct.

A broad range of theorists have recognized that an acquisition theory must allow for linguistic patterns being progressively strengthened during acquisition (e.g., Braine, 1971, 1988a, 1988b; MacWhinney, 1978; Pinker, 1984, 1989b; Plunkett & Marchman, 1991). However, there has been surprisingly little discussion of the nature of the strengthening process. Braine (1971, 1988a) posited that input features are registered in a memory in which pattern consolidation is a function of frequency of registration and in which patterns tend to lose strength over time. That is, a rule gets stronger as it is used to

---

[5]Sometimes, particularly in the case of the locative-alternation errors, there is a long period of correct use of a verb prior to any error. Bowerman (1982b) and Braine, Brody, Fisch, Weisberger, & Blum (1990) explain the time lag in essentially the same way: Children begin by learning an argument structure for each verb individually and therefore begin using them correctly. At some later point they acquire the two canonical schemas that specify the possible arrangements of postverbal arguments for this class of verb. Errors then appear because the argument structure of a schema can come into competition with that of the lexical entry.

analyze input and decays when not used. Quite apart from its possible role in preemption, some such mechanism is essential to an acquisition theory. First, it allows an acquisition model to be sensitive to input frequency, as real children acquiring a language are. Second, it accounts for learning despite imperfections in the input that could ruin an all-or-none learning model (e.g., occasional ungrammatical or misheard input, irregularities, child misunderstandings—these may be registered when they occur, but, being repeated infrequently or not at all, they tend to be soon forgotten, i.e., their consolidation decays to zero). Third, it provides a natural mechanism for expunging rules that were erroneously learned or have become obsolete—they are forgotten as their consolidation decreases to zero (see Braine, 1988b, for extensive discussion of the merits of such a mechanism over an alternative proposal of Pinker, 1984).[6]

There is some empirical support in an old miniature-language study for the existence of a uniqueness preference somewhat like the one posited. In the study by Braine (1965), subjects listened to strings of the forms *aXb* and *pXq* (*a, b, p, q* were words, X represented a class of 18 different items). Subjects learned this in two stages. First, they learned the positions of the items without yet registering the *a–b* and *p–q* contingencies. At this point, they accepted strings of the form *aXq* and *pXb* as in the input list; that is, they had an overgeneral grammar. They then retreated from this overgeneral grammar as they registered that *a* at the beginning went with *b* at the end, and similarly, that *p* at the beginning went with *q* at the end. It is very unlikely that subjects positively identified that there were *no* strings that began with *a* and ended with *q* nor any that began with *p* and ended with *b*. Rather, it seems that when subjects noticed that there were lots of strings

---

[6]In addition, a strength mechanism with the properties discussed can account for the otherwise rather mysterious fact that, in the absence of input, young children forget languages very quickly, much faster than adults: Although young children learn second languages better than adults, adults remember them much better over long periods of non-use than children do. For instance, the first author and his 4-year-old son were both exposed to Hebrew for a year in 1965–66. At the end of that time the son could converse freely with his nursery-school peers, but the father's ability to interact in Hebrew was quite limited. Six months later, however, the son's ability to understand Hebrew was completely gone, and his speaking was limited to counting a few low numbers; the father's command of Hebrew was essentially unchanged. Similar experiences are common. In Israel, the first author met many families who came from North African countries as native French speakers. The youngest children had typically lost their French despite the fact that French was commonly spoken by the adults in the home; retention of French seemed primarily a function of the age of the child on arrival in Israel.

Such data are, of course, anecdotal; it would be very worthwhile for someone to document the facts. However, these anecdotal data indicate that there is a huge age difference in language retention, one that, unfortunately, has had almost no discussion. The difference would receive a natural explanation if speed of decay were larger in young children than in older children and adults. Such a parameter difference also predicts that, because children would retain details poorly, the ratio of pattern learning to rote learning will be greater in children than adults (cf. Johnson & Newport, 1989), and it could thus help account for children's superior initial learning.

of the form *a–b* and *p–q*, they took it that there were none of the form *a–q* and *p–b* until such time as they heard some (which of course they never did). In that case, it is appropriate to say that the non-noticed possibilities were preempted by the noticed ones. That is to say, the subjects were operating with a uniqueness preference that belongs to the same family as the proposed unique argument-structure preference.[7]

Recently we have been engaged in pilot studies aimed at evaluating whether preschool children and adults show a unique argument-structure preference and the extent to which they rely on narrow range semantic constraints in assigning argument structures to novel verbs. We argue that if, following Pinker (1989a), children and adults are sensitive to narrow semantic constraints on verb alternations, they will make a novel verb belonging to an alternating narrow conflation class alternate freely and will not allow a novel verb to alternate if it belongs to a nonalternating subclass. However, if children and adults are oblivious to semantic constraints of a narrow sort but have a unique argument-structure preference, we expect that, if they are continually exposed to a novel verb in one kind of sentence frame only, they will eventually—perhaps after a period of alternation—settle into using the verb in the sentence frame in which they have heard the verb. In other words, we expect subjects eventually to follow adult models fairly consistently, regardless of a verb's narrow conflation class membership.

In two pilot experiments 13 preschoolers (mean = 4;8, range 3;8–5;9) and 18 undergraduates were introduced to two novel verbs that belonged to a narrow conflation class of causative/intransitive verbs that usually alternate in English (i.e., the manner-of-motion verbs). In addition, the subjects were introduced to two novel verbs that belonged to nonalternating narrow conflation classes (i.e., transitive verbs of causation of directed motion and intransitive verbs of motion in a lexically specified direction). The actions associated with the novel manner-of-motion verbs were (a) the bouncing motion of objects attached to the bottom of a Slinky held at one end by the experimenter and (b) the wobbly twirling motion of wooden objects set in motion on top of a pedestal. The two actions associated with directed-motion verbs consisted of (a) going down a pole into a nest either by sliding or jiggling and (b) going down a zigzag slide either by rolling, sliding, bouncing, or a similar motion. To discourage subjects from classifying our novel directed-motion verbs as manner-of-motion verbs, each directed-motion verb was introduced with several objects that moved in a variety of ways. Because children often substituted the expressions *going down* or *falling* for the

---

[7]Of course, it would be absurd to speak of argument structure for the words of a semantically empty system; however, we suggested earlier that the unique argument-structure preference should be taken as including a unique subcategorization-frame preference also. One could view the subjects as learning something like subcategorization frames for the words, for example, *b* occurring in the frame *a*X—and *q* in the frame *p*X—.

novel directed-motion verbs (e.g., "I'm making the rat go down," "It's going down into the nest," "They are both now falling down"), we have some evidence that children did not perceive the novel directed-motion verbs as denoting manners of motion. Likewise, children sometimes used English manner-of-motion verbs (e.g., *turn, spin, swing*) in their descriptions of the actions corresponding to the novel manner-of-motion verbs, indicating that the children were attempting to describe the manner in which the objects were moving.

Each novel verb was introduced in a particular sentence frame so that half of the verbs in each semantic class were introduced in causative sentence frames and the remaining half were introduced in intransitive sentence frames. For each manner of introduction, sentences were varied so that the actor argument was the subject of the sentence half of the time and the patient or theme argument was the subject of the sentence half of the time. Thus, for verbs introduced transitively, half of the sentences heard by the subjects were in the active voice (e.g., "John sebbed the ball into the box"), and half were in the passive voice (e.g., "The ball was/got sebbed into the box"). For verbs introduced intransitively, half of the sentences involved canonical intransitive usage (e.g., "The mouse mished into the nest"), and half were periphrastic constructions with the verb *make* (e.g., "Judy made the mouse mish into the nest").

After subjects had been introduced to each of the novel verbs in a variety of sentences, they were asked a series of questions that encouraged them to put a particular argument in subject position when responding to the probe questions. Agent questions (e.g., "What are you doing?") were used to elicit responses with the actor/agent argument as sentence subject (i.e., either a transitive usage in the active voice or an intransitive periphrastic *make* construction). Patient/theme questions (e.g., "What is the ball doing?" or "What is going on with the ball?") were used to elicit responses with the patient or theme argument as sentence subject (i.e., a transitive usage in the passive voice or an intransitive usage). Neutral questions (e.g., "What's happening?") were asked to uncover spontaneous usage.

The results of the experiments with both preschoolers and adults provided no evidence that narrow conflation classes play a role in constraining subjects' usage of novel verbs. The extent to which subjects' usage of the verbs mirrored the adult models was not affected by the semantic subclass of the verbs. That is, subjects were equally likely to alternate between causative and intransitive sentence frames for all verbs, regardless of whether the verb denoted a manner of motion or motion in a lexically specified direction. Although there were considerable differences in performance between subjects, the experiment conducted with adults provided some evidence for the existence of a unique argument-structure preference: About half of the adults followed the assigned transitivity of the novel verbs in their spontaneous usage and in response to the probe questions. These subjects clearly registered the argument structures in which the novel verbs appeared and closely matched their own usage to the experimenter's usage. On the other hand, the remaining subjects' behavior was quite idiosyncratic. Some of these subjects used both causative and intransitive sentence frames with a majority of the verbs, whereas other subjects showed preferences for using either causative or intransitive sentence frames without regard to the manner in which the verbs were introduced. In these cases it was unclear whether the adults actually registered the verbs' argument structures as introduced by the experimenter.

The results of the experiment with children indicated that, although there was a general bias towards using the argument structure modeled by the experimenter, most subjects were willing to use a majority of the novel verbs in both causative and intransitive sentence frames. However, the transitivity of the children's responses was related to the nature of the probe questions. As in prior work (e.g., Braine, Brody, Fisch, Weisberger, & Blum, 1990), most of the children tended to use causative sentence frames to answer agent questions and intransitive sentence frames to answer patient/theme questions. In general, passive sentences and *make* constructions were considerably less frequent in the child data as compared to the adults. Thus, the results of the study suggest that children's usage of novel verbs primarily reflects pragmatic demands to have a particular argument in subject position. It may be that children have difficulty switching flexibly between alternative sentence constructions (e.g., passives and actives, intransitives and *make* constructions) in response to conversational demands, with the result that they are prone to overextend the more familiar causative and intransitive sentence frames to meet discourse needs.

In these pilot experiments, the duration of exposure to the novel verbs was quite short (two sessions in the case of the adults, four sessions half the length of the adult sessions for the children). Our theory predicts that as the amount of exposure to the novel verbs increases, the subjects' response patterns will converge on their response patterns for familiar nonalternating English verbs. However, we have not yet tested this prediction. Consequently, although we believe that our data must count against the narrow-conflation-class theory, we cannot yet claim that the data provide much support for the unique argument-structure preference we propose. Further work with longer exposure periods is needed.

HOW THINGS STAND AT PRESENT

Despite the differences, there are some important points of similarity between the theories. Both theories posit the same initial generalization stage in children's learning: Children acquire canonical sentence schemas (or broad conflation classes) that define argument structures that are possible and understandable but nevertheless not fully productive. Moreover, in both theories the use of the schemas is constrained by what is contained in the lexical entry of a verb. For both theories, it follows from the principle that canonical schemas are not fully productive rules, that coinages that conform to the schemas usually reflect one-shot performance errors or, rarely (in adults), nonce coinages for rhetorical or metaphorical effect.

Although both theories posit that a large number of the argument-structure errors reported in the literature, especially by Bowerman (e.g., 1988), represent performance errors, there is some disagreement on this point by others, notably by Bowerman herself. Errors on the *spray-load* alternation are relatively few, even in Bowerman's data, and thus seem readily interpretable as performance errors or as due to semantic misanalyses (Gropen et al., 1991b; Pinker, 1989a). Errors on the other alternations are also fairly rare in most corpora (see for instance, Pinker's [1989a, p. 319] discussion of the frequencies in the CHILDES corpora [MacWhinney & Snow, 1985]), and they seem similarly interpretable as occasional performance errors. However, errors of the causative use of intransitive verbs are quite common in Bowerman's data and particularly common for a few intransitive verbs, such as *stay* and *go*. Unfortunately, because Bowerman did not record correct uses, one cannot compare the relative frequencies of correct and incorrect usage. (To the extent that the relative frequencies are similar, it would favor the idea that the errors are based on a productive rule, or that the particular verbs have been misclassified as being optionally transitive.) Although no firm conclusion is possible, the frequency of errors on *stay* and *go* are sufficiently high over a period of some months to make it plausible that Bowerman's daughters did temporarily misclassify a few verbs as optionally transitive. That raises the question whether either theory provides a mechanism whereby a child can recover from such a misclassification.

It seems apparent that Pinker's theory does not have such a mechanism. In his theory, the only potential mechanism would be semantic reanalysis, that is, correction of a mistaken meaning for a verb. However, that mechanism is inapplicable because nothing suggests that Bowerman's daughters had wrong meanings for *stay* and *go*. Pinker would therefore have to claim that such misclassifications do not exist, or argue that on the rare occasions that errors arise they are always corrected explicitly—someone must always explain the error to the child. The latter explanation is very unlikely in the case of Bowerman's data because she studiously refrained from correcting her children's language. Our theory does have a possible mechanism for eliminating misclassifications: Everything learned is subject to decay unless instances of it are re-encountered by the child in the language they hear. Whether such a decay mechanism can provide an adequate explanation for the disappearance of erroneous marking from a lexical entry depends on the particular parameters and conditions of the strengthening mechanism discussed earlier, which are currently unknown. Nevertheless, in principle, according to our theory such misclassifications could disappear as a result of nonreinforcement from the language heard.

As this chapter indicates, the problem of explaining why children make argument structure errors and how they stop making them is unresolved. Although the two theories discussed have much in common, there are crucial differences in the nature of the mechanisms proposed to be available to children acquiring a language. The semantic criteria approach as developed by Pinker (1989a) makes the assumption that children are capable of partitioning verbs into narrowly defined sets of alternating and nonalternating verbs. If a novel verb belongs to an alternating narrow conflation class, the language learner knows that it is licensed to alternate even if he or she has not heard it used in both argument structures of the alternation. If, however, the novel verb belongs to a nonalternating narrow subclass, the language learner will use the verb conservatively, matching his or her usage to that of adult models. As noted earlier, the role of the narrow range rules in constraining verb usage is problematic and has yet to receive any empirical support; in fact, the results of our pilot experiments suggest that narrow conflation classes do not play a role in constraining verb usage for children or adults. On the other hand, the notion of a unique argument-structure preference makes intuitive sense (although experimental demonstration is lacking), given that children are clearly biased toward using verbs in the argument structures in which they have heard the verbs used. We also adopt the independently motivated assumption that a verb's argument structure has a strength or solidity that is a function of how often the verb has been heard with that argument structure. In addition, there is reason to assume that there is an increase with age in flexibility in switching between sentence constructions to meet conversational demands to have particular arguments as subject or object. With these three assumptions, our theory can account for the disappearance of overgeneralization errors.

ACKNOWLEDGMENTS

Some of the work included in this chapter was supported by a grant (HD 20807, Project 2, Martin Braine, Principal Investigator) from the National Institute of Child Health and Human Development. We thank the principals, teachers, and children at City and Country School, Greenwich House Preschool, and West Chelsea Early Learning Center for their helpfulness. We also thank Melanie Cioppa, Monica Martyak, and Annie Avery for assistance with running subjects in the exploratory work reported.

REFERENCES

Baker, C. L. (1979). Syntactic theory and the projection problem. *Linguistic Inquiry, 10,* 533–581.

Berwick, R. C. (1985). *The acquisition of syntactic knowledge.* Cambridge, MA: MIT Press.

Berwick, R. C., & Weinberg, A. (1984). *The grammatical basis of linguistic performance.* Cambridge, MA: MIT Press.

Bowerman, M. (1974). Learning the structure of causative verbs: A study in the relationship of cognitive, semantic, and syntactic development. *Papers and Reports on Child Language Development, 8.* Stanford, CA: Stanford University Department of Linguistics.

Bowerman, M. (1978). Systematizing semantic knowledge: Changes over time in the child's organization of word meaning. *Child Development, 49,* 977–987.

Bowerman, M. (1982a). Evaluating competing linguistic models with language acquisition data: Implications of developmental errors with causative verbs. *Quaderni di Semantica, 3,* 5–66.

Bowerman, M. (1982b). Reorganizational processes in lexical and syntactical development. In E. Wanner & L. R. Gleitman (Eds.), *Language acquisition: The state of the art* (pp. 319–346). New York: Cambridge University Press.

Bowerman, M. (1983). How do children avoid constructing an overly general grammar in the absence of feedback about what is not a sentence? *Papers and Reports on Child Language Development, 22.* Stanford, CA: Stanford University Department of Linguistics.

Bowerman, M. (1987). Commentary: Mechanisms of language acquisition. In B. MacWhinney (Ed.), *Mechanisms of language acquisition* (pp. 443–466). Hillsdale, NJ: Lawrence Erlbaum Associates.

Bowerman, M. (1988). The 'no negative evidence' problem: How do children avoid constructing an overly general grammar? In J. A. Hawkins (Ed.), *Explaining language universals* (pp. 73–101). Oxford: Basil Blackwell.

Braine, M. D. S. (1965). The insufficiency of a finite state model for verbal reconstructive memory. *Psychonomic Science, 2,* 291–292.

Braine, M. D. S. (1971). On two types of models of the internalization of grammars. In D. I. Slobin (Ed.), *The ontogenesis of grammar: A theoretical symposium* (pp. 153–186). New York: Academic Press.

Braine, M. D. S. (1988a). Modeling the acquisition of linguistic structure. In Y. Levy, I. M. Schlesinger, & M. D. S. Braine (Eds.), *Categories and processes in language acquisition* (pp. 217–259). Hillsdale, NJ: Lawrence Erlbaum Associates.

Braine, M. D. S. (1988b). *Language learnability and language development* (review of S. Pinker, 1984). *Journal of Child Language, 15,* 189–199.

Braine, M. D. S., Brody, R. E., Brooks, P. J., Sudhalter, V., Ross, J. A., Catalano, L., & Fisch, S. M. (1990). Exploring language acquisition in children with a miniature artificial language: Effects of item and pattern frequency, arbitrary subclasses, and correction. *Journal of Memory and Language, 29,* 591–610.

Braine, M. D. S., Brody, R. E., Fisch, S. M., Weisberger, M. J., & Blum, M. (1990). Can children use a verb without exposure to its argument structure? *Journal of Child Language, 17,* 313–342.

Brown, R., & Hanlon, C. (1970). Derivational complexity and order of acquisition in child speech. In J. R. Hayes (Ed.), *Cognition and the development of language* (pp. 11–53). New York: Wiley.

Clark, E. V. (1987). The principle of contrast: A constraint on language acquisition. In B. MacWhinney (Ed.), *Mechanisms of language acquisition* (pp. 1–33). Hillsdale, NJ: Lawrence Erlbaum Associates.

Clark, E. V. (1988). On the logic of contrast. *Journal of Child Language, 15,* 317–335.

Dell, F. (1981). On the learnability of optional phonological rules. *Linguistic Inquiry, 12,* 31–37.

Demetras, M. J., Post, K. N., & Snow, C. E. (1986). Feedback to first language learners: The role of repetitions and clarification questions. *Journal of Child Language, 13*, 275–292.

Erteschik-Shir, N. (1979). Discourse constraints on dative movement. In T. Givon (Ed.), *Syntax and semantics: Vol. 12. Discourse and syntax*. New York: Academic Press.

Gathercole, V. C. (1987). The contrastive hypothesis for the acquisition of word meaning: A reconsideration of the theory. *Journal of Child Language, 14*, 493–531.

Gathercole, V. C. (1989). Contrast: A semantic constraint? *Journal of Child Language, 16*, 685–702.

Gentner, D. (1978). On relational meaning: The acquisition of verb meaning. *Child Development, 49*, 988–998.

Green, G. M. (1974). *Semantics and syntactic regularity*. Bloomington, IN: Indiana University Press.

Gropen, J., Pinker, S., Hollander, M., Goldberg, R., & Wilson, R. (1989). The learnability and acquisition of the dative alternation in English. *Language, 65*, 203–257.

Gropen, J., Pinker, S., Hollander, M., & Goldberg, R. (1991a). Affectedness and direct objects: The role of lexical semantics in the acquisition of verb argument structure. *Cognition, 41*, 153–195.

Gropen, J., Pinker, S., Hollander, M., & Goldberg, R. (1991b). Syntax and semantics in the acquisition of locative verbs. *Journal of Child Language, 18*, 115–151.

Hochberg, J. (1986). Children's judgments of transitivity errors. *Journal of Child Language, 13*, 317–334.

Ingham, R. (1992). *Learnability and cognition: The acquisition of argument structure* (review of S. Pinker, 1989). *Journal of Child Language, 19*, 205–211.

Johnson, J. S., & Newport, E. L. (1989). Critical period effects in second language learning: The influence of maturational state on the acquisition of English as a second language. *Cognitive Psychology, 21*, 60–99.

Levin, B., & Rappaport Hovav, M. (1991). Wiping the slate clean: A lexical semantic exploration. *Cognition, 41*, 123–151.

MacWhinney, B. (1978). The acquisition of morphophonology. *Monographs of the Society for Research in Child Development, 43* (1, Serial No. 174).

MacWhinney, B., & Snow, C. (1985). The Child Language Data Exchange System. *Journal of Child Language, 12*, 271–296.

Markman, E. M. (1989). *Categorization and naming in children*. Cambridge, MA: MIT Press.

Mazurkewich, I., & White, L. (1984). The acquisition of the dative alternation: Unlearning overgeneralizations. *Cognition, 16*, 261–283.

Merriman, W. E., & Bowman, L. L. (1989). The mutual exclusivity bias in children's early word learning. *Monographs of the Society for Research in Child Development, 54* (3–4, Serial No. 220).

Moerk, E. (1983). *The mother of Eve as a first language teacher*. Norwood, NJ: Ablex.

Morgan, J. L., & Travis, L. L. (1989). Limits on negative information in language learning. *Journal of Child Language, 16*, 531–552.

Nelson, K. (1988). Constraints on word learning? *Cognitive Development, 3*, 221–246.

Pinker, S. (1984). *Language learnability and language development*. Cambridge, MA: Harvard University Press.

Pinker, S. (1989a). *Learnability and cognition: The acquisition of argument structure*. Cambridge, MA: MIT Press.

Pinker, S. (1989b). Markedness and language development. In R. J. Matthews & W. Demopoulos (Eds.), *Learnability and linguistic theory* (pp. 107–127). Dordrecht: Kluwer.

Plunkett, K., & Marchman, V. (1991). U-shaped learning and frequency effects in a multi-layered perceptron: Implications for child language acquisition. *Cognition, 38*, 43–102.

Slobin, D. I., & Bever, T. G. (1982). Children use canonical sentence schemas: A crosslinguistic study of word order and inflections. *Cognition, 12*, 229–265.

CHAPTER FOURTEEN

Hedgehogs, Foxes, and the Acquisition of Verb Meaning

Michael Maratsos
Gedeon Deák
University of Minnesota

HEDGEHOGS AND FOXES
AS THEORETICAL ANIMALS

There are a number of very interesting discussions in this volume of papers, and naturally it is only possible for us to comment on some central problems relevant to some, not all, of them. In particular, we discuss the general nature of word learning, and non-object word learning in particular, in light of the hedgehog–fox continuum, which we propose to impose metaphorically upon psychological problems and proposals in general. In particular, we argue that verblike meanings and their acquisition have a more foxlike and less hedgehoglike nature than concrete object nouns; we also examine two of the major proposals that aim to simplify the acquisition of verb meaning and seek to point out the greater degree of flexibility in acquisitional procedure that seems central to the acquisition of such meanings.

Hedgehogs and Foxes: An Initial Introduction
and Quick Transmutation

The philosopher Isaiah Berlin (1954) originally introduced the metaphor of hedgehog and fox as a way of understanding the different kinds of philosophical and intellectual theories people have. In particular, if there are no humans around, hedgehogs and foxes are successful animals who characteristically succeed in different ways. As Berlin saw it, a hedgehog (or porcupine, in America), succeeds by having one thing that it does and doing it all the time. That is, it has quills for protection. A fox, on the other hand, succeeds by doing many different kinds of things and by flexibly choosing or doing somewhat different things to fit new situations. According to Berlin, human intellectual figures can be thought of in light of this distinction. Plato and Marx, for example, were essentially hedgehogs. They each thought one basic problem or process is the fundamental one; for example, for Plato it was the existence of Platonic eternal forms and their shadow reflections in the real world. Foxes include people like Machiavelli or Aristotle, who wrote about many different kinds of things in solving or treating problems.

Like All Metaphors, the Metaphor Can Be Taken Too Seriously

No reader of the dialogues can fail to see Plato's foxlike abilities in intellectual maneuvering. Yet there is some real justice in the metaphor: Some thinkers give much more of an impression of finding one central idea to be central, whereas others find a number of diverse ideas, structures, processes, or procedures to be more equally ranged with or against each other. However, as the subheading advertises, we subvert Berlin's original analysis a little for our own purposes. We distinguish between more or less hedgehog versus foxlike psychological domains of investigation and, in parallel, more or less hedgehog versus fox kinds of accounts of how children acquire and use the subject matter of these domains.

The basic distinction we want to set up is between psychological structures or processes that can be compared on two main dimensions: how much of the process can be fairly well captured by an algorithm versus requiring a lot of on-the-spot, relatively spontaneous thinking; and processes or structures that can be captured by a relatively small number of stable structural parts of relatively small numbers of different kinds versus ones in which diversity of elements or procedures, or both, is central. The first kind of structures—relatively highly algorithmized, a relatively small and organized set of central elements—we call hedgehog structures. The second kind of processes—hard to algorithmize, a relatively large and diverse set of contributing elements—we call fox activities. We do not claim that the world of psychological processes can be neatly divided up into processes that are either fox or hedgehog processes, for some problems require mixing the relevant characteristics. However, we think the overall distinction provides a useful heuristic for gaining perspective.

To take some examples (claims made here largely on the basis of intuition) grammar, for all its complexity, is more of a hedgehog function. Pragmatics, the use of language for social purposes, requires more foxlike, on-the-spot problem solving activities. First, grammar. Without losing track of how much diversity there is in grammar, it still seems reasonable to say that much of the core of grammar seems to involve a fairly small set of primitive kinds of elements, categories, and processes. These lead to plausible proposals that there may be a fairly limited set of basic properties of grammar, which children may furthermore innately know. (Note we are not saying it is thereby proven that children have innate knowledge of this small number of basic properties, just that it is plausible to propose it.) Even the set of meanings that can figure conspicuously in grammatical processes like word order and morphology seems to be reasonably limited when compared to all the existing meanings (Maratsos, 1989; Pinker, 1984; Slobin, 1985; Talmy, 1985). Furthermore, a speaker who knows the grammar of a language has a highly algorithmized process for how to use that knowledge. When we produce a new sentence, we are not really required to make many original or spontaneous decisions, given an original meaning to be conveyed. It is hardly what we would usually call a problem-solving situation in the usual sense; that is, it is likely the speaker will succeed without the benefit of some unusual or improbable grammatical insight.

On the other hand, consider pragmatics and pragmatic acts. Of course, there are some basic principles behind pragmatics. Some of these were outlined by Grice (1975): "Be truthful," "be informative," "be sincere," "be relevant." Even when these principles are violated, as in politeness, which can require us to say things we do not believe or can require us to make small talk that is not meant to be informative, the conversational scenario is played out as though the participants were being Gricean. Politeness, done successfully, requires the conversants to act as though they believed each other to be truthful, sincere, and informative (Brown, personal communication). However, the application of Gricean principles is a fox activity. For example, consider the principle that one should be informative. What are the algorithms or rules that tell a person how to be informative in a particular situation with a particular person? Figuring out what is informative to someone else requires figuring out what the other person already knows (or is likely to know), which may involve using what one knows (or guesses) of the other person's history, appearance, manner of speech, previous remarks in the conversation, basis of current acquaintance, purpose of the present conversation, and any number of other factors. For that matter, one must figure out how much information the other person wants, maybe they don't feel like hearing much new. It is extremely doubtful that there is an standard algorithm for doing this, as there are algorithms telling how *dog, cat,* and *chase* can be put together into sentences if the dog did the chasing and the cat was chased. Similarly, consider a pragmatic act like convincing, which is surely a central social use of language. What convincing is may be specifiable; but what are the algorithms for convincing someone? True, one knows one is supposed to say something with supporting considerations in such a way that the other person comes to believe what one says. But this is not exactly a how-to-do-it list. Convincing other people is (we think, anyway) an obvious candidate for an activity in which fox processes take up more of the bulk than hedgehog processes; it is not easy to say much about how anyone learns to do it, either.

Of course, in particular situations, people may attempt to turn a fox problem into a hedgehog problem, to their own advantage. People selling particular products, for example, are typically interested in working out general strategies that can be taught to the sales corps. For the most part, however, both the application and development of skill in using pragmatic competence have a great deal of foxlike nature about them: Many elements of different kinds are used, and it is necessary to do some spontaneous on-the-spot figuring that is hard to algorithmize.

Our guess is that the fox–hedgehog distinction applies to many problems. In particular, it is likely that the ability to give a name to a set of problems tends to make people think the set is a hedgehog entity, when in reality most of its interest is in hard-to-specify fox activities. Just to mention one case briefly, problem solving covers a wide variety of situations that have a little bit in common, namely, the necessity of devising steps to reach a goal. However, problems differ so much in their nature and requirements that this says very little of interest about how particular problems are solved. Saying a human can solve (some) problems says very little, typically, about how he or she solves a particular problem because of the diversity of the problems. Moreover, we do not call something a problem-solving situation unless it requires the organism to make up something a bit new or unexpected. It is not a problem for us to make up a sentence about a dog chasing a cat or, under ordinary circumstances, to figure out how to get an envelope moved from one desk to another.

In any case, what does this distinction, which is no doubt more complicated and conditional than our treatment implies, have to do with word meaning and its acquisition? As we see it, much current work in word meaning acquisition, such as that by Markman (1992), Golinkoff, Hirsh-Pasek, Mervis, Frawley, and Parillo (this volume), or Lederer, Gleitman, and Gleitman (this volume), appears to comprise attempts to make word meaning acquisition, like grammatical acquisition in accounts like that of Chomsky (1986), a hedgehog process. Because we think that in all likelihood a great deal of the domain of word meaning itself is more of a fox, the current approach seems to be an attempt to turn a fox into a hedgehog.

How has this come about? A number of major arguments have been transferred from the acquisition of grammar literature. First, there is the decision problem: Given the input data, too many possible hypotheses are available about the data, exemplified in word meaning by Quine's (1960) well-known discussion of the *gavagai* situation. Second, there is the velocity problem: Children appear to be very quick. In word meaning, the relevant findings are that children seem to acquire around 6 or 7 words a day during the preschool years (Carey, 1978) and that in some experimental situations, children seem to fast-map some or occasionally much word meaning from single situational exposures (Carey, 1982; Markman, 1989).

The response, as in grammar, has been to emphasize a number of hedgehog possibilities. The child must operate with internal heuristics or principles to reduce the decision task (e.g., Markman, 1992), and a relatively small number of such principles may be able to cover a great deal of ground quickly (Chomsky, 1986; Golinkoff et al., this volume). In principle, however, hedgehogs as we have described them—a fairly small number of primitive elements and procedures, algorithmic process for application or combination—do not have to be fast or slow in particular. One can have a slow hedgehog. For example, many theories in classical learning, such as operant conditioning, in effect comprise slow hedgehogs: A few simple principles applied over time in regular fashion achieve the result. Current word meaning approaches, however, clearly favor fast hedgehog procedures: A relatively small number of algorithmically applied principles and heuristics like object bias, whole-object assumption, taxonomic principle, mutual exclusivity can resolve a great deal of word meaning quickly. This approach, with some supplementation (discussed later), has had some success in dealing with concrete object words, and in this volume authors like Golinkoff et al. attempt to apply it to non-nouns as well. Simultaneously, the syntactic bootstrapping approaches outlined in Lederer et al. (this volume) are essentially attempts to call in that well-known neighborhood hedgehog, syntax, to solve apparently foxlike problems of verb meaning such as role participants or non-actional meaning relatively swiftly and efficiently.

There is little evidence that evolution itself (unlike theorists) requires utter consistency in a system. Thus, we do not think it necessary to disclaim the usefulness of various forms of principles, constraints, or general tendencies to insist on the foxlike nature of word meaning and of nonsubstantives in particular. However, given that hedgehog principles by nature are generally more theoretically appealing and easier to think about and specify (science itself is a massive attempt to convert the foxlike nature of apparent diversity into a hedgehog; physics has managed this in some domains with some success), hedgehog accounts will always sit better in the mind. It is inherently appealing, therefore, to exaggerate their range of applicability in any problem. Complementarily, foxlike appeals to the child's ability to assess, for example, what is pragmatically meant or relevant in a situation are naturally harder to specify in detail, even if they are fully valid.

In general, we believe that for various reasons, exaggeration of the applicability of (fast) hedgehog explanations has occurred in current work on word meaning, along with an underestimate of the role of slower sifting-over-time processes that must account for a great deal of word meaning acquisition, especially for nonsubstantives. In the following sections we begin to support these claims by critical examination of a small cluster of propositions. First, we inspect the hypothesis that verblike meanings share a great deal in common with the hedgehog-amenable domain of simple concrete object nouns (Golinkoff et al., this volume). We stress reasons for thinking that compared to substantive nouns, verblike meanings are more diverse and more difficult to specify in general and thus are less likely to be captured by fast hedgehog procedures. Second, we examine the hypothesis that syntactic bootstrapping is necessary for circumventing foxlike pragmatic processes in children's acquisition of mental predicates (Lederer et al., this volume). In doing so we look briefly at a problem with employing syntactic bootstrapping to solve certain argument role problems (see Rispoli, this volume, for extensive critical examination). In these examinations, we reexamine the basic velocity and decision problems to see whether it is inevitable that fast hedgehog solutions are required by the known data and by logical considerations.

THE BASICS: WHAT ARE WE CONTRASTING, ANYWAY?

We note that throughout this volume, there is no settled notion of what *verb* means, either grammatically or semantically, but especially the latter. There is good reason for this. Across the world's languages, the words that linguists call verbs differ in some basic grammatical privileges and in the semantics they cover.

In fact, it is unlikely that verb versus noun is really the important distinction underlying most of the discussions in this volume. What is more likely the central distinction is that between what have traditionally been called substantive nouns and virtually everything else. A substantive is a word that refers by itself, without requiring implicit reference to other entities or qualities. For example, whether or not this is really true, one has the feeling one can talk about a dog or a table and refer to relatively self-complete entities. On the other hand, consider the word *hit*. Hitting cannot exist without a hitter and something or someone hit. Similarly, the word *in* refers to a relation between necessary other entities (roughly, a container and something contained). Often the entities whose properties or relations are given by the non-noun are the *arguments* of the non-noun, and the word that describes or relates them is the *predicate* of the argument(s).

In fact, however, not all nouns are substantives. For example, the word *game* implies and requires the notion of players; *trip* requires takers of the trip and destinations. "We went to Morocco" is very analogous to "our trip to Morocco," in which *our* and *to Morocco* specify the taker and destination arguments of *trip*. Many concrete object nouns are similar in nature. Plato remarked that *father* is a relational word, not a simple substantive—a father automatically implies an offspring; no one can be a father by himself. Similar arguments can be used for *mother, patient* (which does not just mean a person who is ill), and other social role nouns.

Golinkoff et al. try to make some clear general semantic distinctions between nonobject nouns and corresponding verbs; for example, nouns are claimed often to refer only to a result, whereas verbs can be used to refer to intermediate processes in an event, as in their discussion of *arrival* versus *arrive*. However, one can talk about ongoing processes in games, trips, and so on; one can discuss the ongoing destruction of the city or say "during the destruction." Indeed, even for *arrival*, we have no problem saying "the arrival of the army went on all day" or "during the arrival of the troops."

There is also no reliable semantic distinction that differentiates various groups of non-nouns. This is perhaps easiest to see in cross-language comparisons. For example, the intransitive verbs of English reliably refer to actions (e.g., *run, walk, die*), but in other languages, intransitive verbs may include the meanings "be unpopular," "be at fault," "be cold," "be warm," "be happy," "be afraid," and many other intransitive stative meanings. We cite these examples for languages that still retain a verb–adjective distinction; in languages in which there are no separate adjectives and all major predicate terms are grammatically verbs, all meanings usually covered by adjectives in English are expressed by main verbs.

The problem of analyzing the reliable and non-reliable differences among types of nouns, verbs, adjectives, prepositions, and so on, could go on for a long time. We simply assert that the most consistent distinction in this volume is the distinction between intuitively simple substantive concrete object nouns like *dog* and *table* versus nonsubstantives, which we take to include non-nouns like *hit, break, like, sad, angry, on,* and *popular,* and also many nouns like *bath* or *trip* (see Nelson, this volume, for interesting data on such event nouns). In our discussion, *concrete noun* refers to a relatively clear substantive as opposed to a non-noun or a relational noun.

ARE VERBLIKE MEANINGS (NONSUBSTANTIVES) ACQUIRED LIKE CONCRETE NOUNS?

As we remarked previously, many believe that the acquisition of concrete substantive nouns has a considerable amount of fast hedgehog character. Golinkoff et al., while discussing some of the differences between nonsubstantives and concrete nouns, asserted that there are principles highly analogous to those proposed for concrete noun acquisition that can be readily and successfully generalized to many verbs, at least the subclass of event-word verbs. Although there is some appeal in their proposals, we think that there are many problems in attempting these generalizations. In treating the problems, it is useful to start with a brief demonstration that one of the aspects of concrete noun analysis is central to the utility of hedgehog principles for them: the availability of a potentially definable and workable privileged level of classification, the Basic Object level. Without something like this level, the other heuristics proposed for concrete nouns fail to cover much ground. In subsequent discussion, we address the significance of the fact (noted by Golinkoff et al.) that there is no successfully proposed corresponding Basic Event or Basic Action level.

Why is the Basic Object level (or something like it) so important for concrete noun acquisition? The reason is simple. Without it, the other set of familiar proposed principles covers practically no analytic ground at all. Let us list the principles suggested by Markman (1989, 1992). (We do not presuppose here that this set is correct, although it may be; we only suppose it for the sake of discussion here.) These principles include the Object Bias (i.e., assume a novel word refers to an object), the Whole Object bias (i.e., guess that a word referring to an object refers to the entire object, rather than one or more of its parts or properties in isolation), the Mutual Exclusivity principle (i.e., assume, as a first guess, that a class of objects has a single word to refer to it), and the Taxonomic Principle (i.e., assume a word refers to a taxonomic rather than a thematic category. See Markman, 1992, or Golinkoff et al., this volume, for explanation of the taxonomic principle). Why are these not very useful without something like the Basic Object level (or related shape bias; Landau, Smith, & Jones, 1988)? Suppose a word has been guessed (correctly) to refer to a particular whole object, or rather to a taxonomic category to which the object belongs. Obviously giving the word some kind of category description is necessary in order to get anywhere. Otherwise the word may refer just to that particular object and not generalize at all.

However, simply saying the word has to refer to some taxonomic category for the object is practically useless. For example, suppose a child is learning his or her first word that refers to a concrete object. Concrete objects themselves comprise a taxonomic class, so the child might assume the word refers to any concrete object. This assumption is not really specific enough to be very useful, and there is no evidence that any child has ever construed any first word this way. In fact, "taxonomic category" says much less to define what kind of thing one is talking about than seems generally thought. Taxonomic category just means things that are like in kind, which means things that share some attribute in common. A perfectly good—and highly meaningful—taxonomic category, for example, is "anything that can be counted as part of the Gross Domestic Product." (Anyone who wants to argue this is not an ecologically valid or important category can consult the list of presidents for whom a one or two percent decrease in this category has been politically troublesome or fatal.) "Thing used to produce farm products" is a taxonomic category. "Thing with a curve in its shape somewhere" defines a taxonomic category. "Thing that I like to look at" defines a taxonomic category. "Thing with large brown eyes and slightly asymmetrical ears" defines a taxonomic category. Indeed, one can decide a word refers to a whole object taxonomic category and have gained no particularly useful ground at all. It is no difficulty to show that adding Mutual Exclusivity adds little to the problem.

In practice, "taxonomic category" implicitly means "basic object level taxonomic category," which happens to give a useful intention for most object words. Thus, a child seeing a chair and hearing "chair" is thought to guess that *chair* applies to the chair and other members of the basic object level chair. This is a good guess, compared to all the other taxonomic category guesses that can be made, given that the nouns used around the child most commonly categorize at the basic level. The child can do this presumably because "basic object level" refers to a privileged natural level of categorization. It is furthermore typically (at least it can be hoped) definable by a fairly general cognitive–perceptual metric: the highest level of categorization of concrete objects for which one can readily imagine an average. For example, consider the levels of categorization "jet," "airplane," and "vehicle," which ascend in generality. Most people feel they can meaningfully form an average picture or shape for jets or airplanes but not for vehicles in general. Thus, "airplane" is relatively concrete (one can imagine an average shape) and general (it is the highest such level) at once. Children may form on a nonlinguistic basis a natural basic object categorization system for the objects in their world and supplement the previously described assumptions with this system. Of course, one must further specify how humans see shapes and average shapes, but this is at least a conceivable task (see Biederman, 1988, for a proposal on the basic constituents of shape perception that tends naturally to give the Roschian basic object level). The shape bias proposed by Landau et al. essentially refers to the possibility of analyzing such an overall general shape in dealing with concrete objects; without such an overall grounding, simply saying one generalizes object names on the basis of shared shaped would be about as unhelpful as the above principles without some kind of basic object level assumed.

We do not assume that the current form of basic object categorization is the right form or that all the problems have been worked out. Rosch and Mervis (1975) noted, for example, that different cultures may have different basic levels for some objects: Whereas "tree" is basic for most English speakers, different specific trees turn out to be the relevant level for some cultures, with "tree" overly general. It seems that proposals using such a level are at least plausible proposals and can potentially cover a great deal of the concrete noun sphere, although of course they do not work for nouns like *weapon, toy, food, animal,* and so on (nouns of a type for which supplementary learning situations have been proposed by supporters of principles or constraints accounts (see Markman, 1992).[1]

We note here briefly that the same recourse to Basic Object level categorization that is necessary to give any utility to proposals like Mutual Exclusivity and the Taxonomic Principle, properly applied, saves much of proposals like the Principle of Contrast and the Gricean account of the related phenomena from the otherwise compelling criticisms made by Merriman et al. (this volume). Briefly, if the Gricean assumption that the other speaker is being informative is supplemented by a notion of informativeness that includes a natural basic object taxonomy as a central way of dividing up the world into informational packets, the explanations given by Gathercole (1987) can be resuscitated for the same class of basic object level concrete object nouns that anyone achieves heuristic success with. As far as we can tell, incorporation of some natural shared basis for categorization, like the basic object level, is necessary for any heuristic fast hedgehog account to make much headway.

Event Words and Object-Related Principles

How much are events like concrete objects? Golinkoff et al. (this volume) wrote an interesting proposal to extend concrete noun principles to event words by analogy. They discussed differences between concrete object nouns and event words but stressed the helpful similarities. We stress the differences, or question some of the straightforwardness of the applicability of the analogies. In doing so, we reinforce the intuitive impression that event words really are more difficult to pin down quickly than concrete object words.

Whole Objects and Maximal Events. One of the most useful assumptions about object words is that a word that refers to an unnamed object refers to the object as a whole rather than to some limited part or property (like a fragment of its shape, or its texture, or its color, and so on). Golinkoff et al. believe there is a corresponding principle for parsing the world of events—that the child tends to assume an event word refers to the Maximal Action. In worrying about this problem, they bring up another very important problem: Actions are often, perhaps typically, composed of subactions. For example, consider the deceptively simple event phrase *pick up* (*pick* is the

---

[1]The assumption of a simple and absolute primacy of basic object level concepts in taxonomies has been questioned in a number of places, including arguments about whether all basic objects can be fit into a uniform taxonomy, whether the basic level can be formalized, whether basic objects really are a naturally privileged conceptual level, whether they are developmentally privileged, and a number of other difficulties (e.g., Joliceur et al., 1984; Mandler & Bauer, 1988; Medin, 1983; Murphy, 1982; Murphy & Wisniewski, 1989; White, 1982). We think there is still likely to be something special about basic level objects, and the presence of a special widespread categorization basis is central to the success of fast hedgehog accounts, whatever the eventual basis turns out to be.

verb, but *pick up* is the semantic unit). In picking something up, one moves one's hand toward it, shapes the fingers so they will be able to grasp it, closes the fingers around the object so that when the hand is moved from the location of the object, the object will go with the hand. Obviously there are a great many subactions here, and there may be more. The movements of each finger may be separate actions, and so on. Yet we intuitively feel all these actions are united into a unitary scheme of picking up the object, and *pick up* refers to this larger scheme. In theory, if a word *guz* is used to refer to this event, the child may think *guz* refers to any subaction, a subaction sequence, or the whole sequence. The maximal action principle is that the child will guess the word refers to the largest action sequence. It will work, of course, if there are indeed clear definable divisions of the world of events into maximal events and if such divisions are what people are talking about when they use most simple action words (though naturally proposals must be made for words that do not correspond to maximal events, just as is necessary for concrete object words that do not refer to average-shape definable concrete nouns).

A priori, what reason is there to be confident that action words have such simple maximal definitions? Intuitions are what are available on this point currently, and our intuitions are not very hopeful. The world of events does not seem to us to segment very neatly into simple, clear, isolated clusters, for intention can unite highly separable actions or segment highly fused actions. *Eat* refers to a subpart of the usual maximal action sequence, which we take to be someone putting something in someone's mouth, the latter then chewing, swallowing for the purposes of relieving hunger. (Does one eat a button or swallow it? We would say swallow, unless one is deluded; we may swallow some chewed gum but won't be eating it.) In fact, the right reference for *eat* does not include the part about putting the food in the mouth; people can eat food even if they do not put it in their mouths themselves. We note also that if *eat* is somehow a natural maximum, *chew* and *swallow* are not, although they seem like natural enough action words.

Problems like those for *eat* are not very hard to find. For example, *throw* apparently does not include picking up the object to be thrown nor even necessarily the object actually hitting anything (*I threw the ball at the wall* seems to indicate that *throw* means setting the object into motion, leaving out its achieved endpoint as something to be specified or not by another phrase). *Drink* only refers to the action of swallowing the liquid, as far as we can tell, even if there is a natural maximal action sequence that includes getting it to the mouth in a container. Is it part of a natural maximal action sequence to count someone going to the store to buy something to drink, or holding a glass under the faucet to get water, or getting something out of the refrigerator?

For other reasonably concrete action words, the problem of natural perceptual boundaries seems fairly impossible. For example, where is the perceptually natural action sequence for words like *fight* or *play* or *game?* These are natural enough action words, but the events they can refer to can include many pauses and stops. (Such words, of course, are only a prelude to eventual action-event words like *war* or *industrial revolution.*) Our guess is that for action-event words, much of the action beginning–end boundaries are provided partly by convention and partly by the understood goals and intentions of the actors. *Pick up* segments as a whole because the purpose is to use the subactions as part of an action of removing an object from a location (so if one pauses when the hand is around the object and then lifts it, one is still picking up). Our guess is that figuring out the beginnings and ends of verbally referred-to perceptual sequences requires figuring out the goals relevant in the situation and comparing different uses of the same event word over different uses. It seems doubtful that such boundaries are commonly obvious in the same way as are the boundaries of many objects.

Basic Objects and Mutual Exclusivity: Event-Word Counterparts? For a large group of concrete object words, there is at least potentially the prospect that something like highest average perceptual shape provides a reasonable means of categorizing objects naturally, although other heuristics would have to be used to handle the many nouns for which this was not the right analysis. Golinkoff et al. (this volume) noted, however, that something like a basic action level does not exist, although they state hopes for the combination of maximal action with shape analysis and semantic component analysis for event verbs. As discussed previously, the proposition that there is a straightforward maximal action for a large number of physical event words deserves some scrutiny, at the least. What about the nonbasic actional nature of event words? Why is this so, and what does the lack of such a basic level entail?

The reason there is no such level, at least currently, is that basic verbs or basic event words readily include words that refer to the same events in different yet overlapping ways. The basic object level, at least, is one at which a group of mutually exclusive, largely perceptually definable words refer to nonoverlapping categories that usually do not refer to other basic object level categories. *Table* does not include *chair* or *lamp* (although of course all of these words overlap with the nonbasic word *furniture*, which has no good perceptual average). Because basic object nouns are the most common nouns, the child guessing such natural, nonoverlapping category meanings will work out a large part of the noun vocabulary at least. However, these criteria just do not apply very well for event words, or even just verb event words. There are many common event words that seem basic enough but do not refer to any particular perceptual shape at all. Different event words may refer quite reasonably to the same action sequence, and it is hard to find privileged natural levels of categorization even within purely perceptually defined verbs.

We call shape event words by the word *movie*, just to make clear that we are referring to a sequence of perceptually definable actions (although naturally the movie is not perceptually complete). Movie words probably include words like *walk, run, wave*, and perhaps *eat* (with reservations to be noted) and *stir*. What are some non-movie event verbs or nouns? *Play* and *game* are such words, for there are no particular movies that can be run to illustrate these; any number of action sequences can be *play* or *game*. Similarly, *go, make, move, break, get, fix, hurt* (in the sense of hurting someone else), *do, find, give, put*, and *turn on* (a machine, device) are all semantically basic words—many of which appear in rather early vocabulary (Bloom, 1991; Tomasello, 1992)—that do not connote some kind of average perceptual movie sequence that can be concretely defined. *Go*, for example, means that someone or something changes its location (a result); one can go by plane, by car, by jumping, by crawling, by walking, by running, and so on. It is not a movie verb. Similarly, one can break something by dropping it, hitting it with something, pulling out a spring, crushing it in the hand, sitting on it, kicking it, hitting something else with it, throwing it, and so on. *Break* refers rather purely to a result, with no particular movie sequence (although only certain classes of action sequences are allowed as breaking sequences). *Fix*, the reverse of *break*, also has no particular corresponding set of average actions, nor does *make*, which means to bring something into being by some sequence of actions that have no particular definition. *Mix* means to get the components mixed up, whether by shaking, stirring, leaving on a vibrating surface, or another such action. Nearly all of these words have specifications of possible relations between agent and action sequence and result, but they do not entail a particular movie sequence that can be given a basic perceptual average, unlike good movie verbs—or unlike good basic object shape nouns, analogously. (Their non-movie nature can only be compounded by their many metaphorical uses, e.g., "go figure," "make a mess," "break tradition," "get a quick fix," "I was moved [emotionally]," etc.)

It is impossible to say these are not in all other senses basic verbs. They are commonly used, sometimes more commonly than the corresponding movie verbs. For example, *go* is probably the most common way of referring to someone changing his or her own location, not *run* or *walk* or some other movie verb. *Break* is probably more common than words like *smash* or "hurl against the wall so that (whatever it is) falls into pieces" or "bang on the floor so that (whatever it is) no longer moves the (whatever it is) part the way it used to." The movie verbs do not feel privileged vis-à-vis the result verbs, nor do the result verbs feel particularly privileged vis-à-vis some movie verbs. In fact, despite the overwhelming tendency in the literature to treat these as mutually exclusive classes, it is common enough for verbs to mix result and movie features. For example, the verb *to hand* (someone something) refers both to a result (i.e., an object changes location or possession from one person to another) and to a particular perceptually definable action; it is done with the hand (except when used more metaphorically, as in "they handed over the suspect"). The verb *throw* refers both to a movie sequence and to a result: An object changes location from the hand to somewhere else. If someone goes through throwing motions but keeps the object in the hand, it was not thrown. Changes of location, of course, are results that are also movie results in some degree because they entail at least a change of perceptual array corresponding to something moving. An example is the verb *move*, which is a result verb meaning to change the location of something by any means one likes (one can use the hand or bump it with one's head), but the result must be a change in location of the moved object. Similarly, when one boils a liquid, whether by putting it on a stove, holding a burner under it, or putting it in a vacuum, there is a characteristic bubbly result that is part of our meaning for *boil*; otherwise it is just evaporation. Eating defined properly, we think, involves both movie parts (e.g., some kind of solid food passing down through a passage) and non-movie parts (e.g., goal of satisfying hunger). In the end, it is probably hard to specify what eating is. If someone is fed by intravenous feeding, we do not say they are eating; the goal of satisfying biological processes is not enough. But jellyfish eat (we think), although they do not have mouths, exactly. Somehow *eat* seems to have movie components and intentional components, although they are not easy to specify. (We note that *feed* has practically no movie components; one can feed an organism by intravenous feeding, putting food in its mouth, putting it directly into the stomach, or somehow arranging for nutrients to soak through the skin in a nutrient-saturated atmosphere.)

As these examples show, action meanings also violate any reasonable form of Mutual Exclusivity. The same action can be easily referred to by different verbs: "he walked to the store"—"he went to the store," "he gave her the ball"—"he handed her the ball," "he smashed the plate"—"he broke the plate," "he had lunch"—"he ate lunch," (*have* is commonly used in a sense that covers part of the meanings of *eat* or *drink*), "he grabbed the hat"—"he got the hat." (Note that these examples do not violate a claim for Contrast. The meanings of the verbs are different, but the same action can definitely be described by different verbs, whereas it is not usual for a given object to be described by two different nouns, whether contrastive or not). It is also common for verbs to refer to overlapping parts of a common action: "he said it loudly,"—"he yelled it," "he got the hat,"—"he picked up the hat,"—"he held the hat," and so on. Some of these overlaps do not arise from the movie–result alternation but simply from the fact that there are often perfectly good verbs for both larger action sequences and subparts. For example, part of picking something up is to grasp it, to hold it, and so on, which are all perfectly good submeanings. Which part of the sequence or how much one wants to refer to seems largely dependent on the speaker's interests and intentions at the time (although this requires larger discussion beyond the scope of this chapter).

One way investigators have implicitly tried to simplify this set of problems and to resuscitate a relative of fast hedgehogs is to try to find a bias or constraint on children's preferences for interpretations of action verbs, either to find a bias in favor of movie (perceptual) interpretations (e.g., Gentner, 1978) or to find a bias in favor of result interpretations. Golinkoff et al. (this volume) tend to favor the movie bias because movies are more analogous to the shape characteristics of basic concrete objects. Behrend (this volume) noted that the evidence is mixed in some ways but also noted that a few studies of artificial verbs tend to favor a result bias. We would like to discuss some reasons that this kind of attempt to find an overall preferential bias does not seem likely to solve the basic problems and may even obscure the nature of underlying processes.

First, many of the studies do not show children clearly favoring one interpretation at all. Researchers tend to find some group differences favoring one kind of interpretation or the other and declare a .60–.40 split to show a winner. The studies usually show various children using both movie and result interpretations in some degree. In all probability, whether one even gets a winner in one direction or the other probably depends on things like the salience of the result versus the movie for the particular actions being studied. All things considered, it is unlikely that a careful study of the available results would show any clear overall bias of useful strength. In fact, the most extensive study of nonobject early predicate words available, Tomasello's diary study of his own child (Tomasello, 1992), shows both result and movie verbs to be common in her speech by 24 months of age.

Second, it does not really matter that much if there is a bias. Both movie and result features are basic features of core verbs. A child who guesses a movie description wrongly has to have a way of changing to a result description and vice versa for a child who guesses a result description wrongly. The proper analysis of action words as a group must involve the analysis of related uses of the word over a number of a situations, given the describability of most situations by more than one natural word. The natural perceptual parsing given by concrete basic objects is not available.

Third, given that many verbs have both result and movie components, it is absolutely necessary for children not to follow the strategy that a successful first biased guess is enough. Suppose a verb has both movie and result components, and a biased child guesses the movie components. Both, of course, are always present in the future experienced uses of the verb. If the child's strategy is to make a guess and to exclusively prefer the movie interpretation if it continues to be successful, the result components will never be noticed. Vice versa for an initial successful result guess for an action word that also requires movie components. In fact, it would be best to record both movie and result components and see how these play out against future experienced uses, rather than to make an exclusive guess of one or the other initially. If children do not do this, they still need a way of adding the relevant neglected features even to a successful initial biased guess.

Our point is that even basic action verbs do not show the straightforward potential for perceptual parsing, including mutual exclusivity and a natural segmentation, that concrete objects with the basic object and whole object makeup afford the theorist. A thorough working through the problems (which we cannot do here) readily shows that for verbs, fast hedgehog guesses analogous to those that succeed with basic objects do not work. Moreover, theorists ought, we think, to be impressed by the facts: The core action vocabulary is not organized as straightforwardly as the core concrete object vocabulary. Something is very likely different about the mentality involved in the conceptualization of simple objects and actions. There must be a fairly strong relation between this fact and the fact that concrete object words are reliably found in one grammatical category (nouns), whereas concrete action words can be verbs or other form classes (e.g., "he kicked the ball"—"he gave the ball a *kick*," or counterparts like *go, travel,* and *trip*).

Thus, although our chief concern here is to open up the problems with concrete-object-word-derived fast hedgehog methods (which tend not to succeed with nonbasic object concrete nouns), the fact that some of the most central aspects of basic action organization do not map onto the perceptual world as straightforwardly as objects is itself a clue that deeper acquisitional processes are likely to be different (see Choi & Bowerman, 1991, and Gentner, 1982, for important related discussion of actional semantic problems; Maratsos, 1990, 1992, discusses apparent consequences of the object–nonobject difference for the nature and acquisition of the relevant grammatical form classes).[2]

---

[2]Our guess is that there is much else to discuss here. For example, concrete object nouns keep their basic semantic character even as they are combined with other grammatical elements, but basic elements of action verb meanings readily change as grammatical combinations around them change. For example, tense-aspect and argument alternations can change some verbs from processes into achievement-result meanings, as in the differences between "he is climbing" and "he climbed the mountain." Although agentive–nonagentive differences in predicates are usually localized in the predicate word itself, changes in wider context often alter this as well. For example, it is peculiar to give, as a command, "know the answer," but saying "know the answer by tomorrow at five" is much less odd. Similarly, saying "be in the living room" is odd, but "be in the living room when I come back" is all right. Time allotted can change whether or not some state or activity is controllable, as well as other meaningful aspects signaled by the arguments of the predicate; controllability is not a function of the predicate word per se. Nonconcrete object words show all kinds of lability in basic semantic properties of this kind, but it is not clear how much analogous lability basic concrete object words show.

To summarize—and what we are summarizing has only been suggested rather than thoroughly shown—we disagree with the claims by Golinkoff et al. (this volume) that simple concrete object noun heuristics, which can conceivably achieve fast hedgehog results with a core domain of concrete substantive nouns, can be readily generalized in fruitful fashion to the realm of action verbs. We do not disclaim the possibility that there are some analogies (e.g., there is some natural relation between shape for concrete nouns and movie sequences for some verbs), but even when the analogy can be made, it rarely works very simply. For example, the case that there are natural maximal action sequences even for movie verbs seems to us to be much less likely. In other cases, the analogy is weak, as with the analogy from basic object constitution to semantic components. Even the simplest facts about the relation of movie and result components undoes the straightforward applicability of many fast hedgehog proposals, and indeed, they point to something different being at work. It is possible that further analysis and research with actional meanings will show there are some perceptually natural parsings of aspects of movie sequences, for example, as input to further inferential and inductive processes. We emphasize, however, the necessity of doing much more assessment of the aspects of the situation that are cognitively or pragmatically central to the intentions and interests of the speaker and listener, a basic fox activity (see Tomasello, this volume, and Rispoli, this volume, for related discussions). We also think that something likely to be central is the process of sifting out information on related uses of predicates, rather than simply being able to make a good initial detailed guess based on a natural perceptual analysis like that available for basic object words (see Behrend, this volume, for some related discussion, although Behrend appears ambivalent about this problem).

THE DECISION AND VELOCITY PROBLEMS REVISITED

We trace the rise of fast-mapping hedgehog accounts to two central arguments, the velocity problem and the decision problem: Children learn many words quickly and are quite accurate considering all the alternatives that are theoretically possible; they must have a fairly simple set of structured heuristics that allow them to capture a great deal of word meaning quickly and accurately. In the light of what we said previously to deny the obvious applicability of fast hedgehog solutions to a wide range of nonbasic object substantives, what is to be said about these nevertheless central problems? It is not simply a matter of space constraints that prevents us from giving any kind of complete answer; we do not claim to know any kind of detailed adequate answer. But we can comment on some central aspects of the problems, with suggestions about where future analysis and research might partly divert themselves.

Consider the velocity problem. Children are learning six to nine word meanings a day; consequently, they must be able to map a great deal of word meaning appropriately from a small amount of exposure. Two considerations show that children need not be mapping as much information as quickly as this apparent fact implies. First, let us grant the possibility that a good deal of reasonably accurate fast mapping does sometimes go on. We emphasize the possibility that much of this works because of children's foxlike abilities to use a variety of sources of information—pragmatic, cognitive, social, evaluation of the current situation, and a certain degree of natural dovetailing of interests and salience for the child and the speakers from whom the child learns words. Such foxlike processes are not, of course, as scientifically attractive to deal with as hedgehoglike processes (see previous discussions), but they are quite likely to be important in children's ability to map situational and word use information. Nor, of course, do we exclude from such to-be-combined sources whatever information can be gotten at least heuristically from sources like grammatical use or semantic interpretations of words in particular sentence contexts.

Second, however, it seems likely to us that there is much more sifting of information over time for individual words than the current literature implies. Fast-mapping approaches that consider how many words for which children achieve some sort of useful meaning tend to assume that children are getting the meaning for each word very quickly, in the sense of approaching a complete description. Children would only have to be moving so quickly on each word if they proceeded in serial fashion, that is, nearly finishing each word before moving on to the next. Although this is a convenient method for highly focused conscious learning such as medical students must do in learning anatomy terms, it is not the required method for young children. Instead, what they could be doing—and in fact no doubt are doing in some degree—is working on a great many words in parallel, adding information to each word over time until some criterion for adequate specification has been reached or until some equilibrium of meaning is reached. Such a procedure requires a great deal of long-term memory storage capacity (as opposed to the limited short-term memory capacity people bring to focused conscious processing), and it is known that both children and adults have such capacity, often in surprising detail. Adults, for example, can recognize members of sets of hundreds of photographs following a delay of weeks. Children do very well in analogous tests (Siegler, 1992). Large long-term storage capacity, the ability to call up some material quickly for on-the-spot processing and revision, and the ability to add current information to such a store allow the supposition that children can work on many words in parallel over a period of time, rather than having to capture most of the meaning for each in single exposure serial decision process.

In all likelihood, apart from the difficulty of short-term consciousness in naturally apprehending or intuiting a large memory capacity working on many words in parallel over time, there is another investigator-based reason for preference for fast-mapping hypotheses, and that is convenience of experimental study. Studying slow-mapping procedures requires repeated experiments on the same children, with repeated input and testing over time, something difficult to do; indeed, currently only diary studies on individual children give somewhat suitable (and still spotty) results. Fast-mapping hypotheses are naturally studied in single-presentation experimental procedures, which are much more convenient for everyone. Thus, giving greater importance to fast-mapping processes happens to make the study of word meaning acquisition more experimentally amenable.

Haunting all of these problem of velocity is an additional consideration: Most of the evidence for how many words children learn to comprehend must be based on comprehension tests. However, a person does not have to comprehend very much about a word's meaning to pass many comprehension tests, like those on the Peabody Picture Vocabulary Test. Often fairly gross knowledge is enough to distinguish correct choices from distractors. Without taking away from children's likely ability to deal with a great deal of information at once, it is a useful caution not to assume that children are learning six to nine words a day to the level of specification an adult naturally assumes.

This leaves the decision problem, which emerges in various forms. First, even children's early spontaneous word uses tend to look fairly accurate (see Ingram, 1989, for an excellent summary of early word meanings), despite some well-known errors; therefore, they must be largely accurate in their assessment of word meanings. This argument implicitly assumes that children begin to use a word very quickly after forming some initial meaningful entry for it; thus, if their use is impressively accurate, their initial entry must be impressively accurate (and thus must have been highly constrained). However, we do not know that children necessarily start to use a word quickly after making an initial entry for it. Current work on comprehension versus production, for example, indicates that children probably comprehend about 50 words at the time they use one. This implies that some set of processes may keep words in a state of being adjusted before spontaneous use begins to emerge. Time is left for sifting processes to result in increased accuracy of word meaning.

More broadly, however, decision arguments rest upon logical grounds. The possible number of hypotheses is so great that the child's hypothesis generation and decision procedures must be somehow limited by internal structures and heuristics.

Some anti-constraints writers seem to try to solve the problem by recruiting the child's ability to make appropriate pragmatic and social decisions about what is relevant in context or to make use of general cognitive structuring decisions available elsewhere or parent-child implicit cooperation (and obviously, we are not against the validity of positing such processes). The probability of extensive long-term sifting processes for much of word meaning also suggests that the child has time to sift out differing possibilities using input evidence and therefore requires less constrained hypothesis and decision processes.

Someone who favors the Limits–Constraints approach can readily point out that such responses only push the problem into other domains. Pragmatic decisions about what someone else thinks is relevant or central have the same logical decision problems. If children can somehow profit from interaction with helpful adults and peers, both they and the adults (or other children) can successfully limit their interpretations of what the other in the conversation is up to in the first place. Long-term sifting and induction processes, whatever they may be, also can in theory reach many decisions other than the ones actually reached, apparently with some consistency, by the language acquirers of the social community. Indeed, such a theorist may reply that what looks like a (sometimes patient) fox is really at best a large bunch of industrious hedgehogs who may move around a lot. To paraphrase John Ross' use of the William James "Turtles" story (Ross, 1967), it is constraints all the way down.

Viewed in this larger perspective, the Limits proponent must be correct. Science (which is what we are supposed to be trying to do) is inexorably deterministic. Its own refuges from determinism currently are probability substituted for strict determinism and indeterminism due to measurement problems. Free will and spontaneity are simply illusions, incomprehensible. Whatever one proposes the organism does, it is always possible to propose the organism does something else instead, and thus implicitly every theory about human behavior or development is a constraints or limits or innate heuristics theory (including, for example, S–R behaviorist theory, which prided itself on how constrained its account of organic functioning is). Nevertheless, there is a considerable difference between a very fast, domain-specific, quick-acting hedgehog that uses only a few simple principles and a large indeterminate group of hedgehogs that probably operate across various domain boundaries, both quickly and slowly, using a wide variety of elements, heuristics, procedures, and inductive and inferential processes. In fact, it is not clear that a proper analysis would show what could properly be called a bunch of hedgehogs at all, although whatever is shown naturally has to be limited somehow in the end.

Of course, we would not want to push a concrete metaphor too far. Fox–hedgehog is a mnemonic and theoretical heuristic, not a Platonic distinction. We have not attempted to eliminate the Decision problem at all, only to show that word meaning is much more of a foxlike problem than many accounts imply, that slow mapping probably takes care of more work than is currently stipulated, and that nonsubstantives are even more likely to have these characteristics than substantive concrete nouns, for which fast hedgehog procedures have indeed been proposed with at least some plausibility.[3]

NONACTIONAL MEANINGS AND GRAMMAR

Whatever the problems of perceptual analysis for basic event words, they are even worse for verbs and predicates more broadly, for the simple reason that these are not confined to movie sequences and concrete results. Many predicates refer to various mental qualities. These include perceptions, cognitions, feelings, and evaluations (including moral and aesthetic evaluations), which are essentially mental, unobservable acts or states. Relevant verbs include, in English, *see, want, think* (in related meanings, *think of* something, *believe* something to be true), and nonverb meanings as in *sad, sure, nice* (i.e., an evaluation of people that expresses an attitude of the speaker), *maybe* (expressing the speaker's view that something is possible but not certain), *should* (expressing a view that something is morally or factually required or necessary), and so on. We note again that across languages, such meanings are not necessarily in one grammatical form class or another. For mental predicates, the same meaning (e.g., "want") can be encoded by an auxiliary verb in some languages, a main verb, an adjective, or even a morphological marker on the main verb. Concepts like "be sad" or "be happy" can be encoded by main verbs in other languages. Even within languages, highly similar concepts are commonly expressed by words in different form classes, such as *should—better* (e.g., *he better go*)—*have* (*to*)

---

[3]A question we have been asked, very reasonably, is how one can study foxlike processes. As far as we can tell, the answer is not encouraging: By definition, foxlike processes are harder to study and likely to be less satisfactory to study even when progress is made. A core implication of hedgehog proposals is that the discovery of something that the organism is doing will cover a great deal of explanatory territory. By definition, discovering something that a fox is doing does not necessarily cover much territory at all, for it is only one of many things the fox does. Fox processes may also be harder to find because each one covers less of what the fox does and occurs proportionately less often. Furthermore, even a complete fox description would be a long list of elements and processes and the ways in which they somehow (perhaps often unpredictably) interact, which is simply cognitively less appealing than a short list of basic principles that apply algorithmically. The problem, however, is that just because fox processes are less methodologically or theoretically appealing, they are not necessarily valid or central; undue exaggeration of or concentration on hedgehog processes and proposals will inevitably give a distorted view of the organism we are trying to elucidate. The undue prominence of syntax as a central process of language acquisition, for example, seems to us partly a consequence of the hedgehog–fox differences between syntax and pragmatics.

(e.g., *he has to go*) all express some kind of moral necessity felt by the speaker.

Lederer et al. (this volume) are struck, as many observers have been, by the highly nonphysical nature of these meanings. They are essentially, in the end, unobservable, having to be inferred somehow from a combination of situational analysis, verbal context, cognitive understanding of others, and so on—or so it has seemed to most people. They may have observable correlates, but these correlates are not perfectly reliable and more important, do not comprise the actual meanings of the words. One may be sad without looking sad or look sad without being sad. Such oppositions would be impossible if *sad* meant an external expression or some other observable physical array. The possibly observable correlates are even slighter for words like *maybe* or *think* or *should*, although there are doubtless some statistical tendencies.

Lederer et al. suggest that such meanings are too complex and require too much inference for children to understand them strictly by interpreting word uses in contexts. (It has never been easy to propose accounts of how children figure out words that refer to non-overtly perceived sensations, even in an organism that suspects other organisms have such feelings on possibly nonlinguistic grounds.) They suggest that children use the fact that such predicates take sentence complements as a grammatical cue that non-physical meanings are involved. Thus, even *want*, which appears commonly with non-sentences as its second argument (e.g., "I want an apple; I want that cup"), is analyzed as a true mental predicate because of its use with sentential complements, as in "I want (to eat this)," or "I want (them to go)." The idea is presumably that for a verb to take a true sentential argument, it has to be a mental predicate. Then the mental predicate meaning derived from grammatical analysis can be read back even into simple uses like "I want that dog," which otherwise on grounds of pure grammar are like uses such as "I eat this apple."

Clearly the idea here is to use a hedgehoglike system (i.e., grammar and the system of sentential complements) to solve what looks like a fox problem: How children ever figure out in context that a word is referring to a mental predicate or some other submerged meaning that by definition does not refer to an external action or appearance. It looks as if without some kind of grammatical aid, they have to make a complex inference based on a combination of prior context, what is at issue, what the speaker is likely to be remarking on, what internal feelings, cognitions, and perceptions are like, how others would experience them, when they would comment specifically on them, what else is encoded in sentences, and so on.

There are actually a number of questions here. Most modestly, can a child who knows the grammar of his or her language use grammatical information to discover that a predicate is a mental predicate? Can a child learn mental predicates without such grammatical complement help? In fact, the answer to the second question has to be that children can, contrary to Lederer et al.'s claim as we understand it. We list a few reasons for this.

First, one cannot figure out the grammar in the first place without figuring out the nature of some mental predicates. In Lederer et al.'s account, it appears presupposed that the child can figure out that sentences that are constituents of other sentences are indeed sentence complements without knowing that the predicate of the main clause is a mental predicate. However, it is not clear how this can be done. Sentences can appear as parts of other sentences without being complements, and the difference in markers in English is very slight or nonexistent; in many languages, it has been or still is nonexistent. For example, causative result sentences introduced by *so that* can appear after verbs: "I'm yelling so that he'll come." There is not much obvious structural difference between "I'm hoping that he'll come" and "I'm yelling so that he'll come." The surface marker is whether *that* or *so that* is used. Obviously there is no innate knowledge that *so that* does not signal a true sentence complement but *that* does. How does someone learning English figure out that *so that* introduces a coordinated noncomplement sentence that is not the true argument of a main clause predicate, whereas *that* (sometimes) introduces a complement, that is, a true argument of a higher predicate? As far as we can tell, one must at least sometimes analyze the relation of the introduced sentence. And as far as we can tell, this means that, for example, the child has to determine by analysis that a clause like *that he will come* is a complement because it is the argument of a mental predicate. That is, at least early in acquisition, the child can only analyze which grammatical sentence forms are complements and which are some other kind of constituent sentence form by analyzing the broader meaning framework of sentences to derive the small difference among complement and noncomplement markers.

Second, sometimes this is not adequate because there is no reliable difference to analyze. For example, the most common complement form after infinitive-taking verbs like *want* is a subjectless *to*-clause, as in "I want to eat the apple." In such clauses in English, the form is *to* + VP. However, *to* + VP is also used for purpose infinitive clauses that follow main verbs without referring to mental predicates: "I ran (to get away)." In terms of surface grammar, "I ran (to get away)" is a great deal like "I want (to get away)," but obviously *ran, want,* and *to get away* are related in very different ways.

Third, the strategy of reading back complement-taking forms onto simple predicate forms is a rather dangerous strategy because languages are full of homonyms; thus, this strategy is misleading or at least does not work very well. The strategy we mean here is that of inferring that *want* in *I want an apple* is a mental predicate because it is likely to be one in "I want to eat an apple." It is true that *want* has similar (but not identical) meanings when it takes a simple

NP or a complex NP, but this is not a universal. Consider *have*, as in "I have an apple" and "I have to eat an apple." The second *have* refers to necessity, whereas the first refers to simple possession. Similarly, "I've got to go" and "I've got an apple" both use *got* but only the complement-taking form means necessity. Also consider the relation between "it suddenly hit me that she wasn't coming" and "the ball hit me." Sometimes both predicates are mental but do not have the same meaning, as in "I know he is happy" versus "I know him." *Know* can mean acquaintance when used with simple NP objects, which it does not mean when used with sentence complements.

Fourth, many mental-type meanings are carried by words that are not taking some kind of sentence complement in any obvious way. For example, consider the word *maybe* in English, as in "maybe he'll come." It is not exactly clear just what *maybe* means, but it clearly refers to a mental state of the speaker. *Probably* in "he'll probably come," has the same meaning. *Better* in "he better come" has a considerable amount of mental predicate meaning, without obviously taking *be come* (its semantic argument) as a sentence complement. In other languages, meanings like "want" may be encoded by an auxiliary verb or even by a morphological marker on the main verb (Langacker, 1973). Slobin (1985) noted a language in which the speaker refers to strong emotional response by adding a particle to the end, which children learn to do quite early (this particle has no main predicate counterpart that takes sentence complements). In English (and any number of other languages), many mental predicate trait terms typically do not take any complements, including words like *intelligent, agreeable, nice* (e.g., "she's nice, isn't she" refers to a speaker's mental feelings toward someone, among other things), *smart, stupid,* and so on. These words are typically used just like other simple adjectives (e.g., "he's stupid," "he's tall") in their immediate sentence contexts.

Fifth, in many languages, sentence complements may look exactly like noncomplements (already noted for infinitive purpose or true argument complement clauses, as in "I want to get away" and "I ran to get away"). In older English, "so that" meanings were communicated by *that*, as in "I ran that he might not catch me." In modern Chinese, many sentence constituents can be chained with no marking at all; therefore, literal translations are "he want escape," "he run escape" (he is running to escape), "he happy sing" (he is happy to sing), and so on. Can it be any clearer that the job of figuring out that the main predicate of a sentence is a mental predicate that takes a true argument complement must be done by the children's ability to interpret in context? (Can one propose that the child can figure out that a predicate cannot be a mental predicate taking a complement because it has a clearly known nonmental predicate meaning? That is, *I run escape* cannot have *run* as a mental verb because *run* refers to a well-known physical action. The problem here is the many mental-like predicates that have simple nonmental forms but still take mental predicate forms as well: "I got a ball," "I got to find this." It would be a mistake to infer that the meaning of the second *got* could be a mental necessity predicate because one knows the first *got* refers to simple possession).

Finally, it seems unlikely that a child exposed only to a language without complements, hearing sentences like "I'm happy" or "I'm sad" or "I want this" will never figure out by him- or herself that such predicates do not refer to physical actions or appearances. It should be noted that we are not saying such knowledge of grammatical-semantic correspondences are not used by speakers whose language at least sometimes makes such correspondences. In English, if one hears "I'm nizz that Mary is here," if one has figured out the adjective + sentence complement structure of English, one can guess that *nizz* refers to some kind of feeling or mental attitude or reaction. (As we noted previously, figuring out the that + S structure of English complements requires analysis of mental predicates.) Of course, this would not work for all languages and does not work for all mental predicates (e.g., *better, maybe*, or *probably*). However, if the language has such correspondences, we are sure that speakers can figure them out and use them to make future learning easier.

We also need to point out another way in which we think hedgehog-bootstrappers tend to overstate their case in their domain. Quite simply, take the sentence above, "I'm nizz that Mary came." Perhaps one could infer that *nizz* refers to some kind of mental reaction because adjectives that take sentential complements in English usually do (maybe always do). But how much of the job is this? There is a tremendous range of subtlety in how many reaction and trait meanings there are. Brown (1985) noted that English has 2,000 terms describing different kinds of personal traits alone, not counting mental predicates like *want* or *need*, which do not denote stable personal traits. Knowing that something refers to some kind of nonphysical, mental trait is not exactly the end of the trail, and it is hard to see how someone could figure out the rest of meaning without considerable cognitive and pragmatic inference from the actual contexts of word use (including meanings conveyed by other parts of the conversation and also assumptions about shared evaluations, feelings in different situations, and so on). Bootstrapping accounts often say, in effect, "this gives the child a good start on the problem," implying that this start is the crucial part. We see no reason to accept that this is so. The problem of how one goes on to make decisions or sift out possibilities about the highly developed cognitive, emotional, attitudinal, moral, and other subtleties of mentally oriented predicates seems at least as crucial, if not more so (although ultimately, what is crucial depends on the taste of the investigator).

Thus, we find it impossible to believe children cannot figure out mental predicate meanings without grammatical bootstrapping; indeed, it is absolutely necessary that they figure out many mental predicates without the aid of grammatical bootstrapping. Even when possible semantic–grammatical correspondences are known, they do not decide all cases of mental–non-mental predicate distinctions. Even if grammatical bootstrapping applies, it accomplishes less than is claimed for it, given the great variety of mental predicate meanings, for each of which the exact meaning must still be figured out by use of foxlike pragmatic–social–cognitive procedures plus whatever sifting-over-time processes are required.[4]

CONCLUSIONS

To summarize briefly, we have suggested a metaphor, that of fox versus hedgehog, for considering aspects of a broad range of psychological problems and acquisitional processes. We think that much of the current work in word meaning overemphasizes fast hedgehog acquisitional proposals, which seem reasonably promising in the special (although very important) case of basic object level concrete substantives but less so for dealing with nonconcrete substantives, the central topic of this volume. More detailed analysis suggests that much of nonconcrete object noun acquisition itself must recruit fox processes and also processes of sifting-over-time to account for children's ability to acquire this highly variegated set of meanings—a set that seems to exist without having a convenient basic object-like level of analysis and often refers to highly nonconcrete, nonevent meanings like those of mental predicates. We do not deny the basic hedgehog point that somehow children's inferential and inductive processes must be inherently structured and limited, but these limits are probably not to be successfully enumerated by a relatively small set of algorithmically and quickly applied heuristics or hypotheses for a wide variety of nonsimple object meanings. Finally, only time will tell if the right way to think of our word-learning fox is as a very large hoard of sometimes patient hedgehogs, but if a single animal metaphor is required, we think a fox will survive better than an impatient hedgehog in these nonbasic object environs.

ACKNOWLEDGMENTS

We acknowledge the helpful remarks and information supplied by Michael Tomasello during the writing of this chapter.

---

[4]Tomasello (1992), in his longitudinal diary study of his child, found many mental predicates in her vocabulary at 24 months, before grammatical complement use appeared to any extent. Indeed, mental predicate words like *want* and *like* appear extensively in early lexicons (e.g., see Braine, 1976). Of course, we do not know how much comprehension of sentence complements children have early on, but these early uses are certainly compatible with learning mental predicates when little or no sentence complement grammar is known.

REFERENCES

Berlin, I. (1954). *The hedgehog and the fox.* London: Weidenfeld & Nicholson.

Biederman, I. (1988). Aspects and extensions of a theory of human image understanding. In Z. Pylyshyn (Ed.), *Computational processes in human vision: An interdisciplinary perspective* (pp. 117–142). Norwood, NJ: Ablex.

Bloom, L. (1991). *Language development from two to three.* Cambridge, England: Cambridge University Press.

Braine, M. D. S. (1976). Children's early word combinations. *Monographs of the Society for Research in Child Development, 41,* 1–104.

Brown, R. (1985). *Social psychology: The second edition.* Glencoe, IL: The Free Press.

Carey, S. (1982). The child as word learner. In J. Bresnan, M. Halle, & G. Miller (Eds.), *Linguistic theory and psychological reality* (pp. 264–293). Cambridge, MA: MIT Press.

Choi, S., & Bowerman, M. (1991). Learning to express motion events in English and Korean. *Cognition, 41,* 83–121.

Chomsky, A. N. (1986). *Knowledge of language.* New York: Praeger.

Gathercole, V. (1987). The contrastive hypothesis for the acquisition of word meaning: A reconsideration of the theory. *Journal of Child Language, 14,* 493–531.

Gentner, D. (1978). On relational meaning: The acquisition of verb meaning. *Child Development, 49,* 988–998.

Gentner, D. (1982). Why nouns are learned before verbs: Linguistic relativity versus natural partitioning. In S. Kuczaj (Ed.), *Language development* (Vol. 2, pp. 31–53). Hillsdale, NJ: Lawrence Erlbaum Associates.

Grice, H. P. (1975). Logic and conversation. In P. Cole and J. L. Morgan (Eds.), *Syntax and semantics: Vol. 3. Speech acts.* New York: Academic Press.

Ingram, D. (1989). *First language acquisition: Method, description and explanation.* Cambridge, England: Cambridge University Press.

Jolicoeur, P., Gluck, M. A., & Kosslyn, S. M. (1984). Pictures and names: Making the connection. *Cognitive Psychology, 16,* 243–275.

Landau, B., Smith, L. B., & Jones, S. S. (1988). The importance of shape in early lexical learning. *Cognitive Development, 3,* 299–321.

Langacker, R. (1973). *Language and its structure.* New York: Holt, Rinehart & Winston.

Mandler, J. M., & Bauer, P. J. (1988). The cradle of categorization: Is the basic level basic? *Cognitive Development, 3,* 247–264.

Maratsos, M. (1989). Innateness and plasticity in language development. In M. Rice & R. Schiefelbusch (Eds.), *The teachability of language* (pp. 105–126). Baltimore: Paul Brookes.

Maratsos, M. (1990). Are actions to verbs as objects are to nouns? On the differential semantic bases of form class categories. *Linguistics, 28,* 1351–1380.

Maratsos, M. (1992). How the acquisition of nouns may be different from that of verbs. In N. Krasnegor, D. Rumbaugh, R. Schiefelbusch, & M. Studdert-Kennedy (Eds.), *Biological and behavioral determinants of language development* (pp. 37–55). Hillsdale, NJ: Lawrence Erlbaum Associates.

Markman, E. (1989). *Categorization and naming in children.* Cambridge, MA: MIT Press.

Markman, E. (1992). Constraints on word learning: Speculations about their nature, origins, and domain specificity. In M. R. Gunnar & M. Maratsos (Eds.), *Modularity and constraints in language and cognition. The Minnesota symposia on child psychology* (Vol. 25, pp. 59–102). Hillsdale, NJ: Lawrence Erlbaum Associates.

Medin, D. L. (1983). Structural principles in categorization. In T. J. Tighe & B. E. Shepp (Eds.), *Perception, cognition and development: Interactional analyses* (pp. 202–231). Hillsdale, NJ: Lawrence Erlbaum Associates.

Murphy, G. L. (1982). Cue validity and levels of categorization. *Psychological Bulletin, 91,* 174–177.

Murphy, G. L., & Wisniewski, E. J. (1989). Categorizing objects in isolation and in scenes: What a superordinate is good for. *Journal of Experimental Psychology: Learning, Memory, and Cognition, 15,* 572–586.

Pinker, S. (1984). *Language learnability and language development.* Cambridge, MA: Harvard University Press.

Quine, W. V. (1960). *Word and object.* Cambridge, MA: MIT Press.

Rosch, E. (1979). Principles of categorization. In E. Rosch & B. Lloyd (Eds.), *Cognition and categorization* (pp. 1–36). Hillsdale, NJ: Lawrence Erlbaum Associates.

Rosch, E., & Mervis, C. (1975). Family resemblences: Studies in the internal structure of categories. *Cognitive Psychology, 7,* 382–439.

Ross, J. R. (1967). *Constraints on variables in syntax.* Bloomington: Indiana University Linguistic Club.

Siegler, R. (1992). *Children's thinking* (2nd ed.). Englewood Cliffs, NJ: Prentice-Hall.

Slobin, D. I. (1985). Crosslinguistic evidence for the language-making capacity. In D. I. Slobin (Ed.), *The crosslinguistic study of language acquisition.* Hillsdale, NJ: Lawrence Erlbaum Associates.

Talmy, L. (1985). Lexicalization patterns: Semantic structure in lexical forms. In T. Shopen (Ed.), *Language typology and syntactic description: Vol. 3. Grammatical categories and the lexicon* (pp. 84–121). New York: Cambridge University Press.

Tomasello, M. (1992). *First verbs: A case study of early grammatical development.* Cambridge, England: Cambridge University Press.

White, T. G. (1982). Naming practices, typicality, and underextension in child language. *Journal of Experimental Child Psychology, 33,* 324–346.

Author Index

Subject Index

A

Action scope
  continuity, 206
  Korean motion verbs, 206
  saliency, 206
Action scope principle, 205–207, 215
Action words, *see* Verbs
Arguments, 333, 382
  structure acquisition, 307, 309, 322

B

Bootstrapping effect, 13, 56, *see also* Syntactic
  bootstrapping

C

Canonical sentence schemas, 355–356, 372–
  373
  early learning stages, 368
  unique argument-structure preference the-
    ory, 365–367
Categorical scope principle, 194, 198, 202,
  207–211, 215
  errors, 208–209

extension, 210–211
Korean language, 208–209
perceptual similarity, 208
preferential-looking paradigm test, 209–210
semantic components, 209–211, 213
syntactic bootstrapping, 209
syntactic frames, 210
taxonomic assumption, 208
verbs, 208
Causality, notion, 35
Children, *see also* Toddlers
  change perception, 35
  intentional agent concept, 41–42, 55
  movement imitation, 34–35
  multiword speech, 23–24, 46–52
    verbs, 49
  noun disambiguation, 148–159, 180
  object movement perception, 35
  object names, 3–5
  possession concept, 41–42, 48–49, 55
    movement, 43, 53
  referential capability, 254
  self-concept, 30–32, 42–44, 49, 53–55
  semantic development patterns, 67–68,
    77–78
    English language, 69, 73–74
    parental input, 69–74